T0328539

HARD RIGHT TURN

Hard Right Turn

Assassination of the American Left
- A History

Jerry Carrier

Algora Publishing
New York

Library of Congress Cataloging-in-Publication Data

Carrier, Jerry, 1948-
    Hard Right Turn: Assassination of the American Left - A History / Jerry Carrier.
      pages cm
    Includes bibliographical references and index.
      ISBN 978-1-62894-177-7 (soft cover: alk. paper)—ISBN 978-1-62894-178-4 (hard
cover: alk. paper) ISBN 978-1-62894-179-1 (eBook) 1. Right and left (Political science)—
United States. 2. Radicalism—United States—History. 3. United States—Politics and
government. I. Title.
    JC574.2.U6C36 2015
    320.510973—dc23

                              2015027708

Printed in the United States

This book is dedicated to Jessica, Jamey, Amy, Adam, James, Ryan and Kym
in the hope that their America will be better.

Author's Note

Some readers may find my chronicling of America's past sins somehow unpatriotic. They may feel that I dislike my country. But I write these things because it is my country and my ship for which I seek to steer a better course. I may be perceived as radical by some but I will give you these words from H.L. Mencken: "The notion that a radical is one who hates his country is naïve and usually idiotic. He is, more likely, one who likes his country more than the rest of us, and is thus more disturbed than the rest of us when he sees it debauched. He is not a bad citizen turning to crime; he is a good citizen driven to despair."

Table of Contents

Introduction

> "It is a bitter reality, brought into vivid focus by five years of Obama, that the Left is an immobilized and politically impotent force at the very moment when the economic inequalities engineered by our overlords at Goldman Sachs who manage the global economy, should have recharged a long-moribund resistance movement back to life."—Jeffery St. Clair, American journalist

> "When fascism comes to America, it will be wrapped in the flag and carrying the cross."—Sinclair Lewis

> "The biggest lie of all is that capitalism is democracy. We have no way of understanding democracy outside of the market, just as we have no understanding of how to understand freedom outside of market values."—Henry Giroux, American cultural critic

The term "the left" was first used as a political designation during the French Revolution when the Jacobins sat on the left in the National Assembly and the Girondins on the right. The left is best defined as movements, organizations, and individuals, who promote: the equality of all humans, a fair and equitable division of wealth and power, support for the poor and disadvantaged, and a commitment to action to advance these causes.

America is a country with politics to the right of the center; just how far right is subject to debate. There really is no longer an American left, as it has been systematically destroyed. Most believe liberals to be the American left, but liberals are much more centrist than leftist and they are certainly no counterweight to the powerful American right.

In the late 1940s and during the 1950s, many liberals like Hubert Humphrey, Bob La Follette Jr. and Adlai Stevenson eagerly participated with the right in the destruction of the left. It was Humphrey who wanted to put all socialists in prison camps and authored legislation to do so in the McCarran Act. During the 1960s there was a very brief resurgence of the left, but it died a painful death and the liberals who took their place were capitalists and political centrists, and they were unmoved by the plight of the left. The liberals were also still very dedicated to the existing establishment which was firmly entrenched to the capitalist free market right. Today the right hurls insults at liberal and moderate politicians calling them "socialists" or "communists," although the people shouting these insults along with most other Americans have little idea what those things really are or what they actually mean, nor are they aware that they were long ago completely destroyed in the name of national security in the mid twentieth century.

America has determinedly destroyed the left over the last hundred and fifty years. It was done legislatively, often illegally and even violently. Leftist leaders were jailed for their thoughts, assassinated or were driven out of the political process. The constitution and the law were ignored or suspended to allow this to occur on many occasions. This is not some conspiracy theory; America's history is indisputable on this subject, but few Americans know or appreciate this history or its consequences.

There were many false claims that the left were destroyed because of false claims of left-wing violence or "imminent threats" to the government. In reality there were very few threats to the government or acts of violence. In fact many on the left were anti-war, isolationists, peace activists, and many were followers of Thoreau and Gandhi and they believed in passive non-violent resistance. And the few incidents of violence attributed to the left like the 1886 Haymarket strike or even the 1968 Democratic Convention in Chicago were later shown to be rightwing police riots.

The campaign to destroy the left was about political and religious purity and rightwing bias. There was never any real chance of a leftist coup to overthrow the government in right of center America. In the US we should be much more afraid of her fascist tendencies than any left-wing takeover. The deliberate destruction of the left was never about real threats. It is an on-going myth that we have to trade liberty and suspend the constitutional rights of the left and others for security reasons. It is as Benjamin Franklin said, "Those who surrender freedom for security will not have, nor do they deserve, either one."

America has much less tolerance in its politics and religion than even in its very limited racial, ethnic, or class tolerance. And while many of the actions taken by the government and others against the left were illegal and even unconstitutional, history is always written by the victors and this past is mostly unknown, forgotten, or unrecognized by the American people who naively believe they live in a free country where people are allowed to believe and to do what they freely choose.

And because there is no longer an American left, the US keeps sliding ever further to the right. There is no counterbalance. There is no other side. There is no real debate. And with no debate the ultra conservative right, capitalism and the rich and powerful are unchallenged, unchanging, and intolerable to ideas, thoughts, and actions outside their very narrow self-serving interests. The great American experiment is no longer real, but is rather a stagnant pool of putrefying myths, which is why American society and the welfare of the common people are in decay.

CHAPTER 1. DEFINING THE AMERICAN LEFT

"It still remains unrecognized, that to bring a child into existence without a fair prospect of being able, not only to provide food for its body, but instruction and training for its mind, is a moral crime, both against the unfortunate offspring and against society."—John Stuart Mill, *On Liberty*

"Civil government, so far as it is instituted for the security of property, is in reality instituted for the defense of the rich against the poor, or of those who have some property against those who have none at all."—Adam Smith

"A socialist is just someone who is unable to get over his or her astonishment that most people who have lived and died have spent lives of wretched, fruitless, unremitting toil."—Terry Eagleton Professor of Cultural Theory at the National University of Ireland and the University of Manchester

"Many people consider the things government does for them to be social progress but they regard the things government does for others as socialism."—Chief Justice Earl Warren

What is the American left? Most standard definitions of the left include anarchists and civil libertarians (many of which have recently allied with the right), labor and unionists, socialists, communists, and recently environmentalists. However the American right's definition of the left includes any type of radicals, atheists, liberals and moderates and many include women, gays and minorities as part of the left. And some conservative rightwing pundits also compare the left to fascists, although by definition fascism and Nazism are rightwing doctrines and much closer to America's conservative right than is commonly believed. The right may greatly dislike socialism, but historically, as we shall see, they have not had the same disdain for fascism and National Socialism.

Even libertarians, who at one time were closely aligned with the anarchists and are now advocating rightwing action, were at one time part of the left. They now feel more comfortable and prefer to be classified with the American right because of their strong anti-government and anti-regulatory attitudes. The American right is about absolute elitist power for the wealthy and doesn't really want the libertarians except to support their ideas of unregulated capitalism.

I believe the definition that I included in the introduction to be the most historically accurate definition of the left which is defined as movements, organizations, and individuals, who promote the equality of all humans, a fair and equitable division of wealth and power, support for the poor and disadvantaged, and a commitment to action to advance these causes.

In historical terms the groups most associated with the left were the labor unions, civil libertarians, socialists, and communists. While most Americans understand something about labor unions, they have difficulty defining the other groups. Many people have very little understanding of socialism or communism and assume the cold war model of the dictatorship of Stalin in the USSR represents all of leftist thinking. Communism in the Soviet Union has more to do with Russian history and transferring the obedience of the powerless Russian serfs and peasants from the czar to a totalitarian state and the oligarchy more than it has to do with Marxist thought. It is amusing to note that Karl Marx would likely have been as appalled by Stalinism, Maoism and the dictatorship in North Korea, at least as much as most Americans. Marx was a journalist. He firmly believed in freedom of speech and of the press, and he wrote many newspaper editorials about free speech and the press. He greatly disliked any form of authoritarian government, particularly since he was constantly harassed, deported and threatened with arrest by many of them, especially his own Prussian government. Most people today would be shocked to know that Marx was not a big fan of government authority, was a firm believer in democracy, and wrote with passion that "Democracy is the road to socialism."

Adam Smith and his free market economic policies is a hero of rightwing America, but his quote at the beginning of this chapter could have been a quote from Marx. And while it is fair to argue that perhaps the Marxist philosophy is an unattainable utopian concept, it is grossly unfair to think that Marx advocated despotism or was opposed to individual liberties. Marx disliked capitalism because he believed it enslaved the working class and middle class and made them wage slaves and limited their freedoms. He believed that capitalism would always lead to a grossly unfair division of wealth that would place many in slave-like poverty to support a few men of wealth. He believed capitalism was contrary to individual liberties because money and the powerful would use their wealth and power to rule over the common people, and there is much truth to this in twenty-first century America.

Marx was also against private ownership of property and believed that a truly democratic state would more fairly govern a nation's resources than a few wealthy men. Marx said, "Even an entire society, a nation, or all simultaneously existing societies taken together . . . are not owners of the earth. They are simply its possessors, its beneficiaries, and have to bequeath it in an improved state to succeeding generations."

And while most of us believe in private ownership of property and unlimited wealth, many others in the rest of the world believe this in much lesser degrees. While many would argue for a complete laissez-faire system of private ownership, others see advantages to having some controls, regulations, or public ownership of national resources.

Recently the right has even shown a growing dissatisfaction with social support systems such as Social Security, public pensions, and medical care. They have argued against traditional American public systems like the post office and even the public schools. They advocate charter schools to rob the public schools of their funding. They now insist private is always best. The right's bias against public systems is in stark contrast to the desires of the founding fathers like Benjamin Franklin who created and championed some of our most cherished institutions such as the post office and public schools, including the public university.

However, even in parts of conservative America, there is still a belief in some public ownership or the US wouldn't have a national park or a national forest system. If, for example, Yellowstone were a private property, it would likely look more like Las Vegas or a Disney theme park than a nature park today, and private industry would likely harvest Old Faithful as a geo-thermal energy site. Even Wally Hickel, a staunch conservative Republican businessman who served as the Governor of Alaska and as Nixon's Secretary of the Interior, called public lands "the commons." He strongly advocated that the Arctic and its vast resources, the atmosphere, all waters and the oceans and the fish within them should never be in private ownership because he believed they belong to the future of all mankind.

In 2008 with the near collapse of the global market and economy, Americans also learned what the consequences of unregulated capitalism would be, as Alan Greenspan the chief advocate of unregulated capitalist markets testified before Congress that his belief in free markets was "flawed."

The beliefs of most of the people of the world are somewhere in between complete laissez-faire unregulated capitalism and the complete public ownership of all property. And the difference between communism and socialism is also by degrees with socialists believing in some level of private ownership, and communism believing in mostly or total public ownership. In Western Europe the balance has been made at varying levels, with Social Democracies having higher levels of public control and ownership. This is particularly true in Scandinavia where they enjoy excellent economic success and a high standard of living, or did until American capitalist greed collapsed the global markets in 2007.

The right dislikes and belittles these European social democracies, but then they also disdain American institutions such as the post office, Social Security, Unemployment Insurance, Medicare, the Affordable Care Act and Welfare, including SNAP (food assistance to the poor), as unwanted and unneeded socialism. They believe the poor and disadvantaged deserve their fate. They avow a firm belief in "the survival of the fittest," falsely attributing this philosophy to science and to Charles Darwin. It was actually the conservative politician/sociologist Herbert Spencer who, without benefit of science, originated the concept of survival of the fittest. While at the same time the right disavows Darwin's theories of evolution and natural selection in favor of their faith-based creationist theories, they oddly endorse Spencer's ideas and attribute them to Darwin, and as much as the wealth and the power of the United States are concentrated into the hands of fewer and fewer people, the right blindly sees this as "survival of the fittest" and a hallmark of American success.

The economic wellbeing of most of Americans deteriorated after the right destroyed the left. It is not a coincidence that, as the unions disappeared, living-wage jobs with health and retirement benefits also disappeared. As socialist and communist influences were removed from the debate, so too was any real question as to the degree of concentration of private ownership and wealth in the hands of a few that may be healthy for a society, or what the proper role of government or regulations would be in making sure there is fairness, and so it all gets worse.

The definitions of left and right are really very simple. Capitalism is a system where capital or money rules. Communism is a system where all or most property is owned by the state as a whole. Socialism in varying degrees is that middle ground that seeks a balance between public and private ownership and control. Anarchists and libertarians believe that government is at the root of all evil. Republicans and conservatives, Democrats and even liberals are mostly free market capitalists. Currently there is very little balance or even a substantial debate about the American economic system and this is not good. It is as Supreme Court Justice Louis Brandeis said, "We can have democracy in this country, or we can have great wealth concentrated in the hands of a few, but we can't have both."

Left vs. Right

"Advocates of capitalism like to appeal to the sacred principles of liberty, which are embodied in one maxim: The fortunate must not be restrained in the exercise of tyranny over the unfortunate."—Bertrand Russell

"It could fairly be said that the U.S. is increasingly out of step with the rest of the world. As our neighbors to the south elect left-wing or even socialist governments, we are lurching further to the right, as Europe becomes less engaged to the Church, we are becoming more fundamentalist."—Graydon Carter, American journalist

The American left and right have differences other than private vs. public ownership. In economic terms the right favors individual acquisition of wealth with the left favoring equitable distribution. The right believes that wealth should be distributed to the "fittest" or those deemed deserving, which are frequently seen as those that a Christian god has already determined to be deserving, while the left believes in wealth distribution by merit, fairness, equality, and need.

In cultural terms the right views America as primarily or solely as a capitalist and Christian nation, while the left believes in free thought and the separation of religion and the state. The right views America as an Anglo-Saxon Eurocentric culture, while the left views America as diverse and multi-cultural. The right wants an English only nation, while the left sees the benefits of a multi-lingual society. The emphasis of the right is primarily on economic contributions, while the left favors social contributions. The right favors religion and faith, while the left favors humanism, environmentalism, science and intellectualism. The outlook of the American right tends to be exclusive, while the American left is inclusive. The right favors tradition and the status quo, while the left favors progress and change. The right measures individuals by status and wealth, while the left measures each by their self-worth. The right sees things in black and white, the left in shades of gray. The right sees the left as overly critical of America or as unpatriotic, while the left sees the right as delusional and apologists for the wealthy and the status quo. The right sees the left as Soviets or Maoists, while the left sees the right as fascists.

Chapter 2. The Birth of Equality

Jean-Jacques Rousseau 1712–1778

> "The first man who, having fenced in a piece of land, said 'This is mine,' and found people naive enough to believe him, that man was the true founder of civil society. From how many crimes, wars, and murders, from how many horrors and misfortunes might not any one have saved mankind, by pulling up the stakes, or filling up the ditch, and crying to his fellows: Beware of listening to this impostor; you are undone if you once forget that the fruits belong to all and that the land belongs to no one."—Jean-Jacques Rousseau, *Discourse on Inequality*

If you want to understand politics and the American left, you have to understand Jean-Jacques Rousseau and his philosophy. Rousseau said, "No man has any natural authority over his fellow men. "And with this simple philosophy Rousseau became a major inspiration to the American, French and even Russian revolutions. He is sometimes credited with being the inspiration behind Europe's constitutional monarchies. He inspired Franklin, Jefferson and Karl Marx. Rousseau was a very religious man, but he was also the first to advocate religious tolerance, campaign against religious excesses and to promote the separation between church and state. He was the main inspiration for Jefferson's writings on freedom of religion.

Rousseau was born in Geneva, Switzerland, into a middleclass family. His mother died nine days after his birth, and his father abandoned him at the age of ten; in later life he developed a suspicion that people were conspiring against him, likely as response to these tragic circumstances, and also to his having to flee from France because of his political writings. Scottish philosopher David Hume would later sympathetically write: "[Rousseau] has not had the precaution to throw any veil over his sentiments; and as he scorns to dissemble his contempt for established opinions, he could not wonder that all the zealots were in arms against him. The liberty of the press is not so secured in any country ... as not to render such an open attack on popular prejudice somewhat dangerous."

Rousseau was a man of contrasts and never a well-liked figure. Napoleon said of him, "It would have been better for the peace of France if this man had never existed." In perhaps his most noted political work, *Social Contract*, written in 1762, Rousseau pronounced the people sovereign, and wrote that one citizen was as equal as any other. Although he was a religious man he disliked the politics of churches and organized religion, and he wrote that organized religion was a form of tyranny. Rousseau proposed a communal society where he claimed that each person would enjoy the protection of a common force while remaining as free as they were in the state of nature. These writings would greatly influence Karl Marx a century later.

There are some major controversies in Rousseau's writings. The primary conflicts were between his concepts of general will and common interest. Most of the so called democracies, both capitalist and the social democracies like those in Scandinavia, interpret Rousseau's writings in their favor, insisting general will is what the citizens of a state have decided together in a democratic process. But the Soviets interpreted Rousseau's general will of common interest as the incarnation of the citizens' common interest as determined by the dictates of the state on their behalf. As a consequence capitalist and social democracies and communist governments have all claimed Rousseau was on their side.

In his book *Liberal Fascism: The Secret History of the American Left, From Mussolini to the Politics of Meaning*, the rightwing conservative political commentator Jonah Goldberg traces fascism to the philosophy of Rousseau who, he says, "properly deserves to be called the father of modern fascism." Most would argue there is very little basis of support for Goldberg's claim. Goldberg also argued that Rousseau was an atheist, saying, "It followed, moreover, that if the people were the new god, there was no room for god Himself.... Loyalty to the state and loyalty to the divine must be seen as the same thing."

Goldberg's claims that Rousseau was an atheist actually destroyed the rest of his argument because it has no absolutely no basis in Rousseau's writings. Rousseau was a religious man; he described god as the "existence of a mighty, intelligent, and beneficent divinity, possessed of foresight and providence." He certainly never argued that "there was no room for god." But then, to begin with, Goldberg's overall argument that the left is the same as the fascist right, and that President Wilson and Roosevelt were fascists, are nonsensical rightwing radio and television ear candy; intellectually this is all a nonstarter. The American right, not the left, has always had fascist leanings, and by all political definitions fascism is a function of the far right, not the left.

It is the right that has a history of supporting fascism. In the 1930s, for example, a large proportion of the American right supported the rise of Hitler and the Fascists; this included Prescott Bush the father and grandfather of two presidents. Prescott Bush and his wealthy American and German friends were the people who helped finance Hitler and the Nazis' rise to power and they profited from them. Hitler's supporters also included the American air hero Charles Lindbergh, and America's most famous industrialist Henry Ford. Both of these men received medals from Hitler and Nazi Germany for their support, as did the infamous American Catholic priest Father Coughlin, the forerunner to the modern day rightwing televangelists. Ford also financed the German American Bund, the Nazis in the United States, and he financed Father Coughlin's fascist activities. Many on the American right supported Hitler, the Nazis and fascism until America went to war.

Most misinterpretations of Rousseau's writings come from his statements about "general will." Rousseau wrote of three different types of general will that need consideration by the state. The first is the individual or private will that is governed by a person's selfish interests. The second is the individual's identification to the collective will and for the collective good which may at times cause conflict with the individual will. It is the Rousseau's collective will that is sometimes misinterpreted as the state's right to define the common will. The third is a general will that identifies with a subset of the population, such as race, ethnicity, religion, etc. that may not be shared by the society as a whole.

Rousseau argued that, under the right conditions and subject to the right procedures, citizen legislators would construct just laws that correspond to all these common interests. He wrote that the laws of the state must be general in application and universal in scope, and argued that the law cannot apply to particular individuals or groups, but that they must apply to everyone equally within the state. And these writings of Rousseau are what influenced the creation of American and French democracies and the European constitutional monarchies.

Rousseau was not a fascist and would have been appalled by Nazi Germany. Rousseau took the view that to give away your general right to rule yourself to another person or to any legislative body constitutes a form a slavery, and that to recognize such an authority would amount to an abdication of morals. These strong beliefs came from Rousseau's hostility to the monarchy, but it has also been argued that this principle applies to the election of representatives to governments just as well, even where those representatives are subject to periodic re-election.

However, in understanding Rousseau's writings a reader must also take into account when they were written. It must also be noted that in the case of representative government, Rousseau would have been arguing in the hypothetical because except for some North American Indian tribes a universal representative government did not exist at the time of his writings. It should also be noted that if Rousseau felt it was slavery and immoral to give away the right to rule yourself, then he would not have been a supporter of either fascist or communist dictatorships.

In *Discourse on the Arts and Sciences*, Rousseau argued that the arts and sciences were not always beneficial to humankind because they did not always address basic human needs but were mostly created for the enjoyment and vanity of the upper classes. Although this was certainly somewhat true in the eighteenth century, it is a part of Rousseau's writing that to both the right and left find to be the most controversial part of his philosophy. Rousseau was against the concentration of wealth in the hands of the few and he believed that too much luxury, including art, had contributed to the corruption of man and his civil societies. Similar themes were later explored by the American economist Thorstein Veblen in his *Theory of the Leisure Class*.

In addition to inspiring Franklin, Jefferson and Marx, Rousseau was an important influence on the German philosopher Immanuel Kant. A portrait of Rousseau was said to be the only image on display in Kant's house. Rousseau and Kant were the primary influences on the writings of Georg Wilhelm Friedrich Hegel, who was an inspiration to the philosophies of Karl Marx and Friedrich Engels. Hegel's *Phenomenology of Spirit* in 1807, also drew upon both Rousseau's and Kant's ideas and in turn both Marx and Engels were influenced by this work, particularly by Hegel's discussion of the master–slave dialectic which inspired Marx's thoughts about the proletariat vs. bourgeoisie.

Like Rousseau, there are also parts of Hegel's writings that are also claimed by people on the left and right. On the political right Hegel's writings on civil society became a description for all non-state aspects of society, including culture, society and politics. On the left, it became the foundation for Marx's economic theories. Hegel's writings about civil society are much like Rousseau's writings on general will, in that both the left and right interpret them in their favor. The historian Alexis de Tocqueville was also greatly influenced and inspired by Rousseau, Kant and Hegel.

Hegel and German Idealism 1770–1831

"When liberty is mentioned, we must always be careful to observe whether it is not really the assertion of private interests which is thereby designated."—Georg Wilhelm Hegel

"The history of the world is none other than the progress of the consciousness of freedom."—Georg Wilhelm Hegel

"We are all of us very good at self-persuasion and I strive to be alert to its traps, but a version of what Hegel called 'the cunning of history' is a parallel commentary that I fight to keep alive in my mind."—Christopher Hitchens

Hegel's influence is represented by two opposing camps. The Right Hegelians, the allegedly direct disciples of Hegel at the University, who advocated Protestant orthodoxy and the political conservatism of the post-Napoleon Restoration period. The Left Hegelians, also known as the Young Hegelians, which included Karl Marx and Friedrich Engels, interpreted Hegel in a revolutionary sense, leading to atheism and supporting a liberal democracy in politics. The Left Hegelians also spawned Marxism, which inspired many global movements, including the Russian Revolution, and Mao and the Chinese Revolution. Hegel also inspired Communitarians, a philosophy that emphasizes the connection between the individual and the community, and the duty an individual has for the overall community.

Georg Wilhelm Friedrich Hegel was born on August 27, 1770, in Stuttgart. His father was a civil servant. His mother was the daughter of a well-known lawyer at the High Court of Justice. When he was thirteen his mother died, most likely of influenza, and his father almost perished from the illness as well; he survived but didn't regain his full health.

At age of three Hegel attended a primary school called the "German School." When he entered the "Latin School" two years later, he already had a good command of Latin, having been taught by his mother. During his schooling and adolescence Hegel was known as a voracious reader, always making copious notes about his readings. At the age of eighteen Hegel entered a Protestant seminary attached to the University of Tubingen.

At the seminary Hegel discovered that he was not religious. He envisaged his future as a man of letters, a philosopher who would teach philosophy. It was during this time that he watched the unfolding of the French Revolution with enthusiasm and a keen interest. It had a great impact on his future writings. After he received his theological certificate from the Tubingen Seminary, Hegel became tutor for an aristocratic family. During this period he began writing, and he composed a text, *The Life of Jesus*, and a book-length manuscript called *The Positivity of the Christian Religion*. Both were much more critical of the Christian religion than their titles would lead prospective readers to believe.

Hegel moved to Frankfurt in 1797. While he was there, Hegel composed the essay *Fragments on Religion and Love*. In 1799, he wrote another essay entitled *The Spirit of Christianity and Its Fate*, a criticism of Christianity which remained unpublished during his lifetime. Also in 1797, the unpublished manuscript *The Oldest Systematic Program of German Idealism* was written in Hegel's hand — but it is thought to have been a joint work with two other friends from the seminary, the poet Friedrich Holderlin and the philosopher Friedrich Wilhelm Joseph Schelling. In 1801 Hegel came to Jena University at the encouragement of his friend Schelling, who held the position of Extraordinary Professor. In 1802, Schelling and Hegel founded the *Kritische Journal der Philosophie* (Critical Journal of Philosophy), to which they each contributed pieces until their collaboration ended when Schelling left for a position in Wurzburg in 1803. In 1805, the University promoted Hegel to the position of Extraordinary Professor.

These academic positions were unsalaried and the little money he had from his family was soon gone. Hegel was now under great pressure to get a salaried academic position and to finish his book, the long-promised introduction to his philosophy. As he was putting the finishing touches to the *Phenomenology of Spirit*, Napoleon engaged Prussian troops on October 14, 1806, in the Battle of Jena on a plateau just outside the city. On the day before the battle, Napoleon entered the city of Jena. Hegel said of Napoleon afterward, "I saw the Emperor, this world-soul, riding out of the city on reconnaissance. It is indeed a wonderful sensation to see such an individual, who, concentrated here at a single point, astride a horse, reaches out over the world and masters it . . . this extraordinary man, whom it is impossible not to admire."

Although Napoleon chose not to close down Jena University as he had other universities, his attack devastated the city and most of the students deserted the university. This made Hegel's financial prospects even more desperate. In March 1807, Hegel moved to Bamberg, where he had an offer to become editor of a newspaper, the *Bamberger Zeitung*. Unable to find more suitable employment, Hegel reluctantly accepted. In November 1808, Hegel was appointed the headmaster of a school in Nuremburg, a post that he held until 1816, and while at the Nuremberg school he adapted his recently published *Phenomenology of Spirit* for use in the classroom.

Hegel's career as a philosopher and a man of letters accelerated after the publication of his second major work: the *Science of Logic*. He received offers of a post from the universities of Berlin and Heidelberg; Hegel chose Heidelberg and moved there in 1816.

Most academics agree that Hegel was an atheist. Though indoctrinated in Lutheranism as a child, Hegel rejected Christianity in his college years. In his early writings, he inveighed against religion. But because of his desire to get a university position Hegel hid his atheism and his anti-authoritarianism. Robert Solomon explains why in his book *From Hegel to Existentialism*: "Hegel really did have a secret, and . . . it has been well kept. The secret, abruptly stated, is that Hegel was an atheist. His 'Christianity' is nothing but nominal, an elaborate subterfuge to protect his professional ambitions in the most religiously conservative country in northern Europe." Terry Pinkard in his book *Hegel a Biography* states, "Hegel was desperate for a professorship, and to get a position he needed a book." Hegel knew that writing a book that openly espoused atheism would have destroyed his career before it began, so his book was highly nuanced.

Robert Solomon also pointed out that: "Hegel had seen Spinoza's *Ethics* widely condemned in Germany. He had seen Kant, whom he considered to be unquestioningly orthodox, condemned and censored by the narrow-minded regime of Frederick Wilhelm II. He had seen Fichte dismissed from the University of Jena for views that were (incorrectly) considered atheistic."

Hegel sought a professorship back at the University of Jena and, being aware of Fichte's dismissal for atheism, he chose to disguise his writings. The *Phenomenology of Spirit* was a book that espoused atheism by covertly redefining god as the spirit of humanity. Solomon offers this explanation: "What then does Hegel's conception of god admit, which any atheist would not? To say that god exists is no more than to say that humanity exists. That is atheism."

Hegel's master and slave dialectic, which is also called lordship and bondage, is the most widely discussed passage of Hegel's *Phenomenology of Spirit*. In *Phenomenology of Spirit* freedom is the release from bondage to god, religion, and to religious superstition. Freedom is when man becomes an atheist, finally recognizing that he and not the supernatural god of religion is the true god. Hegel's Master and Slave Dialectic can be summarized as follows: The master or lord encounters, and subdues or defeats a person who becomes his slave. But the master ultimately becomes totally dependent on the slave, just as god's existence depends on man's belief in him, so the slave will eventually become the master, and man will become god.

Marx and Engels, both Young Hegelians, were very deeply influenced by Hegel's master and slave dialectic.

CHAPTER 3. FROM MERCANTILISM TO CAPITALISM

> "The economic system (neo-mercantilism) we are now creating in (Adam) Smith's name bears a far greater resemblance to the monopolistic market system he condemned ... (and) opposed as inefficient and contrary to the public's interest ... than it does to the theoretical competitive market system he hypothesized would result in optimal allocation of a society's resources."—David C. Korten, *When Corporations Rule the World*

> "Capitalism is a pure religious cult. Perhaps the most extreme there ever was."—Walter Bendix Schönflies Benjamin, German philosopher and essayist

> "Large Societies can only function economically if they have a redistributive economy in addition to a reciprocal economy. Goods in excess of an individual's needs must be transferred from the individual to the central authority, which then redistributes the goods to the individuals with deficits."—Jared Diamond, *Guns, Germs, and Steel.*

The British economist Adam Smith is the father of modern capitalism, particularly American capitalism. Smith's world was dominated by the Mercantilists. Mercantilism was really a nationalistic extension of feudalism and was the economic doctrine that a government's control of foreign trade is of paramount importance for ensuring the wealth and military security of a country. It was based upon and demanded that a nation have a positive balance of trade. Mercantilism dominated Western European economic policy and political thought from the sixteenth to late eighteenth centuries. Mercantilism in its simplest form was about bullionism, the acquisition of precious metals, primarily gold and silver, by merchants and their governments. It was supposedly about the circulation of money and growing the nation's wealth, but in reality it encouraged monopolies, hoarding and a concentration of wealth. The mercantilist disdain towards economic regulation was the same as feudalist attitudes, and mercantilism was really a commercial extension of agricultural feudalism.

In the American colonies British mercantilism was an alliance between the British government and the British merchants. The merchants were frequently given monopolies and became partners with the government with the goal of increasing British political power and wealth to the exclusion of other empires, particularly the Spanish, French and Dutch. The British protected their merchants with their navy and attacked other nations' merchant vessels even in times of peace by secretly promoting piracy. The British kept the other nations' merchants and traders out of their colonies with trade barriers and regulations. They also subsidized some colonial industries in order to maximize the flow of resources and goods from the colonies to Britain and to maximize the sale of British goods back to the colonies, while they sought to minimize imports from other nations to the colonies. Smuggling and piracy became a favorite American colonial industry in the eighteenth century when Americans sought to circumvent the English restrictions on trading with the French, Spanish and Dutch for their own gain.

The British goal of mercantilism was to run trade surpluses so that gold and silver would pour into London. The British government also took more than its fair share of colonial trade through duties and taxes. British goods were also sold at artificially high prices to the colonies with a nice profit for the British merchants at the expense of the colonists. The British and their merchants also set artificially low prices for purchased colonial goods and resources, which had the effect of further encouraging smuggling and piracy. These unfair economic limitations were a significant factor pushing the colonies to claim independence. Economic decisions were more important than concerns about personal freedoms and liberties as the root cause of the American Revolution.

Adam Smith was opposed to such mercantilist controls and argued in 1776, in his book *The Wealth of Nations,* that Britain and the merchants would prosper more if a free market was allowed to exist without these trade barriers and restrictions. In addition to a free market, Smith wrote that the wealth of a nation depended upon the productivity of labor and the number of laborers who are usefully or productively employed. Smith also assumed that the economy would automatically achieve full employment if the market was operating freely, a belief which has proven to be very problematic.

One of Smith's concerns as he wrote about free markets was that they soon tended to become dominated and controlled by the rich and powerful, as they had during the feudalist period. He wrestled with this and never fully justified how a capitalist free market could work. In the end Smith couldn't find a reason to prevent a free market from becoming dominated by the rich and powerful, and since he was a religious man, he turned to a higher power, writing that "[man] neither intends to promote the public interest, nor knows how much he is promoting it....He intends only in his own gain and in this, as in many other cases, he is led by an invisible hand." The followers of Smith would use this "invisible hand theory" to imply that either god or some kind of natural law was guiding the rich and the economy to do what is right. Unfortunately, economics is a cultural phenomenon where neither nature nor god plays any role. As John Stuart Mill wrote, the distribution of wealth: "Is a matter of human distinction solely. The things once there, mankind, individually or collectively, can do with them what they like."

The writings of Adam Smith were well received in the American colonies because Smith advocated free trade without barriers, tariffs or taxes which had stifled colonial trade, prices and growth. It affected both the economic activities of the middleclass Yankee traders and the American Southern aristocratic plantation owners like Jefferson and Washington.

However as Marx would later state in *Das Capital*, capitalism like mercantilism is distinguished by almost exclusively private ownership and by the concentration of the means of production and wealth in the hands of very few. In modern America, wealth and the means of production are indeed very concentrated in the hands of a very few. Capitalist economies have shown themselves to be systems with very uneven distribution of wealth and the conundrum of the American right is that the "free market" and unchecked capitalism have historically produced many more losers than winners.

Typically in capitalist economies less than one percent of people own more than half of the nation's productive capacity and most of the wealth. This is especially true in the United States. Common mathematical models of such distributions include power-law distributions, exponential distributions, and mixtures of the two, and all show the same results. In reviewing these distributions in capitalist societies, it becomes clear that a few people will own hundreds of thousands or sometimes millions of times more than the average person does. One common mathematical formula for comparing nations with each other in terms of their unequal wealth distribution is called the Gini Index or Ratio. This ratio shows that the United States has about the same inequitable wealth distribution as many very poor third world countries.

According to Karl Marx, the treatment of labor (working people) as a commodity leads to people valuing things more according to their price rather than their usefulness, and this leads to an expansion of the system of commodities. Marx observed that some people bought commodities in order to use them, while others bought them in order to sell elsewhere at a profit, and some bought commodities because they were rare or in fashion. These are clearly left-over elements of mercantilism. They are also the unfortunate foundation for the modern American consumer economy, where much of what we buy is because Madison Avenue controls the wants and desires of the American people. Americans purchase goods to keep up with their neighbors and buy things they really can't afford in the hope of appearing higher in class or status than they are.

Later writers expanded upon the roots of capitalism, further defining what it is. In 1904, in *The Protestant Ethic and the Spirit of Capitalism*, German sociologist Max Weber wrote that the Protestant ethic was an important factor in the economic success of Protestant groups in the early stages of European capitalism. Weber believed that worldly success could be interpreted as a sign of eternal salvation under Calvinism. Calvinism emphasizes a religious duty to make good use of all the god-given resources that are at each individual's disposal. And it follows that an individual's wealth is therefore a sign that person is more favored by god than others. It is an extension of the European Divine Right of Kings which claimed that: I am king because god made me king, and you are a poor peasant because god choose you to be, and who are we to question god? This concept of predestination is hard-wired into capitalism.

On September 10, 2006, *Time* magazine published an article, *Does God Want You To Be Rich?*, which stated that a good majority of Americans believed that god decided who was rich or poor. This concept of predestination is also hard-wired into the collective consciousness of the American people. It is a significant basis for the American Christian-Capitalist belief system and the American class system.

Weber's work is reflected later by the American historian Samuel Eliot Morison who wrote in *The Oxford History of the American People*, "Puritanism was hewed out of the Black Forests of feudal Europe and the American wilderness. Puritan Doctrine taught each person to consider himself a significant, if sinful, unit, to whom god had given a particular place and duty, and that he must help his fellow men. And, "Puritanism appealed to merchants because they taught that man could serve god as well in business or a profession, as by taking Holy Orders."

Capitalism would be tied to the Protestant Ethic of hard work and thrift. It would become a cultural universal and the preeminent American religion or belief system. It is why capitalism and the religious right are so firmly cemented together. It is why they vehemently hate the irreverent left and see them as a challenge to their religious beliefs. Henry Ford, the American industrialist, would reaffirm this by saying, "There can be no conflict between good economics and good morals, as we know anything that is economically right is morally right."

English historian R.H. Tawney expanded on Weber's thesis in his *Religion and the Rise of Capitalism* in 1926 and argued that political and social pressures and the spirit of individualism with its ethic of self-help and frugality were significant factors in the development of capitalism.

More recently the author Ayn Rand attempted to write a moral defense of capitalism, one we might call overly romantic, in her libertarian novels; she argued for free market capitalism with no regulation and won converts on the American right like the Chairman of the Federal Reserve Bank, Alan Greenspan. He was so enamored with Rand that he had the novelist stand beside him at his swearing-in ceremony as Chairman of the Council of Economic Advisors in 1974. Greenspan remained a follower and a believer of Rand until well after her death in 1982. However, the collapse of the free market economy in 2007–2008 forced even Greenspan to admit to Congress that this was a flawed philosophy. He said to Congress, "Yes, I've found a flaw. I don't know how significant or permanent it is. But I've been very distressed by that fact."

Others on the right haven't been as quick to learn. Conservative Republican Congressman Paul Ryan, the self-proclaimed budget guru of the political right and the Republican Vice Presidential candidate in 2012, also attributes his philosophical and economic foundation to the overly moralistic libertarian fiction of Ayn Rand.

The rightwing pundit Ann Coulter asked: "Why is it so difficult for people to grasp the advantages of a free market?... the capitalist system here in America managed to produce a society in which the poorest citizens have televisions, refrigerators, telephones, and the opportunity to appear on the Jerry Springer Show." Coulter freely admits to her intellectual shortcomings and biases as she has also said, "I'm a Christian first, and a mean-spirited, bigoted conservative second, and don't you ever forget it." Unfortunately many of the people Coulter disdains in her first quote also don't have adequate food, shelter or medical care.

One of the failings of capitalism is that where it has been excellent at producing cheap consumer goods such as cell phones and televisions, unfortunately the basics such as food, transportation, housing and particularly medical care, are unaffordable for too many. It is why American poor people have televisions and other electronics. And because of these cheap amenities it is also why many Americans don't consider these people as poor as say someone in rural Africa earning less than a dollar per day but who have crude but adequate food and shelter.

Karl Marx was one of the few economists to recognize and explain this contradiction. He noted that the basic needs of people would differ from country to country and from rural to urban. The necessities for survival in inner-city Milwaukee will not be the same as in rural Africa. A destitute family in Milwaukee may own a television, but it doesn't mean they are wealthier or better off than a rural African family making less than a dollar per day: they may have never seen television, but they may have adequate food, shelter and a safe place for their family to survive. And while some will continue to argue that the poor Milwaukee family could sell the television to get money for food, the resale of inexpensive electrical appliances or other cheap consumer goods is not a very profitable or realistic option. Some will also argue that the Milwaukee family should have bought food instead of the television to begin with, but this too fails to recognize that poverty and income in poor American households is not static; it usually fluctuates. And where a family may have been able to pay rent, buy food and still afford to buy a television at one time, it doesn't mean that they will be able to afford the necessities going forward. Over half of the American people live paycheck to paycheck and a loss of job, loss of a spouse, or an illness in their family is frequently the cause of American poverty. Health care bills are the top cause of bankruptcy in America. Confucius said, "In a country well governed, poverty is something to be ashamed of. In a country badly governed, wealth is something to be ashamed of."

The Free Market, Milton Friedman and the Chicago School

> "I am in favor of cutting taxes under any circumstances and for any excuse and for any reason."—Milton Friedman.

> "The theories of Milton Friedman gave him the Nobel Prize; they gave Chile General Pinochet."—Eduardo Galeano, Latin American journalist and writer.

> "Fascism should more appropriately be called Corporatism because it is a merger of state and corporate power."—Benito Mussolini

Capitalism took a decided right turn when the "free market" economists of the "Chicago School," also known as the "Chicago Boys," came to prominence starting in the 1950s. Today these policies are worshiped by conservatives and the American right. Even so-called moderate politicians like Bill and Hillary Clinton abide by their principles, which is why the Clintons dismantled Roosevelt's New Deal AFDC Program for the nation's poor children.

Milton Friedman and his policies were the foundation of "Reaganomics" and George W. Bush's "Ownership Society." They are the policies that controlled Clinton and inspired George W. Bush's nation-building and his quest to "privatize" Social Security. They are the reason Republicans want to destroy Social Security, Medicare and even the US Post Office. They are the policies that economically and politically hamstring Barack Obama.

The Chicago School sought to dismantle the New Deal and to refute Thorstein Veblen and Keynesian economics. They are proponents of a laissez-faire "free market" and seek the abolishment of all market regulations, taxation and government supports. They are against unions, minimum wage, Social Security, Medicare, environmental regulations, and any type of government social program, even public schools. They wish to dismantle the US Post Office, public school systems, and national parks. They believe all these to be government interference in their magical free market. Naomi Klein in her book *Shock Doctrine, The Rise of Disaster Capitalism* gives an excellent account of the Chicago School and their failings.

Here is a listing of some prominent figures associated with the Chicago School and their beliefs:

- Robert Fogel was one of the "Chicago Boys." Fogel preposterously argued that pre-Civil War slaves in the South had a higher standard of living than the White workers in the Northern states. He believed this apparently justified Southern economics and his arguments that the government should stay out of these affairs. He also argued that the building of the railroads in the 19th century with the assistance of government was a gross mistake and that they didn't contribute to meaningful economic growth. This theory has been denounced by many as inventing a justification for slavery. It may also be noted that the railroads were actually the largest employer in America during its industrial era and contributed enormously to American wealth.

- Ronald Coase, another well-respected "Chicago Boy," was a strict libertarian and believed that laws and regulations are not as necessary "as lawyers and government believe." He felt that the government should do nothing, pass few laws and no regulations, and let individuals and corporations find the best solutions on their own.

- George Stigler was the developer of "Capture Theory" which claims that in an efficient market, the government and industry regulators will soon become captured by the industry they are regulating, and therefore regulatory agencies are redundant and unneeded.

- Richard Posner advocated that law and justice should be about efficiency, because in a world of scarce resources waste should be regarded as immoral. Therefore resources and goods should be allocated to those who would use them the most efficiently, meaning the corporations and the wealthy.

- But the most influential and the man who caused the most damage was Milton Friedman. Friedman was a capitalist zealot. His almost religious belief in a capitalist free and unregulated market was so strong that he was willing to see mass poverty and unemployment, war, mass murder, and torture used to meet his goals. Although he didn't participate in these activities directly, he did cause, inspire, advise, condone and encourage those who undertook these evils on his behalf. The torturous regime of Augusto Pinochet in Chile was his first client and his inspiration. He inspired the coup that overthrew the democratic government of Chile. He advised the Chilean government and Pinochet personally, and some of his "Chicago Boys" actually took positions in the government within hours of Pinochet taking power. The previously mentioned book by Naomi Klein documents this quite well.

Friedman and the Chicago School were also involved with the military coups that destroyed the democratic governments of Argentina and Brazil. They were also involved in Uruguay. They became the financial and economic advisors to these torturous and repressive regimes. They strongly encouraged further repression to achieve their economic goals when the local populations objected to their economic systems. They advised harsh military crackdowns on any groups or individuals who disagreed with their vision. They saw these nations as their living laboratory to demonstrate the wisdom of their economic theories at any cost.

They failed miserably. In Chile, where Friedman and his acolytes spent the most time, the economy crashed in shambles. Unemployment went from about 3% under the former democracy to about 30% under the military dictator Pinochet. Under the guidance of the "Chicago Boys" the country went into hyperinflation. They destroyed all financial regulations and the unregulated corporations and speculators then raided the Chilean economy, causing a national debt of about $14 billion. Prior to Pinochet, Chile was a prosperous country with a poverty rate of about 9%, much less than the poverty rate in the United States; it became poverty stricken under the Chicago Boys' guidance and about half of the Chilean people, 45%, sank into poverty during these free market experiments. Food became scarce and unaffordable to many. Pensions and medical assistance from the government stopped on Freidman's advice.

The economic catastrophe only stopped when Pinochet realized that Chile was headed for total economic ruin and he stopped implementing Friedman's and the "Chicago Boy's" theories. Uruguay, Brazil and Argentina all had similar results under Friedman and the Chicago School's direction. It was economic disaster. As one of Friedman's Latin American critics said of him, "Thousands of people were imprisoned so that his markets could be free."

Despite these bloody coups, torture and gross economic failures the growing neoconservative movement still enthusiastically embraces the philosophy of Friedman and the Chicago School. The philosophy of Friedman became the foundation of conservative and Republican politics. The Chicago School's policies were implemented in the US with zeal by Presidents Reagan, Bush Sr., Clinton, and Bush Jr. and particularly by Treasury Secretary Alan Greenspan. And the result was a rapid and widening gap between the rich and poor, as the wealth was concentrated in the top one percent. It also brought about the massive failure of the unregulated markets in 2008, which nearly destroyed the economy of the United States and much of Europe. Even Greenspan, a staunch advocate of Milt Freidman's policies, had to admit to Congress that his desire to achieve unregulated free markets had been wrong. Unfortunately, conservatives and Republicans still fanatically push the Friedman and Chicago School agenda.

Kevin Phillips, The Reincarnation of a Rightwing Conservative

> "This country is facing an enormous economic and financial crisis. The notion that you can reform the tax system to give more tax breaks to the people at the top and that's somehow going to light a fire under an economy that's weakening in a lot of places is, I think, ridiculous."—Kevin Phillips

> "....[Y]oung people unskilled in mathematics, addled by credit cards, and weaned on so-called intelligent design...will somehow retool American science for another generation of world industrial leadership."—Kevin Phillips sarcastically commenting on rightwing economic and education policies

Kevin Phillips was a campaign strategist for Richard Nixon's 1968 presidential campaign, and his signature work for that successful campaign became the basis for a book, *The Emerging Republican Majority*, which became the political playbook of the rightwing conservative Republican Party in national politics from then to the present. His predictions of shifts in voting patterns in presidential elections, and thoughts on how to manipulate them, proved accurate and helped win the presidency for Nixon, Reagan and both Bushes, and eventually resulted in the Republican takeover of Congress in 1994. Phillips accurately predicted the political shifts of what are now called red and blue states and set a strategy on how the Republicans could manipulate the voters to their advantage. Kevin Phillips and Patrick Buchanan were also responsible for the design of the Republican Southern Strategy whereby the Republican Party embraced the Southern biases and the politics of race and religion to become the preferred party of the South. As a result the Republican Party was eventually captured by White rightwing Christians and it has now become a rural and regional Southern party. This strategy permanently disaffected African-American, Latino, Asian-American, Native American and even women voters, which may lead to the Party's eventual downfall.

Phillips decided to research and write about the economic successes of this Republican political coup that he helped engineer. His research was eye-opening for him. He discovered the consequences had been the reverse of what he thought. He found that his policies were not contributing to American prosperity but were instead directing America's wealth into the hands of far fewer people. He also found that these policies were destroying the middleclass.

After these discoveries Phillips became disenchanted with the right and their economics. Phillips then became a scathing critic. His transformation started with the research and writing of his book *The Politics of Rich and Poor: Wealth and Electorate in the Reagan Aftermath* which he wrote in 1990. Phillips began to compare the contemporary economy to two other eras of unchecked capitalism, the Gilded Age and the Roaring Twenties. The book infuriated the right by showing that their "capitalist free market" policies had unfairly and dangerously concentrated wealth at the expense of most of the American people, and Phillips became persona non grata with conservatives and Republicans. In 2002, he wrote *Wealth and Democracy: A Political History of the American Rich*, which completed his reincarnation; some consider the book to be an American classic. The book was an expansion of *The Politics of Rich and Poor* and warned about the unprecedented concentration of wealth and power. It also gave a history of economic bubbles and predicted an economic catastrophe, which came in 2008.

In 2004, he wrote *American Dynasty: Aristocracy, Fortune, and the Politics of Deceit in the House of Bush*, which criticized both Bush presidents and the tendency of Americans to crave and re-elect "royal" families without merit like the Bushes and the Clintons. In 2006, he wrote *American Theocracy: The Peril and Politics of Radical Religion, Oil, and Borrowed Money in the 21st Century*, which looked at the role of religion, oil power, and the financial industry on the politics of the American right. And in 2007, he authored *Bad Money: Reckless Finance, Failed Politics, and the Global Crisis of American Capitalism*.

The writings of Phillips provide excellent analysis and criticism of power, politics and capitalism, and are even more astonishing because they were written by the man who had created the blueprint that created that power. In a rather extraordinary way it was Phillips' apology for helping to create the Frankenstein that almost killed the American economy.

Long before Phillips, the American economist Henry George said, "What has destroyed every previous civilization has been the tendency to the unequal distribution of wealth and power."

Chapter 4. Communism

"For us in Russia communism is a dead dog. For many people in the West, it is still a living lion."—Aleksandr Solzhenitsyn

"For us there are two kinds of people in the world, there are those who are Christians and support free enterprise, and there are the others."—Secretary of State John Foster Dulles at the height of the Cold War

"The same rightists who decades ago were shouting, 'Better dead than red!' are now often heard mumbling, 'Better red than eating hamburgers.'"—Slovoj Zizek, Slovenian sociologist and philosopher

"I still call myself a communist, because communism is no more what Russia made of it than Christianity is what the churches make of it."—Folk singer and philosopher Pete Seeger

"From each according to his ability, to each according to his needs," is probably the signature statement by Karl Marx that best describes his utopian economic philosophy. Communism is based upon the basic idea that private property is usually at the expense of everyone, and that common ownership of property is to the benefit of everyone. It is not a new concept and pre-dates Marxist writing and thought. Marx actually attributed the original communist societies to the pre-history hunter gather tribes who lived in communal societies and to early Christian sects. The first writings on the subject were not from Marx, but came from Plato who wrote about the idea of common ownership in *The Republic*. Along with Plato's *Republic*, the writings of Rousseau particularly *Social Contract*, and Hegel greatly influenced Marx and he was also influenced by his partner Friedrich Engels.

Karl Marx and Friedrich Engels

> "The individual is handicapped by coming face to face with a conspiracy so monstrous he cannot believe it exists."—J. Edgar Hoover on Marxism

> "The problem with Marxism is the proletariat isn't going to rise up against capitalism and consumerism. The only time they'll rise up is during a commercial break to either go to the bathroom or grab more beer."—Jarod Kintz, American writer

Karl Marx was born in 1818 as the son of a German Jewish lawyer Hirschel Marx. When Karl was a child, Hirschel converted to Protestantism in an attempt to avoid the German anti-Semitism and persecution that was very common at this time. Karl Marx was a promising student, and upon completing his early schooling he began to attend the University at Bonn to study law like his father. However, Marx began to run with a wild crowd and ran up significant debts; he was also almost killed in a duel. His father paid off his debts and forced him to transfer to the more quiet and staid Berlin University. The move was transforming as Marx returned to being an excellent student. He also began to idolize one of his lecturers, Bruno Bauer, whose atheism and socialist political opinions enchanted Marx. It was Bauer who introduced Marx to the writings of Hegel. Bauer had known and admired Hegel, who had been the professor of philosophy at Berlin University until his death in 1831.

In 1838 Marx's father died and he was forced to earn his own living. With Bauer's help he became a university lecturer. He completed his doctoral thesis at the University of Jena, and Marx hoped that Bauer would also help find him a teaching post. However, in 1842, Bauer was terminated from the University for his outspoken atheism. His dismissal embittered Marx, who was also an atheist. Bauer's constant trouble with the authorities because of his atheist views also helped to radicalize Marx.

Marx became a journalist and editor of the newspaper *Rhenish Gazette*. He began writing socialist articles and his newspaper became politically very controversial. His criticism of the government caused the Prussian authorities to ban the publication and forced Marx to leave Prussia. However, years later Marx would return to Germany and revive this newspaper.

After the newspaper was banned, friends warned him that he might be arrested. Marx quickly married the woman he was courting, Jenny von

Westphalen, and they moved to Paris where he accepted the post of editor of a new political journal, the *Franco-German Annals*. Among the contributors to this socialist journal were his old mentor Bruno Bauer, Russian anarchist Michael Bakunin, and the radical son of a fairly well-to-do German industrialist named Friedrich Engels.

If Marx gave birth to communism, then it was fathered by Engels. In 1845, Engels published *The Condition of the Working Class in England*, which may be fairly described as the first significant communist writing. Engels was the son of a German middleclass businessman. Early in his education Engels fell in love with the works of Hegel and became one of the Young Hegelians, a group of Germans who saw Hegel's philosophy as the key to forming a fair and just egalitarian society. This group also included Karl Marx, although the two would not meet until later.

In 1842, when he was just twenty-two, Engels' parents became so concerned about his political radicalism and his open hostility to the upper classes that they sent him to work in Manchester, England, thinking that the change in geography might result in a change in politics. However in Manchester Engels met a young working class Irish woman, Mary Burns, who was a more radical leftist than he was. Engels was enchanted by her. The two became life-long monogamous partners. They never married because both were atheists and disdained religion, and they refused to have a Christian religious ceremony dominate their relationship. Burns is credited with showing Engels the working conditions of the English and Irish workmen that led to his writing *The Condition of the Working Class in England.*

When Karl Marx met Mary Burns, he too was also enchanted with her. Later, upon learning of her young death at the age of forty-seven, he wrote to Engels that Mary Burns was one of the "best natured and witty" people he had ever known. After Mary's death, Engels lived with Mary's younger sister Lizzie, whom he later married on his death bed so that she could legally inherit his money and possessions.

In 1844, on a trip back home to Germany, Engels first met Marx, at the Café de la Régence on the Place du Palais. Marx had read and published some of Engels' writings in the *Franco-German Annals*; he was impressed with him and had arranged their meeting through letters. The two immediately became close friends and decided to collaborate on their writings. Engels shared Marx's views on capitalism and after their first meeting he wrote that there was virtually "complete agreement in all theoretical fields." After publishing their first article together in Paris, *The Holy Family*, the Prussian authorities banned *Franco-German Annals* in Germany and put pressure on the French government to expel Marx from the country. In January of 1845, Marx fled France for Belgium and Engels accompanied him.

In Belgium Marx used up the last of his money and in August of 1845, Marx joined Engels in Manchester, England. Engels began to support Marx and his family in England with the royalties of his book and arranged for other socialist sympathizers to make donations to support Marx. During this time Marx and Engels used their time to study and more fully develop their economic and political theories, while continuing to write.

Both Engels and Marx returned to Brussels in 1846, where they set up a Communist Correspondence Committee. They began to organize and link together the socialist leaders in Europe. During this time some socialists in England who were influenced by Marx's ideas held a conference in London where they formed the Communist League. Engels attended the conference on behalf of Marx to help shape the organization. In 1847, the Communist League outlined the goals of their organization, namely "the overthrow of the bourgeoisie, the domination by the proletariat, the abolition of the old bourgeois society based on class antagonisms, and the establishment of a new society without classes and without private property." In 1848, Marx and Engels co-authored *The Communist Manifesto* to further define the Communist philosophy.

Following the publication of the Communist Manifesto, the Belgian government expelled Engels and Marx. They returned to Paris and stayed there briefly before moving to Germany, where they recreated the newspaper *Rhenish Gazette*. The men hoped to use the newspaper to encourage socialism among the German people.

Engels helped Marx form a socialist organization called the Rhineland Democrats. In September of 1848, several of the leaders of the group were arrested, but Engels managed to escape to England. Marx continued to publish the *Rhenish Gazette* until he was expelled in 1849, and then he too returned to England. The Prussian authorities applied pressure on the British government to expel the two men so they could be arrested and imprisoned, but the British Prime Minister, John Russell, refused on the grounds of freedom of expression. The two men moved to London with their families. Money soon became an issue and Marx, Engels and their families fell into poverty. Because of these hard times Engels reluctantly and quietly returned to work for his father at his business in Prussia. However, he kept in constant contact with Marx, and they corresponded with each other with two or more letters per week. Engels also regularly sent money to his impoverished friend. Despite all his financial and political problems, Marx continued to write and in 1867 the first volume of *Das Kapital* was published.

Marx began work on the second volume of *Das Kapital* in 1871, with help from his sixteen-year-old daughter Eleanor. She was home schooled by her father and at sixteen already had a very detailed understanding of economics, capitalism and communism. She would later to play an important role in the British labor movement. When Eleanor left home to take a job as a school teacher, his writing slowed to almost a halt. However, when Marx and his wife became very ill, Eleanor returned home to nurse them and also helped her father finish his second volume. Eleanor Marx was never really recognized for her work and her contributions to communist doctrine, just as Mary Burns was never credited for the significant role she played in Engels' writings. This was not completely the fault of Marx and Engels, as these were times dominated by men, and women's opinions were not taken as seriously. This was true of even Marx, who said, "Anyone who knows anything of history knows that great social changes are impossible without feminine upheaval. Social progress can be measured exactly by the social position of the fair sex, the ugly ones included."

The end of Marx's life was not a happy one, due to illness and poverty. He wrote to Engels a year before his death to say it was a life not worth living. Marx died in London in 1883. Engels devoted the rest of his life to editing and translating and promoting Marx's writings, including the second volume of *Das Kapital.* Engels used Marx's notes to write a third volume that was published in 1894, and shortly after this Friedrich Engels died, in 1895.

Communism aside, the two men made considerable contributions to the art and science of economics. These two men of bourgeois upper middle class backgrounds gave up what would have been comfortable lives, had they followed in their father's professions. Instead they chose a life of persecution and poverty to pursue what they thought was justice for the greater mass of working class people. Their efforts were admirable, whether or not you agree with their viewpoints and their utopian politics. These are two men who changed the world. Their ideas and writings are still debated for their meanings today.

Gus Hall, The American Communist

> "Socialism in America will come through the ballot box."—Gus Hall

> "Communism is a religion that is inspired, directed and motivated by the Devil himself who has declared war against Almighty God."—Reverend Billy Graham

He was born Arvo Kustaa Halberg in rural northern Minnesota in 1910. He later changed his name to Gus Hall to be more American. His parents were Finnish immigrants and, like many Finns, he and his parents were active members of the International Workers of the World, sometimes referred to as the "Wobblies." He spoke both Finnish and English fluently. He came from a large, poor family with ten children and at age fifteen he went to work in the northern Minnesota lumber camps and iron mines to help support his family.

In 1927, at the age of seventeen, he was recruited into the Communist Party USA (CPUSA) and became an organizer for the Young Communist League. In 1931, he was given the opportunity to go to Moscow and study at the International Lenin School. Upon his return he moved to Minneapolis and became a union activist. In 1934, he was jailed for six months for being an organizer of the Minneapolis Teamsters' Strike. The strike became violent when the Minneapolis Police were encouraged to use excessive force to break up the workers' protest. It was a police riot and then Hall and other union leaders were unfairly blamed for the violence.

Afterward he moved to Ohio to organize steel workers. He became involved with John L. Lewis and helped organize the Congress of Industrial Organizations, (CIO), which would later merge with the American Federation of Labor to become the premier American labor organization, the AFL-CIO.

In 1937, Hall became more active in the CPUSA and became the Communist Leader of Cleveland. He ran for Governor of Ohio as a communist and received a small number of votes. In what many believed were trumped up charges, he was sent to jail for election fraud in 1940 and spent 90 days in Jail.

He voluntarily joined the Navy in World War II just after Pearl Harbor. He served the entire war in the Pacific and was honorably discharged in 1946. After the War, he was elected to the National Executive Board of the Communist Party USA.

In 1948, under the Smith Act, Hall was convicted of advocating Marxism, which the government said was the same as "the act of teaching the violent overthrow of the US Government." In fact Hall never sought nor advocated the overthrow of the government and said, "Socialism in America will come through the ballot box." After he had served five years in prison, he was released on bail while the Supreme Court reviewed the Smith Act. In 1951, the Court upheld the Smith Act and his conviction. Hall told friends that the ruling was unconstitutional and decided he would not return to prison. He skipped bail with three other convicted communists and went to Mexico. They were caught and sent to prison for another three years. The Supreme Court later reversed their decision, finding that the Smith Act and Hall's conviction were unconstitutional, and he was released. He had served a total of eight years in prison for a wrongful and unconstitutional conviction.

After his release, Hall became the General Secretary and Chairman of the Communist Party USA. In the early 1960s, the government was again attempting to send Hall to prison, under the McCarran Act this time, for being a communist. The Supreme Court also later found this Act to be unconstitutional, but first, the State of New York used the McCarran Act to revoke Hall's driver's license and to otherwise harass him for being a communist. In 1959, he was awarded the Order of Lenin, the highest civilian award in the Soviet Union, for his wrongful imprisonment, courage, suffering and contributions to communism. This further enraged the American government.

When not in prison, Hall and the CPUSA were constantly harassed throughout the 1950s. On May 27, 1956, US Treasury agents seized the Communist Party newspaper *The Daily Worker* for nonpayment of taxes. At the same time they raided communist party offices in New York, Newark, Chicago, Detroit, Los Angeles, Philadelphia and San Francisco.

In the 1960s, Hall attempted to democratize the Communist Party USA and to merge it with the growing new American left movement and the anti-war movement. Unlike the Soviet Union, he envisioned an American communist democracy but was unsuccessful in attracting many people from the anti-war or civil right movements. He also strongly advocated peaceful co-existence between the United States and the Soviet Union, and the abolishment of nuclear weapons; these stances earned him the reputation of a "dangerous peacenik" among the likes of J. Edgar Hoover.

In 1964, Hall and the Communist Party USA supported Lyndon Johnson for president because Hall feared that a Goldwater presidency would bring nuclear war with the Soviet Union. Hall also visited the Soviet Union on many occasions in the 1960s and 1970s, and some American communists and socialists, and others, thought he had become a Soviet apologist. Hall endorsed the communist governments of Cuba and Vietnam, but he also severely criticized the Communist governments of China and North Korea because of their lack of freedoms, but he ignored these issues in his admiration of the USSR.

Communism is different in different places. It is not the same uniform evil conspiring against the United States that Americans like to believe. One thing that Americans of the right and left share is that they are not very good at understanding that governments, communist or otherwise, are shaped by the cultures and histories of the countries they govern. The Russian czars and the Russian Orthodox Church, for example, were many times harsher to their people than most of the monarchies of Western Europe. The Russian serfs were no better than slaves and were considered property of the Russian aristocracy. The Russian peasants were forced into blind obedience of the czars and the Russian Orthodox Church. The Russian communist government also demanded the blind loyalty of the Russian peasants and easily received it as the peasants merely transferred their loyalties from one master to another. And likewise, after the Soviet Union collapsed, the new Russian "capitalist democracy" has not been as successful or as open as those of Western Europe or even as those of other Eastern European governments. Local history shapes local governments differently. This explanation is not to give horrific dictatorships like Stalin's USSR a pass, but rather it explains why they came to be and why communism and capitalism are both different from place to place.

The democracies of Asia and Africa aren't the same as Western European or American democracies. The socialist democracies of Scandinavia, for example, are far different from the American capitalist model. Personal freedoms and private ownership in one culture may be seen as acts of intolerable selfishness in another. Forms of government are therefore difficult to compare from country to country. Most Americans tend to naively believe their capitalist system is the only viable model for everyone. It should also be noted that all governments evolve over time, sometimes for the better and sometimes for the worse. It also should be noted that socialism and democracy are not mutually exclusive, as many Americans think.

Starting in 1972, Hall ran four times for President of the United States on the Communist Party USA ticket. Hall was a civil rights advocate; he blamed capitalism for slavery and the oppression of Blacks. In 1980 and 1984, Professor Angela Davis, the Black power advocate, was his running mate. The highest vote total he obtained in these elections was about one percent, in 1976, and most of this vote was a Watergate protest rather than a vote for the CPUSA. After 1984, state election laws became more demanding and it became financially impossible to raise the money necessary to be on each state's ballot and to run a national campaign as a small party. These financial requirements soon excluded all minor parties from real participation in American national politics.

In 1987, it was revealed that Morris Childs, Hall's longtime friend and deputy, had been an undercover agent for the FBI all along. The revelation devastated Hall. A few years later, in 1991, Angela Davis led a large number of members to split with the CPUSA to form their own socialist party. Hall and the CPUSA never recovered. Gus Hall resigned as party chairman in 2000, shortly before his death.

Angela Davis

> "I think the importance of doing activist work is precisely because it allows you to give back and to consider yourself not as a single individual who may have achieved whatever but to be a part of an ongoing historical movement."—Angela Davis

"I never saw myself as an individual who had any particular leadership powers."—Angela Davis

Angela Davis was born in 1944, into a Black middleclass family in Birmingham, Alabama. Both her parents were college educated. Her mother was an elementary school teacher and her father was a high school teacher who also owned a service station in the Black section of the city. She was one of four children. Her brother, Ben Davis, played professional football for the Cleveland Browns and Detroit Lions. Her mother was a national officer and leading organizer of the Southern Negro Congress. The Southern Negro Congress, formed in 1937, was an anti-fascist civil rights organization that J. Edgar Hoover claimed was "communist inspired."

In high school Davis applied to and was accepted into an American Friends Service Committee program that placed Black students from the South into integrated schools in the North. She and her parents chose Elisabeth Irwin High School in Greenwich Village in New York City. There she joined a Communist youth group, Advance. She also met children of some of the leaders of the Communist Party USA.

Davis was an excellent student and was awarded a scholarship to Brandeis University, where she was one of only three black students in her freshman class. She became enchanted with the philosopher Herbert Marcuse at a rally during the Cuban Missile Crisis and then became his student. She would later say that "Herbert Marcuse taught me that it was possible to be an academic, an activist, a scholar, and a revolutionary." She worked part-time to earn enough money to travel to Europe before she went on to attend the eighth World Festival of Youth and Students in Finland. These Youth Festivals were labeled "communist" by the US State Department during the 1960s. When she returned home in 1963, she was interviewed by the FBI about her attendance at the festival and questioned about her communist leanings. It was at this time that Davis came under permanent FBI surveillance.

During her second year at Brandeis, she decided to major in French. Davis was accepted into a special program that allowed her to spend her junior year in France. She attended classes at Biarritz and the Sorbonne. In Paris, she lived with a French family. It was in France that she received news of the 1963 Birmingham Church bombing killing four little girls by the members of the Ku Klux Klan. She was personally acquainted with the young victims' families and it deeply affected her.

Upon her return to Brandeis, Davis realized that her major interest was in philosophy, and she attended another course by Marcuse. According to Davis, he helped her to get into the University of Frankfurt in Germany for graduate work in philosophy. In 1965, she graduated magna cum laude and was a member of Phi Beta Kappa.

After completing her graduate work in Germany, Davis stopped in London to attend a conference called The Dialectics of Liberation. A Black contingent at the conference included the American activist Stokley Carmichael. Although Davis was attracted to Carmichael's fiery rhetoric, she later wrote she was disappointed by his Black Nationalist sentiments and his rejection of communism as a "white man's thing."

Davis returned to the United States and followed Marcuse to University of California at San Diego and earned her master's degree from the San Diego campus and then her doctorate in philosophy from Humboldt University in East Berlin.

Davis became an assistant professor of philosophy at the University of California at Los Angeles (UCLA) and became known as a civil rights advocate, a radical feminist and a communist. She also became an official in the CPUSA and an associate of the Black Panther Party. In 1969, at the insistence of then Governor Ronald Reagan, the Board of Regents of the University of California fired Davis for her membership in CPUSA. The courts then ruled it was unconstitutional to fire Davis for being a communist and she was reinstated. Governor Reagan and the Regents continued to search for ways to fire Davis. They finally accomplished this on June 20, 1970, when they trumped up charges for what they claimed was "inflammatory language" that she had used in four different speeches.

Davis now became a national figure, speaking out against racism and the Vietnam War, and she was also a loud feminist advocate. During this time she came under more intensive and daily surveillance by FBI and the Nixon Administration. She was included on Nixon's infamous enemies list.

In 1970, Davis purchased a few guns for defensive purposes. She gave them to the Black Panthers. On August 7, one of these weapons was used by a seventeen-year-old boy to take over a Marin County California courtroom to free and arm two defendants and to take hostages in their escape. The boy and the two defendants were later killed by police. In the shootout, Judge Harold Haley was killed and two other hostages were wounded. The court later charged Davis with "aggravated kidnapping and first degree murder in the death of Judge Harold Haley" and issued a warrant for her arrest.

Soon after, Davis fled California, telling friends that she didn't think she could get a fair trial. On August 18, 1970, four days after the initial warrant was issued, the FBI director J. Edgar Hoover made Angela Davis the third woman to appear on the FBI's Ten Most Wanted List. She later wrote that during this time she hid in friends' homes and moved from place to place at night. On October 13, 1970, FBI agents found her at the Howard Johnson

Motor Lodge in New York City. President Richard M. Nixon personally congratulated the FBI on its "capture of the dangerous terrorist Angela Davis."

On January 5, 1971, after several months in jail, Davis appeared at the Marin County Superior Court and declared her innocence before the court, saying, "I now declare publicly before the court, before the people of this country that I am innocent of all charges which have been leveled against me by the state of California." Davis again stated that she had bought weapons for the Black Panthers to defend themselves and that she was not part of the kidnappings or murder. Davis was tried before an all-White jury who returned a unanimous verdict of not guilty. This verdict enraged J. Edgar Hoover and the Nixon administration. Davis aggravated their anger by also accepting an invitation from Fidel Castro to visit Cuba after her release.

During her incarceration, leading up to the trial, Davis received harsh treatment and was segregated as a prisoner in solitary confinement. She felt this was grossly unfair treatment of someone who was not convicted and was merely awaiting trial. She said the unfair treatment by the FBI, the courts and law enforcement changed her. Davis became an advocate for prison and judicial reform and fought against what she called "the United States prison-industrial complex." She also became a strong opponent to capital punishment. She would become well known internationally for these causes.

In 1980 and 1984, Davis ran for Vice-President along with the leader of the Communist Party USA, Gus Hall. Davis viewed her candidacy as a protest against American oppression of free choice although she knew she had little hope of achieving significant results. Understanding the futility of her candidacy, she urged her supporters to vote for the Democratic Party against the rightwing Ronald Reagan.

CHAPTER 5. RELIGION

"Communism has decided against God, against Christ, against the Bible, and against all religion."—The Reverend Billy Graham

"I thought that communism, the tyranny of communism, was an abomination and I beseeched God to bring that terrible evil down and he did. It was a great triumph, it took a while, but it happened."—Reverend Pat Robertson taking credit for the fall of the Soviet Union

"For Europe, the fall of Communism has to be taken into account, and the fact that in the fight against Communism the recovery of Europe's Christian roots was the driving force."—Rocco Buttiglione, Italian Catholic politician

"The trouble with Communism is the Communists, just as the trouble with Christianity is the Christians."—H. L. Mencken

In America, the war against the left and against communism was as much about religion as it was about economics. When Karl Marx said, "Religion is the sigh of the oppressed creature, the heart of a heartless world, and the soul of soulless conditions. It is the opium of the people," American Christians saw this as a direct attack on their faith. The American right still lives in fear and behaves irrationally as if the left, the socialists, Jews, Muslims, intellectuals and scientists, are all secretly conspiring to forbid their religion. The religious oppression in the Soviet Union, now long gone, only augmented these fears.

Even mainstream American Christians, including Dr. Martin Luther King Jr., feared communism would undermine Christianity. King said, "Communism is the only serious rival to Christianity. Such great world religions as Judaism, Buddhism, Hinduism, and Mohammedanism are possible alternatives to Christianity, but no one conversant with the hard facts of the modern world will deny that Communism is Christianity's most formidable rival." Ironically King was accused of being "a communist" at the time he spoke these words by FBI Director J. Edgar Hoover and others on the right. Hoover was so obsessed with the notion that King was a communist that he wiretapped King and had the FBI investigate King's supposed communist ties many times. When his agents always failed to find any connection between King and the communists, Hoover angrily reassigned those agents to the worst duties possible, according to Anthony Summers in his book *Official and Confidential, the Secret Life of J. Edgar Hoover*.

The left's opposition to capitalism, Karl Marx's atheism, and the harsh practices of Lenin and Stalin are the reasons most Americans have a hatred for the left. It is also partially why capitalism has become married to Christianity to form what is now the national religion in America.

Russian communists had a great fear of Christianity. The Russian Orthodox Church, which was dominated by the czars and the aristocracy, was used to keep the religious Russian peasants in their place and supporting the monarchy. According to the Orthodox Church, the peasants' role was to serve god and their masters without question. This concept of the divine right of the czar was so strong in Russia that when the communists came to power, they banned the church for fear of a counter-revolution from the peasants. Vladimir Lenin led a purge of the religious establishment, banning religion in the Soviet Union and arguing beyond Marx's original intentions (Marx had said, "Atheism is a natural and inseparable part of Marxism"). However, atheism is not the rule in all communist countries, as Communist Cuba remains predominately Catholic and Communist Vietnam is predominately Buddhist. Even in Communist China, religion has remained and made a significant comeback.

Although Americans saw religious persecution in communist Russia and China as one in the same, religion in communist China was also different. Mao Zedong was said to have been raised in Confucianism and Taoist traditions, but he had personally rejected religion for communism. However Mao's own thoughts, while devoted to communism, also contained many philosophical influences from Confucianism and Taoism, and his writings in his little *Red Book* reflect these strong religious influences.

Communist China also treated religion differently than the USSR. For many years in China there was a sort of a cold tolerance of religion, although it was not condoned by the state. China did take harsh actions when a religious movement was deemed to be encroaching upon the power of the state.

There were periodic political conflicts between the communist state and religion, such as with the Buddhists of Tibet. That movement was backed heavily by the CIA and was seen in China as a separatist revolt and not a religious movement. China, like many Western governments, also had their problems with the Muslims, particularly in their western provinces. Excesses were also committed during the Cultural Revolution (1966–1976), when religious and university intellectuals were highly suspected of treason and were treated extremely harshly, including ordinary teachers and many of the country's local leaders. The Cultural Revolution was a time of gross intolerance for anything that the young radical revolutionaries did not consider pure Maoist doctrine. The Chinese government later apologized for the horrible excesses committed by young radicals and promised to institute reforms.

Recently the Chinese communist government has allowed and has even somewhat encouraged a Chinese religious revival. On January 21, 2011, President Hu Jintao visited a Confucius Institute in Chicago shortly after his meeting with President Barack Obama at a state dinner at the White House. And in a sign of government approval, less than a week before President Hu's state visit in 2011, a new eight-meter bronze statue of Confucius was erected in Tiananmen Square in Beijing in front of the National Museum of China, directly opposite Mao's portrait, in recognition of Confucian influence on Mao. Today in China regular religious services, books and television programs about Confucian teachings and other religions have become very popular. Like their American counterparts, some of these religious authors and "evangelists" have become extremely famous and wealthy. Religion is thriving in communist China, including Christianity.

The conflict between American Christians and the communist Chinese came as a result of the China Lobby. The China Lobby was an American religious movement seeking to spread Christianity and capitalism to what they considered "pagan" China beginning in the late nineteenth century. It was religious colonialism. The China Lobby was a group of mostly former American Christian missionaries and American ex-patriots in China, along with the Rockefeller Foundation, who began to identify with and support the Chinese Nationalist movement led by Chiang Kai-shek in the 1920s. The principle reason for this support was because of Chiang's conversion to Christianity and his lip service to a capitalist democracy. These missionaries began in the 1920s to organize and lobby Congress to recognize the Chiang's Nationalist movement in China. They asserted that Chiang Kai-shek's conversion was proof that Chiang and his Nationalist movement would bring the entire Chinese population into Christianity and that China would then function as an American puppet state. It was American/British Christian colonialism at its worst.

Their efforts redoubled in 1937 with the outbreak of the Sino–Japanese war. A good number of missionaries and Christian groups were organized to influence US policy on behalf of China between 1937 and 1941. The most important was the American Committee for Non-Participation in Japanese Aggression, also known as the Price Committee. In 1938, they were angered by the US government's inaction in the face of Japanese aggression in China. Frank and Harry Price, the sons of a prominent missionary P. Frank Price, gathered a small group of men, including some powerful people in the American press like Henry Luce (the son of a missionary and founder of *Time* and *Life* magazines) and his wife Claire Boothe Luce, to support Chiang's China. They also persuaded Minnesota Congressman Walter Judd, who was a former medical missionary in China, to be the group's speaker, and employed an American propagandist to lobby for Chiang's Chinese Nationalist government. They launched a successful campaign to stop the flow of American goods and critical resources to Japan. Their organization also secretly received illegal financial support from the Chinese government, and they were, in legal terms, acting as foreign agents lobbying the US government. They became formally known as "The Friends of China." They would become more infamously known as "The China Lobby."

Before Japan allied with Germany, the Friends of China were also connected to other rightwing organizations including the American Fascists and other groups sympathetic to Hitler. William J. Goodwin was as a lobbyist for China and the Friends of China. In the 1930s Goodwin was also closely affiliated with the rightwing racist Christian Front and with the American fascist Gerald L. K. Smith; like them, Goodwin was also an anti-Semite and a Hitler apologist. He was also an ally of the anti-Semite Nazi priest the Reverend Charles E. Coughlin of Detroit, a Catholic who was the forerunner of the modern rightwing televangelist. At his peak Coughlin had hundreds of thousands of listeners on a network of a hundred radio stations promoting anti-Semitism, fascism, Hitler, and anti-union causes.

The Friends of China used the most sophisticated propaganda and public relations methods available at the time including mass mailings, press releases, speaker tours, petition drives, and developed leaders in churches, universities and civic organizations across the United States to lobby on behalf of China. They generated enormous pressure intended to force Roosevelt to oppose Japan and support Chiang's Nationalist Christian government. This pressure was responsible for President Franklin D. Roosevelt's decision in July 1939 to notify Japan that the United States intended to terminate the ongoing commercial treaty between the two nations. The cancellation of the treaty created economic sanctions that cut off iron ore, petroleum and other critical resources to Japan. This ultimately led to the Japanese decision to attack Pearl Harbor.

During the war the China Lobby constantly reminded the American people of the long suffering of Chiang Kai-shek and his Chinese allies, and they filled the press with stories of Chinese resistance and greatly exaggerated the heroism, leadership and Christianity of the of Generalissimo and his wife Madame Chiang Kai-shek. The entire American media, including, Luce's *Time Magazine*, the American public school system's *Weekly Reader* for American children, the movie theatre newsreels, and commercial radio spots, were used to portray Chiang and his wife as the spirit of free China with greatly exaggerated references to their dedication to Christianity and their love of an American style democracy. In truth Chiang Kai-shek and his wife were never more than incompetent, greedy opportunists. Chiang was a warlord.

Meanwhile Mao Zedong was hardly mentioned in the American press, even though he was by far more successful than Chiang militarily and, more importantly, much more popular in China. General Joseph "Vinegar Joe" Stilwell, the American commander of the Chinese forces during the war, knew both Chiang and Mao very well as they served with him. His reports back to Washington said that Chiang was corrupt and incompetent. He reported that Chiang's soldiers would frequently sell their weapons to the Japanese for profit. He said that by contrast Mao was a very good leader, a capable general, was honest and naturally attracted many followers. He said that Chiang was not a natural leader and Stilwell correctly predicted Chiang would also be inept when it came to building a nation.

These comments got Stilwell into trouble with the China Lobby. Stilwell predicted to his superiors that Mao, not Chiang, would lead China after the war despite any US efforts, and this assessment further infuriated the blind and wishful-thinking China Lobby. Their anger turned vengeful and they eventually forced Roosevelt, who was very ill at the time, to relieve General Stilwell of his command in China, despite the fact that the US State Department and most US diplomats in China also strongly agreed with Stilwell's assessment. (They too would be replaced after the war at the urging of the China Lobby and the Dulles brothers.) And while the fall of China to the communists in 1948 may have come as a shock to the China Lobby and many Americans, it wasn't a surprise to General Stilwell who was unquestionably America's most prominent authority on China at the time. Ironically the China Lobby and the Republican Party then blamed General Stilwell and the State Department for "the loss of China," although they and not Stilwell were primarily responsible for the coming rift between China and America.

Stilwell had correctly predicted that Mao would rule China. Stilwell had also wanted America to ally with Mao and China against Russia, and he knew this was possible as China and Russia had been historical competitors. He saw Mao and China as a buffer between the USSR and the rest of Asia, and he argued that they would be a strong ally against the USSR. Unfortunately, the religious biases and wishful thinking of the virulent anticommunists of the China Lobby and the Dulles brothers prevented this from happening.

The China Lobby had thought they could recreate China as a Christian-Capitalist American outpost. Had General Stilwell and the State Department been listened to and had America allowed him to ally with Mao's China, the Cold War would have been very different. It would have likely prevented the war in Korea and, possibly, in Vietnam.

Despite congressional and public sympathy for Chiang, and the intimidating efforts of the powerful China Lobby, the Truman Administration and the State Department were still prepared to recognize the People's Republic of China and to allow it to take the Chinese seat in the United Nations. Truman persisted in this effort until early 1950, when the China Lobby found an ally in the infamous Senator Joseph R. McCarthy. They began to intimidate and threaten anyone in Congress dealing with the communists, implying they were traitors. However Truman and his administration still ignored the China Lobby and were still steadfastly proceeding with plans to recognize communist China.

The outbreak of war in Korea curtailed Truman's plans and any hope of American–Chinese reconciliation. General Mac Arthur convinced President Truman that if he invaded North Korea, the Chinese would not and could not respond. He was wrong. When the army from the People's Republic of China counterattacked, that ended any attempt by Truman to recognize or work with China. MacArthur accomplished what the China Lobby and Senator Joe McCarthy could not: he put an end to any American cooperation with the Chinese. MacArthur was an ambitious man with presidential dreams and he didn't believe Truman would have the courage to fire him; Truman did. Mac Arthur became an overnight hero among the China Lobby and the American right and briefly toyed with the idea of running for president in 1952, but he was an arrogant man and failed to attract a political following.

The Korean War created paranoia in the United States, which lent credence to McCarthy's unreasonable charges of communist treason in the State department and the military. Too many people allowed his attacks to be taken more seriously than they should have been. McCarthyism and the Korean War destroyed any possible accommodation with the People's Republic of China for decades. It also created a hostile standoff on the Korean peninsula that persists to this day, although the US and China have resumed diplomatic relations.

The China Lobby was filled with the hypocritical Christian rightwing, but none more so than Senator Joseph McCarthy. McCarthy was a dishonorable charlatan. He ran his first senate campaign shortly after World War II by calling himself "tail gunner Joe" to appeal to the emotions of voters and their pride in the returning heroes. It was a lie. A tail gunner on a B-17 was one of the most dangerous and heroic jobs in World War II, but Joe McCarthy was actually a supply officer who had falsely claimed a Purple Heart a result of an injury he received in a drunken party aboard a supply ship hundreds of miles from any combat. McCarthy a German–Irish Catholic from Wisconsin and also disgracefully ran his senate campaign on "the myth of the holocaust" to appeal to Wisconsin's large German Catholic community.

McCarthy was unremarkable in his first term as senator. He was missing from the Senate floor during much of their proceedings as he was battling alcoholism, and according to some historians he also had a morphine addiction. At the end of his term he was struggling to find a reason that would get him re-elected and was persuaded by his friend J. Edgar Hoover and an anti-communist Catholic priest to dedicate his campaign to anti-communism. According to several biographies, his friend Joe Kennedy, the father of Jack and Bobby Kennedy, was also persuasive in this regard. McCarthy briefly dated Joe Kennedy's two daughters and became friends with Bobby, who also took a job working for him. McCarthy became godson to Bobby's daughter.

Overnight McCarthy became an anti-communist zealot. From 1951 to 1953, McCarthy was advised and supported by William J. Goodwin, the former fascist and China lobbyist and J. Edgar Hoover. He enthusiastically joined the ranks of the China Lobby, and on their behalf succeeded in driving some of the State Department's best diplomats from China and from the State Department in disgrace. He even discredited such foreign policy luminaries as Dean Acheson, General George C. Marshall, John S. Service, and Owen Lattimore in the process.

According to McCarthy and the China Lobby, China had been lost to the communists because disloyal Americans and communist-atheist traitors who had prevented Chiang Kai-shek from receiving the aid with which he could have held China. They claimed that "Chiang was never unleashed." They further claimed that American soldiers died in Korea because they had been betrayed by disloyal and stupid liberal traitors in the State Department and communists in the military who had turned China over to the communists. General Stilwell was again vilified by McCarthy. It was not until the 1960s and the revulsion against the war in Vietnam that some of the men denounced during the McCarthy era were finally vindicated.

Some people did attempt to blunt McCarthy and the China Lobby. In April 1952, Republican Senator Wayne L. Morse of Oregon introduced into the Senate pages of Chinese documents outlining the plans of Chiang's Nationalist regime to bribe and buy influence with the US Congress and policy makers. Some of the documents referred to cooperation with Goodwin, the China Lobby spokesman; Congressman Walter Judd; and California Senator William F. Knowland, who was so single-mindedly consumed with Chiang and Nationalist China that he was referred to jokingly by his Senate colleagues as "the Senator from Formosa." American communist paranoia was at its peak and Morse's revelations of influence buying and bribery fell on deaf ears in Congress; these documents were never really considered.

The China Lobby's determination to keep the People's Republic of China out of the United Nations intensified and a powerful new pressure group was created to retain the seat for Chiang's Nationalist regime, which was now ridiculously relegated to the small island of Formosa with no hope of ever coming to power in mainland China. In 1953, the new group began with a petition drive and called itself "The Committee of One Million against the Admission of Communist China to the United Nations." After collecting a million signatures, the organizers disbanded in 1954, but they reorganized and did it all over again in 1955. The second time even Liberal Democrats signed their names to the new petition, including Senators Paul Douglas of Illinois, William Proxmire of Wisconsin, and Hubert H. Humphrey of Minnesota.

In 1960, Ross Y. Koen, a young professor in California, prepared to publish his dissertation, *The China Lobby in American Politics*, revealing the lies and deception they had practiced. However, the book was never distributed. The Nationalist Chinese embassy reportedly threatened legal action against the publishers for what they claimed were defamatory statements in the book, and this along with the power and persuasion of Luce and the China Lobby and the CIA succeeded in frightening the publishers to stop publication, making a lie of America's claim of freedom of speech and press.

The China Lobby is alive and well in the neo-cons of the present. In the 1970s and 1980s, when President George H. W. Bush, was playing tennis and began to lose, he would threaten his opponent that he would "unleash Chiang." The expression is a nod to the China Lobby myth that General Chiang Kai-shek was in Formosa straining at the leash to return to retake China, but was held back by the timid politicians of the American left. Bush gave this political bias to his sons.

In September 2005, in the *Gainesville Sun*, Governor Jeb Bush reportedly said the following at a swearing in ceremony that made Marco Rubio the Florida Speaker of the House: "Chiang is a mystical warrior. Chiang is somebody who believes in conservative principles, believes in entrepreneurial capitalism, believes in moral values that underpin a free society. I rely on Chiang with great regularity in my public life. He has been by my side and sometimes I let him down. But Chiang, this mystical warrior, has never let me down." Bush then unsheathed a sword and gave it to Rubio as a gift. "I'm going to bestow to you the sword of a great conservative warrior."

Joe McCarthy and the China Lobby are a blood stain on American democracy. In 1956, during the McCarthy era, in a wave of Christian jingoism, the words "In god we trust" were adopted by Congress as the official motto of the United States as an alternative or replacement to the original United States motto, "E Pluribus Unum." At this time, in another act, "In God we trust" was added to the paper currency, and the phrase "one nation under God" was added to the Pledge of Allegiance, thereby insulting and denigrating American agnostics, atheists, Jews, Buddhists, Muslims and other non-Christians.

Ironically, the original Pledge of Allegiance was written by Francis Bellamy, a Baptist minister and an American socialist, in 1892. He said it was created "At the beginning of the 1890s when patriotism and national feeling was at a low ebb. The patriotic ardor of the Civil War was an old story...The time was ripe for a reawakening of simple Americanism and the leaders in the new movement rightly felt that patriotic education should begin in the public schools." Bellamy wasn't advocating it as a Christian call to arms.

In post World War II America, atheists were considered with communists as one in the same. Until a Supreme Court decision in 1961, atheists were restricted from holding public office, serving as witnesses in court, or serving as jurors by many state constitutions. However atheists were still required to declare they belong to "one nation under god" in the Pledge of Allegiance and to "solemnly swear" to god in taking some public oaths. A belief in the Christian religion was required of Americans in the post war to prove their Americanism.

In 1959, Madelyn Murray filed a case, *Murray v. Curlett*, on behalf of her son William J. Murray, who was being forced to attend Bible readings in a public school and was being harassed by his teachers and the school administrators for refusing to participate.

The case was consolidated with another case filed by Edward Schempp, who sued a Pennsylvania public school district that was forcing his son to pray in school. The consolidated case is usually cited as *Abington School District v. Schempp*, although arguably *Murray v. Curlett* became the more famous of the two. The case was argued before United States Supreme Court on February 27 and February 28, 1963. In a bi-partisan decision the Court decided eight to one in favor of Murray and Schempp, declaring public school-sponsored Bible reading and prayers in public schools in the United States to be unconstitutional. The ruling had immediate political impact. The reaction from the religious right was loud and angry. Congressman George W. Andrews of Alabama said of the Supreme Court, "They put Negros in the schools and now they have driven god out!"

Vietnam, a Religious War

"Let them burn and we shall clap our hands.....His barbecuing was not self-sufficient because imported gasoline was used."—Madame Nhu's comments to the press on June 8, 1963, after the Buddhist monk Thich Quang Duc died by self-immolation to protest Diem's and his Catholic government's persecution of the Buddhists in Vietnam.

"This war in Vietnam is, I believe, a war for civilization."—Francis Cardinal Spellman

"Television brought the brutality of war into the comfort of the living room. Vietnam was lost in the living rooms of America, not on the battlefields of Vietnam."—Marshall McLuhan

"The United States has set up hundreds of military bases in many countries all over the world.....The longer the US aggressors remain in those places, the tighter the nooses around their necks will become."—Mao Zedong 1958

According to Richard Barnet in Intervention and Revolution, The *United States in the Third World*, on January 14, 1954, the CIA reported to President Eisenhower that the main French military garrison at Dien Bien Phu was down to six days' supply of rations and would either be overrun or be forced to surrender. President Eisenhower considered seriously the possibility of a large-scale US military intervention to assist the French. The China Lobby and others had warned that if Vietnam fell to the communists, Thailand and the rest of Southeast Asia and Indonesia would fall like dominoes. This became known as the "Domino Theory." Eisenhower appointed a committee comprised of the Joint Chiefs of Staff, CIA Director Allen Dulles, and Roger Kyes, the Deputy Secretary of Defense, to develop a plan for Vietnam. On April 7 the President told a press conference that the loss of Indochina, like "falling dominoes," India, Japan, Indonesia, and the Philippines would follow, as well as the small countries that bordered Vietnam.

Eisenhower gave Vice President Richard Nixon the job of gaining support from the press for an eventual conflict in Vietnam. Nixon held many "private" and "off-the-record" press briefings on the situation. Nixon was later commended by President Eisenhower "for awakening the country to the seriousness of the situation."

Reporter Richard Rovere, in his column The Washington Letter, on April 8, 1954, said it was "one of the boldest campaigns of political persuasion ever undertaken by an American statesman. Congressmen, political leaders of all shadings of opinion, newspapermen, and radio and television personalities have been rounded up in droves and escorted to lectures and briefings on what the State Department regards as the American stake in Indo-China." He also reported that the dominoes were falling so fast in these briefings that he wondered whether the Eisenhower Administration thought that the United States could survive a communist victory in Indochina.

The China Lobby came out in full force to "save" Vietnam. They became so obnoxious, proclaiming that this was a Maoist intervention, that President Eisenhower feared they would push him into a full war with China and publicly cautioned there was "no incontrovertible evidence of overt participation by Chinese troops in the Indo-China conflict."

After the Vietnamese communists defeated the French at Diem Bien Phu, an international conference was opened in Geneva, Switzerland, in April of 1954 and lasted into late July. The conference was to decide issues about both Korea and Vietnam. The major participants included the United States, Great Britain, France, the USSR, and China. Secretary of State John Foster Dulles, after securing the agreement of Britain and France, established the Southeast Asia Treaty Organization, SEATO, a regional collective-security organization designed to prevent any further communist advances in Asia. Against Dulles and the Americans, the conference agreed to partition Vietnam into a socialist North and a "free" South. They did likewise in Korea. Dulles was disappointed with the split and explained this setback to Senator William Knowland as the Geneva talks were dragging to a close, saying, "The problem is where to draw the line . . . we are confronted by an unfortunate fact that most of the countries of the world do not share our view that communist control of any government anywhere is in itself a danger and a threat."

The Geneva Accord prohibited sending foreign military personnel to either of the two Vietnams and banned contributing any arms and munitions to them, and further prohibited the two Vietnams from entering into foreign military alliances. The United States ignored the Accords and violated the treaty by doing all three. The Americans provided military advisors, and paid most of the cost of running the country and virtually the entire bill for outfitting the entire South Vietnamese army and the police. Between the years 1955 and 1956, the United States supplied the South Vietnamese armed forces with $2 billion in military supplies and built their standing army to a strength of two hundred and fifty thousand. They were also trained by the Americans. It was truly an American-created country and army.

The French, at American insistence, accepted Ngo Dinh Diem as the Premier of South Vietnam in June, 1954, at the Geneva Conference. The French thought he was a poor choice and said so. Diem was an odd man. He spoke French almost as well as he did Vietnamese. Diem was a strong anticommunist and he was a very devout Catholic. He was in fact a Catholic monk who had taken a vow of celibacy to dedicate himself to a life in the Catholic Church; he was also very conservative in his personal habits. He came from a prominent Vietnamese family with strong Catholic ties that boasted a number of Catholic bishops.

Diem had served as a French civil servant in Vietnam and was noted for his anti-communism. He was instrumental in putting down a peasant communist revolt in 1930 and 1931. He was appointed Interior Minister under the French puppet ruler Bao Dai. Diem lobbied for an independent Vietnamese legislature but was rebuffed by the French and threatened with arrest, which he never forgave.

During the next decade he immersed himself in the Catholic Church. When the Japanese invaded Vietnam, he tried but failed to persuade the Japanese regional government to create an independent Vietnam. In 1944, when it was discovered that he had worked with the Japanese, the French ordered his arrest, but the Japanese helped him to escape disguised as one of their military officers to Hanoi. He met Ho Chi Minh in Hanoi where Ho attempted to convert him to communism, but the Catholic Diem declined. Diem blamed the communists for the death of his brother and could not reconcile his Catholicism with communism. He moved south and lived with his brother Ngo Dinh Thuc who was the Catholic Bishop of the Vinh Long diocese. Thuc was well connected in Catholic politics; he had studied in Rome and was friends with the politically-connected American Catholic Francis Cardinal Spellman.

John Cooney, in his book The American Pope: The Life and Times of Francis Cardinal Spellman, said Spellman was vehemently anti-communist. Spellman once said that "a true American can neither be a communist nor a Communist condoner" and that "the first loyalty of every American is vigilantly to weed out and counteract Communism and convert American Communists to Americanism." Spellman also believed that all unionists and American labor leaders were communists. In 1949 when the gravediggers went on strike for higher wages, he accused them and their union of being communist-atheists. On March 14, 1949, in Time Magazine Spellman was quoted saying that the strike was "an unjustified and immoral strike against the innocent dead and their bereaved families, against their religion and human decency."

In 1927 Spellman established a close lifelong friendship with Archbishop Eugenio Pacelli during a trip to Germany. It was a profitable friendship as Pacelli was later elected Pope Pius XII in 1939. As one of his first acts he appointed Spellman Archbishop of New York.

Like Spellman, Pope Pius XII was a vehement anticommunist and right-wing sympathizer. He was a supporter of the fascists. He negotiated the Reichskonkordat with Hitler in which the Catholic Church recognized and entered into an agreement with the German Nazis. This horrific act caused Father Franziscus Stratman, the senior Catholic chaplain at Berlin University, to write at the time, "The souls of well-disposed people are in a turmoil as a result of the tyranny of the National Socialists, and I am merely stating a fact when I say that the authority of the bishops among innumerable Catholics and non-Catholics has been shaken by the quasi-approval [by the Catholic Church] of the National Socialist movement." Pope Pius XII was also a strong supporter of Mussolini and the Italian fascists.

Spellman's connections to Pope Pius XII earned him the nickname "the Powerhouse." His power was also enhanced by strong friendships with many wealthy Americans and politicians. Spellman strongly supported the China Lobby and Senator Joe McCarthy. He also defended McCarthy's 1953 investigations of "Communist" subversives in the federal government. He believed and gave credence to McCarthy's unfounded charges of communist conspiracies in America.

In 1950 Spellman was impressed with Diem, who he found to be a right-wing Catholic and anti-communist like himself. He developed a fast and strong relationship with him as he already knew Diems family and had befriended Diem's brother while they both studied together in Rome.

In 1950, Diem went to the United States and lived at Spellman's Maryknoll Seminary in New Jersey. Spellman helped Diem get an audience with the Pope in 1951. Diem and Spellman wanted to see a Catholic-capitalistic Vietnam and made plans to accomplish this with the blessing of the Vatican and Pope Pius XII, who shared their anti-communist zeal. After his Papal visit and with the Pope's blessings, Spellman introduced Diem to many American dignitaries who then also became supporters. Among them were Supreme Court Justice William O. Douglas, most of the China Lobby, and the so-called master of counterinsurgency and guerilla warfare, General Edward Lansdale of the CIA, a fervent Catholic and anti-communist who had developed cooperative ties to the Catholic Church while conducting his CIA duties and assignments.

When William O. Douglas first met Diem in Washington in 1951, he took an immediate liking to him for his anti-colonialism and said, "He is honest and independent and stood against the French influence." Douglas then introduced Diem at a breakfast meeting to Senators Mike Mansfield and John F. Kennedy, who also became Diem supporters.

When the Geneva Conference was convened in 1954, Diem's brother Ngo Diem Luyen was chosen to represent Vietnamese Emperor Bao Dai. With the lobbying of the Vatican, the China Lobby, the CIA and Diem's other supporters, Secretary of State John Foster Dulles persuaded Bao Dai to name Diem as the South Vietnamese Prime Minister. The appointment was widely condemned by French officials who felt that Diem was an incompetent, reclusive monk. French Prime Minister Pierre Mendes-France declared him to be a "Catholic fanatic" and prophetically warned of potential problems between Diem and Vietnam's large Buddhist majority. These warnings were ignored by the Americans, and Diem was chosen. Diem would soon become known in Southeast Asia as "the American puppet without strings."

Edward Lansdale was with the clandestine Office of Strategic Services (O.S.S.), the forerunner of the CIA, from almost the beginning. He was a journalist until then. After the war he remained with American intelligence, using a cover as an Air Force officer. His World War II service was classified having served in numerous sensitive posts. After World War II, Lansdale became Chief of the Intelligence Division in the Philippines. According to Sterling and Peggy Seagrave in their book Gold Warriors: America's Secret Recovery of Yamamoto's Gold, Lansdale led the "recovery" of a large cache of gold and money amassed by Japan during their occupation of the Philippines. This money along with confiscation of the wealth amassed in Nazi Germany helped the United States to covertly finance the CIA and the Cold War against the Soviet Union.

In 1948 Lansdale left the Philippines for a stateside post as an instructor at the Strategic Intelligence School. However, in 1950 Philippine President Elpidio Quirino personally requested that the US government reassign Lansdale back to the Philippines to combat the popular and growing communist revolution by the Hukbalahap, more commonly known as "the Huks." Lansdale worked directly with Raymond Magsaysay, the Philippines National Defense Director, and the two became close friends. It was largely Lansdale's and the CIA efforts that brought Magsaysay to the presidency of the Philippines in 1953.

In the Philippines, Lansdale also allied with the Catholic Church and Pope Pius XII to defeat the Huks. According to Major Andrew E. Lembke in a paper published by the US Army Combat Institute Press in 2001 entitled Art of War Papers, Lansdale, Magsaysay, America, and the Philippines, A

Case Study of Limited Intervention Counterinsurgency, the Papal Nuncio of the Philippines, Signor Emilio Vagnozzi, by order of the Vatican, gave support to Magsaysay's presidential campaign through Catholic Action, the Church's voter education program. The Catholic Church also played a major role in convincing the Philippine people to not support the Huk rebellion, and they financed and led in the reeducation and conversion of the Huk rebels to support the Magsaysay government.

The success of Lansdale in the Philippines was on the minds of the Pope, the China Lobby, Secretary of State John Foster Dulles and his brother CIA Director Allen Dulles as the French defeat at Diem Bien Phu was occurring and Vietnam was falling to the communists. Lansdale was sent to Vietnam in 1953 as part of a team under General John W. O' Daniel serving as his guerilla and counterinsurgency advisor. The book, The Quiet American by Graham Greene was supposedly inspired by Lansdale in Vietnam.

In 1954 to 1957 Lansdale was put in command of the Saigon Military Mission. In this position he began to shape what would become the Republic of Vietnam. True to his China Lobby roots and with the assistance of the Catholic Church, he began to create a Christian-capitalist nation.

Before the Geneva Convention partition of Vietnam into North and South, the majority of Vietnam's Catholics lived in the north. This was a problem for Lansdale and Diem as they saw the Catholics as the base support of their new Christian-capitalist nation. Ironically Hanoi's large Catholic population was also an on-going source of problems for Ho Chi Minh. In an unusual agreement between Ho, the Americans and the Vatican they conspired to move the Catholics south. For Ho and the communists they agreed so they could consolidate their power in the North and rid themselves of their largest opposition. The Americans and the Vatican needed the Catholics to support Diem's fledgling South Vietnamese government.

The plan was called "Operation Passage to Freedom" and eventually saw up to one million North Vietnamese go south, almost all of them Catholics. It wasn't an easy task. The Catholics were content to live in Hanoi, even under communism. Lansdale led a propaganda campaign to encourage as many Catholics to move south as possible. The Catholic Church was an accomplice and through their priests they promoted slogans such as "Christ has gone south" and "the Virgin Mary had departed from the North," and alleged that anti-Catholic persecution under Ho Chi Minh would soon follow.

However the Catholics were still slow to respond and they were still not moving to the South in large numbers, so the Catholic Church, at Lansdale's direction, began to claim that the United States might use nuclear weapons on Hanoi and that any Catholic who stayed in the North would be committing the unpardonable sin of suicide. When Hanoi's communist newspapers at the direction of Ho began hinting at this possibility, over sixty percent of northern Catholics moved to Diem's South Vietnam, providing him with a source of loyal support. The US Navy was used to transfer these refugees south. In some cases Navy personnel were dressed up to look like priests to assure the Vietnamese refugees that they were under safe Catholic care.

In 1955 in a rigged election backed by Lansdale and the CIA, Ngo Dinh Diem was elected over Bao Dai, the reigning monarch. The election was overseen by Diem's brother, Ngo Dinh Nhu. Campaigning for Bao Dai was prohibited, and Dai's supporters were also frequently attacked by Nhu's men. Diem recorded an implausibly high ninety-eight percent of the vote a result that could have only been obtained through fraud. It was fraud as the total number of votes exceeded the number of registered voters by over 380,000. There were only 450,000 voters registered in Saigon, but supposedly 605,025 voted for Diem. Lansdale had warned Diem that these suspicious high numbers would only lead to accusations that Diem had rigged the elections, but Diem was padding these numbers in anticipation of the unification elections with the North.

According to the Geneva Accords, Vietnam was to undergo elections in 1956 to reunify the country. The communists were heavily favored to win these elections. American estimates were that Ho would likely receive eighty percent of the total vote. Diem and the Americans cancelled the elections claiming that they could not be satisfied that they would be fair. Diem also justified this cancellation saying that South Vietnam was not a party to the Geneva Accords. Diem rationalized the electoral cancellation by claiming that the 1956 elections would be "meaningful only on the condition that they are absolutely free" and claimed that the communists would not allow them to be.

At the urging of the United States and Great Britain, Diem then proposed the elections be held under the strict supervision of the United Nations, knowing full well that this plan would be rejected by the Soviet Union and Ho Chi Minh. He knew that elections would then not be held and he could use the lack of the unification vote as a justification for his remaining in power until one was held.

Madame Nhu, the wife of Diem's younger brother, was South Vietnam's de facto First Lady. She was also a fervent Catholic. She led the way in Diem's social programs to reform Saigon society in accordance with the values of the Catholic Church. Brothels and opium dens which had been legal under the French were closed. Divorce, birth control and abortion were made illegal according to Catholic doctrine, and adultery laws were strengthened. Diem won a crime war with the help of CIA bribes and US military power over the private army of the Binh Xuyen, an organized crime syndicate operating brothels and gambling houses. They had enjoyed the freedom to operate under the French. Diem also received assistance from the CIA and the US military in dismantling the private armies of the Cao Dai and Hoa Hao religious sects, which controlled parts of the country.

Diem wanted a total Catholic society and he forcibly replaced many non-Catholic civil servants, teachers, and military officers with the Catholic refugees from the North. Most of those replaced were Buddhists. Under Diem the Buddhists in the army were also denied promotion if they refused to convert to Catholicism. Surveys of the religious composition of Vietnam at the time estimated the Buddhist majority to be between seventy and ninety percent. The Buddhists began to demonstrate against Diem's pro-Catholic government. The demonstrations were ruthlessly putdown by his brother Nhu, using the Army and his national police force. In protest Buddhist monks began to immolate themselves in public places drawing American television cameras and world attention to Diem's religious intolerance.

As a fanatic Catholic, Diem was passionately anti-Communist and he viewed communists as satanic. His government tortured and killed communist suspects on a daily basis believing they were doing god's work. According to historian Gabriel Kolko in his book *Vietnam: Anatomy of a Peace*, about 12,000 suspected opponents of Diem were killed between 1955 and 1957 and by the end of 1958 an estimated 40,000 suspected communists and other political prisoners had been jailed and many of them tortured. The United States has denied involvement in these actions but it was Lansdale and the CIA that advised and assisted Diem at the time, and it was they who put him in power and protected the regime. It was Lansdale who strongly advised him to put down any dissention and protests with brute force and in some situations the US supplied that force. Diem also showed the Buddhists and other Vietnamese where his true loyalty lie as he ordered the white and gold Vatican flag flown over government buildings and at all major public events in South Vietnam.

All these anti-Buddhist actions and the jailing, murder and torture of dissidents only served to make the communists more attractive to the average South Vietnamese. Diem's pro-Catholic government was viewed as foreign and Diem as "America's puppet without strings."

South Vietnam in reality was a new American colony. In the United States Diem's Vietnam Republic was the dream come true of the Catholic Church, the Dulles brothers and the China Lobby. It was a Christian-capitalist American puppet state in Asia. But it could only last as long as America was willing to station a fighting force of up to a half million soldiers to assure its survival against the will of the Vietnamese people. In the end it made little difference. The resultant war by the US to preserve their puppet state killed and maimed millions while the inevitable outcome came to pass anyway. The Vietnam War was fought for nothing.

Chapter 6. Class

"The history of all hitherto existing society is the history of class struggles."—Marx and Engels, *The Communist Manifesto*

"Socialism never took root in America because the poor see themselves not as an exploited proletariat but as temporarily embarrassed millionaires."—John Steinbeck

Predestination and class play a major role in the history of American economics and culture. This is a subject that I wrote a great deal about in my two previous books, *The Making of the Slave Class* and *Tapestry, The History and Consequences of American Culture*, but a very brief chapter in this book is also necessary.

Economics and politics are more about class than most of us think. There seems to be a pattern in working class political preferences. In under-developed and poor countries, the working class tends to be more to the left, while in industrialized nations the working class seems to be more to the right. Rightwing authoritarianism plays a part in this, which is a subject that is discussed in detail later in this book, but it basically means that there is a penchant for people to hang on to customs, religion and traditions (like Christian Conservatives in the US) and they will support powerful rightwing authorities who ensure this continuation. Later we will also look at the authoritarian personality disorder which explains why this occurs.

Developed places also tend to have significant middle classes that are interested in preserving the status quo, and they frequently are the deciding factor in which way the politics will lean. The gap between the working class and the leisure class in the US is growing rapidly, and the middle class is shrinking. Does this mean America could lose its rightwing bias and begin to go left, or will it mean that the oppressed working class will be powerless to bring change against the wealthy leisure class and their control of the military and the police? It also begs the question, what is the role of predestination and religion in political preferences?

Currently the working class, particularly the White working class, tends to favor rightwing politics. A look at the numbers leading up to the 2012 presidential election between President Obama and Mitt Romney shows these working class preferences. Just before the election, Governor Mitt Romney held a double-digit advantage over President Barack Obama among all White working-class voters, 48% for Romney and 35% for Obama. However, the preferences of the middleclass voters varied by race, gender, religion and by region.

Religious, gender and regional differences also play unique roles the class system. Romney enjoyed a two to one advantage over Obama among White working class Protestant voters (56% to 27%). However White working class Catholic voters were more narrowly divided 44% for Romney to 41% for Obama.

Romney held a commanding 40-point lead over Obama among white working-class voters in the South with 62% for Romney and just 22% for Obama. However, the gap between the two candidates with white working-class voters in other states was considerably less than in the South. In the West Romney led 46% to Obama's 41%. In the Northeast, Romney had 42 to Obama's 38%, and in the Midwest Obama actually led 44% to Romney's 36%.

White working class men favored Mitt Romney over Barack Obama by a margin of nearly two to one at 55% for Romney to 28% for Obama, but White working class women were evenly divided between Romney and Obama.

Like the Steinbeck quote at the beginning of this chapter, it is oxymoronic for these White working class voters to vote for a leisure class man who advocates rightwing policies that are not in their financial interests, particularly considering that many are in poor financial health. Approximately two-thirds of White working class Americans report that they are in just fair or poor financial condition. One in five White working-class Americans have no health insurance of any kind. More than one-third, 36%, of White working class Americans are insured through government programs like Medicare and Medicaid, but ironically most are politically opposed to the Affordable Health Care Act and what they deride as "government medical care." And most of them have many more nonmedical financial and social problems than White middleclass Americans. White working class people have the following problems: 49% have experienced home foreclosures, 32% have reported problems with crime, and 17% claim to have problems due to racial tensions.

Some of this support by the poor and working class for candidates who advocate for more favorable policies for the leisure class is due to a belief in predestination. Many poor American Christians tend to believe, as their forefathers did, in the Divine Right of Kings, in which a ruler asserts that "I am king because god made me so, and you are poor because god made you so—and who are we to question god?" Many poor and working class Americans believe that god determines who is rich and who is poor, and they show the same favoritism to political policies that favor the rich even when it is against their interests and welfare. It is interesting to note that working class people of color are likely to be politically more moderate and left-leaning than the White working class, but they can also be conservative on single issues such as gay rights or gun control. Working class African-Americans are one of the most religious groups in the US, according to the Pew Survey on American Religion. In general this group does not endorse the left, as even their hero the Rev. Dr. Martin Luther King Jr. said, "Communism is the only serious rival to Christianity." They tend to be more conservative on issues other than gay rights and gun ownership, such as women's rights.

Religious people of any class are more likely to lean right. This is likely due to rightwing authoritarianism in response to what some Americans see as a decline in Christian values. The Pew Survey shows that 50% of Americans who attend church weekly state they are conservative, 31% say they are moderate and only 12% say they are liberal or left-leaning, with the rest not answering. Americans who say religion is not important affiliate as follows: 19% are conservative, 38% moderate and 36% are left-leaning or liberal.

Chapter One

CHAPTER 7. THE BEGINNINGS OF THE AMERICAN LEFT

"It could fairly be said that the US is increasingly out of step with the rest of the world. As our neighbors to the south elect left-wing or even socialist governments, we are lurching further to the right. As Europe becomes less engaged to the Church, we are becoming more fundamentalist."—Graydon Carter, American journalist

"It is well enough that people of the nation do not understand our banking and monetary system, for if they did, I believe there would be a revolution before tomorrow morning."—Henry Ford

"I think being a liberal, in the true sense, is being non-doctrinaire, non-dogmatic, non-committed to a cause, but examining each case on its merits. Being left of center is another thing; it's a political position."—Walter Cronkite

The Harmonists

The first American socialists were religious socialists. George Rapp was the founder of the religious sect called by various names as the Harmonists, Harmonites, Rappites, or the Harmony Society. Rapp was born in Germany. He was a deeply religious as a young man and he had very strong opinions. He had a number of religious convictions that differed from his church. He was also a socialist. When these differences appeared to be irreconcilable, Rapp quit attending church services and taking communion. He accused his former church of being more interested in materialism than religion.

Rapp believed that Christians should not aspire to owning material goods; he believed that all material goods should be owned in common to benefit the entire Christian community. He began to attract a group of devoted followers in Germany and as a group they eventually emigrated to the United States, where over time they established three communities: Harmony, Pennsylvania; New Harmony, Indiana, and Economy, Pennsylvania.

The industrious Rapp founded Harmony, Pennsylvania, in 1804 as America's first communal and socialist society. In 1805, he formally established his new religious order, the Harmony Society, and he and his followers lived in Pennsylvania for about ten years before selling their community for a profit to the Mennonites in 1814. They moved to the edge of US settlement in Indiana, where they established the colony of New Harmony.

In 1824, despite economic success, the group decided to sell their property for a profit and to return to Pennsylvania and start over. They sold New Harmony to Robert Owen, a Welsh industrialist and social reformer. He purchased the town in 1825 with the intention of creating another socialist utopian community; however, it failed after just two years.

The Harmonists moved back to Pennsylvania and founded the town of Economy. The name has since been changed to Ambridge. The Harmonists were very good at business. All three of their settlements were financially very successful and contained various profitable communal business enterprises including a clothing factory, sawmill, tannery, vineyards and a distillery. They had even built and operated a successful hotel in Harmony. In Economy the group also aided the construction of the Pittsburgh and Lake Erie Railroad. They established the Economy Savings Institution and the Economy Brick Works, and operated the Economy Oil Company, the Economy Wood Mill, the Economy Lumber Company, and even donated some land in Beaver Falls for the construction of Geneva College. The society exerted a major influence on the overall development of Western Pennsylvania. While in Economy the group also decided to adopt universal celibacy as a religious practice, and they slowly died out.

The 1848 Revolutions

In 1848, much of the Western world erupted in revolution. In all over fifty countries had major disturbances. Contrary to what was thought at the time, these were individual revolutions in each nation with no coordination or cooperation among the revolutionaries from the different countries. While the causes for revolution in each country were different, there were some common factors. In most places there was a widespread dissatisfaction with old elite political leadership and the aristocracy. In general there was widespread dissatisfaction with the economic conditions of the masses, and there were demands for more participation in governmental decisions by the people affected and rising expectations for democracy.

These civil revolts coincided with an upsurge of European nationalism, and following these uprisings there was a conservative backlash and a re-grouping of the wealthy, the aristocracy, the army, and many loyalist peasants in reaction to the revolutionaries.

The uprisings were led by various, usually unorganized, coalitions of reformers, including both the middle class and working class, but these were short lived. Thousands of people were killed in these revolts, and in most cases the leaders were eventually killed or forced into exile and the uprisings largely failed. However, they did succeed in achieving the abolition of serfdom in the old Austro-Hungarian Empire, in ending the absolute monarchy in Denmark, and finally ending the monarchy in France. The revolutions were most significant in France, Prussia, Poland, Italy, and the Austro-Hungarian Empire. Interestingly, some uprisings occurred in Latin America, but not in Russia, Great Britain, Spain, Sweden, Portugal, or the Ottoman Empire.

Although these rebellions were in favor of greater freedoms and democracies, in the aftermath of the 1848 revolutions a permanent suspicion spread in many Western governments. The false idea that the revolts may have been coordinated, and that socialists, communists, anarchists, and unions had secretly planned them, was unnerving. In the West, particularly in the United States, many people also came to believe that these forces were capable of creating revolution at a moment's notice to threaten any existing government. This paranoia was strongest in the United States and may have been aggravated by the polarization of the country leading up to the Civil War.

The Oneida Community

The Oneida Community was a socialist religious commune founded by John Humphrey Noyes in 1848, in Oneida, New York. The community believed that Jesus had already returned in AD 70, making it possible for them to bring about the perfect life that Christians believe will come to fruition with the return of Jesus. They believed themselves to be free of sin and materialism. They believed that they could achieve perfection in this world and not just in Heaven.

The Oneida Community were communists, espousing communal ownership of all property and possessions. In addition to Oneida there were some smaller Noyes-inspired communities in Wallingford, Connecticut; Newark, New Jersey; and in Putney and Cambridge, Vermont. The Oneida community's original eighty-seven members grew to several hundred by 1852. However the smaller communities dissolved by 1854, except for the Wallingford branch, which operated until it was destroyed by a large tornado in 1878. The Oneida Community dissolved in 1881 and eventually became a profitable joint stock company making silverware called Oneida Limited.

Early Marxists and Unionists

The first non-religious American socialists were German Marxist immigrants who arrived from Prussia following the 1848 revolutions. Joseph Weydemeyer, a German colleague of Karl Marx, came to New York in 1851. He established the first Marxist journal in the US called *Die Revolution,* but it was short-lived. In 1852, he also established the *Proletarierbund,* the Workers Party, which would later become a labor organization, the American Workers' League. It was the first Marxist organization in the US, but it too was short lived, having failed to attract any native English-speaking membership.

William H. Sylvis was a pioneer American union leader. Sylvis is best remembered as a founder of the Iron Molders International Union and in 1866 the National Labor Union, which was one of the first American union federations attempting to unite workers of various professions into a single national organization.

William Sylvis was an Irish-American from Pennsylvania. He considered himself an American patriot and was a loyal to the Union during the Civil War. Early in the war, Sylvis recruited a regiment on behalf of the Union Army. He then had to decline the offer of a commission as the officer to lead this unit due to his wife's strong pacifist objections. However, several months later, he established another company composed of Philadelphia iron molders, and he overcame his wife's objections and served as a sergeant during the war with this unit.

After the Civil War ended in 1866, Sylvis created the National Labor Union. However, due to his service he was in poor health, and he was unable to attend their first national convention. Also in 1866 the "First International Congress" was held in Geneva, Switzerland. Sylvis had helped to organize this first attempt to unite communists, socialists, and unionists. However Sylvis was still too ill to attend the event and sent his representatives along with some members of the National Labor Union to represent the United States workers. William Sylvis died in 1869 at the age of forty-one. Without his dynamic leadership, the National Labor Union did not survive. The International Congress also fell apart as political disagreements, conflicting priorities and distrust between the many factions destroyed the organization by 1876.

In the 1870s, a large wave of German speaking immigrants came to the United States, bringing with them a substantial group of followers of Ferdinand Lassalle, a German-speaking Polish Jew who was the founder of German socialism. Unlike Marx and his adherents, Lassalle believed that the state was an independent entity, an instrument of justice essential for the achievement of the socialist program. He wanted to use existing governments and not to destroy them as was advocated by the anarchists. While Lassalle was a radical, he was not a revolutionary. Unfortunately Lassalle was killed in a duel at the age of thirty-nine, just as he was achieving political recognition. The Social Democratic Party of Germany he founded, based upon his philosophy, survived, and his followers also came to America to spread his ideas. In 1876, Lassalle's followers joined briefly with American Marxists to form The Workingmen's Party of the United States (WPUS), despite their conflicting ideologies about government.

The WPUS was mostly composed of foreign-born working class people. They represented a combination of socialist ideas from both Lassalle and the Marxists. The socialists wanted to form a Socialist political party to advance their agenda through the political and electoral process, but the Marxists wanted to end the capitalist system and the government and to create a new system. However, both the socialists and the American Marxists found common ground in creating and supporting the unions. They also strongly advocated strikes and boycotts, but they were both strongly opposed to violence or revolution.

The WPUS had weak leadership and little influence in politics at either the national or local level. Much like the International Workingmen's Association before it, the WPUS was widely viewed as a small group of utopian dreamers. However, during a railroad strike in 1877, the WPUS came to be led by the charismatic and well-spoken American journalist Albert Parsons. America was surprised by this new-found union power when Parsons was able to attract strong nationwide support for the striking railroad workers.

Despite national popular support the WPUS was mostly unsuccessful in the national railroad strike. However on August 6, 1878, they had gained enough popularity to capture five seats in the Kentucky state legislature. As the word spread of these victories around the country, it encouraged more "Workingmen's Parties" to be formed in cities around the country, some of these were chartered by Parsons and the WPUS while many others remained independent.

Albert & Lucy Parsons

"If there was no evidence to show that I was legally responsible for the deed, then my conviction and the execution of the sentence is nothing less than willful, malicious, and deliberate murder, as foul a murder as may be found in

the annals of religious, political, or any other sort of persecution."—Albert Parsons

Albert Richard Parsons was born in 1848 in Montgomery, Alabama. His father came from Maine to set up a shoe factory in Birmingham. His family were prominent American Yankees and he was a direct descendent of two of George Washington's Revolutionary War officers, Major General Samuel Holden Parsons, and a Captain Parsons who was wounded at Bunker Hill.

Albert's parents died when he was a boy and he went to live his older brother William who owned a small newspaper in Tyler, Texas. He also lived for a short time with an older sister in Waco, Texas. At the age of twelve he became an apprentice at the *Galveston Daily News*, where he worked as he later described it, "as an indentured servant until outbreak of the (Civil) War."

At the age of thirteen, the son of northern Yankees, was anxious to leave his apprenticeship and he volunteered for duty on a Confederate ship as a cabin boy. He served aboard a converted passenger steamship called the Morgan. He later joined an artillery company as a powder boy, which supported an infantry unit that was led by another brother. After his first enlistment at the age of about fifteen he joined a cavalry unit commanded by his oldest brother William and served as a scout. At the end of the war his brother gave him a mule for his service, and he traded it for forty acres of corn that he harvested to pay for six months tuition at Baylor University in Waco, Texas which had been chartered in 1848.

After a year of college he started his own newspaper, the Waco *Spectator*, in 1868. He became a Republican, supported Reconstruction and started speaking out for the rights of the former slaves. He quickly made many enemies, including the powerful Ku Klux Klan. He eventually lost his newspaper because of these views and the subsequent local boycotts of his business.

In 1869, Parsons got a job as a traveling correspondent and as a business agent for the *Houston Daily Telegraph*, during which time he met Lucy Eldine Gonzalez. They married in 1872. Lucy was born in 1853. Her parents were Black slaves who were of mixed Mexican, Native and African-American heritage. The marriage only served to make him an even more controversial figure in Texas as inter-racial marriage was considered a crime and it put them both in danger. The Klan had threatened and was preparing to kill the two of them and Albert Parsons and Lucy were forced to flee Texas for Chicago.

In Chicago, Parsons got a job as reporter with the *Chicago Times*. In 1874 Parson's concerns for oppressed people led him to become interested in labor politics and he began studying socialism and communism. He began to believe that these were the only forces dedicated to helping both labor and oppressed peoples. Parsons later stated that his studies had convinced him that "the complaints of the working people against the society were just and proper" and he came to believe that the treatment of poor people in the urban North and the Black slaves in the South were the same kind of oppression. He saw both as slavery.

Lucy Parsons became an advocate in many social causes, but in particular on behalf of political prisoners, people of color, the poor and women. She was an intelligent, well-spoken and very literate woman. Her intelligence infuriated many White men of influence because of her race, gender and her unapologetic outspokenness. She began writing for two newspapers, *The Socialist* and *The Alarm*. The later newspaper was the journal of the International Working People's Association (IWPA) that she and Albert Parsons helped to found in 1883 shortly after they both gave up Republican politics as too conservative. The Parsons came to see that the Republican Party was deserting its progressive roots and they began to observe it growing more conservative. This movement was the start of the modern conservative Republican Party.

In April 1876, Albert Parsons attended the final convention of the National Labor Union (NLU), held in Pittsburgh. At this convention the union men divided from the more radical revolutionary wing to establish the Working Men's Party of the United States, which then soon merged with the Social Democratic Party to which Parsons was a member. This organization would later rename itself the Socialist Labor Party of America at their 1877 convention in New Jersey where Parsons provided much of the leadership and also attended as a delegate.

Parsons was a strong advocate for change through the ballot and ran for elective office in Chicago and the State of Illinois many times as a socialist. In his first attempt in 1876, he ran for Chicago Alderman and received an impressive six thousand votes. In 1877, he ran for Clerk of Cook County and narrowly lost. He ran two more times for Chicago Alderman and twice for Clerk of Cook County and once for US Congress from Chicago, and although he had well-run campaigns, he failed to get elected. He ran as a socialist in these elections.

A major railroad strike took place in 1877. About a week after the strike began, Parsons was asked to address a large crowd of about 30,000 workers who had gathered at a mass demonstration on Chicago's Market Street. Parsons gave a powerful speech to the assembled strikers on behalf of the Workingmen's Party. The next day due to pressure from the railroads, Chicago's wealthy businessmen, and corrupt Chicago officials, the *Chicago Times* fired Parsons for the speech which they claimed was inflammatory.

The morning after being terminated, Parsons went to the offices of the leading German newspaper, the *Chicagoer Arbeiter Zeitung* (Chicago Worker's News) to apply for work. He was found there by the Chicago police and was brought to City Hall where he was brought before the Chief of Police and a crowd of what were said to be some of the city's "leading citizens." Although they lacked any reason to charge Parsons, he was humiliated, threatened, belittled and harassed for about two hours, with the Police Chief asking Parsons if he didn't "know better than to come here from Texas and incite the working people to insurrection." Parsons denied any such action, noting that he had run for office, that he believed in the ballot and had urged the workers not to strike but to go to the polls to elect new representatives. The police Chief threatened Parsons, telling him that his life was in danger and that he had better leave Chicago. He then released him as the crowd derided him and called for him to be hanged. The afternoon papers including the *Chicago Times* reported that Parsons was arrested for inciting the crowd to riot which was untrue, but this lie has followed him from that day.

Judge Thomas Drummond of the United States Court of Appeals was overseeing numerous railroads that had declared bankruptcy in the wake of the railroad stock bubble and the Panic of 1873. On July 24, after Parson's speech to the strikers, the judge became concerned that a strike at this time could further hurt the railroad's viability. He ruled that "A strike or other unlawful interference with the trains will be a violation of the United States law, and the court will be bound to take notice of it and enforce the penalty."

Judge Drummond ordered federal marshals to arrest the leaders of the strike, and he then tried them for contempt of court. He asked for federal troops to break the strike. The workers of Chicago revolted and the Mayor of Chicago then rounded up five thousand local volunteer vigilantes and thugs to help restore order. The City received the National Guard and federal troops on July 25, and they along with the police and the vigilantes began to violently break up the strike with events reaching a peak the following day. The violence was mostly caused by the vigilantes, the troops and police against the strikers. They are remembered as the "Battle of the Viaduct" because of their proximity to the viaduct on Halsted Street. The headline of Parson's former employer, the *Chicago Times* claimed, "Terrors Reign, the Streets of Chicago Given Over to Howling Mobs of Thieves and Cutthroats."

The violence of the Vigilantes, the troops and police to end the strike resulted in the deaths of nearly twenty striking men and boys and wounded hundreds of others. There were no deaths and few serious wounds among the vigilantes, the police or troops. In his speech Parsons had strongly advocated elections, not violence, but he was falsely blamed for the violence anyway.

At this time most workers worked twelve hours a day, six days per week. Parsons began to aim his activism at establishing an eight-hour work day and a five-day week. In January 1880, the Eight-Hour League of Chicago sent

Parsons to a national conference in Washington, DC, where he launched a national lobbying movement aimed at coordinating efforts of labor organizations to win and enforce an eight-hour workday. In October of 1883, Parsons was a delegate to a convention in Pennsylvania which established the International Working People's Association, the organization to which he would belong for the rest of his life.

In the fall of 1884, Parsons and his wife Lucy launched a weekly newspaper in Chicago they called *The Alarm*. The first issue was October 4, 1884, and 15,000 copies were printed. It was four pages with a price of five cents. *The Alarm* listed the International Working People's Association as its publisher and touted itself as "A Socialistic Weekly." Parsons and Lucy Parsons were both contributors as writers and editors.

Parsons now began to lose faith in the elective process. He wrote, "My experience.... taught me that bribery, intimidation, duplicity, corruption, and bulldozing grew out of the conditions which made the working people poor and the idlers rich, and that consequently the ballot-box could not be made an index to record the popular will until the existing debasing, impoverishing, and enslaving industrial conditions were first altered."

He became an anarchist and wrote, "The Anarchist believes in peace, but not at the expense of liberty. He believes that all political laws are enacted only to force men to do those things they would not naturally, or if left untrammeled. Therefore he considers all political laws as violations of the laws of nature, and the rights of men.... He believes that all governments tend to more laws, instead of less, and that therefore all governments ultimately become despotisms."

The eight-hour day campaign was progressing and Parsons, with Lucy and their two children, led approximately 80,000 people down Michigan Avenue on May 1, 1886, in support of the eight-hour work day. This is regarded as the first-ever May Day Parade to be held. Over the next few days 340,000 laborers joined the strike for an eight-hour day in Chicago. Parsons was called to Cincinnati, where another 300,000 workers had struck on a Saturday. On Sunday he addressed the rally in Cincinnati and participated in a second huge parade.

Another massive strike in support of the eight-hour work day occurred in Chicago. Two days later police opened fire on the striking workers at the McCormick Reaper Works and killed six of the strikers. A rally was organized at the Haymarket to protest the six unnecessary killings and the police violence. Parsons was asked to speak at the rally but had declined to speak, fearing there would be violence. As things calmed down, he later changed his mind and eventually spoke to the crowd. The Mayor of Chicago was present and said later that it was a very peaceful gathering. The Mayor and others left when it looked like it was going to rain. Albert Parsons, Lucy and their children also left the rally when the weather began to suddenly change, because they were worried about their children.

The rally ended around ten that evening and long after Parsons and the Mayor had left, just as the audience was drifting away, a large group of policemen came and forcefully told the crowd to disperse. A bomb was thrown into the crowd at the square and exploded, killing one policeman and wounding people attending the rally. Many later said the bomb had come from the police; the bomb thrower was never found. Gunfire then erupted which resulting in seven fatalities in the crowd and many others wounded. The police began firing indiscriminately. Some policemen were wounded and died. These were blamed on the crowd; however, it was discovered later that the police fatalities and most of the police wounds were from other police officers firing into the crowd. It was indeed a police riot.

The police arrested Parsons and seven other men after the events in the Haymarket. All the men were socialists. The authorities accused them of being promoters of radical ideas and said that they could have been involved in a conspiracy. Parsons was accused of inciting a riot. He worried about the police murdering him (as the police chief had threatened, the last time he was detained). He also worried that a crowd of vigilantes would hang him, as they had warned they would do, and he fled to Waukesha, Wisconsin.

Parsons turned himself in on June 21 to stand in solidarity with the other accused men and to defend his actions and beliefs. William Perkins Black, a corporate lawyer, led the defense of the accused. He bravely persisted despite a series of death threats from the police and others. He was later ostracized by his legal peers and lost all his business for having defened Parsons and the others.

Before and during the trial, multiple witnesses testified that none of the eight men had committed any violence nor had they ever advocated violence. Black offered as proof of Parsons' non-violent intentions the fact that had even brought his children to the rally. Black also noted that Parsons was not present when the bomb was thrown and had left with his family the same time as the Mayor. Despite all this testimony, they were all were found guilty.

Only one was sentenced to 15 years in prison, while the rest of them were sentenced to death. Two asked for clemency and their sentences were commuted to life in prison on November 10, 1887. The Governor immediately lost popularity for that act and lost his political support. On that same day, one prisoner killed himself in his cell with a blasting cap hidden in a cigar, to avoid hanging. The next day Albert Parsons and three others were executed by hanging. The three men serving prison sentences later received pardons from another Illinois governor who granted their freedom from incarceration on June 26, 1893. The Governor and many others had come to recognize the injustice and the unfairness of the convictions and the executions and realized that the Haymarket was a police riot.

Parsons had been told he could have had his sentence commuted to life in prison rather than death, but he refused to write the letter asking the governor to do that; he said that this would be an admission of guilt that would justify their treatment of him. Parsons said it would have been dishonorable and would justify his accuser's illegal actions.

From his prison cell Albert Parsons wrote his farewell in the *Alarm* on November 5, 1887: "And now to all I say: Falter not. Lay bare the inequities of capitalism; expose the slavery of law; proclaim the tyranny of government; denounce the greed, cruelty, abominations of the privileged class who riot and revel on the labor of their wage-slaves. Farewell."

He attempted to make a last minute speech, but cruelly the executioner hanged him before he could say his last words. Albert Parsons is buried in the Forest Home Cemetery in a plot marked since 1893 by the Haymarket Martyrs Monument in Forest Park, Illinois. On February 18, 1997 it was designated a National Historic Landmark, and on April 26, 2002, it became listed on the National Register of Historic Places. It is a small apology for killing a man who committed no crimes and who had dedicated his life to others.

Following her husband's 1887 execution, Lucy Parsons became more active. The Chicago police would later describe her as "more dangerous than a thousand rioters." She remained an activist in the anarchist and socialist movements and became one of the first feminist activists in the new Women's Movement. She was often arrested, threatened and harassed for giving public speeches or distributing activist literature. She continued championing the labor cause, and because of this she came into ideological conflict with some of her mainstream feminist contemporaries because she said that capitalism, class and racial politics were also responsible for suppressing women's rights.

In 1905, Lucy participated in the founding of the International Workers of the World (IWW), and she began editing the *Liberator*, a socialist newspaper that supported the IWW in Chicago. Her focus shifted to class issues, poverty and unemployment, and she organized the Chicago Hunger Demonstrations in January 1915, and was able to enlist the American Federation of Labor, the Socialist Party, and even Jane Addams's Hull House to participate in a huge demonstration on February 12 of that year. Parsons led some of the first sit-down strikes in the United States and later a series of workers sit-down strikes in Argentina. She also helped defend labor activists and African Americans, such as the Scottsboro Nine, unjustly accused of crimes.

In 1925, she began working with the National Committee of the International Labor Defense, an organization which included many communists. Although her membership is disputed and despite the fact that the Communist Party of America has never claimed Lucy Parsons as a member, some biographical accounts claim that Parsons joined the Communist Party USA in 1939.

Parsons continued to give fiery speeches in Chicago's Bughouse Square well into her 80s, where she inspired people like writer Studs Terkel. Parsons died on March 7, 1942, in a house fire in Chicago. After her death, the Chicago police illegally seized her library of over fifteen hundred books and all of her personal papers. She is buried near her husband. In 2004, the City of Chicago named a park after her.

The Decline of the Anarchists

"Every anarchist is a baffled dictator."—Benito Mussolini

"I'm not an anarchist. I believe in government."—Keith Olbermann, television analyst

The heyday of the Anarchists in America was about 1881 when they split with the socialists to form the Revolutionary Socialist Party. By 1885, they had seven thousand official members and many more followers. Interestingly, today's rightwing libertarians developed from the American anarchists. Most anarchists, like Albert Parsons, were also peace advocates, which also gave rise to today's isolationist libertarians.

The American anarchists were inspired by the International Anarchist Congress of 1881 in London. There were two federations of anarchists in the United States that became affiliated. A convention of anarchists in Chicago formed the International Working People's Association of which Albert and Lucy Parsons were founding members. The group included mostly German immigrants and union advocates and it became known as the Black International. The other group was from San Francisco and they formed the International Workingmen's Association called the Red International which was said to be the anarchist's association for those who leaned toward the communists.

After the Haymarket Police Riots in Chicago in 1886 and the American press campaign to make it appear that the anarchists and not the police had caused the violence, public opinion turned against anarchism. Very little violence can be attributed to American anarchists, who were mostly self-proclaimed pacifists. However the Assassination of President William McKinley by a mentally ill man became the decisive turning point in the demise of the anarchists in the United States.

Leon Frank Czolgosz was born in Alpena, Michigan, in 1873. He was the son of Polish Catholic immigrants and was one of eight children. The family was poor. When he was ten he went to work at the American Steel and Wire Company with two of his older brothers, but they were fired after the workers went on strike for higher wages. He continued to work at various factories and witnessed a number of labor strikes that were all ended by police violence against the workers and he became interested in the anarchist movement. He was a shy loner who had difficulty making friends and was not interested in girls. He had a falling out with his family when he told them he was giving up Catholicism.

He had an obsessive personality and totally immersed himself in anarchist and socialist literature. And after hearing a speech by the nationally known anarchist, Emma Goldman, he went to her home and introduced himself as "Nieman," meaning "no man," which Czolgosz romantically thought was a heroic name. He begged to join her in the anarchist movement. She was leaving on a trip, and although she thought he was a strange young man, she hastily introduced him to a couple of anarchist friends before she left. Czolgosz was indeed a strange young man and failed to make any lasting friendships, even in this group of people he admired and desperately wanted to please.

Czolgosz saw that there was a great injustice in American society and it inflamed his persecution complex and made him paranoid and angry. He believed inequalities in the American government had allowed the wealthy and the powerful to enrich themselves by exploiting the poor, including his family. He began to hate the government. He saw government as the root of all evil. Czolgosz was a very disturbed young man who had seen violence and had been bullied from early age. He became obsessed with notions of revenge against all bullies and dreamed of a grand gesture against the government. When he read that King Umberto I of Italy had been shot dead by the anarchist Gaetano Bresci, he was envious. He had read that when Bresci was arrested, he told the press that he had "decided to take matters into his own hands for the sake of the common man." Czolgosz fell in love with this incident and he decided to copy the crime.

In 1901, Czolgosz traveled to Buffalo, New York, the site of the Pan America Exposition where he knew President McKinley would be speaking and greeting the public. On September 6, he went to the exposition armed with a .32 caliber revolver he had purchased four days earlier for $4.50. Czolgosz approached McKinley as the president was standing in a receiving line inside of an exhibition called the Temple of Music, where he was greeting the public. It was about four in the afternoon when Czolgosz reached the front of the line. McKinley extended his hand and Czolgosz slapped it aside and shot the President in the abdomen twice. The first bullet ricocheted and lodged in McKinley's jacket, but the other seriously wounded him. Members of the crowd immediately attacked and began to beat Czolgosz as McKinley slumped backward. McKinley recognized that Czolgosz was mentally unbalanced and pleaded, "Go easy on him boys. He could not have known." Although the shot was not fatal, McKinley died eight days later of an infection from the wound.

At his pre-trial hearing Czolgosz answered that he was pleading "guilty," but the presiding judge, Truman C. White, questioning his sanity, overruled him and entered a "not guilty" plea on his behalf. Czolgosz refused to cooperate or to speak with his attorney or to testify in his own defense. He never spoke a word at his trial. His lawyers were unable to prepare a proper defense since Czolgosz refused to speak to either one of them. As a result, his lead attorney Loran L. Lewis argued at the trial that Czolgosz could not be found guilty for the murder of the president because he was insane at the time. In his statement to the jury, Lewis noted Czolgosz's refusal to talk to his lawyers or cooperate with them and said it was a sign of paranoia and insanity. And while he admitted his client's guilt, and he said that "The only question that can be discussed or considered in this case is whether the act was that of a sane person." Lewis also added, "If it was [an act of a sane man], then the defendant is guilty of the murder," and concluded, "If it was the act of an insane man, then he is not guilty of murder but should be acquitted of that charge and would then be confined in a lunatic asylum."

Czolgosz had already been tried and found guilty in the American press and in the court of public opinion; the majority of the American public wanted a guilty verdict and an execution. The prosecutor, Thomas Penney, stressed Czolgosz's anarchist affiliations as the motive, and he asked the jury to acknowledge the majority of the people's demand for a quick trial and execution.

Czolgosz was convicted on September 24, 1901, after the jury deliberated for only one hour. On September 26, the jury unanimously recommended the death penalty. Czolgosz remained darkly silent and showed no emotion at all upon his conviction and death sentence. When he was asked by the judge if he wanted to make a statement, he just very slowly and silently shook his head no. On October 29, 1901, just a month and a half after McKinley's death, Czolgosz was executed in the electric chair at the age of twenty-eight.

In the American press it seemed as if "the anarchists" and not Czolgosz were on trial. By emphasizing his anarchist ties, the prosecution and the press succeeded in placing the focus on anarchists. Afterward, anarchist leader Emma Goldman was arrested on suspicion of being involved in the assassination, but she was eventually released due to insufficient evidence. Goldman made it worse when she denied the charges but said that although the president shouldn't have been killed, she thought that McKinley was the "president of the money kings and trust magnates." Her remarks were strongly disavowed by most other anarchists, who felt that Czolgosz's actions and Goldman's insensitive remarks about McKinley had done mortal damage to the peaceful non-violent anarchist cause, and that concern proved to be prophetic. Violence and anarchism were now permanently tied together in the minds of most of the American people.

Dr. Lloyd Vernon Briggs, who later became the Director of the Massachusetts Department for Mental Hygiene, reviewed the Czolgosz case in 1901 on behalf of Dr. Walter Channing, the coroner, shortly after Czolgosz's death. Briggs concluded that Czolgosz was "a man who had been suffering from mental illness for many years. He said that Czolgosz "was not medically responsible and in the light of present-day psychiatry and of modern surgical procedure, there is a great question whether he was even legally responsible for the death of our President."

Eugene V. Debs

> "It is better to vote for what you want and not get it than to vote for what you don't want and get it."—Eugene V. Debs

"Years ago I recognized my kinship with all living beings, and I made up my mind that I was not one bit better than the meanest on earth. I said then, and I say now, that while there is a lower class, I am in it, and while there is a criminal element, I am of it, and while there is a soul in prison, I am not free." This quote from Debs summarizes his world view. Eugene Victor Debs was born in 1855 in Terra Haute, Indiana. His parents were wealthy French immigrants. He was raised in a very upper middleclass household and was named after his parent's two favorite writers, Eugene Sue and Victor Hugo.

Debs dropped out of school at the age of fourteen and found a job in a factory making railroad cars as a painter and cleaner. After two years he left for a railroad job as a fireman on a steam locomotive. He became a member of the Brotherhood of Railroad Firemen (BLF). He left that after three years and found a job in a grocery supply company and stayed there for four years while attending college at night, but he retained his BLF membership and was active in the union during this time. This included serving as the Brotherhood's delegate from Terra Haute to their national convention. Debs was elected the associate editor of the BLF's monthly publication, *Firemen's Magazine*, in 1878. Two years later, he was appointed the Grand Secretary and Treasurer of the BLF and was also made editor of the *Firemen's Magazine* in July 1880.

Debs was also keenly interested in politics. During his work with the union he had also became a prominent figure in local politics and he served two terms as Terre Haute's city clerk from September 1879 to September 1883. In the fall of 1884, he was elected to the Indiana Assembly as a Democrat, serving for one term.

Debs left the BLF in 1883 to found the American Railway Union (ARU). It was one of the first unions for unskilled workers in America. A year later Debs made national headlines with a successful strike against the Great Northern Railway winning almost all the demands he had asked for and assuring the union's position as the bargaining agent for many of the Great Northern employees. Later that year the Pullman Company of Chicago said that because of falling revenue due the economic Panic of 1893, they were cutting the wages of their employees by about twenty-eight per cent. The wages that Pullman paid were very low to begin with and these wage cuts would have put most of these workers into poverty. The workers, some of whom were already members of the American Railway Union, appealed for support from the union at its convention in Chicago. Debs cautioned them that the ARU was too weak to take on the all the railroads, the Pullman Company and the federal government whose mail cars were made by Pullman. The membership overruled Debs and they decided to support the Pullman employees in a strike. The ARU Board then decided to expand the strike from Chicago to St. Louis, which brought out over 80,000 railroad workers on strike. Although Debs had urged them to not strike, he bowed to their wishes and he agreed to lead the strike.

On July 9, 1894, *The New York Times* ran the following article and its sentiments were echoed in many newspapers across the nation: "Organized labor makes a miserable showing in its attempts to give aid and comfort to the Anarchists at Chicago....The truth is that every labor union man in the City of New York knows that he becomes a criminal the moment he puts himself on the side of Debs or attempts to sustain him by quitting work to show sympathy for the strikes and the riots Debs has provoked. When he sent his dispatch to the railway laborers in Buffalo Debs became a misdemeanant under the Penal Code of this State....He is a lawbreaker at large, an enemy of the human race. There has been quite enough talk about warrants against him and about arresting him. It is time to cease mouthings and begin. Debs should be jailed, if there are jails in his neighborhood, and the disorder his bad teaching has engendered must be squelched."

Newspapers and editorialists at the time said, "All of the best people" are against these "union hooligans." The groups who most opposed Debs and the strikers were the government, middleclass merchants, professionals, wealthy industrialists and business owners, bankers, and rural people who had little idea of what railroad and industrial life was about. Most working class people on the railroads, in other transpiration jobs, in the mills and factories and utility plants, who were working twelve hours, frequently seven days a week, for very low pay, understood. The 80,000 people who were on strike certainly understood.

Although Debs was a reluctant leader, the strike came to be known as "Debs' Rebellion." He fought the railroads by establishing a successful national boycott of Pullman train cars and persuaded other workers not affiliated with the strike to also refuse to work on Pullman railcars.

In response to the boycott and the strike the Pullman Company and the railroads persuaded the US Government to intervene and they obtained a court injunction against the strike on the thin grounds that the strikers had obstructed the US Mail which was carried on the Pullman cars. President Grover Cleveland sent the US Army and ordered them to "physically break" the strike. The Army did this with brute military force. They attacked the unarmed picketing strikers and opened fire on them killing thirteen and wounding many others in their first encounter. The strikers reacted in anger at the death and violence and retaliated by vandalizing and damaging millions of dollars' worth of railroad property.

In the aftermath, thousands of strikers were fired and blacklisted by the railroads and by many other industries. Those on the list were permanently banned from working in American industry or the railroads ever again. Debs was arrested and brought to federal court on charges of contempt of court for leading the strike. He was represented by Clarence Darrow, who was at the time a well-paid corporate lawyer for a railroad company. However Darrow was so outraged by the injustice that he switched sides to represent Debs. Darrow made a substantial financial sacrifice in order to represent Debs. He lost many clients. And although Darrow did an excellent job, Debs was still found guilty for violating the injunction and was sent to prison in Woodstock, Illinois.

Prior to his prison sentence Debs had been a fairly moderate Democrat, but the strike and his unfair prison sentence changed him. He began to read socialist literature and became a socialist while in prison. He also read Karl Marx, and was particularly fond of *Das Kapital* which was given to him by a visiting socialist newspaper editor. He would later say: "I began to read and think and dissect the anatomy of the system in which workingmen, however organized, could be shattered and battered and splintered at a single stroke. The writings of Bellamy and Blatchford early appealed to me. The Cooperative Commonwealth of Gronlund also impressed me, but the writings of

Katusky were so clear and conclusive that I readily grasped, not merely his argument, but also caught the spirit of his socialist utterance and I thank him and all who helped me out of darkness into light."

Debs had married Kate Metzel in 1885, just before going prison. After Debs' release from prison, he started his Socialist political career. Debs persuaded his ARU membership to join forces with a socialist group to found the Social Democracy of America. Debs and Martin J. Elliott, his Board Chair, along with his running mate Jon Harriman, were the first federal office candidates for the fledgling Socialist party. They ran for US President, Vice President and Congress in 1900. Debs received 87,945 votes and became nationally recognized as the nation's leading unionist and socialist.

His wife, Kate Metzel Debs, strongly disagreed with his new found socialism. She had very little time or patience for politics, but they remained together despite their political differences. Irving Stone would later write a biography about the two called *Adversary in the House* because he was so entranced by the dynamics of this strong-willed couple with very strong opposing viewpoints. The couple later built and moved into a comfortable home at 451 North Eighth Street, in Terre Haute, Indiana, which is now a National Historic Landmark of the National Parks Department in the Department of Interior and is also an official historic site of the State of Indiana. The house serves as the Eugene Debs Museum.

In 1901, Social Democracy split into two factions and Debs led the majority faction to found the Social Democratic Party. He was elected chairman of the Executive Board of the National Council and the governing board of the party. Debs was an uncomfortable leader and disdained publicity. He designed the party as a collective leadership rather than having a single person governing its actions. However, Debs' position as chairman and his national reputation among unionists and socialists alike made Debs their unquestioned leader. Although he was never comfortable with his leadership role, he was still very charismatic.

Debs remained active in politics. He was the Social Democratic Party candidate for president in 1904, 1908, and 1912, and also ran in 1920 from a prison cell where he was sentenced for his anti-war protests during World War I. In 1916, he also ran for Congress in his home district in Indiana. In the 1904 election, Debs received 402,810 votes and he finished third overall. In the 1908 election, Debs received a slightly higher total of votes, collecting 420,852. In 1912, Debs ran for president and more than doubled his total from 1908 to receive 901,551 votes. In 1920, from prison, his total was an incredible 913,693 votes which remains the all-time high for any American socialist presidential candidate.

Despite Debs' success as a genuine third party presidential candidate, he was very disillusioned with politics. Some of his disillusionment was perhaps due to his wife's influence and her genuine dislike and disdain for all politics. Union organizing remained Deb's greatest passion and it was where he spent most of his time.

In 1905, in Chicago, Debs and few other union leaders including Big Bill Haywood (the leader of the Western Federation of Miners) and Daniel De Leon (the leader of the Socialist Labor Party) held what Haywood called the "Continental Congress of the working class." Haywood said at the time, "We are here to confederate the workers of this country into a working class movement that shall have for its purpose the emancipation of the working class." And Debs stated, "We are here to perform a task so great that it appeals to our best thought, our united energies, and will enlist our most loyal support; a task in the presence of which weak men might falter and despair, but from which it is impossible to shrink without betraying the working class." And out of these lofty speeches the International Workers of the World (IWW) was founded. They were sometimes called "the Wobblies."

The IWW was built on the basis of uniting the unskilled workers of industry, and at first this worked well, but after a half dozen years a rift developed between the unionists and the politicians of the Socialist Party. It started when the elected wing of the Socialist Party, led by Victor Berger and a few other socialist elected officials, became irritated with the disparaging speeches by Haywood against all politicians. In December of 1911, Haywood told an audience at New York's Cooper Union that elected socialists were "step-at-a-time people whose every step is just a little shorter than the preceding step."

Haywood genuinely disliked politicians and felt they were always more interested in their political careers than in the plight of the working class. He said it was better to "elect the superintendent of some branch of industry, than to elect some congressman." In response, Berger and the elected socialists attacked the IWW and the unionists as "purely anarchistic." By comparing the unionists to the anarchists, they succeeded once again in raising American fears about potential anarchist violence. These attacks were particularly aimed to discredit Big Bill Haywood.

The rift presented a dilemma for Debs, who was a leader in both the IWW and the Socialist Party. The final straw between Haywood and the Socialist Party came during the Lawrence Textile Strike when Haywood became disgusted by the decision of the local elected officials in Lawrence, Massachusetts to send the police to physically break the strike. They did so by using their clubs on mothers and children who had joined their husbands and fathers on strike. Haywood was outraged and in a heated response publicly declared that "I will not vote again until these injustices end."

Haywood was purged from the National Executive Committee of the Socialist Party. Debs was the only person who could have saved Haywood, and although he disagreed with their decision, after a mild protest he deferred to the other committee members. Debs always preferred communal and consensus decisions.

Part of his acquiescence in this decision was also that while Debs greatly admired Haywood and his integrity, the non-violent Debs greatly feared that the passionate Haywood would someday match the police violence with worker violence.

The decision on Haywood was very typical of Debs' leadership. Although Debs was idolized as a leader of both the unionist and socialist movements, he never wanted or liked the spotlight or to be in the role as the sole decision maker. In 1906 he stunned a Detroit audience by saying, "I am not a Labor Leader. I do not want you to follow me or anyone else. If you are looking for a Moses to lead you out of this capitalist wilderness, you will stay right where you are. I would not lead you into the Promised Land if I could, because if I led you in, someone else would lead you out. You must use your heads as well as your hands, and get yourself out of your present condition."

After Haywood's expulsion and his split with the socialists Debs still openly admired and remained friends with Haywood and the IWW. In 1906, when Haywood was on trial for his life in Idaho, Debs boldly defended him and described him to the press as "the Lincoln of Labor."

Debs was not only anti-violence, he was also a pacifist and vehemently anti-war. In the build up to World War I Debs was an isolationist and said that war was an industrialist's invention to further their own profits from the blood of many. He greatly angered President Woodrow Wilson, and the President would later refer to Debs as "a traitor to his country." He directed his Attorney General A. Mitchell Palmer to silence or imprison him which he did.

Debs began an anti-war campaign that would later be almost identically copied by the anti-war activists during the Vietnam War in the 1960s and 1970s. On June 16, 1918, while World War I in Europe was taking the lives of tens of thousands, Debs made a dramatic speech in Canton, Ohio, disavowing the war and urging young men to give peaceful and passive resistance to the military draft. The speech was covered extensively by the American press and despite the fact that Debs had carefully worded his speech in an attempt to comply with the newly enacted Espionage Act; he was arrested by Attorney General Palmer's federal agents on June 30. He was then charged with ten counts of sedition, principally because he advocated in his speech that men should avoid the military draft.

His trial defense team was very weak and they called no witnesses and presented no evidence, asking instead that Debs be allowed to address the court in his defense. Although it was an unusual request it was granted by the judge who was under some political pressure by the Wilson Administration and Attorney General A. Mitchell Palmer to get a quick resolution. Debs spoke for two hours about his pacifist and anti-war beliefs and said he was a conscientious objector.

Debs was found guilty on September 12, 1918. At his sentencing hearing two days later, he again addressed the court in a speech which has become a courtroom classic. Heywood Broun one of the more respected journalists of that time and who was no fan of Debs, said the speech was "One of the most beautiful and moving passages in the English language. He was for that one afternoon touched with inspiration. If anyone told me that tongues of fire danced upon his shoulders as he spoke, I would believe it."

The most quoted part of Debs' speech was the opening, "Your Honor: Years ago I recognized my kinship with all living beings, and I made up my mind that I was not one bit better than the meanest on earth. I said then, and I say now, that while there is a lower class, I am in it, and while there is a criminal element I am of it, and while there is a soul in prison, I am not free."

Debs was sentenced on November 18, 1918, to ten years in prison at the age of sixty-three. He was also disenfranchised for life meaning it would be a federal crime for him to vote or participate in any election.

He served his time in federal prison in Atlanta. Debs was such a pleasant and unpretentious man that he was well regarded by the prison officials and the inmates alike. But he was not a young man and his health rapidly deteriorated in the rough prison conditions. Despite his health and imprisonment he ran for president in 1920 from his cell and received his best election results while running against the popular Republican Warren Harding.

On December 23, 1921, because of his very poor and rapidly deteriorating health, President Harding commuted Debs' sentence to time served effective Christmas Day. Debs arrived in Terre Haute on Dec. 28, 1921. He was given a tremendous welcome by over a thousand friends who greeted him on his return to his hometown. Debs spent his last days trying to recover his health, which was severely damaged by his prison confinement and a lack health care.

In his final years, he made a few speeches, but he wrote many articles. At the age of seventy, Eugene V. Debs died on October 20, 1926. His death left a void. The American unions and the American socialist movements never found another charismatic leader of his caliber. He was the last of his kind.

He was buried in Terre Haute and ten years later his wife Kate died and was buried beside him.

Debs was a man born into upper middleclass comfort who had dedicated his entire life to the working class and the labor causes of providing living wages, creating a five-day work week, and working for pension and health benefits. In recognition of these contributions the US Department of Labor named Debs as a member of its Labor Hall of Fame in 1990.

Big Bill Haywood

> "If one man has a dollar he didn't work for, some other man worked for a dollar he didn't get."—Big Bill Haywood

> "The mine owners did not find the gold, they did not mine the gold, they did not mill the gold, but by some weird alchemy all the gold belonged to them!"—Big Bill Haywood

William Dudley Haywood was born February 4, 1869. He was known as "Big Bill Haywood," and was a founding member and leader of the Industrial Workers of the World (IWW). He was also a member of the Executive Committee of the Socialists Party of America. During the first two decades of the 20th century, he was involved in many important labor battles. These included working with the United Mine Workers in the Colorado Labor Laws disputes, the Lawrence Textile Strike, and many other textile strikes in Massachusetts and New Jersey.

Haywood liked to call his philosophy "socialism with its working clothes on." He was an advocate of a labor philosophy that favored organizing all workers in an industry under one union, regardless of the specific trade or skill level. This was in contrast to the many craft unions at the time. He was a civil rights advocate and he strongly believed that workers of all races, religions and ethnicities should be equal in pay and stature, which clashed with many other union leaders at the time. According to Haywood, the IWW was "big enough to take in the Black man, the White man; big enough to take in all nationalities, an organization that will be strong enough to obliterate state boundaries; to obliterate national boundaries."

His strong preference for confrontational strikes over passive negotiation and his disdain for elected officials eventually alienated him from the Socialist Party. This and his disdain for socialist politicians were the cause of his dismissal from the Party in 1912. He was not afraid of confrontation and Haywood was frequently the target of prosecutors. His trial for the murder of Idaho Governor Frank Steunenberg in 1907 drew national attention. He was eventually acquitted as the charges against him had been trumped up by the police and the mine owners. The Governor's actual murderer was Harry Orchard. It was discovered during the trial that he was a paid informant of the mine owners who at the time were in a contentious dispute with Haywood and the other leaders of the United Mine Workers.

During the First Red Scare, in 1918, Haywood was one of a hundred members of the IWW convicted by the Wilson Administration of violating the Espionage Act of 1917. He was jailed for being a socialist, which the government claimed made him a threat to the national security. While out of prison during an appeal of his conviction, Haywood came to believe he could not receive a fair trial and fled to the USSR. He spent the remaining years of his life in Russia. And so the man who Debs had called "the Lincoln of Labor" was run out of the country because of an illegal act that made being a socialist in America a traitor.

Mary Harris "Mother" Jones

> "If they want to hang me, let them. And on the scaffold
> I will shout Freedom for the working class!"—Mary Harris
> "Mother" Jones

Mary Harris was born in Cork, Ireland in 1837. She left Ireland for Canada with her parents during the Potato Famine. She received a Catholic education in Toronto before moving to Monroe, Michigan, where she was a teacher in a Catholic school. She then moved to Chicago and opened a dressmaking shop. She married George Jones and moved with him to Memphis. Her husband was a foundry worker and active in the union.

Her life was hard and tragic. During a yellow fever epidemic in Memphis, she lost her husband and all of her four children who were all under the age of five at the time. She left Memphis and returned to Chicago, where she reopened her dressmaking shop. After four years she lost her business and home in the Great Chicago Fire.

She believed strongly in the right of working people to earn a living wage. She became interested in union work and joined the Knights of Labor as an organizer. After the Knights of Labor disbanded, she became affiliated with the United Mine Workers Union and joined the Socialist Party of America. She became a strike organizer for the Union and was notoriously good at her work.

She gained a national reputation for organizing the wives and children of striking workers in demonstrations on their behalf. She became known in the American press as "the most dangerous woman in America." This phrase was coined by a West Virginia district attorney, Reese Blizzard, in 1902. He made this claim at her trial for violating a court injunction banning meetings by striking miners. Blizzard was quoted in the press as saying to the court,

"There sits the most dangerous woman in America. She crooks her finger and twenty thousand contented men lay down." The union men and women she represented fondly called her "Mother Jones."

Jones was ideologically separated from most of the other women activists and she opposed the passage of the Nineteenth Amendment. She was strongly opposition to abortion, and after losing her four young children she couldn't imagine any circumstances where she could condone the termination of a pregnancy. She also believed strongly that women were subservient to men, as her Catholic upbringing had taught her, and she believed that women should concentrate on their children. She did not support women's suffrage.

Jones failed to see the contradiction in her own life, although she was in what was thought of then as a "male-only occupation." She was quoted as saying that "You don't need the vote to raise hell." She said she believed that women should be home with their children and believed that men should have a living wage to allow them to do so.

In 1901, workers in Pennsylvania's silk mills went on strike. Most of the workers were children, mostly young girls, and they wanted safer and better treatment. They were also demanding to be paid adult wages. It was during this strike that Jones became a life-long advocate against child labor. In 1903 Jones organized children who were working in mills and mines in Pennsylvania, to participate in the "Children's Crusade." She organized a march from Kensington, Pennsylvania, to Oyster Bay, New York, the hometown of President Theodore Roosevelt. They arrived with banners saying "We want to go to School and not the mines." Mother Jones made the press aware that many of the children had missing fingers and other disabilities from their hazardous work in the mills and mines. Her first attempts to get press coverage of these working conditions failed, as many of the newspapers were under the control of the mill and mine owners. However, through her persistence, she made the public aware of these conditions and garnered enough public outrage that the strike was successfully settled on the behalf of labor.

In 1912, Mother Jones arrived in West Virginia on behalf of the United Mine Workers. She began organizing during a conflict between the local coal miners and a large private army hired by the mine owners. The mine owners managed to get martial law declared in the area to break the miners' strike. Jones was arrested on February 13, 1913. She was brought before a military court and accused of inciting riots and conspiring to commit murder among other nebulous charges. She refused to speak or recognize the legitimacy of the military court. She was found guilty and sentenced to twenty years in the state penitentiary. After eighty-five days of confinement she developed a very serious case of pneumonia and was released. The US Senate then decided to investigate the conditions in the West Virginia coal mines.

The Senate investigations and pressure from Congress eventually brought the needed reforms. The poet Carl Sandberg claims that the "She" in the song *She'll Be Coming Around the Mountain* was a tribute to Mother Jones and her work improving the West Virginia coal mines.

Several months after her victory in West Virginia and a recovery of her health, Jones went to Colorado to the site of another labor conflict. The Colorado miners were on strike for better wages and conditions. She was arrested again during this conflict and served time in jail. When she was released, she was forcibly escorted out of Colorado and told not to come back or she'd face arrest and a long prison term.

Shortly after Jones was forced out, the Colorado National Guard attacked the striking workers' tent camp. It became known as the Ludlow Massacre. The Colorado National Guard killed twenty-five people, including two women and eleven children. The children were asphyxiated and burned to death in their tent after the Colorado Guard set it ablaze. In retaliation for the Ludlow Massacre, the miners armed themselves and attacked dozens of mines over the next ten days. They destroyed property and engaged in several skirmishes with the Colorado National Guard, which by some accounts resulted in the loss of perhaps as many as 199 miner's lives.

John D. Rockefeller Jr., the primary owner of the mines, was blamed for these deaths in the press. As the public anger at Rockefeller grew over the incident, he decided to invite Jones to meet with him personally in his office in New York. After the meeting Rockefeller, who desperately wished to improve his tarnished public image, visited the mines. He met with the miners and made many reforms suggested by Jones and the United Mine Workers.

Jones remained a union organizer for the United Mine Workers well into the 1920s and continued to speak on union affairs until her death. She released her own account of her experiences in the labor movement in *The Autobiography of Mother Jones*, which was published in 1925. She died in 1930 at the age of eighty-seven.

Mary Harris Jones left her mark on both American and Irish culture. *Mother Jones Magazine* is an American left leaning magazine named after her. It features investigative reporting and articles on politics, the environment, human rights, and culture. The song *Union Maid* written and performed by the folk singer Woody Guthrie celebrates Jones. And in 2012, in Cork, Ireland, the Mother Jones Festival was held in the city to celebrate the 175th anniversary of her birth, with numerous international guest speakers.

Floyd Olson, Elmer Benson, and Minnesota's Farmer Labor Party

"The poor frequently protest being governed badly; the rich protest being governed at all."—Floyd B. Olson

Floyd B. Olson was born November 13, 1891, on the north side of Minneapolis, Minnesota. He was the only child of Scandinavian parents. Like many in the neighborhood, his family was poor working class. The North Side Minneapolis neighborhood where Olson grew up was also the home of a large Orthodox Jewish community. Olson's friendships with some of the local Jewish families led him to serve as a "shabbos goy," which is a gentile assisting Jews on the Sabbath by performing household functions like starting fires for heat, cooking, etc. that the Orthodox Jews were not permitted to do on their Sabbath.

Olson picked up Yiddish from these childhood associations with his Jewish neighbors. Years later when he entered politics he still spoke the language fluently and used it while campaigning among Jewish groups. He was one of the first Minnesota politicians and one of the first US governors to appoint Jews to office and he had a number of Jewish advisors in his campaigns and while serving in elected office.

(An interesting side note: the author's grandfather Albert Carrier was a neighbor and a childhood friend of Olson's. He was an Irish Catholic boy who also served as a "shabbos goy" and could also speak Yiddish, and his brother, the author's great uncle, Jack Carrier, later served as Olson's top aide and was the first secretary of the Minnesota Democratic Farmer Labor Party.)

After graduating from high school in Minneapolis in 1909, Olson went to work for the Northern Pacific Railway with his childhood friends Albert and Jack Carrier. The next year, he enrolled at the University of Minnesota. However, he left after only a year, during which he was constantly in trouble for wearing a derby hat in violation of school rules for dress and for refusing to participate in mandatory ROTC drills. After leaving the university he returned to the workforce doing unskilled labor jobs; he became a member of the International Workers of the World.

In 1913, Olson enrolled at William Mitchell College of Law and earned his degree in 1915. That same year, he met and married Ada Krejci and became a practicing lawyer. In 1919, Olson was hired as an Assistant Attorney in Hennepin County, Minneapolis. The following year he was promoted to Hennepin County Attorney after his boss was fired for accepting bribes. He became interested in politics and he helped form the Committee of 48, an organization that attempted to draft the progressive Senator Robert La Follette from Wisconsin to run for president on the Progressive Party ticket.

(Another interesting side note: the author's son-in-law is currently a senior partner in what was Robert La Follette's old law firm. La Follette's desk is still on display in their Madison, Wisconsin law offices.)

La Follette declined to run in 1920, but he would later run on the Progressive Party ticket in 1924. That same year, Olson ran in Minnesota the Democratic primary for the local seat in Congress but lost.

As Hennepin County Attorney Olson quickly earned a name for himself as an able prosecutor and a champion who relished going after crooked businessmen. He also bravely took on the then powerful Ku Klux Klan in a well-publicized case that earned him respect from both Jews and Catholics, however because of this he also he also received serious death threats. The Klan had become a dominate force in many Midwestern states at this time, and the Grand Dragon of the entire Klan was from Indiana and had elected the Governor. However, Olson persisted and his strong actions kept the Klan from coming to power in Minnesota. Olson was easily reelected to the position in 1922 and 1926.

In 1923, Olson brought a case against the leaders of a conservative business organization, The Minnesota Citizen's Alliance, who were dedicated to suppressing unions by preserving right-to-work laws. After the Alliance hired an organized crime hit man to bomb the home of a union leader, Olson's investigation and prosecution of the Citizens Alliance made him a hero to the Minnesota Labor movement. They encouraged him to run for the Farmer Labor Party's 1924 gubernatorial nomination. La Follette appreciated that Olson had tried to draft him to run for president four years earlier and openly endorsed him and campaigned for him for Minnesota governor increasing his status.

Minnesota at that time was heavily dominated by the Republican Party. The Republicans had a safe majority in Minnesota and it had been so since the Civil War. But despite this Olson did very well and received forty-three percent of the total votes to Republican Theodore Christianson's forty-eight percent. It was a surprisingly good showing in Republican Minnesota. The Democratic candidate came in a distant third place with six percent. Although Olson had lost this election, his strong showing set up the Farmer Labor Party as a legitimate second party alternative to the Republicans and made Olson the undisputed leader.

Olson was asked by the Farmer Labor Party to run for governor again in 1928, but he declined, and the Farmer Labor candidate lost by a significant margin in the Republican landslide that accompanied Herbert Hoover's presidential election.

In the wake of the stock market crash and the beginning of the Great Depression in 1929, the Farmer Labor Party made a significant effort to draft Olson to run for Governor in 1930. He accepted and easily won the election. He formed a strong political coalition of farmers, unions and labor, and also successfully recruited small businessmen, and added them to his growing

Catholic and Jewish base. It was a coalition that would bring the Farmer Labor Party to dominance in Minnesota. When the Farmer Labor Party merged with the Democratic Party to form the Independent Democratic Farmer Labor Party, this Party would go on to dominate Minnesota politics into the twenty-first century. This independent party would later affiliate nationally with the Democrats, but it has remained independent to this day. As this is written the current Minnesota Governor, a majority of both houses of the Minnesota Legislature, both US Senators and five of eight Minnesota members of Congress belong to the Independent Democratic Farmer Labor Party.

Olson swept to a landslide victory in the 1930 election, receiving fifty-nine percent of the total votes in a four-way race and winning eighty-two of the state's eighty-seven counties.

At the time Olson assumed his office, the Minnesota Legislature was officially nonpartisan, but in reality it was dominated by very conservative Republicans who opposed Olson and his progressive platform. However Olson was so popular and such a skilled politician that he managed to enact the vast majority of his legislative agenda. During his three terms as governor Olson proposed and the legislature passed bills that instituted a progressive income tax and created a social security program for the elderly before the federal Social Security legislation was passed. He also expanded the state's environmental and conservation programs. He was the first governor to guarantee equal pay for women. He guaranteed the right of the unions for collective bargaining, instituted a minimum wage, and created an employer paid unemployment insurance program. Under Olson's tenure Minnesota became the most progressive state and has largely remained so.

Olson was able to accomplish this because of his popularity and his fearlessness to accomplish his goals. In its April 24, 1933, issue *Time* magazine quoted Olson speaking from the steps of the Minnesota capitol: "I am making a last appeal to the Legislature. If the Senate does not make provision for the sufferers (unemployed) in the State, and the Federal Government refuses to aid, I shall invoke the powers I hold and I shall declare martial law.... A lot of people who are now fighting these measures (unemployment, and social security) because they happen to possess considerable wealth will be brought in by provost guard and be obliged to give up more than they would now. There is not going to be misery in this state if I can humanly prevent it. . . Unless the federal and state governments act to insure against recurrence of the present situation, I hope the present system of government goes right down to hell."

Despite his success the changes Olson wanted the most was legislation that would have put all of Minnesota's electric utilities under public ownership as many of the smaller and rural electric companies were already co-ops or municipally owned. He also wanted Minnesota's natural resources such as the iron, copper and nickel mines, the grain elevators, and meatpacking plants under public ownership. But this legislation never stood a chance of passage even in Minnesota with the popular Governor demanding it.

In 1935, Olson was asked by the Progressives to run for President in 1936. He declined and persuaded the progressives to support Roosevelt. Roosevelt was grateful and told Olson that if his Farmer Labor Party ever wished to affiliate with the Democratic Party he would help make that happen. Roosevelt kept his word even after Olson's death and the two parties merged in 1944 and the DFL was allowed to remain independent but still affiliate nationally with the Democrats.

On November 18, 1935, Olson announced his intention to run against longtime incumbent Minnesota US Senator Thomas Schall. When Senator Schall unexpectedly died following the following month in an auto accident, Olson as governor appointed his friend Elmer Benson the interim successor to Senator Schall, and Benson promised that he would not run for the seat in the 1936 election.

As Olson began to campaign in 1936 for the Senate he suddenly became sick. At first it was diagnosed as stomach ulcers; however it was later revealed as stomach cancer. Olson's last public appearance was on June 29, 1936 where he gave stump speech in Minnehaha Park in Minneapolis. The next day he returned to the Mayo Clinic for treatment but it was too late. He died there on August 22, 1936. He was just forty-four years old. Minnesota's champion of the working class was dead.

Shortly after Olson died, Minnesota Highway 55 was renamed the Floyd B. Olson Memorial Highway in his honor by the Minnesota Legislature. His house in North Minneapolis is now on the National Register of Historic Places. In 2004 a proposal by the conservative Republicans who greatly disliked Olson and his anti-capitalist ways sought to rename the Olson Highway after President Ronald Reagan but this proposal was met in Minnesota with widespread public condemnation and was soon abandoned.

Elmer Benson was born in 1895, in Appleton, Minnesota. He was a good student and after high school he attended and graduated from William Mitchell College of Law. After law school Benson served for a year in the US Army during World War I. He decided to not practice law after returning from the war and became a banker and businessman.

He became interested in politics and became a close ally of Governor Floyd B. Olson who helped orchestrate Benson's political rise. Olson appointed Benson state Commissioner of Securities before choosing him to replace Thomas Schall in the United States Senate upon Schall's death. Benson served in the Senate until November 3, 1936.

After Olson's premature death from cancer in 1936, Benson ran for governor and was elected by the largest margin in state history. He served from January 4, 1937, to January 2, 1939. He lost his bid for reelection in 1938. His defeat in 1938 is seen as a setback for progressive politics in Minnesota. In 1940, he ran for the United States Senate against Henrich Shipstead, an incumbent senator who had recently defected from the Farmer Labor Party to join the Republicans. Benson took second place, in a race that also involved a Democrat, and Shipstead was reelected. Benson again ran for the Senate in 1942, and but was defeated by a Republican in a four way race.

Despite these losses Benson still had significant power within the DFL and the national Progressive Party and he managed the 1948 presidential campaign of Henry Wallace. He left politics after the 1948 election and went back into business. He died in 1985.

Benson has been accused of being a communist on many occasions. In May of 1984, shortly before his death, a book review of *The Heyday of American Communism* by Hal Draper implied that Olson and Benson had deliberately allowed the communists to take over the Farmer Labor Party. Benson wrote a strong letter to the editor denying his allegations: "I was the Governor of Minnesota during 1937 and 1938, the beginning period of the Popular Front outlook of the Communist Party. I'm sure that communists did participate in the Farmer-Labor Party at this time and also in the farm and union movements. However, the statement in Draper's review that the Communist Party "took over" Floyd B. Olson, who preceded me as Governor, is sheer exaggeration. The reviewer's further allegation that I 'continued in Olson's path, giving communist organizers money for organizing...' is a further elaboration of the same exaggeration. I don't know if the basis for the innuendo that the Farmer-Labor Party became almost an extension of the Communist Party lies in the book itself or in the mind of the reviewer; but, in any event, the innuendo should not be allowed to stand without challenge."

The Farmer Labor Party merged with the Democrats in 1944, but remains today an independent party separate from the National Democratic Party. The Minnesota Democratic Farmer Labor Party, DFL, has included some very influential politicians in American politics including: former Vice Presidents Hubert H. Humphrey and Walter Mondale, and Senators Gene McCarthy and Paul Wellstone, and currently Senators Amy Klobuchar and Al Franken, and Congressman Keith Ellison the nation's first Islamic member of Congress.

The Liberals Join the American Right in the Destruction of the American Left

"Communism is the death of the soul. It is the organization of total conformity, in short, of tyranny, and it is committed to making tyranny universal."—Adlai Stevenson

Liberals have been painted by the American right to be thought of as leftist politicians. Liberals for the most part are not of the American left, most are moderates and centrists, they strongly support free market capitalism and disdain both socialists and communists. No better example of this was one of the most liberal American politicians, Hubert Horatio Humphrey. He greatly disliked socialism and communism. Humphrey was an ardent capitalist and worked on and passed the McCarran Act to make being a communist in America a felony. He personally wrote and added a piece to the bill to detain and imprison all socialists and communists. The Humphrey clause to the McCarran Act was what one aide to President Truman labeled as the "concentration camp bill." It was vetoed by President Truman on Constitutional grounds, but his veto was overridden by Humphrey and the Congress. Humphrey and liberal democrats did a great deal to destroy the American left.

Humphrey was born in Wallace, South Dakota, about forty miles from the Minnesota border on May 27, 1911. He was the middleclass son of a small town pharmacist. He attended the University of Minnesota and became a pharmacist and returned home to work in his father's drug store in 1931. He worked there until 1937 and then left to attend Louisiana State University and received a Masters Degree in Political Science in 1940. Humphrey tried twice to join the military during World War II, but was rejected for medical reasons. He returned to Minnesota and during the war he became the state assistant director of the War Manpower Commission. In 1940, Humphrey was a Republican and supported Wendell Willkie for President.

In 1943, Humphrey became a political science professor at Macalester College in St. Paul and ran for Mayor of Minneapolis but lost by a small margin. In 1944, he helped with the merger that founded the Democratic Farmer-Labor Party, (DFL) merging Minnesota's Democratic Party with the then dominate Farmer-Labor Party. In 1944–45, he made a national name for himself by leading a campaign expelling socialists and communists from the DFL. In 1945, the anti-communist Humphrey ran for Mayor of Minneapolis on the DFL ticket and won gaining almost two thirds of the vote.

In 1947, while he was Mayor, Humphrey joined with Eleanor Roosevelt, economist John Kenneth Galbraith, labor leader Walter Reuther, historian Arthur Schlesinger Jr., theologian Reinhold Niebuhr, author Joseph Lash, and Wilson Wyatt who was in Truman's cabinet and later Governor of Kentucky, to form the Americans for Democratic Action, (ADA) a liberal political action group who were committed anti-communists. Humphrey was the Chair of the ADA in 1949 and 1950. In 1947, he also made speeches and campaigned to make communism illegal and to make it a felony for anyone to espouse or advocate for communism in the United States.

In 1948, Humphrey was elected to the US Senate from Minnesota. In 1950, he helped the Republicans in Congress pass the McCarran Act over President Truman's veto. The act made being a communist a felony. It was then that Humphrey also personally sponsored and wrote the nefarious clause of the Act that would detain suspected communists in "camps for subversives" which became known as the "concentration camp bill." The McCarran Act was used to send fellow Minnesotan Gus Hall and other American communist party leaders to prison for no other crime than being communists and to threaten and intimidate many other left-wing political dissidents during what has now become known as "the McCarthy era." Humphrey earned the nickname of "The Happy Warrior" for his cold war persecution of American communists.

The US Supreme Court ruled unanimously in 1965 that the McCarran Act was unconstitutional and said that it deprived Americans of freedom of speech and assembly. However by the time they acted most of the permanent damage to the American left had already been done. The left had been destroyed.

In addition to persecuting people for their political beliefs Humphrey also did some good things. He was a passionate civil rights advocate. In 1948, Humphrey's proposal of ending racial discrimination was included into the party platform at the Democratic National Convention despite strong opposition from Southern Democrats. He gave one of his most notable speeches on the convention floor demanding the Democratic Party "walk into the sunshine of human rights." His speech caused the delegations from Mississippi and Alabama to walk out of the convention. Because the Southern Democrats bolted the convention Humphrey was able to get a majority of the votes to pass the civil rights plank in the Democratic Party's platform.

The Southern Democrats revolted. They formed the Dixiecrat Party and ran Senator Strom Thurmond for President, believing that Truman could not beat Governor Dewey without the "Solid South" and they were greatly shocked when Truman won. Humphrey was given credit for moving Civil Rights forward and for helping Truman win showing the Democrats they could win without the South and that they could still win when supporting civil rights. Humphrey was also the author of the Civil Rights Act of 1964. He wrote it at the request of President Johnson when he was Johnson's Vice President.

Humphrey was also a politician who could set aside higher ideals for political expediency. In 1964, during Freedom Summer, Mississippi Blacks and a few Whites organized and elected a desegregated State delegation to the National Democratic Convention to challenge the all-White segregated Mississippi delegation at the Convention. They scrupulously followed all the party rules in creating their delegation. The Desegregated delegation looked as if it would succeed in unseating the all-White delegation by getting a majority of the convention to vote in their favor. However it would be at the cost of enraging the Southern delegations which threatened to walk out. President Johnson was angry because he felt this event was overshadowing his convention nomination. He worried that it would offend his Southern voters.

Rita Schwerner, the young wife of Richard Schwerner, one of three civil rights workers who were killed by the Ku Klux Klan in Mississippi in 1964, was one of the organizers of the desegregated delegation. She had succeeded with the help of the press to force a meeting with President Johnson to plead the case of seating the desegregated Mississippi delegation. Johnson took offense at this forced meeting and in a taped telephone conversation, after his meeting with Schwerner, he told J. Edgar Hoover that Rita Schwerner was "a troublemaker and a communist." Hoover agreed and said that the Civil Rights movement was filled with communists.

Johnson then told Hubert Humphrey that if he wanted to be Vice President to make sure that the desegregated Mississippi delegation was not seated at the convention. He didn't want a sideshow with the Southern delegations walking out. Humphrey, with the help of Walter Mondale, made sure that the desegregated Mississippi delegation lost the vote and was not seated. This event has largely been forgotten because Johnson and Humphrey also passed the Civil Rights Act of 1964, which has led many to sing the praises of their commitment to Civil Rights.

Humphrey was re-elected to the Senate in 1954 and again in 1960. He was elected the Senate Majority Whip in 1961. In 1964, Humphrey became President Johnson's Vice Presidential choice and they won in a landslide election. Humphrey was not a novice to presidential politics. He ran for president and was nominated in 1952. He ran in 1960 against Kennedy and Johnson, losing to Kennedy in the primaries. Humphrey was also strongly in the mix as the Democratic vice presidential nominee in 1956 and 1960. He finally won the presidential nomination in 1968 and lost in a very close election to Richard Nixon. After serving as Vice President and after his failed bid for the presidency in 1968, he returned to the Senate when Minnesota elected him again in 1970. Humphrey also ran for the Democratic presidential nomination in 1972, but he dropped out in the primaries because of his previous support of the Vietnam War when it became obvious that the growing anti-war sentiment in America would cost him too many votes. Even in 1972 Humphrey still opposed any peace agreement in Vietnam that would allow any communist sharing of the government in South Vietnam. He remained a fervent anti-communist to his death. Because of his stand on Vietnam, many of Humphrey's friends and allies, and young voters and university students abandoned him. His war policies became a political handicap.

Privately Humphrey's support for the war was softening, but he had difficulty reconciling this with his anti-communism. In 1967, he voiced some of his concerns about the war to President Johnson. According to Carl Solberg in his biography: *Hubert Humphrey: A Biography*, Humphrey's critics didn't know that Johnson had reacted angrily to Humphrey's doubts about the war and he threatened Humphrey. Johnson warned Humphrey that if he publicly expressed any doubts or if he opposed any of his Administration's Vietnam War policies, he would destroy his political career along with any chance Humphrey had to become President.

After Johnson decided to not seek the presidency in 1968, he again warned Humphrey that he would strongly oppose his nomination at the 1968 Democratic Convention if he did not support the war efforts. Humphrey acquiesced to Johnson's threats. Humphrey narrowly lost his election for president in 1968 to Richard Nixon largely because of his support of the Vietnam War, and as incredible as it may seem today, Nixon was seen at that time by many as "the peace candidate."

Humphrey briefly campaigned for the presidency again in 1976, but he dropped out despite significant support when he was diagnosed with terminal cancer. Humphrey is sometimes credited with persuading President Jimmy Carter to choose his former aide Minnesota Senator Walter Mondale as his running mate in 1976. Humphrey died on January 13, 1978. Before he died, he called and invited President Nixon to attend his funeral, which the then disgraced and reclusive Nixon did. Humphrey's wife Muriel was appointed by Minnesota Governor Rudy Perpich to serve the remaining months of his last term in the Senate.

Hubert Humphrey is but one example of many liberals who were vehemently anti-communist and assisted the American right in illegally suppressing "communists", socialists and others on the American left. Historian Mary S. McAuliffe in her book *Crisis on the Left: Cold War Politics and American Liberals 1947–1954*, argued that most liberal intellectuals excluded Communists "from the arena of permissible public debate and, as a result, lost sight of vital civil liberties."

Humphrey himself did not lose sight of these civil liberties, but rather deliberately sought to have the rights of communists and socialists abolished. He was joined by the Americans for Democratic Action and many other liberal colleagues in doing this. The liberals assisted the right in killing the American left.

Liberals justified their actions by making the comparison that the excesses of the left were the same thing as the excesses of the right and that communism and socialism were like fascism. They likened Hitler and Stalin as despots therefore categorized them the same in all other aspects. In *The Age of McCarthyism: A Brief History with Documents,* historian Ellen Schrecker said that American liberals increasingly saw "few distinctions between Stalin's crimes and Hitler's and stressed the similarities rather than the differences between Communism and fascism." American liberals failed to understand the difference between Stalinism, communism, or socialism and they assumed that the goal of all leftist philosophy was to produce a Stalinist style totalitarian state by violent revolution. It is akin to arguing that all conservatives want a fascist dictatorship modeled on Hitler's Germany.

This odd and twisted blurring of fascism and the left by liberals and the American right has continued today with rightwing pundits like Rush Limbaugh calling women's rights advocates "feminazis," and other rightwing writers and speakers like Jonah Goldberg who oddly accuse Franklin Roosevelt the American left of being "fascists." These beliefs also belie some of the American right's history of supporting and advocating fascism during Hitler's rise to power. It also belies that many on the American right have a love of unquestioned authority and blindly push for law and order and advocate for a strong military or police state.

In his book *The Politics of Hope,* Arthur Schlesinger Jr. defined liberalism and its opposition to the left, and liberalism's unquestioned support of capitalism, when he said, "In general, liberalism opposes socialism when socialism is understood to mean an alternative to capitalism based on state ownership of the means of production."

Some former liberal intellectuals like Paul Krugman have moved even further toward the America right and assert that free market capitalism can provide better solutions than what he has called "top-down economic planning and Keynesian economics." Krugman stated in *Fortune Magazine,* in 1999, that the current state-dominated monopolies such as energy distribution and telecommunications would benefit by more by private ownership in the free market. He said he believed they would improve their efficiency. What he fails to mention is that such privatization would also maximize profits to a few owners at the expense of the consumer. He fails to acknowledge that these kings of monopolies would likely limit the choices and services available to those consumers in order to achieve even greater profits. He also appears not to understand that these capitalists, once in control of such monopolies, would also then spend untold millions of dollars lobbying the government for less and less regulation and oversight, for more control, and possibly even government subsidies and tax breaks to grow their profits ever larger, as all large privately-owned industries in America tend to do. Americans have forgotten the lessons of the trust busting Theodore Roosevelt who ended the Gilded Age, a period in American history that allowed the rich and their monopolies to run amok and control most of America's resources and the economy, and to concentrate wealth in ever fewer hands.

An excellent summary of what the liberals and the American right did to the American left was written in an essay entitled, *Anti-communism in the 1950s*, by historian Wendy Wall, for the Guilder Lehrman Institute of American History. She wrote:

> In 1950, fewer than 50,000 Americans out of a total US population of 150 million were members of the Communist Party. Yet in the late 1940s and early 1950s, American fears of internal communist subversion reached a nearly hysterical pitch. Government loyalty boards investigated millions of federal employees, asking what books and magazines they read, what unions and civic organizations they belonged to, and whether they went to church. Hundreds of screenwriters, actors, and directors were blacklisted because of their alleged political beliefs, while teachers, steelworkers, sailors, lawyers, and social workers lost their jobs for similar reasons. More than thirty-nine states required teachers and other public employees to take loyalty oaths. Meanwhile, some libraries pulled books that were considered too leftist from their shelves. The banned volumes included such classics as *Robin Hood*, Henry David Thoreau's *Civil Disobedience*, and John Steinbeck's *The Grapes of Wrath*.

Chapter 8. The Hard Right Turn

> "The American fascists are most easily recognized by their deliberate perversion of truth and fact. Their newspapers and propaganda carefully cultivate every fissure of disunity, every crack in the common front against fascism."—Vice President Henry Wallace

> "When fascism comes to America it will be wrapped in the flag and waving a cross."—Sinclair Lewis

The Republicans and the Christian Right

The Republican Party began their journey into rightwing Christian politics in the post-Civil War Years. They began to assert that the Democrats were the party of "Rum, Romanism, and Rebellion." "Rum" meant that the Republicans began to strongly support and advocate for the prohibition of alcohol, while the Democrats believed that the government should stay out of moral issues. "Romanism" referred to Roman Catholics, especially Irish and German-Catholic Americans, who were strong supporters of the Democratic Party. And "Rebellion" stood for the Democrats of the Confederacy who supported secession from the union and were referred to as the "solid South" for their loyal support for the Democratic Party until Richard Nixon developed his Southern Strategy for the Republican Party.

After the Civil War the Republicans were in firm control of the nation, but over time the political trends began to favor the Democrats, as the German and Irish Catholic immigrants came to outnumber the Republicans in many northern congressional districts. During the 1880s and 1890s, the Republicans struggled against the Democrats, winning several close elections and then losing two to Grover Cleveland in the presidential elections of 1884 and 1892.

The religious lines between the two parties were sharply drawn with Methodists, Congregationalists, Presbyterians, and Scandinavian Lutherans, tightly linked to the Republicans. In sharp contrast, liturgical groups, especially the Catholics, Episcopalians, and some German Lutherans, who looked to the Democratic Party for protection from Republican legislative moralism, especially concerning Prohibition. They also looked to them to also protect their parochial schools from Republican and government interference. The Baptists, especially in the South, remained solidly Democratic even though they were very sympathetic to Republican legislative moralism.

Prohibition was one of the largest differences between the two parties. In the North over half of the voters were Methodists, Scandinavian Lutherans, Presbyterians, Congregationalists, and Disciples of Christ who largely believed the government should be used to reduce social sins, especially the prohibition of alcohol.

There were also other cultural issues tied to this religious alignment. Foreign language and parochial schools, particularly for Catholics, became important politically because of these sharp religious divisions between the Republicans and Democrats. The Catholics saw Republicans and their protestant moralism as a threat to their Catholicism, and German, Irish, Poles and other Catholic ethnic groups and Jews saw the growing anti-immigrant movement among Republicans as a threat to their ethnicity and their continued growth and prosperity.

In December 1875, the Republican Speaker of the House, James G. Blaine, proposed a joint resolution that became known as the Blaine Amendment. It was an amendment that on the surface appeared to support the separation of church and state, but in reality was an attempt to regulate and reduce the number of Catholic and parochial schools in America. It also sought to stop federal efforts to mandate that the states provide free public education for all children.

The act stated: "No State shall make any law respecting an establishment of religion, or prohibiting the free exercise thereof; and no money raised by taxation in any State for the support of public schools, or derived from any public fund therefore, nor any public lands devoted thereto, shall ever be under the control of any religious sect; nor shall any money so raised or lands so devoted be divided between religious sects or denominations."

The effect was to prohibit all support, public and private, for religious schools—particularly Catholics and Jews, and sought to abolish the requirement for states to provide public education to all children. The Bill was also hypocritical because it also deliberately failed to address the issue of mandatory Protestant training for all students, including Catholics and Jews, in most public schools at this time. The bill passed the House but failed in the Senate. Although it never passed Congress, Blaine and the Republicans were seen as anti-Catholic and anti-Semitic. However, Blaine's amendment served its intended purpose of rallying most Protestants to the Republican Party. The only large groups of Protestants still loyal to the Democratic Party were the Baptists and the Southern Evangelicals of the Solid South.

The Roman Catholics, German Lutherans, Episcopalians, and Jews comprised over a quarter of the vote and they began to strongly support the Democrats. They wanted the government to stay out of the morality business and to quit interfering with their parochial schools.

Prohibition debates and referendums heated up party politics in most states, and prohibition was finally passed in 1919 and served as a major issue between the "wet" Democrats and the "dry" Republicans until it was repealed in 1933. One of the more ironic outcomes of Prohibition was that it gave rise to organized crime, particularly the Mafia which became many times more powerful during this time, and America's morality movement actually caused a drastic decline of morals and encouraged lawlessness during Prohibition.

The Republican Party controlled the presidency throughout the 1920s, running on platforms of opposing the League of Nations, promoting American isolationism and anti-immigration laws, enacting high trade tariffs, the promotion of big business interests, and to keep prohibition. Warren Harding, Calvin Coolidge, and Herbert Hoover were resoundingly elected in 1920, 1924, and 1928 respectively. The breakaway efforts of both Republican liberals Teddy Roosevelt and Senator Robert La Follette failed. In 1924, La Follette ran for president but failed in his efforts to stop a landslide for Coolidge. It was the last serious attempt to unite liberals in the Republican Party.

The pro-business policies of the decade seemed to produce an unprecedented prosperity for the rich and leisure class, but it also widened the gap between the rich and poor and created many poor. This unquestioned pro-business attitude lasted until the stock market crash of 1929, which brought about the Great Depression and the decline or ruin of many fortunes as well as the decline of the family farms and the small businesses on America's Main streets.

Although the Republican Party did very well in large cities and even among urban Catholics in the presidential elections of 1920 and 1924, it was unable to hold those gains in 1928, when Governor Al Smith of New York, an Irish-Catholic, ran as the Democrat. Smith carried the majority in most northern and Midwestern large cities but still only won Massachusetts and six states of the Deep South against Herbert Hoover.

However in 1932, after the stock market crash Roosevelt and the Democrats won by carrying the Catholics and Jews and by retaining Al Smith's majority in the large cities. He was also able to attract labor, farmers and small business owners. The large central cities became Democratic strongholds and have largely remained so, but the Republicans continued to dominate the wealthy suburbs and most rural areas.

The Depression cost Hoover the presidency and resulted in the 1932 landslide election of Franklin Roosevelt and the Democrats. Roosevelt's New Deal Coalition controlled American politics for most of the next two decades, through the presidential administrations of both Roosevelt and Truman. The Democrats had also made major gains in Congress. Previous to Roosevelt's election, they won in the 1930 midterm elections; this gave them congressional parity with the Republicans for the first time since Woodrow Wilson's presidency.

In the 1934 midterm elections, ten Republican senators went down in defeat, leaving Republicans with only twenty-five senators against seventy-one Democrats. The House of Representatives was split in a similar ratio. Roosevelt's "New Deal" and his progressive legislation creating Social Security, the Fair Labor Standards Act and Unemployment Insurance were heavily criticized by the Republicans in Congress, who likened it to communism and socialism. But the Democrats were now in a solid majority and the Republicans were powerless to stop it. The volume of Roosevelt's legislation, as well as the inability of the Republicans to stop it developed into a bitterness and hatred in the Republican Party which still persists in their politics.

This hatred and bitterness in the 1930s came out in the so-called rightwing "whispering campaign." It was led by rightwing Republicans like newspaper publisher William Randolph Hearst, *Time* magazine owner Henry Luce, industrialist Henry Ford, and the poisonous radio priest, Father Coughlin. They spread anti-Semitic rumors that Roosevelt was secretly Jewish, that his actual name was Rosenfeld, and that he was involved in a Jewish plot to take over the world. They also claimed that he was ill from syphilis, and raised White racial fears by claiming that Eleanor Roosevelt had "a nigger lover" and was an agent for the Russian communists. Roosevelt actually found a written press memo in the press room stating these rumors about his wife as "facts" and he circulated this horrific memo at the next press briefing without comment to a greatly embarrassed the press corps.

In *Maverick Marine: General Smedley D. Butler and the Contradictions of American Military History*, Hans Schmidt wrote that in November 1934, Marine Major General Smedley Butler, at the time the most decorated Marine in US history, testified to a special House of Representatives Committee that he had been approached to participate in a conspiracy which became known as the "Business Plot."

Butler told the committee that Bill Doyle, the Commander of the Massachusetts American Legion and Gerald P. MacGuire a wealthy bond and finance executive told him that a national group of very wealthy businessmen and bankers were assembling a private army of ex-soldiers and others intended to establish a fascist dictatorship during a march on Washington to overthrow President Franklin Roosevelt. Butler claimed that he had been asked to lead this army and refused. Although many Americans and the press initially dismissed the General's claims, the Congress investigated.

MacGuire was asked to testify before Congress and denied these allegations under oath, however the congressional committee was able to verify all the pertinent statements made by General Butler. A final report by a special House of Representatives Committee confirmed many of Butler's accusations about the plot. In the aftermath *Time* wrote, "Also last week the House Committee on Un-American Activities purported to report that a two-month investigation had convinced it that General Butler's story of a Fascist march on Washington was alarmingly true." *The New York Times* reported that the committee "alleged that definite proof had been found that the much publicized Fascist march on Washington, which was to have been led by Major. Gen. Smedley D. Butler retired, according to testimony at a hearing, was actually contemplated."

The hatred by rightwing Republicans and big business about Roosevelt's social policies were also elevated when Roosevelt allowed the inclusion of Blacks and Jews in federal employment. This also alienated many conservative Democrats particularly in the Solid South. The conservative Democrats began joining with the conservative Republicans led by Senator Robert Taft, who was called "Mr. Conservative," to create a conservative coalition. Although they were largely ineffectual during the Roosevelt years they began to dominate domestic issues in Congress after Roosevelt's death.

In 1948, when the Democrats included in their Platform a Civil Rights plank many Southern Democrats fled the Democrats and formed the Dixiecrat Party and ran Strom Thurmond as their candidate for president against Harry Truman. Many thought at the time that the president could not win without the South and assumed that their defection signaled Truman's defeat to the Republicans. However in a surprising election Truman was able to narrowly beat the greatly favored Republican Thomas Dewey. In the election Thurmond had done damage to the Democrats and won four Southern states and also won one Electoral College elector from Tennessee who defected from his pledge to Truman and voted for Thurmond.

After 1948 and the defection of the Dixiecrats, the South began to steadily move toward their own "independent candidates." In the 1964 Presidential election, just after President Johnson and the Democrats passed the Civil Rights Act of 1964, Republican Barry Goldwater easily carried the Deep South for the Republican Party. And with this election the once Democratic "solid South" conclusively shifted their allegiance to the Republicans. Johnson had predicted this with his passage of the 1964 Civil Rights Bill and said that the Democratic Party would "lose the South for a hundred years."

In 1968, Richard Nixon's aides, Kevin Phillips and Patrick Buchanan developed the shameful "Southern Strategy" where the Party of Lincoln would permanently divorce itself from civil rights to attract the bigoted Southern conservatives to switch parties rather than run as independents. It was effective and the once "Democratic solid South" became the Republican solid South. However it came with a price. Black voters have since voted in overwhelming numbers for the Democrats. The strategy also had other consequences and by the 1980s the Southerners and the radical rightwing began to dominate and to completely own the Republican Party. They began to push the Republicans further to the right.

On July 25, 1968, an encyclical written by Pope Paul VI entitled Humanae Vitae banned most kinds of birth control and abortion by the Catholic Church. Democrats had aligned themselves with the Women's movement and were supporters of family planning clinics. The "abortion issue" drove a wedge between the Democrats and the Catholics who had been staunch supporters of the party. Southern evangelicals strongly embraced this Catholic ban on abortions and the Republican Party became the home to the abstinence before marriage anti-abortionists who called themselves "pro-life." Because of the Southern Strategy and the abstinence and anti-abortion movement the Republican Party completed their hard right turn and they were completely taken over by the Christian-conservative moralists and the Southern rightwing.

The Roots of Xenophobia

"In politics, what begins in fear usually ends in folly."— Samuel Taylor Coleridge

The Socialist Party of America (SPA) was created in 1890 by Eugene Debs in a dispute with Daniel De Leon of the Socialist Labor Party. De Leon was a communist and was dismissive of the labor leaders in the party. The SPA was divided between reformers who believed that socialism could be achieved through gradual reform of capitalism and members who thought that socialism could only develop after capitalism was replaced. But most of the

SPA membership largely believed in the gradual replacement of American capitalism. They were not revolutionaries. However like all political groups there was a small minority of hard line radicals who thought that reforms would only come with a great upheaval.

Despite the rhetoric and the inflated fears of the American right, the SPA at the peak of their success in 1912, their presidential candidate received a paltry 5.9 percent of the popular vote. The communists under Gus Hall did much worse. In their best showing in 1976 they only achieved about one percent of the popular vote for president and most of this was a protest vote against the Watergate Scandal and most of these voters were not serious proponents of communism. Socialism and communism were not and would never be a threat to American capitalism which was why it is so strange that America reacted so strongly against them. In the 1920s and 1950s America panicked about "the red menace" and imagined there were secret leftist plots with thousands of coordinated violent revolutionaries behind them and they grew hysterical for fear of a takeover.

At its peak American socialism and Gus Hall and the communist party were never any threat to America or capitalism. The first socialist congressman Victor Berger was elected in 1910. By the beginning of 1912, at the socialist peak there were only 1,039 local socialist officeholders out of tens of thousands, this included mayors, aldermen, and councilmen, and a few state legislators. Milwaukee, Berkeley, Butte, Schenectady, and Flint were the few cities that were actually managed by socialists for a very short time with little dramatic change.

Even in labor and union circles the socialists never attracted a large following. At the peak of socialist power, the socialist challenger to labor leader Samuel Gompers only took one third of the vote in an election for leadership of the AFL. The Socialist Party of America had five English and eight foreign-language daily newspapers, about three hundred weekly newspapers, and a dozen monthlies which gave the impression of a greater influence than they actually had, as all these newspapers had a very small circulation.

America Sees Red

> "Do you honestly think, my fellow citizens, that none of this poison has got in the veins of this free people?....That poison will spread, more and more rapidly until it may be that even this beloved land of ours will be distracted and distorted by it....You have to watch them with secret agencies planted everywhere."—President Woodrow Wilson's stump speech warning about communism in America

> "The Red Scare was a nation-wide anti-radical hysteria provoked by a mounting fear and anxiety that a Bolshevik revolution in America was imminent, a revolution that would change Church, home, marriage, civility, and the American way of Life."—Murray B. Levin, American political scientist

One of America's first hard turns to the right and some of the worst persecution against the American left came from an interesting source. Attorney General A. Mitchell Palmer was a very progressive liberal Democrat, but he was an anti-communist and was also anti-labor. Palmer was born in 1878 in Pennsylvania and was raised a Quaker. He was blindly ambitious and as Attorney General he was easily influenced by a more ambitious aide named J. Edgar Hoover. Palmer was elected to Congress three times and served from 1909 to 1915. He was considered a leader among the liberal progressive Democrats and was elected as a Democratic National Committeeman from Pennsylvania. Many saw his election as a sign that the Democratic Party was swinging away from the conservatives to the liberals and progressives. He was a delegate to the Democratic National Convention in 1912 and supported and worked on behalf of Woodrow Wilson to receive the party's nomination.

When Wilson was elected president he offered Palmer the position of Secretary of War, but Palmer declined citing his Quaker beliefs. He did indicate an interest in being Attorney General, but Wilson had already offered that position to another, so Palmer decided to remain in Congress. Later Wilson offered Palmer a judicial post, but Palmer also turned that down. Wilson then appointed him Alien Property Custodian during World War I and Palmer agreed and served in that position until 1919 when Wilson finally appointed him as the 50th Attorney General of the United States. Palmer was a popular choice with liberal and progressive Democrats and they had strongly campaigned to have President Wilson appoint Palmer to the office even though there were several other much better qualified Democrats under consideration by Wilson at the time.

In his book *Over Here: the First World War and American Society*, David Kennedy says that an anti-left climate started in 1916. President Wilson was a racist and an anglophile. He disliked people of color, Catholics, Jews, and Southern and Eastern European immigrants. He wanted to stop their coming to America. These biases made Wilson anti-immigration and he began to warn against "hyphenated Americans" (foreign born) who he claimed had "poured the poison of disloyalty into the very arteries of our national life." Wilson also said, "Such creatures of passion, disloyalty and anarchy must be crushed out." Wilson was also paranoid about communism and saw these new immigrants as the carriers of what he viewed as a communist disease. It was in this atmosphere that Palmer took office.

The quote from Wilson at the beginning of this chapter summarized his paranoia about a communist plot to take over the American government. In 1918, in response to the Bolshevik Revolution and led by Wilson's revulsion and paranoia, American fears about communism reached a heightened state. Rumors spread that a communist revolution could sweep the world.

In the wake of the Russian Revolution, President Wilson ordered an American Expeditionary force to seize the Far Eastern Russian port of Vladivostok, which was a curious thing for an ally to do. The Russians were our allies at the time in the war against Germany. This became known as the Siberian Expedition. An initial force of 3,000 infantry was sent to Vladivostok and it eventually grew to almost 8,000 men. They occupied the port and surrounding territory for about nineteen months, with the purpose of stopping the spread of the Russian Revolution. Concurrently another force of about 5,000 American troops was sent to invade the northern Russian port of Archangelsk. It was called the Polar Bear Expedition. These expeditions stayed in Russia for over a year. The total number of Americans killed during these two invasions was 424, with no count ever given for the Russian casualties. This was a hot start of what would become America's Cold War with Russia. The British, French, and Japanese also sent some token forces during these American invasions. The invasions had little effect on the communist revolution in Russia.

One of Palmer's first acts as Attorney General was to create the General Intelligence Unit within the Department of Justice to spy on Americans suspected of harboring socialist or communist tendencies. Palmer recruited J. Edgar Hoover to head this new unit. Hoover was a young recent law school graduate who had spent the most of World War I working in and later leading the Justice in Department's Enemy Alien Bureau. It was a fateful decision. Hoover was an over-ambitious groveling sycophant and a passionate anti-communist; he ingratiated himself to Palmer. Hoover was also a rightwing racist bigot and had the ability to encourage the worst in Palmer.

The Immigration Act of 1918 had expanded the definition of aliens that could be deported for cause. It was enacted by the Congress who had reacted hysterically to the Russian Revolution. In October of 1919, the Senate demanded that Palmer explain what they viewed as his complete failure to immediately move against and deport foreign leftist and communist radicals in America. Many in Congress began to become increasingly paranoid about imminent communist plots and a communist revolution in America.

Palmer didn't need much convincing as he had already described communism to Congress as a collection of "atheists, crooks, parlor pinks and scxual perverts." Palmer's reply to the Senate came on November 17, and he played on their fears by describing an imaginary ominous threat by the Bolsheviks against the US government. More than half of Palmer's report, which was actually written by J. Edgar Hoover, spoke about radicalism in the Black community and the new civil rights movement and what the report called "the open defiance" by Black leaders who Palmer and Hoover believed had advocated racial violence and were responsible for the race riots that had occurred that summer. Palmer at Hoover's urging claimed that most Black civil rights leaders were communists or at least communist inspired. Since most of the report had been written by Hoover it greatly reflected Hoover's very strong racist bias. The report contained no supporting evidence to back up these allegations.

The other half of the report blamed unions and union officials. It claimed that the unions were all involved in plots to destroy the American government and claimed the unions were all led by the Soviets. While there were a significant number of self-proclaimed communists and socialists in the unions at that time, most of these were not in leadership positions in the unions and none had foreign ties. There was only a very small group of American communists that had a real connection to the Soviets and most of these were not people in positions of authority. The Soviets did try to encourage labor unrest in the US during this time, but their efforts were very ineffective. Most of the labor unrest at the time was due to poor wages and long work days and weeks. The American labor force and didn't need Soviet inspiration or encouragement.

Lack of evidence to the report's claims didn't deter Hoover. He continued to believe and advocate throughout his life as the Director of the FBI that American Labor and Black leaders, especially Dr. King and other Southern civil rights advocates, were communists. And Despite multiple investigations he never found any evidence to prove his claims against Labor, King or the civil rights movement.

The worst communist fears of President Wilson and Congress was heightened and exaggerated when three Italian followers of the revolutionary Italian anarchist Luigi Galleani carried out a series of small mail bombings against American politicians. Although these bombers were European anarchists and not communists, and despite that these attacks were mostly ineffective and failed in their attempts, they still raised fears of an imminent communist revolution. The bombings did cause some tragedy as a housekeeper for a senator was wounded and night watchman was killed when a bomb went off prematurely. But this incident, which had nothing to do with communism, gave a paranoiac rise to the growing notion that there was a widespread communist conspiracy in America that was attempting to violently overthrow the government. Wilson and the Congress were determined that the Bolsheviks would never accomplish what they had in Russia.

At the urging of Congress and President Wilson, Palmer launched his first raids against the American left on November 1919 and continued them through January 1920. They began with a series of police actions which became known as "the Palmer Raids" which were actually carried out by J. Edgar Hoover. Most of those arrested and detained in the raids were union members, labor leaders or foreign born immigrants, especially Russians and Jews, who were taken into custody solely based on their ethnicity, religion or because of their membership in a labor union. But none of those arrested were ever accused of violence nor were they involved in any plots or any actions advocating violence or the overthrowing of the government. Palmer, citing national security, also denied those arrested and detained by Hoover the right to an attorney. Palmer and Hoover had also allowed the raids to be conducted without search warrants.

The first raid came on November 7, 1919, a date chosen by Palmer and Hoover because it was the second anniversary of the Bolshevik Revolution. Hoover, who Palmer had just promoted as the head of the new Bureau of Investigation, (later to be re-named the Federal Bureau of Investigation) ordered his agents and the local police to execute a series of raids against Russian immigrants in twelve cities. The irony was that many of these Russian immigrants detained were White Russian and had come to the United States because they were anti-communist and were opposed to the Russian communist revolution.

Some of this was also anti-Semitism as many of the Russian immigrants targeted by Hoover were Jews. Wilson, Palmer and Hoover were also anti-Semitic.

Later press accounts reported that many of the Russians that were questioned and detained in these raids were "badly beaten" by the Bureau's agents and the police. They were detained in jail for prolonged periods without being charged with any crime and not allowed to have an attorney. The Russian immigrants also later testified in court that they were also threatened, tortured and beaten during questioning to get them to admit they were part of a communist conspiracy.

During the raids Hoover's agents cast a wide net bringing Russians, labor groups, Jews and even any passers-by who admitted to being of Russian ethnicity or Jews when stopped and questioned by Hoover's men. In one bizarre incident several teachers who were conducting English language night school classes for new Russian immigrants were arrested as communist spies and revolutionaries. Since many of the arrests and raids were without search warrants granted by the courts, many of these actions were later deemed illegal by the courts. Of the 650 who had been arrested in the raids in New York City almost all were released by the courts. In total Hoover and Palmer managed to have only forty-three people deported out of thousands and none of these were communists, violent, nor were any of them a real threat to the government.

During this time Palmer told the US Senate that Hoover had amassed a data base of the names of "60,000 Bolsheviks" who were plotters against America. In reality they were mostly new immigrants, Jews, labor leaders, along with leaders of the fledgling Black civil rights movement. Palmer then asked Congress to pass a new anti-sedition act making it easier for him to arrest, detain and deport these people.

Because of his anti-labor policies Palmer began to have major problems with the growing labor movement. He was forced to deal with a well coordinated nationwide coal strike which he then also blamed on a communist conspiracy. As Palmer became consumed with the national coal strike and other labor disputes, J. Edgar Hoover organized the next raids on Palmer's behalf. Hoover ran amok and arrested between six and ten thousand people as communist conspirators. The courts released most of these immediately but at least thirty-five hundred were again held by authorities in detention for extended periods without charges. Only 556 were eventually deported under the Immigration Act of 1918 as illegal immigrants but none of these deportations were for violence or plotting the overthrow of the government and there was no proof that very many were communists.

One of those deported to Russia was Emma Goldman a Russian immigrant who was an American citizen by marriage. Hoover greatly disliked Goldman because according to him she was immoral. Hoover disliked Goldman because she was Jewish and out-spoken. Goldman was not a communist, but she was an atheist, an anti-war activist, a feminist and birth control advocate, all of which Hoover described as immoral and he called her "the Red Queen of Anarchy." She served time in prison during World War I for encouraging men to avoid conscription on moral grounds. She was never a communist and later wrote two books, *My Disillusionment in Russia* which was published in 1923 and *My Further Disillusionment in Russia*, in 1924 criticizing Soviet communism.

Hoover was a cruel man and was gleefully present when they put Goldman on the ship for deportation. He smirked at her and said, "Haven't I given you a square deal, Miss Goldman?" To which she replied, "Oh, I suppose you have given me as square a deal as you could. We shouldn't expect from any person something beyond his capacity."

As satisfying as it must have been for Hoover to deport Goldman, he was extremely frustrated that only 556 of the over ten thousand he had arrested were deported. Many of those freed owed their freedom to the brave actions of Louis Post, the Assistant Secretary of Labor. Acting in his capacity as the head of the Bureau of Immigration, Post canceled more than 2,000 of Hoover's warrants as illegal. Post had reviewed a backlog of 1600 cases and dismissed over seventy percent of these cases as being without any cause. Post was incensed that some detainees had been held in jail for as long as two months for just having attended a meeting of a labor group. Hoover and Palmer blamed their failures and the dismissal of most of the deportation cases on Post. They claimed that Post was the only thing that had stopped these "communist deportations."

Palmer and Hoover were outraged by what they considered as Post's constant interference. At a Cabinet meeting in April of 1920, Palmer called out Secretary of Labor William Wilson who was Post's immediate supervisor to fire Post, but the Labor Secretary strongly defended him. President Wilson who was in very ill health at the time listened to his feuding cabinet heads and was silent about Post, but he was worried about Palmer's excesses and ended the meeting by warning Palmer "Do not let this country see red."

President Wilson who had encouraged the two men in their campaign against the communists was now worried that Palmer and Hoover were getting carried away and that their anti-communist fervor could lead the country into fanaticism. The Secretary of the Navy Josephus Daniels who made notes of this cabinet meeting thought the Attorney General had merited the President's concern because he felt that Palmer "was seeing red behind every bush and every demand for an increase in wages."

In Boston more than six hundred had been arrested in the raids in January 1920 and were held in an unheated prison at Deer Island for many days. A federal judge in Boston, George W. Anderson, reviewed a writ of habeas corpus filed on behalf of the prisoners held at Deer Island. Hoover was present in Anderson's court to defend the arrests. After hearing a day and a half of damning testimony Hoover left for Washington. He was concerned that Judge Anderson would force him to testify under oath and he was worried about perjuring himself.

Judge Anderson ruled against the Justice Department and Hoover stating: "This case seems to have been conducted under the modern theory of statesmanship: Hang first and try later." Judge Anderson went on to say, "A mob is a mob whether made up of government officials under the instructions of the Department of Justice, or of criminals, loafers and the vicious classes." He freed all the detainees at Deer Island.

Palmer and Hoover were angry at both the legal system and Post for their setbacks. They also ignored President Wilson's warning. In April of 1920, Congressman Homer Hoch, an ally of Palmer and Hoover, accused Post on the floor of the US House of Representatives of having abused his power and called for his impeachment. The House Committee on Rules then decided to ask President Wilson to remove Post rather than impeaching him. Because of this action Post requested and was granted a chance to publicly testify before the Committee. He successfully defended his actions and made a strong case against Palmer and Hoover in front of the press. He said that Palmer and Hoover had violated the basic American rights of freedom of speech and assembly of over ten thousand loyal Americans. His strong words and the positive reaction of the press and public stunned the committee. Post vigorously attacked the unfair accusations and deportations of new immigrants, Jews, and of the labor leaders by Palmer. Congressman Edward Pou, a ranking committee member, praised Post's actions and said, "I believe you have followed your sense of duty absolutely." The House Rules Committee dismissed the complaints against Post and took no further action.

However Palmer and Hoover were not finished with the issue. They called upon the American Legion who then sent letters to President Wilson demanding that Post be fired for aiding and abetting "communists." The President, now very ill, asked his Labor Secretary to address the American Legion's letters. Secretary William Wilson replied to the American Legion, "We will not deport anyone simply because he has been accused or because he is suspected of being a Red. We have no authority to do so under the law." He went on to include in his response, "Mr. Post, I am satisfied, ranks among the ablest and best administrative officers in the Government service."

Palmer and Hoover continued their anti-communist crusade and were supported by most members of Congress and the American Legion. According to Palmer and many in Congress, Hoover had now become the expert on communist spies and radicals in America. Hoover bragged that the agents of his Bureau of Investigation had infiltrated many subversive organizations following the raids of November 1919 and January 1920. He claimed that he and his agents had interrogated thousands of those arrested and read through boxes of their publications and personal records that were seized. Hoover told Palmer that through these interrogations and raids that his agents had uncovered solid evidence of the communist plans for a large plot to violently overthrow of the US government on May Day 1920. He convinced Palmer.

As ludicrous as this was, Palmer believed it was true. He immediately warned Congress and the press that he had concrete proof that a nationwide revolution with mass assassinations, bombings, and general strikes would occur on May 1, 1920. According to the *New York Times* Palmer issued a specific warning to the nation on April 29, 1920, claiming to have obtained a "list of marked men" the revolutionaries would kill in the revolution. He went on to say the American radicals were "in direct connection and unison" with European communists who also planned and coordinated revolutions that would occur the same day all across Europe. He said Europe should be warned.

Newspapers carried headlines of: "Terror Reign by Radicals, says Palmer" and "Nation-wide Uprising on Saturday." Many local police departments went on full alert and some states mobilized their entire militias. New York City mobilized its entire police force of eleven thousand including the reserves and forced them to work for thirty-two straight hours to prevent the City's collapse into revolution. The Boston Police Department mounted machine guns on their automobiles and positioned them around the city to shoot the expected hordes of communist rioters.

When May Day came and passed without even one small incident Palmer became an overnight joke. Newspaper reaction was almost uniform in its mockery of Palmer. They said he was demented and delusional. There were editorial cartoons showing Palmer looking under rocks for communists. Hoover for his part slunk off into the bureaucracy to fight another day and let Palmer take the brunt of criticism while he hid behind the excuse that he had been following Palmer's orders.

Hoover was a horribly self-interested and disloyal man. He told the Congress that he had been under the orders of Palmer. According to Regin Schmidt, in his book, *The Red Scare: the FBI and the Origins of Anti-Communism in the United States 1919–1943*, the ever paranoid Hoover incredibly blamed Post for this failure. He told confidants that Post was a communist and had tipped off the communists, which was why the revolution failed to materialize. Hoover and the Bureau then began keeping a dossier on Post and he periodically had his agents investigate him to try and prove that he had secret communist and Soviet ties.

In an incredibly brazen move Palmer sought the Democratic Party's nomination for President in 1920. In a very crowded field of candidates he presented himself as the most American and the most anti-communist of them all. Campaigning in the Democratic primaries, he metaphorically wrapped himself in the American flag and portrayed himself as America's savior saying: "I am myself an American and I love to preach my doctrine before undiluted one hundred percent Americans, because my platform is, in a word, undiluted Americanism and undying loyalty to the republic." Fortunately most Americans didn't see him as their savior and James Cox won the Democratic nomination, but Cox also lost to the Republican Warren Harding by a very wide margin with Harding winning in most states except the eleven states of the former Confederacy.

The mistakes of Palmer and Hoover did not halt America from moving further to the right. When Warren Harding became President he appointed the corrupt Harry M. Daugherty as Attorney General. Daugherty liked

Hoover's work and he kept him as Director of the Bureau of Investigation and continued to encourage his communist xenophobia.

After the failures of Palmer and Hoover some members of Congress became increasingly suspicious of Hoover and his communist claims. According to Tim Weiner in *Enemies,* Senator Thomas J. Walsh of the Judiciary Committee, who had strongly questioned Hoover's claims, was then investigated by Hoover and the Bureau. It was during this time that Hoover began using the Bureau of Investigation to spy on Congress and the Executive Branch. He began keeping files on members of Congress and the President's cabinet. By 1923, the Bureau at the direction of Daugherty and Hoover also began breaking into the offices and homes of uncooperative members of Congress. They also began opening their mail and tapping their telephones. They justified this by claiming that the communists had infiltrated Congress.

Through his investigations of members Congress Hoover began to amass a treasure trove of these men's secrets and he would begin to use these secrets and their threat of becoming public to blackmail Congress and members of the Executive branch. Hoover became the nation's secret keeper.

The 1920s saw the United States swing far to the right. Race and religious intolerance began to rise. Much of this was due to the record number of new immigrants, many of them Jews and Catholics. It was also caused by the steady migration of Blacks out of the South into the Northern and Midwestern cities in search of jobs in the rapidly growing industrial economy. Because of this migration the Ku Klux Klan expanded rapidly even in northern states. In 1923, the radio humorist Will Rogers lamented in New York City, "I hear where the Ku Klux is comin' into New York. Yes, sir, they're here. I'm no fool—you ain't gonna get me tellin' no jokes about them!"

In the 1920s the KKK's Grand Dragon was from Indiana and engineered the election of Klansman Edward L. Jackson, to be the Governor of Indiana. He then appointed many Klansmen to public office. It has been estimated that nearly one third of the men in Indiana and a majority of elected office holders belonged to the Klan in the 1920s. Most Midwestern states had sizable Klan membership at this time. Protestant ministers in the Midwest were offered free membership and highly prized chaplain status within the KKK organization and many joined. Protestant teachers in the Midwest were also targeted for Klan membership and joined. In 1925, the Klan was so prevalent in the Midwest that W.E.B. Du Bois noted, "There in the Middle West that finer flower of democracy.... I looked for sanity in the United States to come from a democratic appeal to the Middle West. And yet, there in Akron I found the Klan calmly and openly in the saddle. The leader of the local Klan was president of the Board of Education and had just been tremendously busied in driving a Jew out of the public schools. The Mayor, the secretary of the Y.M.C.A., prominent men in many walks of life, were either open Klans-men or secret sympathizers. I was too astonished to talk. Throughout parts of Ohio, Illinois and Indiana I found a similar state of affairs."

On August 8, 1925, over 40,000 Klansmen marched openly clad in full regalia in Washington, DC, to show their political strength.

By the mid-1920s, for the first time, America had more people in the cities than in the rural areas transforming the United States into an urban country. Prohibition came into effect on January 17, 1920, ushering in an era of organized crime financed by illegal liquor sales. It was called the Roar-ing Twenties and the American economy soared, especially for the wealthy. Most Americans were economically optimistic and but their politics became more conservative. And in America the Klan along with many other Ameri-cans began to despise "the outsiders," especially new immigrants and anyone different. It was then that many Americans began openly embracing fascism.

Fascists, Nazis and their American Sympathizers

> "Fascism should more appropriately be called Corporat-ism because it is a merger of state and corporate power."—Benito Mussolini

> "It is Jews who govern the stock exchange forces of the American Union. Every year makes them more and more the controlling masters of the producers in a nation of one hun-dred and twenty millions; only a single great man, (Henry) Ford, to their fury, still maintains full independence."—Ad-olf Hitler in *Mein Kampf*

> "The management of Ford Werke (the Ford Motor Com-pany in German) salutes our Fuehrer with grateful heart, honesty, and allegiance, and as before, pledges to cooperate in his life's work: achieving honor, liberty, and happiness for Greater Germany and, indeed, for all peoples of Europe."—A Ford Motor Company note along with a birthday gift of 35,000 Reichsmarks to Hitler in April 1939

In 1922, Russia was reorganized into the United Soviet Socialist Repub-lics, the USSR. This event also caused much of Europe to swing to the right. Benito Mussolini led a fascist takeover in Italy. By the end of the decade Mussolini's Fascist dictatorship became a partner with the Catholic Church. It was Mussolini and the fascists that gave Vatican City and the Catholics their independence from Italy. He restored the good relations between Ro-man Catholic Church and Italy by enacting the Lateran Treaty. This trea-ty created an independent Vatican City controlled only by the Catholic

Church, rather than by Italy. It made the grateful Catholic Church an ally of the fascists. In addition to granting Vatican City its independence Mussolini was able to further cement the relations between the fascists and the Catholic Church because the Church greatly preferred Catholic fascists over the feared "communist atheists." The Church would also later support the German Nazis, as Hitler, like Mussolini, was also a Catholic and they considered him preferable to the "communist atheists" and the Jews. Hitler, a Catholic, was so sure of this support from the Catholic Church that he prophesized in *Mein Kampf*, "Therefore I am convinced that I am acting as an agent for our creator by fighting off the Jews, I am doing the Lord's work."

On June 16, 1998, the Roman Catholic Church would formally apologize for supporting these fascist governments and for failing to take any action in challenging the Nazi and fascist regimes during World War II. They were also forced to apologize for encouraging and for turning a blind eye toward the extermination of more than six million Jews and others. However in this long awaited apology by the Catholic Church the Vatican still defended Pope Pius XII who led the church during World War II and for his and the Church's role in the Holocaust and the Church's protection of Nazi war criminals after the war was over. In the *Washington Post* the next day Efraim Zuroff, the director of the Simon Wiesenthal Center in Jerusalem said of the Vatican's apology, "It falls quite short of what was hoped for. Unfortunately, it does not unequivocally take responsibility for the teachings of the church that created the atmosphere that ultimately led to the Holocaust, and to the participation of numerous believing persons in that crime."

In 1923, Hitler led his fledgling Nazi Party in a coup and tried to take over the Bavarian and German governments in the Beer Hall Putsch. Hitler was jailed for a year in this failed attempt. It was while in prison that he wrote his book *Mein Kampf*. After prison, Hitler attempted to resurrect his Nazi Party and was able to do so with a great deal of help from wealthy supporters among German and American businessmen.

A German banker and industrialist Fritz Thyssen controlled most of the iron ore and steel business in Germany. He was a business partner of Nelson Rockefeller, the Harriman brothers (Averell Harriman was the New York Governor), and Prescott Bush — the father of George Herbert Walker Bush, and grandfather to George W. Bush. Thyssen and his American partners became the financiers for Hitler and the Nazi Party and were responsible for his rise to power.

According to William Shirer in *The Rise and Fall of the Third Reich*, Thyssen and his partners donated over one million German marks to Hitler and the Nazi Party in their rise to power shortly after Hitler left prison. They also arranged for the Association of German Industrialists, which Thyssen also headed, to donate another three million Marks to the Nazis. Some of this was because of their rightwing bias and their anti-communist sentiments, but much of it was also because Hitler promised to outlaw the unions if he came to power. It was also Thyssen who played the major role in persuading the ill and aging President Paul von Hindenburg to appoint Hitler as Chancellor of Germany.

Former Federal Prosecutor and former US Army Intelligence Officer John Loftus investigated and found evidence that the Bush/Walker, Harriman and the Rockefeller families were heavily and directly involved in financing Hitler and the Nazi government. In his book *America's Nazi Secrets* he wrote that "these long buried US government files demonstrate that the Bush family stayed on the corporate boards of Nazi front groups even after they knew beyond a shadow of a doubt that they were helping the financial cause of the Third Reich. It was all about the money. Nazi Germany is where the Bush family fortune came from, and where the Harrimans and the Rockefellers increased their fortunes to obscene proportions."

According to Stephen Kinzer in his book, *The Brothers, John Foster Dulles, Allen Dulles and Their Secret World War*, much of this American investment with Thyssen was done through the law firm of Sullivan and Cromwell and by its managing partner, John Foster Dulles. He was aided by his brother and law partner Allen Dulles. The brothers were particularly adept at foreign relations, business and intrigue. Their father had been educated in Germany and both had spent time there before and after World War I. The two brothers were the grandsons of one American Secretary of State and the nephews of another. They were both Princeton educated and were students of Woodrow Wilson. In fact both were with Wilson in France at the end of World War I when the reparations against the Germans were levied, and they knew how to get around them to do business.

John Foster Dulles was one of the architects of the Dawes Plan of 1924 which restructured Germany's reparation payments in ways which let American banks and financiers become Germany's largest lenders. The architect then benefited himself and his clients financially with this knowledge. In 1923, the two Dulles brothers became close friends with Hjalmar Schacht. Schacht was an early member of the Nazi Party and was named Germany's Minister of Economic by Hitler when he came to power in 1933. This friendship gave the brothers immediate access to anyone in Nazi Germany including Hitler.

The Dulles brothers were both Christian conservatives and their father was a German educated minister and missionary. They were raised in wealth and with many opportunities. Both had worked for the State Department in their twenties and Allen was the head of US intelligence in World War

I in Bern Switzerland, a role he would again undertake in World War II. One account at the time said that Sullivan and Cromwell and the two Dulles brothers were making their fortunes representing America's wealthiest families by quietly managing their investments in Nazi Germany. In addition to their American clients the investigative reporter Drew Pearson listed many German clients the two brothers also represented in a column and said of John Foster Dulles that he was the chief agent for "the banking circles that rescued Adolf Hitler from the financial depths and set up his Nazi Party as a going concern."

At the conclusion of the war Fritz Thyssen was tried as a Nazi and for being a part of Hitler's inner circle. He was accused of crimes against humanity. His companies had eagerly turned over all Jewish employees and their families to the Nazis. He and his companies also used Jewish slave labor in the 1930s and 1940s provided by the Nazis. Although he denied involvement in the use of Jewish slaves during the war Thyssen did eventually agree to pay 500,000 Marks as compensation in settlement with the courts for using Jewish slave labor.

The Dulles brothers managed to keep the business interests of most of their American clients secret, however reports of Bush, Rockefeller and the others' involvement with Thyssen's seized bank and other businesses have been circulating as rumors in diplomatic and intelligence circles for many years. These Bush, Rockefeller and Harriman connections have also been reported by various mainstream media over the years. On October 17, 2003, the Associated Press reported that according to recently found government documents, that Prescott Bush was a controlling director of the Union Banking Corporation that was seized by the federal government during the war because of its illegal financial support to the Nazi government. It was reported that his bank had also made direct contributions to the NAZI Party and supported Hitler's rise to power. These government documents conclusively show that Bush and his partners (Rockefeller and Harriman) helped bankroll Adolf Hitler's personal rise to power through the bank. The documents prove that the Union Banking Corporation, where Prescott Bush sat as a controlling board member and where he was also part owner, was actually a front for a Dutch bank, Bank voor Handel en Scheepvaardt N.V. which was owned and controlled by the Nazi Fritz Thyssen and his brother along with Prescott Bush.

Both Harriman brothers and Bush were also partners in the New York investment firm of Brown Brothers, Harriman and Co. which handled the financial transactions for the Union Banking Corporation as well as Thyssen's Dutch bank. And along with the Dutch bank financial transactions the Union Bank also controlled and financially supported other Nazi companies through the Dutch Bank voor Handel. All of these assets were confiscated by the US government in October of 1942 under the Trading with the Enemy Act. It is now unquestionably proven that Bush and his wealthy partners were trading with the enemy.

During the 1930s Brown Brothers, Harriman increasingly directed their clients' investments into German companies through the Dulles Brothers at the Sullivan and Cromwell Law firm. The Rockefeller family was the largest investor among these clients and their Standard Oil Company developed a particularly close connection with the German chemical giant I.G. Farben. The corporate giant I.G. Farben was crucial to the Nazi war machine and was also responsible for the creation of the concentration camp technology used by the Nazis to kill millions of Jews and others.

All these illegal investments were carefully and secretly managed by Sullivan and Cromwell and the Dulles brothers. John Foster Dulles would later become Secretary of State under Eisenhower. Allen Dulles would later become the CIA Director under Eisenhower. The brothers were also the lawyers for Thyssen's bank and they also represented Rockefeller and the American investors while also representing many large German firms during this time, including I.G. Farben. They set up cartels for chemicals, steel and nickel without which the German war machine could have never been built.

Early in 1933, both Allen Dulles and his brother attended a business meeting in Germany where most of the large German industrialists agreed to back Hitler's bid for power in exchange for his pledge to break the German unions. Fritz Thyssen chaired this meeting. A few months later John Foster Dulles negotiated a deal with his friend Hjalmar Schacht who was Hitler's Minister of Economics. The deal allowed all German trade with the United States to be coordinated through a syndicate headed by Averell Harriman's cousin at Brown Brothers, Harriman.

There were many other Nazi connections among this group of wealthy Americans. The Hamburg-Amerika shipping line, which Harriman and Prescott Bush's father-in-law George Herbert Walker had owned since 1920, had a particularly high degree of Nazi involvement in all of its operations. It was later proven that the company was actively conducting espionage for the Nazi government and German military in America. In 1934, a congressional investigation revealed the shipping line had become the primary vehicle for spying, propaganda, and bribery in America on behalf of Hitler and the Nazi government. It was also documented that Walker, Bush and Harriman were all aware of this spying.

From 1937 on the Dulles brothers would represent Bush, Walker and the Harrimans in all their covert dealings with Nazi firms. They also performed similar concealment services for the Rockefellers. Rather than divesting themselves of these tainted Nazi assets once America declared war on Germany, Prescott Bush, the Rockefellers and Harrimans used the Dulles brothers to help hide and conceal their ownership in these Nazi businesses. While the firm had decided it was too risky to make further investments in Germany just before the war they agreed to protect and in many cases hide their client's and their own investments in Germany that had already been made.

The Associated Press also reported that, no charges were ever brought against Union Bank's traitorous American directors. The reason why they did not bring charges was because, "The federal government was too busy trying to fight the war," according to Donald Goldstein, a professor of public and international affairs at the University of Pittsburgh and an expert on this era. When Associated Press asked Goldstein why the US Government didn't prosecute all these wealthy men he replied that at that time America "did not have the resources to do these things." He said it was common knowledge that many American businessmen like Henry Ford had strongly supported the Nazis. He also said that the US government also desperately needed the help of these particular men, Rockefeller, the Harrimans and the Dulles brothers because when America declared war it was grossly lacking in any intelligence or knowledge of Nazi Germany or its military. These men knew what the American government needed and they likely cut a deal.

It didn't hurt that when Franklin Roosevelt was Under Secretary of the Navy under President Wilson that he and Allen Dulles developed a friendship and were bridge partners on a passenger liner traveling from the US to France as part of the American Delegation to the Peace Conference at the end of World War I. Roosevelt had also invited the Dulles brothers to the White House shortly after his presidential inauguration in 1933 to advise him on foreign affairs. The Dulles brothers had some influence with the Roosevelt White House and likely used this to broker a deal on behalf of themselves and their clients.

Other events seem to confirm a deal was made. According to Daniel Okrent's book *Great Fortune, The Epic of Rockefeller Center* stated that in 1942 the United States intelligence was woefully lacking in its knowledge of Nazi Germany, but the Rockefeller's and their business partners had an extensive intelligence operation of industrial spies operating around the world, particularly in Germany. Their knowledge went far beyond what the American intelligence or military knew. It went far beyond what the British intelligence knew. Accordingly the Roosevelt Administration desperately needed their information and knowledge.

This was how during World War II Rockefeller Center in New York became known as the "House of Spies" with the British Intelligence Service supplying the Americans some initial organization and leadership, which was staffed with Rockefeller's industrial spies and young like-minded conservative Ivy League businessmen from prominent families forming the Office of Strategic Services (the OSS) the forerunner to the CIA. One of these men was Allen Dulles and it is no coincidence that the former Nazi supporter would later serve as the Director of the CIA under President Eisenhower or that his equally guilty brother John Foster Dulles would also serve Eisenhower as his Secretary of State.

CHAPTER 9. THE COLD WAR AND THE 1950S

"The Cold War isn't thawing; it is burning with a deadly heat. Communism isn't sleeping; it is, as always, plotting, scheming, working, fighting."—Richard Nixon

"Communists and most subversive activities are always attached to labor situations...It is a practical impossibility to divorce communism from labor..."—J. Edgar Hoover

"During the Cold War, we were interested because we were scared that Russia and the United States were going to go to war. We were scared that Russia was going to take over the world. Every country became a battleground."—Fareed Zakaria, American news analyst

"It is based upon a theory that we know more about what is good for the world than the world itself. It assumes that we are right and that anyone who disagrees with us is wrong.....Other people simply do not like to be dominated, and we would be in the same position of suppressing rebellions by force like the British found themselves in the 19th century."—Senator Robert Taft

The cultural period of that we usually think of as the 1950s overlapped the decade preceding it and the decade that followed. This period of cultural conformity that we like to call the 1950s actually lasted from the end of World War II in 1945 until the assassination of John Kennedy in 1963. The killing of Kennedy launched the turmoil of the non-conformist 1960s.

Much of this decade plus was dominated by the Presidency of Dwight Eisenhower. Eisenhower was a much more dogmatic and conniving man than he is given credit for being. He was a religious man who came from a family of Mennonites and Jehovah's Witnesses. Eisenhower later became a Presbyterian. Soon after taking office he said in a national speech, "...without god, there could be no form of American government nor an American way of life." Eisenhower began all of his cabinet meetings with a prayer. He also agreed with his dogmatic Secretary of State, John Foster Dulles, that communism was "an alien faith." Eisenhower, no matter how politically understated and affable, was a dogmatic cold warrior.

He knew and disliked the consequences of war and particularly lamented the high cost of keeping a large Army and Navy. When Allen Dulles his CIA Director and his brother the Secretary of State began to lobby him to conduct a cheaper covert war against communism through the CIA he quickly endorsed the idea, including assassinating foreign leaders. It was Eisenhower who personally approved of these regime changes and assassinations as long as he and the US government had plausible denial. Many people were killed and governments were toppled in these regime changes, including many democratically elected heads of state and non-communist governments. Governments and who opposed American business or American corporations were toppled as being communist or socialist. They were justified by Eisenhower and his Secretary of State as necessary to curb Soviet ambitions. The two men believed anything not allied with them must be part of a communist conspiracy.

In World War I the United States went to war with its Russian ally with two concurrent invasions. President Woodrow Wilson, an avowed anti-communist, ordered the American Siberian Expeditionary force to seize the Russian port of Vladivostok and then ordered the Polar Bear Expedition to take the Russian port of Archangel. This history of the US betraying her Russian ally is repeated again when America began the cold war against the USSR long before World War II even ended.

The Soviets were not blind to this. They believed that the United States and England had delayed the D Day Invasion and refused to develop any other western front until late in the war so that the Nazis and the Russians could annihilate each other before America engaged its troops in Western Europe. And there was some truth to this. General Patton (who was no fan of the Russians) along with other military strategists had suggested that America and England push up through Greece or Italy to join the Russians on the Eastern front, a much easier task it, was thought at the time, than landing in France. However the American and British governments quickly rejected this.

The Russians lost about twenty-seven million people in World War II. Only nine million of these were military combatants. By comparison the United States had a little over 291,000 combat deaths in World War II in both the European and Pacific theaters and comparatively very few civilian deaths. The Russians were very bitter about this.

Stalin, an unusually paranoid person in the best of times, made the uncanny mistake of trusting Hitler. On August 23, 1939 representatives from Nazi Germany and the Soviet Union met and signed the Nazi-Soviet Non-Aggression Pact which guaranteed that the two countries would not attack each other. By agreeing to this pact, Germany had protected its eastern border while making preparations to go to war in Western Europe. In exchange Stalin and the Soviet Union were awarded parts of Poland and the Baltic States. The pact was broken when Nazi Germany attacked the Soviet Union less than two years later on June 22, 1941. Remembering this and the American attacks on Russia in the Polar Bear and Siberian Expeditions during World War I, Stalin was not going to make the same mistake by trusting the Americans at the conclusion of World War II.

The Americans were never going to trust or support the USSR in any meaningful way. This was not because of revulsion toward Soviet brutality or totalitarianism, as America then and now the supports many brutal totalitarian regimes around the world. The lack of trust was a result of American communist xenophobia. During the war America and Britain used the USSR as the anvil to blunt the Nazi war machine, allowing the Soviet Army and Russia and Eastern Europe to absorb most of the damage and casualties. And while it may be true that Stalin and the Soviets were as murderous as Hitler and the Nazis, America was only opposing him because he was a communist and not because he was a despot. As previously mentioned, many Americans before the war had little problem supporting the despotism of Hitler and the Nazis. After World War II America supported despots and dictators all over the world in Asia, Africa, the Mideast and Latin America as long as they were not communist dictators. It was this irrational communist xenophobia that was the root cause of the Cold War and Eisenhower and John Foster Dulles led the way.

The Hard Right Turn, The Dark Knights: The OSS/CIA Set the Tone

> "I'm going to be so much better a president for having been at the CIA that you're not going to believe it."—George Herbert Walker Bush

"I never would have agreed to the formulation of the Central Intelligence Agency back in forty-seven, if I had known it would become the American Gestapo."—Harry Truman

"There exists a shadowy government with its own Air Force, its own Navy, its own fundraising mechanism, and the ability to pursue its own ideas of national interest free from all checks and balances, and free from the law itself."—Senator Daniel K. Inouye

"Is it 'left' to insist that presidents and CIA directors adhere to the law? I don't think so. I think it's American."—Anthony Lewis, *New York Times* Legal Journalist

"We could become the first country to go fascist through free elections."—William L. Shirer journalist and author of *The Rise and Fall of the Third Reich*

Major General Reinhard Gehlen was Hitler's spy master. He had overseen a large organization of more than thirty-five hundred Nazi spies scattered throughout Eastern Europe and the Soviet Union during World War II. He and his top officers were Nazi SS zealots who had committed some of the most atrocious crimes of the war in the concentration camps and in the prisoner of war camps. They were vicious and had proven their effectiveness in their efforts to torture, drug and trick information from prisoners. They became masters of mind control and breaking the human spirit. They were also accomplished at inserting their agents into Russia. They infiltrated not only the Red Army but reputedly even the Soviet General Staff.

The records and techniques that Gehlen amassed during the Nazi regime were deemed invaluable to the Allies, especially to the Joint Chiefs of Staff and a select group of very interested Americans in the Office of Strategic Services (OSS). The right-wing OSS men, especially Allen Dulles, were already preparing for a cold war with the Soviets midway through the war. At the end of the war Gehlen was confident that a suitable arrangement with the Americans could be made for himself and his officers. There were many men in the OSS, like Allen Dulles, who had some pre-war connections and sympathies with Nazi Germany. Allen Dulles was the OSS Station Chief in Switzerland during both World War I and World War II; he and Gehlen had mutual friends in Germany; and Dulles knew his work.

Gehlen had been planning his move for months and he used his connections to Allen Dulles to execute it. He noted in his memoirs that, "Early in 1944 I told my more intimate colleagues that I considered the war lost and

we must began thinking of the future and plan for the approaching catastrophe."

In a pre-planned and pre-negotiated move on May 22, 1945, Major General Gehlen surrendered to the US Army in Bavaria. He was brought to what
had been an interrogation center for the German Air Force. In 1945, the United States Army had just begun to use this place as their interrogation center
and intelligence post. They named it Camp King.

Gehlen was a known commodity to both Bill Donovan the head of the
OSS as well as Allen Dulles. They were both anti-communists and were
eager to interrogate him because of his knowledge and contacts inside the
Soviet Union. They were also aware of his mind control and interrogation
techniques and were very interested in these as well. He offered them his
intelligence methods, his archives and his network of contacts in exchange
for his liberty and the liberty of his Nazi SS officers imprisoned in American
POW camps in Germany. He also brazenly offered to work for them, an offer
they quickly accepted.

The OSS quietly removed Gehlen and his commanders from the official
lists of American POWs and more ominously they removed them from the
war crimes lists where most of them were wanted for their atrocious crimes
against humanity. They "sanitized" or hid their war records behind false
identities and transferred seven of Gehlen's senior officers to Camp King.
Gehlen's intelligence archives were then unearthed and brought to the camp
for examination.

William Donovan and Allen Dulles made the deal with Gehlen to formally work for American intelligence. On September 20, 1945, Gehlen and
his three highest ranking Nazi SS officers were secretly flown to the United
States to begin their secret work for the American intelligence.

Immediately Gehlen proved his worth to them by exposing a number of
American OSS officers who he claimed were secret members of the US Communist Party. In retrospect, their guilt has been doubted as it is now believed
that Gehlen likely accused these Americans to impress his new bosses. It
was just the beginning of Gehlen's deceptions. He and his men told many lies
and actively deceived the Americans on almost every occasion.

According to Annie Jacobsen in her book *Operation Paperclip*, once the decision was made the Joint Chiefs of Staff oversaw the program to hire Gehlen's
organization. They also chose to hire a nefarious group of Nazi scientists and
doctors, all of whom were wanted for crimes against humanity. It was originally called Operation Overcast and President Truman was deliberately kept
in the dark during this time. Later the president was told of only part of the
operation and the Joint Chiefs and the OSS lied and told the president that a
few "rocket scientists" were brought to the United States but that "none of

them were real Nazis." After eight months of operation the Nazi recruitment program was greatly expanded and formally called "Operation Paperclip."

The operation not only included German rocket scientists, but German physicists working on the German nuclear weapons program, along with Nazi intelligence officers like Gehlen, many of whom were SS and Gestapo, and many Nazi medical doctors and scientists who had performed some of the most atrocious human experiments ever conducted. Almost all of these men had committed and were wanted for war crimes. Even the rocket scientist Werner Von Braun the father of the American space program was in reality an early and willing member of the Nazi Party. He was also a voluntary member of the SS. He had used Jewish slave labor in his rocket programs and was linked to the deaths of thousands of concentration camp prisoners. These facts largely remain unknown to most Americans. Although it is still frequently denied in the American press, Von Braun and most of his staff were hard core Nazis and war criminals.

One of Von Braun's staff, Kurt Debus, eventually became the first director of the Kennedy Space Center. Kurt Debus was an ardent Nazi and an enthusiastic member of the SS and proudly wore his precisely tailored SS uniform to work every day in Nazi Germany. He was a bully and he once had a colleague arrested by the Gestapo for not giving him a proper Nazi salute. Debus also oversaw the Jewish slave labor that built Von Braun's V2 rockets. Currently America honors this man at the American Space Club which annually gives "The Kurt H. Debus Award" to honor an American scientist who has made significant contributions to America's space program.

The medical doctors and scientists that were recruited during Operation Paperclip and brought to the United States included a horrific lot. Dr. Hubertus Strughold, who later worked for NASA and who is considered the father of American space flight science, conducted torturous experiments in Nazi Germany on epileptic children in high pressure chambers to simulate the rigors of high altitude flight. These experiments resulted in the deaths and injury to most of these children. After the experiments he killed these children and dissected them to see how his experiments had impacted their bodies. Dr. Strughold was also wanted for numerous other inhumane experiments on prisoners in the concentration camps. The Space Medicine Association of America currently awards the annual "Hubertus Strughold Award," named in his honor, to an American scientist who has made the most outstanding contribution in aviation medicine during the year.

Another scientist, Fritz Hoffmann was a Nazi chemist who also conducted poisonous gas and poison experiments on prisoners in the concentration camps. Most of his test subjects died horrible deaths. He was later brought to the US in Operation Paperclip and became the head chemist in the CIAs assassination-by-poison program.

Another Nazi scientist, Otto Ambrose, developed Sarin nerve gas and was responsible for thousands of deaths in the concentration camps. Although he was convicted of mass murder and slavery at the Nuremberg Trials he was later granted clemency by the Americans and then he was secretly brought into the US and he helped design the US Army's horrific chemical warfare program.

In the late 1940s, in Germany at Camp King a Nobel Prize winning Nazi scientist, Richard Kuhn, revealed to General Charles E. Loucks the use of LSD and detailed the Nazi mind control experiments. General Loucks then convinced his superiors that the potential uses for the US military was significant and he convinced the OSS and the Joint Chiefs of Staff that the results of these mind control experiments were vital and should be continued by the US Army. The Joint Chiefs and the OSS agreed and Dr. Walter Schreiber the Surgeon General of the Third Reich and his deputy Dr. Kurt Blome, both war criminals, were then hired to work for the OSS/CIA on mind control experiments. Doctor Schreiber and Richard Kuhn were eventually brought to the US to the Edgewood Arsenal where these experiments were conducted on hundreds of US soldiers. Many of the Nazi medical doctors that were recruited by the OSS had studied torture and mind control and most of these had been identified as war criminals during the Nuremberg Trials. Several secret US government mind control projects grew out of these Nazi experiments at the Edgewood Arsenal. These projects included Project Chatter in 1947, and Project Bluebird in 1950, which was renamed Project Artichoke in 1951. Ultimately they all became part of the infamous Project MK-ULTRA. Their purpose was to study mind control, interrogation, torture and behavior modification, to develop superior torture and interrogation techniques, and to use mind control to create human robots that could later be subject to the commands of the OSS/CIA. These human robots could then be used as unwitting spies, terrorists, couriers and even assassins. They became eventually known as the "Manchurian Candidates."

Major General Walter Schreiber, the Surgeon General of the Third Reich was a particularly immoral man. Schreiber during the Nazi reign supervised the execution of thousands of prisoners by intravenous lethal phenol injections. His personal records were sanitized by the OSS and he was brought to the US because of his knowledge in chemical and biological warfare. He was paid very well by the US military to do this research on behalf of the US. His knowledge on these subjects was very advanced because the he had already tested most of these horrific weapons on humans in the concentration camps and on prisoners of war. Annie Jacobsen in her book *Operation*

Paperclip uncovered since declassified files that reveal that Schreiber was also double-crossing his American benefactors from the beginning. While he was working for the US military, General Schreiber was also illegally dealing and selling arms and biological warfare information to the Soviets, rogue nations and to various third world warlords.

Since most if not all of the scientists and medical doctors conscripted were war criminals there was a high a potential for embarrassment to the US and the modification of their records to hide their Nazi politics and their heinous crimes was a very high priority. It was done because the Joint Chiefs of Staff and the OSS wanted cover and deniability in the event the public became aware of their Nazi pasts and their war crimes. The records of these Nazis were sanitized by either removing all the records of their atrocities to give them "clean" backgrounds, or by giving the guilty complete new identities. Two of the more interesting individuals doing this sanitation of records were Henry Kissinger and Richard Nixon.

According to John Loftus, "Kissinger, a Rockefeller employee, was recruited as a professional spy by Allen Dulles shortly after the end of the war in Europe. Although there is no evidence that he personally recruited Nazis, Kissinger ran the intelligence file room where records of Nazi recruitment were kept." This is also where their records were sanitized.

According to Anthony Summers in his Nixon biography, *The Arrogance of Power*, in 1945 Allen Dulles also recruited Nixon to work for the OSS to help sanitize Nazi files when he was still in the Navy.

There are no coincidences in politics or espionage. Kissinger would also later work for Allen Dulles while Dulles was the CIA Director in the 1950s and then serve as the Secretary of State under Nixon. According to Anthony Summers, as a reward for Nixon's cooperation in the sanitization of Nazi records Allen Dulles and Prescott Bush also "arranged to finance the ever ambitious Nixon's first congressional campaign against Jerry Voorhis."

In July 1946, Gehlen was flown back to Germany from the US where he began his intelligence work for the OSS by setting up an organization of former German Gestapo intelligence officers near Frankfurt. He later moved the operation near Munich. It was called the "South German Industrial Development Organization" to mask its true nature that it was an OSS undercover intelligence operation and spy ring. Gehlen initially handpicked three hundred and fifty former German Nazi intelligence agents, most were former Gestapo and SS officers and were wanted for war crimes. The Gehlen group eventually grew to four thousand undercover agents, all former Gestapo and SS men. This group was soon to be given the nickname the "Gehlen Organization" by the Americans. They were influential beyond their intelligence. They changed the American agents and it was these Nazis that set the culture of what would become the Central Intelligence Agency. The CIA would soon become like them, a lawless group of fascists.

Trusting the Nazis was tragic in another sense as it was later revealed after the breakup of the Soviet Union that the Nazi agents had lied, provided false information, and accused many innocent people of being traitors including Americans. And many of Gehlen's people were discovered afterward to have been double agents who were also on the payroll of the Soviets. They had caused the American intelligence much more harm than good.

In 2005, an intelligence report to Congress entitled *U.S. Intelligence and the Nazis*, came to the following conclusion: "the notion that the U.S. Military and the CIA employed only 'a few bad apples' will not stand up to new documentation..... There was no compelling reason to begin the postwar era with the assistance of some of those associated with the worst crimes of the war."

The Ratlines

> "The Agency loved (Major General Reinhard) Gehlen because he fed us what we wanted to hear. We used his stuff constantly, and we fed it to everybody else, the Pentagon, the White House, the newspapers. They loved it too. But it was hyped up Russian bogeyman junk, and it did a lot of damage to this country."—Christopher Simpson in his book *Blowback* quoting a senior CIA Agent

> "The Pope secretly pleaded with Washington and London on behalf of notorious criminals and Nazi collaborators."—Journalist Uki Goñi in his revised foreword to his book, *The Real Odessa: How Peron Brought the Nazi War Criminals to Argentina*

They were appropriately called "the Ratlines." The Catholic Church with the knowledge and assistance of the OSS smuggled Gestapo and other Nazis war criminals out of Germany into America, Canada, the Mideast and Latin America. The Ratlines were a system of escape routes for hunted Nazis and other fascists who were forced to flee Germany and other parts of Europe at the end of World War II because of their crimes. According to a number of sources including Mark Aarons and John Loftus in their book *Unholy Trinity: The Vatican, The Nazis, and the Swiss Bankers*, and Michael Phayer in his book, *Pius XII, The Holocaust, and the Cold War*, these escape routes were planned and operated by the Catholic Church, the OSS, and a group of Nazi sympathizers. The culprits were given safe passage and placed in havens in Latin America and other destinations that included the United States, Britain, Canada, and the Mideast. There were two primary routes: the first went from Germany to Spain, then to Argentina; the second from Germany to Rome to Genoa, and then to one of the other many havens. These two routes were at first developed independently but eventually came together to collaborate. The two Ratlines were created and operated by two Catholic Church officials, Father Krunoslav Draganovic and Bishop Alois Hudal.

According to a recently declassified US Army Intelligence report, *The History of the Ratline*, at first US intelligence officers were just passive observers of the Draganovic ratline, but this changed in the summer of 1947 according to the US Army's report. From 1947, the US intelligence forces began to use Draganovic's established network to evacuate its own "visitors" meaning Gestapo and Nazi collaborators. As the report stated these were "visitors who had been in the custody of the 430th Counter Intelligence Corps, CIC, and where their record of war time atrocities were sanitized, and whose continued residence at the camp in Austria constituted a security threat as well as a source of possible embarrassment to the Commanding General."

The Soviet Command had also become aware of the presence of hidden war criminals in Austria and had requested the return of these persons to Soviet custody. The Soviets wanted many of these men for war crimes and atrocities in Russia and Eastern Europe.

The operation of the Draganovic ratline was an open secret among the US, British and Vatican intelligence and diplomatic communities in Rome. And it wasn't just American intelligence assets or scientists that were given cover, sanitized and relocated. A US State Department report of July 12, 1946, listed nine war criminals that were being transported by the ratline who were not American assets, but who otherwise enjoyed Catholic Church support and protection. It was a cooperative effort with the Vatican.

Hundal for his part helped some of the most wanted and horrific war criminals escape. They included the infamous Adolph Eichmann, Franz Stangl the commanding officer at Treblinka, Gustav Wagner the commander of Sobibor, and Alois Brunner commander of the Drancy camp near Paris. Brunner was also responsible for sending most Jews from Slovakia to German concentration camps and to their deaths.

Bishop Hundal justified these acts in his memoirs, "The Allies' War against Germany was not a crusade, but the rivalry of economic complexes for whose victory they had been fighting. This so-called business ... used catchwords like democracy, race, religious liberty and Christianity as bait for the masses. All these experiences were the reason why I felt duty bound after 1945 to devote my whole charitable work mainly to former National Socialists and Fascists, especially to so-called war criminals."

The partnership between the OSS and the Catholic Church that began with the Ratlines was also the start of a strange relationship between the Church and American intelligence. Both the Americans and the Vatican feared the communists. In 1948, the CIA and the Catholic Church would conspire to rig the Italian elections against the communists and socialists in Italy. They would also cooperate to make war against the left-wing HUK rebellion in the Philippines. In the 1950s and 1960s they would again cooperate in creating the Catholic dominated Republic of South Vietnam. The Church also assisted the Americans with intelligence in Cuba. The two American spies most responsible for these cooperative campaigns with the Catholic Church were Allen Dulles and General Edward Lansdale.

The OSS recruitment of the Nazis changed the OSS. Many of the OSS officers had rightwing ideas to begin with and these tendencies were reinforced by exposure to Gehlen and his Nazis. Some of the OSS leadership had also started their careers as Rockefeller's industrial spies and saboteurs, and were already tainted by the world of smuggling, bribery, and theft.

The recruitment of Nazi war criminals like Major General Reinhard Gehlen and his Gestapo into the OSS and CIA was a fateful decision that corrupted the agency and set a culture which remains today. It was if American intelligence had been infected with a rightwing disease. Since the agency had its roots in industrial spying, theft and bribery, this experience promoted a culture that had little regard for the law or moral decency. The OSS had been mentored by British MI-5 and their "license to kill" mentality that believed that anything was appropriate if it was for god and country. This disregard for decent social norms and the law in general was increased as American xenophobia of the left and cold war paranoia came into its zenith in post war America. And this "by any means necessary" culture was only strengthened when the CIA was formed in 1947. CIA agents were encouraged to believe they operated above and outside the law. They were virtually a law unto themselves.

By lying to the President and others in their recruitment of the Nazis, America's intelligence agents and their management felt they had carte blanche to do anything, as long as they could justify this to their anti-communist cause. Many in Washington rationalized that an agency that was not subject to the law was needed in order to defeat the communists and the Soviets. They rationalized that since the Soviets would fight dirty then America needed an intelligence agency that wasn't afraid to fight dirty. Many times presidents and Congress didn't want to know what the CIA was doing and they turned a blind eye. Many other times they were lied to by CIA officials. Americans collectively reasoned that this was all necessary to fight the growing communist menace. This is the same rationalization that is given today in the fight against Islam and other unknown global "terrorists."

In the 1950s American pop culture reflected this over-the-top paranoia. The radio drama *I was a Communist for the FBI* and the television show *I led Three*

Lives played on these fears and spread this paranoia nationwide. Americans seemed to desperately want a super-secret agency that would do anything including commit murder to protect them from what they saw as the growing shadowy "red menace." It is why Ian Fleming's *James Bond* fiction novels became so popular. Fleming was a former British intelligence officer.

As a consequence of very few set boundaries and with its working relationships and exposure to some of the world's worst criminals, the CIA became unhinged and ran amok. During Project MK-ULTRA some of the most heinous crimes were committed in the name of national security. Project MK-ULTRA is the code name of a number of CIA covert operations experimenting in mind control and torture through the CIA's Scientific Intelligence Division. The CIA began to compile and use the methods learned from Nazi medical research in the concentrations camps. They also used the research and methods from the infamous World War II Japanese Medical Experimentation Unit 731, who performed horrific experiments on American, Chinese and Russian prisoners of war. The CIA employed or was in direct partnership with many of the Nazi doctors who committed these crimes, as well as Major General Gehlen's and the Gestapo's torture and drug techniques. Their partnerships were extensive throughout the late 1940s and well into the 1970s.

In a Supreme Court case, The CIA v. Sims, which was argued in 1984 and was decided in 1985, the Court described the scope of MK-ULTRA as follows: "Between 1953 and 1966, the Central Intelligence Agency financed a wide-ranging project, code-named MK-ULTRA, concerned with the research and development of chemical, biological, and radiological materials capable of employment in clandestine operations to control human behavior. The program consisted of some 149 subprojects which the Agency contracted out to various universities, research foundations, and similar institutions. At least 80 institutions and 185 private researchers participated. Because the Agency funded MK-ULTRA indirectly, many of the participating individuals were unaware that they were dealing with the Agency.... Over the years the program included various medical and psychological experiments, some of which led to untoward results. These aspects of MK-ULTRA surfaced publicly during the 1970s and they became the subject of executive and congressional investigations."

Thousands of unsuspecting Americans and some Canadians were victims of these hideous experiments.

Although a good deal of OSS/CIA medical experimentation was done prior to MK-ULTRA in the late 1940s, the program officially began in the early 1950s, and it wasn't "officially sanctioned" until 1953, when President Eisenhower was briefed and was told that the Chinese and Russians were using mind control on American prisoners captured in Korea; because of this Eisenhower agreed with and approved of the program.

However the President did not agree to experiments on unsuspecting or coerced American and Canadian citizens, which was how the program actually functioned. The program operated until it was "officially halted" in 1973, however some have alleged, with some justification that the program has continued as a clandestine operation without Congressional knowledge or approval. Fourteen-year senior CIA veteran Victor Marchetti has stated in a number of interviews that the CIA routinely conducts disinformation campaigns with the Congress and the press, and that the CIA mind control research has continued even after MK-ULTRA supposedly ended. In a 1977 interview, Marchetti specifically said that the CIA claim that MK-ULTRA was abandoned was just another deceptive "cover story."

MK-ULTRA engaged in many illegal activities. It used US and Canadian citizens with mild mental health problems as mind control test subjects without their knowledge and without telling them of the possible hazardous consequences of their "treatments." Many test subjects were horribly harmed by the experiments. MK-ULTRA involved the use of many methods to manipulate people's mental states and alter their brain functions to give them new or multiple personalities. It included the surreptitious administration of drugs like LSD and other mind altering drugs and chemicals. These experiments also used hypnosis, sensory deprivation, isolation, verbal and sexual abuse and humiliation, as well as various forms of torture. Many of these methods were learned from the Nazis, but the CIA and their medical researchers quickly improved upon them.

One of the most bizarre of the 149 subprojects was called Operation Midnight Climax. In this operation the CIA set up several brothels in San Francisco, California, to obtain a selection of men who would be too embarrassed to talk about or reveal their exploitation. The men were unknowingly heavily dosed with LSD by prostitutes who put the drug in their drinks. The brothels were equipped with one-way mirrors and these drugged sex sessions were filmed for later viewing and for blackmailing the men into participating in further mind control experiments.

In other experiments people were also given LSD without their knowledge in food or beverages and then were interrogated under bright lights with doctors in the background taking notes. The subjects were told that their "trips" would be extended indefinitely if they refused to reveal their personal secrets, which were then used against them to control their behaviors. In addition to private citizens, some of the people being interrogated this way were also some CIA employees who were required to participate as part of their jobs.

They also experimented on U.S. military personnel, some voluntary and many coerced. Military personnel who were caught possessing or using illegal drugs or who had committed minor crimes were told to "volunteer" for the drug and mind experiments or face a dishonorable discharge and a long prison sentence. Anyone suspected of leftist philosophy or suspected of working for the communists in the Cold War was also coerced into participation by the FBI on behalf of the CIA. Detained heroin addicts were bribed into taking LSD and other drugs with offers of free heroin.

In addition to LSD, other experiments involved drugs such as Temazepam, which were used under the code name MKSEARCH. Heroin, morphine, MDMA, mescaline, psilocybin, scopolamine, and marijuana, high doses of alcohol, sodium pentothal and ergine were used in other subprojects. Many long-term physical and mental debilitations and deaths resulted from all these drug experiments.

There were even more horrific methods. Donald Ewen Cameron was the first chairman of the World Psychiatric Association as well as president of the American and Canadian Psychiatric Associations. Cameron was a member of the Nuremburg Medical Tribunal in 1946 and 1947 that tried the Nazi medical doctors for their human experimentation and torture in the concentration camps. He was impressed and became very interested in the work of the Nazi doctors. He soon became a promoter of their work. He was recruited by the OSS and worked for them and later the CIA. He was recruited to work on the mind control experiments.

In the 1940s, the OSS was worried that illegal medical experiments in a US mental hospital would be much harder to cover up, so at first the mental hospital experiments were done in Canada and the OSS put Cameron in charge of one of these projects. He became the creator of the "Psychic Driving" concept, which the OSS found particularly interesting. Cameron had been experimenting to correct schizophrenia by erasing existing memories and reprogramming the psyche with new memories or creating new personalities. During the project he commuted from his home in Albany, New York, to Montreal every week to work in a clinic at McGill University. From 1957 to 1964 he carried out MK-ULTRA experiments there. In addition to LSD, Cameron experimented with various other paralytic drugs as well as over-the-top shock therapy at thirty to forty times the normal power. His "Psychic Driving" experiments consisted of putting subjects into drug-induced comas for weeks at a time, up to three months in one case, and using electro shocks to totally erase their memories. While they were in coma or drugged-induced states, Cameron played repetitive tapes of noise, simple statements, or commands through headphones to re-program the victims' brains.

According to Anne Collin's book, *In the Sleep Room: The Story of CIA Brainwashing Experiments in Canada*, his experiments were typically carried out on patients who had entered the clinic for usually very minor problems such as anxiety disorders and women with postpartum depression. Most of his patients suffered permanent and severe mental problems from his experiments. He indeed created new personalities. His treatments also sometimes resulted in the victims' loss of motor skills, including incontinence, forgetting how to talk. And they also caused amnesia, including forgetting their parents and thinking that their interrogators were their parents. This last result was deemed noteworthy by the CIA who have since used interrogation and torture to get their victims to a state where they think that their CIA torturers and interrogators are their parents. These methods have been used on many military and CIA prisoners over the years, most recently in Iraq, Afghanistan and in the War on Terror.

Cameron's patients were brainwashed. His work paralleled British projects in London and Surrey. The British Intelligence Services also experimented extensively on patients mostly without their consent or knowledge and caused similar personality changes and long-term damage. The final objective was to create "Manchurian Candidates" human robots that function normally, but would be pre-programmed to do anything they were commanded to do and to forget everything once the command was completed.

Naomi Klein in her book *The Shock Doctrine: The Rise of Disaster Capitalism*, wrote that Cameron's research and his contribution to the MK-ULTRA project was actually not exclusively about mind control and brainwashing, but also about designing "a scientifically based system for extracting information from 'resistant sources.' In other words, torture."

Cameron's Canadian project was just one of the 149 mind control projects the CIA undertook and their results remain largely classified and unknown. There were MK-ULTRA projects at many of the major universities, in many mental hospitals and clinics, and on many military bases. Some of the people that are claimed to be victims of MK-ULTRA are significant.

Alston Chase published an article in *Atlantic Monthly*, in June 2000, entitled: "Harvard and the Making of a Unabomber," in which she states that Ted Kaczynski was a victim of Harvard's MK-ULTRA program when he was attending the school at the age of sixteen. The evidence to support this is fairly strong as Henry Murray, the Harvard psychiatrist who "treated" Kaczynski for minor mental problems, was the lead researcher in the Harvard MK-ULTRA experiments. Murray also served with the OSS in World War II. He was awarded a grant funded by the US Navy, and his Harvard experiments strongly resembled many other MK-ULTRA mind control projects.

Merry Prankster Ken Kesey, the author of *One Flew Over the Cuckoo's Nest*, says he volunteered for MK-ULTRA experiments involving LSD and other psychedelic drugs at the Veterans Administration Hospital in Menlo Park California. He was referred there by Stanford University to earn tuition money when he was a student. Robert Hunter, a singer-songwriter, translator, and poet best known for his association with Jerry Garcia and the Grateful Dead, said that like Kesey he was a paid volunteer and an MK-ULTRA test subject while at Stanford University. Both men stated that the University lied to them, saying these tests were medically safe and would have no long-term effects. Both have suffered periodic mental problems after these experiments.

Boston mobster James "Whitey" Bulger volunteered for MK-ULTRA drug testing while in prison in exchange for a reduction in the sentence for his crimes. Candy Jones, a fashion model, author, and radio talk show host, also claims to be a victim and was the subject of a book by Donald Bain, *The CIA's Control of Candy Jones.* Jones suffered from periodic bouts of complete amnesia. She believed she was used as a CIA courier while working as an airline stewardess without her conscious knowledge.

Some have alleged that Charles Manson was also product of MK-ULTRA. At the time of his crimes, a new type of LSD known as "Orange Sunshine" was exclusively manufactured for the CIA and the MK-ULTRA program in the 1960s. It was the drug the Manson Family was using before and during their murder spree. The Manson Family also threatened to kill researcher Mae Brussel who was at the time researching the CIA connections to the John Kennedy assassination.

Sirhan Sirhan is another alleged victim. His attorney, Lawrence Teeter, claims that Sirhan was a casualty of the MK-ULTRA program. He and Sirhan's psychologist think that mind control techniques were used to control Sirhan during Robert Kennedy's assassination. They believe he was a "Manchurian Candidate." Sirhan's doctors say he has no memory of that day, even under deep hypnosis, and concluded that it had been externally erased. They believe that a young Sirhan who had sought medical help for minor depression after the death of his sister was programmed by MK-ULTRA experiments.

Michael Meiers in his book *Was Jonestown a CIA Medical Experiment? A Review of the Evidence,* believes that Jonestown was a CIA mind control experimental site, and that the Reverend Jim Jones was another victim of MK-ULTRA. Congressman Leo Ryan, a well-known critic of the CIA, was murdered by Jones and his People's Temple members after he personally visited Jonestown to investigate various reported irregularities.

Seymour Hersh first exposed MK-ULTRA in a *New York Times* article in 1974. He documented the CIA illegalities and experiments on unknowing US citizens. Donald Rumsfeld, then chief of staff for President Ford, and Rumsfeld's deputy, Dick Cheney, who would later be Vice President under George W. Bush, strongly advocated to President Ford that Hersh be fully prosecuted and imprisoned for revealing these heinous government secrets. However, President Ford didn't heed their advice. Instead he appointed a commission chaired by Vice President Nelson Rockefeller, the original owner of the OSS spy ring, to investigate these intelligence improprieties and whitewash them.

Congress insisted on being involved and a Senate Committee chaired by Senator Frank Church also began to investigate. This became known as the Church Committee. In response to their inquiries the CIA immediately destroyed tens of thousands of documents, erasing records of most of the operation. Fortunately some MK-ULTRA records were improperly stored and survived so that we know of some of these crimes. In 1977, John Marks, author of *The Search for the Manchurian Candidate*, filed a Freedom of Information Act request which provided him with many redacted versions of the surviving MK-ULTRA records. This information has confirmed some of the worst alleged atrocities of this illegal CIA mind control operation.

The Hidden History of the Korean War

> "The outlook for peace seems to be getting dull, duller, Dulles."—*New York Post* columnist Frank Kingdon

> "The atrocities that happened here weren't carried out by strangers. It was us, the people who'd once lived together harmoniously in the same village."—Hwang Sok-yung, Korean writer

At the end of World War II the US and the USSR came to the conclusion at the Moscow Conference that Korea, which had been occupied by Japan since 1910, would be jointly administered by the two victors with the USSR in the north and the US in the south. It was not popular with the Koreans who protested both occupations and rioted over these issues until both the USSR and the US asserted military control over their populations. In one such protest in South Korea which became known as the Jeju (Cheju) Uprising of 1948, between 14,000 and 60,000 people were killed by South Korean military with the support and assistance of the US Army.

Korea was supposed to have joint elections in the north and south to let the Koreans decide their fate, but the US and USSR could never agree how to conduct them. The USSR eventually formed a communist government around the dictator Kim Il-sung, and the Americans formed a government around the rightwing, Japanese military educated dictator Syngman Rhee. Both Kim Il-sung and Rhee were violent and cruel despotic strongmen. Kim Il-sung jailed many and consolidated his dictatorship over North Korea. Many of his human rights abuses are well known by Americans. However, the rightwing Rhee was no better.

The American press did not cover the South Korean abuses and instead became accomplices in promoting the US government's propaganda about South Korea. However the world press has occasionally reported about the abuses in South Korea. In November 15, 2008 an article appeared in the *Sydney Morning Herald* which reported on the findings of Seoul's Truth and Reconciliation Commission which for some years had been investigating South Korea's history of rightwing human rights abuses that have been hidden and covered up by the South Korean and American governments for many years.

One of the worst incidents the Commission reported happened in 1948, when Syngman Rhee's new government was installed in Seoul by the United States. The newly installed Rhee ordered his army to suppress a leftist protest on Cheju Island. The South Korean military supported by the U.S. Army gunned down and killed as many as 60,000 local people who were protesting US and South Korean policies. The Commission also reported that by 1950 and before the Korean War had started Rhee at US urging had arrested about 30,000 dissidents who were sent to prison labeled as communists and that he had also arrested another 300,000 people who had disagreed with his policies and imprisoned them in "re-education camps."

On June 25, 1950, Kim Il-sung with support from the USSR and China decided the time was right to take the South by military force. The attack was swift and effective. The North defeated Rhee's South Korean Army and conquered much of the South very quickly, forcing the South and their American supporters into a small area where they made a final stand. It was called the Pusan Perimeter. As Rhee had retreated south his troops began killing those in jail and all those in the re-education camps. Tens of thousands were killed by Rhee's forces as they retreated. Some accounts said that Rhee's army spent more time killing locals and dissidents as they did in fighting the invading army.

The US Army came to Rhee's rescue. The Korean War was officially a United Nations action and although twenty-one countries sent personnel to the war, 88% of the soldiers that fought in the Korean War were Americans. It was in reality an American war, especially after McArthur's big mistake in 1950.

In October 1950, McArthur had assured Truman that if he crossed the 38th parallel and invaded into North Korea that the Chinese wouldn't attack as they had threatened. He said if they did it would lead to an immediate slaughter of their forces. He told Truman he had flown a reconnaissance mission over the area personally. He said at the most the Chinese could get only 60,000 troops across the Yalu River into North Korea if they should consider attacking. At the time of his promises and assurances the Chinese already had 180,000 troops hidden in North Korea and would have a total of 300,000 soldiers in Korea by the time they attacked.

McArthur promised the president that he could invade the North and would have most of the American forces home by Christmas. He also promised that one army division in Korea could be redeployed to Europe by January. The CIA and the Joint Chiefs of Staff strongly supported McArthur's claims to the hesitant Truman. They were all very wrong.

McArthur was rightfully relieved of his command shortly after the Chinese invaded en masse. It prolonged the Korean War three more years only to reach a stalemate in July of 1953, with the 38th parallel still serving as the border between north and south as it had before the war. McArthur's adventurism had cost the Americans three more years of war and untold deaths on both sides for nothing.

During the war the massacre of civilians by Rhee and his American allies were plentiful. Seoul's Truth and Reconciliation Commission is working through no less than 1200 cases, including about 215 incidents in which US and allied air forces deliberately strafed and bombed groups of refugees and other civilians. The victims total at least 100,000 people, which the commission says is a very conservative estimate.

In one incident near Taejon, a short distance south of Seoul, dissidents were shuttled out of the city's jail by the South Korean Army and local police. They were marched with hands bound to the edge of long trenches. They were made to lie down in the trenches and then fired upon with rifles and machine guns. Their bodies were then covered in the shallow ditches. Death squads like this killed continually in this same manner as the North Koreans advanced. Over 7,000 prisoners were executed this way according to the commission. The US Army knew about all these atrocities and had even photographed the incidents but the incidents and the photos were repressed and hidden by the American military and CIA until the information was recently released by the Truth and Reconciliation Commission.

The Commission's findings do not end with Rhee or the Korean War. The commission has detailed many human rights abuses committed by the rightwing South Korean regimes backed by the US from the end of World War II until the early 1990s, including many cases of people being tortured, framed on false treason charges, jailed and executed.

It appears that Kim Il-sung, his son and grandson were not the only bad men in Korea.

The Rosenbergs

> "You sat the Rosenbergs in the electric chair for nothing. We got nothing from the Rosenbergs."—Boris V. Brokhovich, Director of the first Soviet nuclear bomb project

> "If I had known that at the time, if President Eisenhower had known it, he might have taken a different view with regard to her."—Richard Nixon on the probable innocence of Ethel Rosenberg

In January 1950, the US discovered that Klaus Fuchs, a German physicist working for the British in the Manhattan Project, had provided key documents and information about their nuclear bomb program to the Soviets throughout the war. Fuchs identified his courier as an American named Harry Gold, who was arrested on May 23, 1950. Gold confessed and to get a more lenient sentence identified an American Sergeant David Greenglass, a former machinist at Los Alamos, as an additional accomplice. Greenglass under duress to get a more lenient sentence then accused his brother-in-law Julius Rosenberg and perjured himself to also implicate his sister, Rosenberg's wife. He made these accusations as part of an agreement with the FBI in order to get a shorter prison sentence and to protect his wife from any prosecution.

While it is true that Julius Rosenberg passed some US documents to the Soviets, what is also true is that his trial consisted of the government using coercive measures to force witnesses to perjure themselves against him in court. He didn't receive a fair trial. Ethel Rosenberg was an innocent pawn caught up in the anti-communist xenophobia of the times, and the ruthless ambitions of FBI agents and prosecutors who wanted blood, innocent or not. There was also a significant amount of anti-Semitism that followed the Rosenbergs as they were brought to trial.

In 1995, the US government released a series of decoded Soviet cables, which confirmed that Julius had acted as a minor courier for the Soviets but the Soviet files contained no references to Ethel's involvement. The American government chose to single these two out for death sentences, even though all of the other atomic spies who were caught by the FBI in this incident had actually committed much larger crimes and were not executed, including David Greenglass, Ethel's brother. It was Greenglass and not Julius Rosenberg who supplied most of the documents stolen from Los Alamos. He was not given a death sentence and he only served ten years of a fifteen year sentence. Harry Gold, who had identified Greenglass, and who had delivered more secret documents than Rosenberg served only fifteen years in federal prison for being a courier. And the most culpable, the German scientist with British citizenship, Klaus Fuchs, the communist spy that headed this spy ring and recruited them was sentenced to only fourteen years but served just a little over nine years.

Though he initially denied any involvement by his sister Ethel Rosenberg, Greenglass under FBI coercion lied and claimed that Ethel knew of her husband's dealings. He later lied and said she had typed some documents for her husband, although there is no other proof of this other than his coerced statement.

Greenglass became the key prosecution witness in the Rosenberg trial. He later recanted his testimony about his sister's involvement and said it had been forced by the FBI. He stated in an interview in 2001, "I don't know who typed it, frankly, and to this day I can't remember that the typing took place. I had no memory of that at all, none whatsoever."

He said he gave false testimony to protect himself and his wife, Ruth, and said that he was coerced by the FBI and the prosecution to do so. "I would not sacrifice my wife and my children for my sister," He said. However he also said that he didn't realize at the time that his sister would receive the death penalty.

The Rosenbergs were singled out for the death penalty because they had been open members of the Communist Party USA. They had met when they each joined the Young Communist League USA in their teens. During World War II Julius joined the Army Signal Corps and was assigned to the Engineering Laboratories at Fort Monmouth, New Jersey, in 1940. He worked there as an engineer-inspector until 1945. He was fired when the Army discovered his open and on-going membership in the Communist Party USA.

The Rosenbergs were the only two American civilians ever to be executed for espionage during the entire Cold War. In sentencing them to death, Judge Irving Kaufman became enraged saying that he held them responsible not only for espionage, but also for all the deaths of the Korean War. He said, "I believe your conduct in putting into the hands of the Russians the A-Bomb years before our best scientists predicted Russia would perfect the bomb has already caused, in my opinion, the Communist aggression in Korea, with the resultant casualties exceeding fifty thousand and who knows but that millions more of innocent people may pay the price of your treason." It was an incredibly false statement that explodes with xenophobia.

Between the trial and the executions there were widespread world-wide protests and claims of anti-Semitism. The charges of anti-Semitism were widely believed especially abroad. Pope Pius XII appealed directly to President Eisenhower to spare the Rosenberg's lives, but Eisenhower formally refused his request on February 11, 1953. All other appeals were also unsuccessful.

Richard Nixon who was Eisenhower's Vice President at the time would later say that the evidence against Ethel was "tainted." "If I had known that at the time, if President Eisenhower had known it, he might have taken a different view with regard to her."

Julius and Ethel Rosenberg were executed in the electric chair at sundown on June 19, 1953. Julius Rosenberg died after the first electric shock, Ethel did not. After the normal course of three electric shocks, the doctors determined that Mrs. Rosenberg had not yet died and her heart was still beating. Two more electric shocks were applied, and at conclusion eyewitnesses reported that smoke rose from her head in the chamber. The Rosenberg's had two small boys that paid a steep price. They were orphaned by the executions and were tainted so bad that no relatives adopted them. They were later adopted by a high school teacher. In later years they came to realize their father was as guilty as were the others, but they also believe that he was not as guilty as the others who were given jail sentences while their father was executed. They believe their mother, like them, was an innocent victim.

W.E.B. Du Bois

> "To be a poor man is hard, but to be a poor race in a land
> of dollars is the very bottom of hardships."—W.E.B. Du Bois

The US government, the FBI and Senator Joe McCarthy targeted W.E.B. Du Bois, the Black civil rights leader and the founder of the National Association for the Advancement of Colored People (NAACP). Because of his civil rights advocacy and his opposition to nuclear weapons the FBI deemed him a communist. Historian Manning Marable has characterized the government's treatment of Du Bois as "ruthless repression" and a "political assassination."

J. Edgar Hoover and the FBI began to compile a file on Du Bois as early as 1942 because of his civil rights advocacy in forming the NAACP. However the government became more aggressive toward Du Bois in the early 1950s, and it was largely because of Du Bois' was morally opposed to nuclear weapons. In 1950, Du Bois became chairman of the newly created Peace Information Center (PIC), which worked to publicize the Stockholm Peace Appeal in the United States.

The primary agenda of the Stockholm Appeal was to gather signatures on a petition asking governments around the world to agree to ban all nuclear weapons. Du Bois became the American leader of this movement. The US

Justice Department alleged that Du Bois, while working with PIC, was acting as an agent of a foreign state (Sweden) and therefore required Du Bois to register with the federal government as a foreign agent. Du Bois refused saying he was not working in Sweden's interest, but was an American working in America's best interest. He was then indicted for failure to register as a foreign agent.

After the indictment, many of Du Bois' former civil rights associates became afraid of also being accused and they began to distance themselves from him. Shamefully the NAACP refused to issue a statement of support to their founder. He became an isolated man. At a trial in 1951, the case was dismissed because there was absolutely no evidence that Du Bois had ever worked on behalf of Sweden or any other any foreign state or that he was a communist. Although Du Bois was found not guilty of the crime, the government still illegally continued to withhold Du Bois' passport and they withheld it for eight years restricting his travel. They also continued to assassinate his character and to frighten away his former friends and associates.

The Responsibilities Program

The FBI was the agency responsible for the internal security of the United States. At J. Edgar Hoover's instruction they kept files on tens of thousands of Americans who were suspected leftists, socialists, communists or homosexuals. Hoover also considered homosexuals to be a threat to national security which gives an interesting look into the disturbed mind of Hoover who was a homosexual. He wanted these groups driven from government, the military and educational institutions. The information in the FBI files was classified and private and by federal law and was only to be shared with certain individuals of the Executive Branch of the government, particularly the Justice Department. Hoover regularly broke these laws and regularly passed classified and private information to selected members of Congress like Joseph McCarthy and Richard Nixon to assist in their Congressional inquiries and against political foes. For example Nixon used some secret information against Congresswoman Helen Gahagen Douglas who Nixon defeated in a 1950 Senate race by labeling her the "Pink Lady" and accusing her of being a socialist. McCarthy used the secret information in his Senate hearings to embarrass and to terrify his witnesses.

In 1997, an article published in the *Historian* by Cathleen Thom and Patrick Chung, states that Hoover began the covert Responsibilities Program at the FBI in 1951. Tim Weiner also wrote about it in his book *Enemies*. The program sought to expand Hoover's campaign to push leftists, socialists, communists and homosexuals out of the government by illegally giving classified information about these individuals to their political foes, police departments or their employers. Hoover hand selected the employers, Governors and Mayors and local legislators, local police, and even universities to receive this information.

The program was run personally by Hoover through the local FBI Special Agent in charge of that region. Thousands of people were accused as leftists or homosexuals, and this information was used against them politically or used by employers like local governments, universities and private employers to fire these people from their jobs. Much of this information was false and fabricated. The Program ran until 1955, but the files on the individuals were kept by the FBI for twenty-five years after this.

The FBI and the Responsibilities Program also became involved in the State Department. Secretary of State John Foster Dulles allowed Hoover to place one of his agents, Scott McLeod, as head of internal security at the State Department. The FBI then began regularly using illegal wiretaps and other illegal spying methods on the nation's diplomatic corps to purge the State Department of so-called leftists, liberals and homosexuals. Again much of the information was falsified. No one in the State Department was safe and a large number of the Department's employees were affected. Resignations, firings and even suicides occurred as a result of this purge. The purge was carried out under Eisenhower's direct approval in Executive Order 10450 to which specifically sought to rid the federal government of "leftists, homosexuals and drunks."

The Banana Republics

"Fascism is a worldwide disease. Its greatest threat to the United States will come after the war, either via Latin America or within the United States itself."—Vice President Henry Wallace

"The Fruit Company, Inc. reserved for itself the most succulent, the central coast of my own land, the delicate waist of America. It rechristened its territories as the 'Banana Republics' and over the sleeping dead, over the restless heroes who brought about the greatness, the liberty and the flags, it established the comic opera: abolished the independencies, presented crowns of Caesar, unsheathed envy, attracted the dictatorship of the flies."—from the poem *United Fruit Co.* by Pablo Neruda

"Even if the spy Allen Dulles should arrive in heaven through someone's absentmindedness, he would begin to blow up the clouds, mine the stars, and slaughter the angels."—The Soviet newspaper *Pravda*

The term banana republic was first used by the American writer O. Henry to describe the fictional Republic of Anchuria in the book *Cabbages and Kings* in 1904. The book was a collection of short stories inspired by his experiences in Honduras from 1896 to 1897, where he lived while he was wanted in the US for bank embezzlement. The term "Banana Republic" has since become an insulting term to describe mostly Latin American countries with US supported dictatorships that promote US business interests and large-scale plantation agriculture, especially banana cultivation grown at the expense and the exploitation of the local populace. In pure economics terms a banana republic is a country operated wholly for US private profit. They operate as a conspiracy between greedy dictators, the CIA and large US corporations. The local governments are usually American supported and friendly fascist dictatorships. Such was the case in pre-Castro Cuba which was a United States territory until 1948.

The history of these horrible abuses is interesting. In Costa Rica two American railroad tycoons, Henry Meiggs and his nephew Minor Cooper Keith, built a railroad from San Jose to Limon in 1873 after the government had given them the monopoly and the land to build it. They began establishing banana plantations along their Costa Rican railroad to produce food for their workers. This experience led them to recognize the potential of exporting bananas to the United States for huge profits. In a short period of time the banana business soon surpassed their railroad profits.

Keith founded a fruit company which became the United Fruit Company (UFC), operating as Chiquita Brands International. In 1899, it merged with the Boston Fruit Company owned by Andre Preston. By the 1930s through their coercion and bribery, the UFC had gained control of several Central American countries and almost ninety percent of the US banana trade. The UFC flourished in the twentieth century and came to own huge tracks of land and controlled the rail and shipping transportation networks in Central America, Columbia, Ecuador, and much of the Caribbean.

Although it came to compete with the Standard Fruit Company for dominance in the international banana trade, it maintained a virtual monopoly in Central America and the Caribbean. The UFC began to completely dominate the region and its small nations. In 1901, the government of Guatemala "hired" the UFC to manage the country's postal service. In 1913, the UFC created the Tropical Radio and Telegraph Company to control the region's communications. By 1930, it had absorbed more than 20 rival firms, acquiring capital of $215,000,000, and it became the largest employer in Central America. In 1930, Sam Zemurray (who was nicknamed "Sam the Banana Man") sold his Cuyamel Fruit Company which produced bananas and sugar in Honduras to the UFC and retired as a large shareholder. However in 1933, during the

Great Depression, there were concerns that the company was mismanaged and its market value began to plunge. Sam Zemurray staged a hostile take-over. Zemurray moved the company's headquarters to New Orleans. UFC went on to prosper under Zemurray's management until he resigned as president of the company in 1951.

The UFC was rightly accused by many of bribing and coercing government officials to sell them large tracts of land for a fraction of their worth. They forced and received preferential tax treatment and other business monopolies by these governments. They exploited their Latin American workers, paying poverty wages. They also paid little in the way of taxes to the governments of the countries where they operated. Latin American journalists frequently referred to the company as "El Pulpo," the octopus, and leftist parties in Central and South America encouraged the company's workers to sabotage and strike. Not surprising, criticism of the UFC became a common complaint of the leftists, labor, socialists and communists in Latin America.

The list of UFC shareholders is eye-opening. The largest shareholder was the Rockefeller family. John Foster Dulles and the firm of Sullivan & Cromwell had been the legal counsel for the UFC for decades and both John Foster Dulles and Allen Dulles were also major shareholders in UFC. At the same time John Foster Dulles was also the Secretary of State under President Dwight D Eisenhower. Allen Dulles, the brother of John Foster Dulles, was also the Director of the CIA, and they used their influence to control most of these governments. Another major UFC shareholder, John Moors Cabot, came from the same prominent group of Bostonian families that the Dulles and the Cabot-Lodge families came from and was also Assistant Secretary of State for Inter-American Affairs. Cabot's brother, Thomas Dudley Cabot, was the Director of International Security in the State Department and was at one time the President of the UFC. Eisenhower's former aide, General Walter Bedell Smith — the Director of the CIA until 1953, when Dulles took over the position, and Robert Hill, an Undersecretary of State, were both given seats on the board of the UFC when they retired. The CIA was well connected with the UFC. It was a corporation that they directly worked with and was protected by the CIA. It is also a likely secret source of CIA funding.

The CIA Overthrow of Democracy in Guatemala

"What we wanted to do was to have a terror campaign to terrify Arbenz particularly, to terrify his troops, as much as the German Stuka bombers terrified the populations of Holland, Belgium, and Poland at the outset of World War

II."—CIA Agent E. Howard Hunt about the CIA's plan to overthrow Arbenz

The newly democratically elected liberal President of Guatemala, Jacobo Arbenz, implemented socio-economic agrarian reforms in June 2, 1952. These reforms provided that the vast acres of unused prime farmlands that the UFC and a few other multinational corporations had set aside to preserve their monopoly would be bought from them by the Guatemala government at a fair price and then re-distributed to the impoverished Guatemalan people. The UFC believed that this land reform threatened their agricultural monopoly. The corporation owned forty-two percent of the arable land of Guatemala which had been ceded outright or bought for pennies by the UFC from the past military dictatorships of Guatemala, who had been supported and encouraged in their rise to power by the United States and the UFC.

In March 1953, the Arbenz Government re-claimed the idle UFC farmlands, for which the company was paid $600,000. This amount was deemed fair as it was taken directly from the UFC's public tax-declaration of the financial value of the idle farmland that the corporation had filed with the Guatemalan government. It was what the UFC had claimed as the value of the land. The UFC refused this amount and complained to and sought financial redress through the US State Department, which was headed by the large UFC shareholder John Foster Dulles. In 1954, Dulles and the US State Department demanded that the Arbenz Government pay the incredibly unreasonable and unaffordable amount of $15,854,849 to the UFC, for the "true value" of this farmland. The Arbenz Government rejected that demand as ridiculous. They told the US State Department that this was a violation of the national sovereignty of the Republic of Guatemala and claimed the demand was usurious, since the UFC had already previously self-claimed the value of the land at $600,000 for tax purposes.

The UFC, the CIA and the State Department then went on a campaign to portray the Arbenz government as communist or "soft on communism." As a result of the Guatemalan government's refusal to pay the US demanded sixteen million, the US State Department reduced the economic aid to Guatemala. In another crippling move and despite on-going treaty agreements the State Department violated their treaties and unreasonably cut almost all commercial trade with Guatemala. This began to destroy the Guatemalan national economy as eighty-five percent of its exports were sold to the US and an equal percentage of its imports were also bought from the United States. However as the US government began to tighten the economic noose around the neck of Guatemala the other Latin American nations became outraged and they began to support and assist the Arbenz government. As a result the US State Department saw that the economic punishments were not working. So the large UFC shareholder Secretary of State John Foster Dulles had a conversation with his large shareholder brother Allen Dulles the Director of the CIA and decided to take down the Arbenz government.

According to Walter LaFeber in his book *Inevitable Revolutions: The United States in Central America,* Allen Dulles told President Eisenhower that according to the best intelligence that the Arbenz government was "at best a communist friendly" government and may turn communist and ally with the Soviet Union. It was a lie. He told Eisenhower that he would appear weak on communism if he didn't act to prevent this, a charge that all politicians feared as these were the days of the McCarthy communist witch hunts and Eisenhower knew that even a whisper of being soft on communism could have devastating political consequences.

With the President's blessing the CIA began a two prong approach, Operation PBFORTUNE and Operation PBSUCCESS. One operation was a CIA operation to undermine and paint the Arbenz government to Congress and the public as communist and radical, and to assert that this communism was real a danger to spread in Latin American and that it could cripple vital American interests. The second was the CIA and US military operation to overthrow the popular and democratically elected Arbenz government and replace it with a US and UFC friendly fascist military dictatorship.

The CIA and the American military created and trained a small rebel group to overthrow the Guatemalan government. On 29 March 1953, a futile raid against the Army garrison in central Guatemala was launched by the CIA sponsored rebel group led by a Col. Castillo, one of three men whom CIA was considering to install as President of Guatemala after the Coup. However the Guatemalan Army quickly ended their insurrection. The failed attempt resulted in uncovering the CIA's plot and the jailing of its leaders.

The CIA then began a public relations campaign to paint the Arbenz government as "undemocratic" saying that Arbenz was arresting "political opponents." The CIA then lied to the American and the world press about the fact that these men had engaged in armed rebellion to overthrow the duly elected government. This propaganda campaign was effective outside of Guatemala particularly in the US, but largely ineffective in Guatemala and Latin America as a large majority of Guatemalans knew of the revolutionary army's attempt to overthrow their government and had supported the President's jailing of the CIA's revolutionaries.

In Nicholas Cullather's *Secret History: The CIA's Classified Account of its Operations in Guatemala, 1952–1954,* he wrote that it became clear to the Arbenz government that the US was behind the overthrow attempts of Col. Castillo and that they would likely attempt another coup. The Guatemalan government began to bolster their military. At the same time the US immediately cut off all arms to Guatemala from all sources. The Guatemalan fears of another attempt were soon confirmed by a Guatemalan defector from the CIA Operation PBSUCCESS, who confirmed the Castillo insurrection was a CIA plot and warned them of another attempt to come.

The Guatemalan military were unable to get arms to defend themselves from other Western counties as they had been warned off by the US and the CIA. None of these nations dared to violate the US arms embargo to Guatemala for fear of like reprisals. So with little choice, Guatemala was forced to go to Czechoslovakia, where they bought German World War II arms which were then shipped to them on a Swedish freighter. The CIA attempted to stop the ship, but in a comedy of errors they stopped and boarded the wrong ship. The CIA then used the Guatemalan purchase of these arms from a communist country to make a public case that "the Soviet Union was arming a communist friendly government in America's backyard." It was another lie.

In December 1953, the CIA established the operational headquarters of their Guatemalan army of liberation in suburban Florida. They recruited US Air Force pilots who were supposedly "on leave," and professional and mercenary soldiers. They provided military training and established a radio station, "The Voice of Liberation," to broadcast disinformation and propaganda into Guatemala. The CIA also dropped leaflets on Guatemala telling the population "to struggle against the communist atheists and join the rebel patriots." They also falsely claimed that Arbenz was a Soviet puppet and would ban Christianity in Guatemala.

The US Navy launched Operation HARDROCK BAKER, to blockade Guatemala on 24 May 1954. Submarines and surface ships intercepted and boarded every ship in Guatemalan waters and forcefully searched them for "weapons that might support the Arbenz Government." They even searched British and French ships, in violation of maritime national sovereignty agreements, but neither Britain nor France dared to protest. On June 7, 1954, a contingency force consisting of five amphibious assault ships, a Marine helicopter-assault battalion and an aircraft carrier were dispatched to blockade Guatemala and to support an invasion force.

At 8:00 p.m. on June 18, 1954, the CIA mercenary army invaded Guatemala in four groups. The soldiers entered the country at key points on the Honduras and Guatemala border and on the Guatemala and El Salvador border. These multiple attacks were meant to impress the populace that the Republic of Guatemala was being invaded by a large military force, superior to the Guatemalan Army. The CIA thought that the four dispersed groups of their mercenary army would also minimize the possibility of a decisive rout by the Guatemalan Army. They were wrong. The Guatemalans were prepared to fight. An almost identical short-sighted plan, by the same CIA planners, would later be used by the CIA in their gross failure at the Bay of Pigs in Cuba.

It was a CIA military fiasco and the propaganda campaign was a failure as well. The Guatemalans rallied around their elected government to fight the mercenaries. The CIA forces met with decisive failure. Invading on foot and hampered by heavy equipment, the invaders took days or never reached their strategic objectives. One of the CIA units of a hundred and twenty-two mercenaries had a mission to capture the city of Zacapa, and despite outnumbering the defending Guatemalan Army by four to one, they were defeated by a platoon of just thirty men. Only twenty-eight of the one hundred and twenty-two CIA mercenaries survived the battle. Another hundred and seventy CIA mercenaries were defeated when they attempted to capture the port city of Puerto Barrios. The chief of police armed the local men and assigned them defensive positions. They killed or captured most of the CIA mercenaries and the few invaders that survived fled to Honduras. Within three days the Guatemalan Army had found and defeated the rest of the CIA mercenary army.

In the wake of these CIA defeats, the US Air Force then began air raids against Guatemalan military targets and the major cities. The CIA and the US government lied to the press about its participation and claimed the bombing was being done by an independent Guatemalan rebel air force. In reality the pilots were US Air Force personnel "on assignment to the CIA" the aircraft was also "on loan to the CIA" by the US Air Force. It was in reality an attack by the US Air Force. Early on the morning of June 27, 1954, Puerto San Jose was attacked and the US dropped many napalm bombs on the city. The damage was complete and devastating. As part of the collateral damage a British cargo ship, which was being loaded with Guatemalan cotton and coffee was also badly damaged.

After these bombings Arbenz was told that the US Marines and Air Force were standing by and that he would be killed and his country would be invaded and completely destroyed. After seeing San Jose destroyed by napalm bombs and not wishing his country to be destroyed and his people killed, Jacobo Arbenz did what he thought was the honorable thing and he resigned the Presidency of Guatemala to spare his country. He left for exile in Mexico. Eleven days after the Arbenz resignation, the first of five successive US supported fascist military juntas occupied the Guatemalan presidential palace, and each junta was successively more repressive and fascist and amenable to the demands of the US, the CIA and the UFC.

According to Tim Weiner in *Legacy of* Ashes, the CIA developed a list of 58 democratic influential Guatemalan government and military leaders that were then assassinated by the CIA after Arbenz left, to assure that democracy would not re-emerge in Guatemala.

International opinion was aghast about the Guatemalan coup d'état. The French newspaper *Le Monde* and the British newspaper *The Times* attacked the United States' coup as a "modern form of economic colonialism." The Secretary General of the United Nations, Dag Hammarskjöld, said that the paramilitary invasion where the US deposed the elected government of Guatemala was a geopolitical action that violated the human-rights stipulations of the United Nations Charter. The US government and the CIA never forgave Hammarskjöld for these remarks, and they had a long memory.

In October 2011, the government of Guatemala formally thanked and recognized Arbenz for resigning to keep his country from being destroyed by the US military. They formally apologized to Juan Jacobo Arbenz, the son of the deposed President Jacobo Arbenz. The Arbenz family continues to unsuccessfully request an apology from the United States for having overthrown their father and for destroying the democratic government of Guatemala in 1954. The UFC retained their Guatemalan lands and their monopoly.

The American Puppet State of Cuba

"I helped make Mexico, especially Tampico, safe for American oil interests in 1914. I helped make Haiti and Cuba a decent place for the National City Bank boys to collect revenues in."—Marine Major General Smedley Butler

"The administration's attempt to keep us from selling agricultural products to Cuba is an outrage. Cuba is not a threat. That is why we must do more to open Cuba, not less."—Senator Max Baucus

"The Cuban people still live in constant fear of a brutal totalitarian regime that has demonstrated time and again its utter disregard for basic human dignity. The fight for a free Cuba has gone on for far too long."—Mitt Romney 2012

"I don't trust the policy of the United States, nor have I exchanged a word with them, but this does not mean I reject a specific solution to the conflicts. We will always defend cooperation and friendship with all the people of the world, including with our political adversaries."—Fidel Castro 2015 on the possible normalization of US Cuban relations

"I'm going to continue to oppose the ... Obama–Paul foreign policy on Cuba because I know it won't lead to freedom and liberty for the Cuban people, which is my sole interest here,"—Marco Rubio on the 2015 normalization of US and Cuban relations

In the nineteenth century Cuba fought three wars of liberation to gain independence from Spain, the last of which escalated into the Spanish American War when the American battleship, the Maine, was mysteriously sunk and the United States declared war on Spain. After the Americans won their victory which culminated in the Treaty of Paris, Cuba became an American protectorate. However, Cuba's future independence was also assured by the treaty although no exact date was given. Many in the US preferred Cuba to remain an American territory, none more so the United Fruit Company. UFC holdings in Cuba included banana plantations along with sugar mills and sugar cane fields. Americans also owned rum distilleries and the hotels and casinos in Cuba.

At the beginning of the nineteenth century, slavery was abolished in Cuba by Spain. In the early nineteenth century Cubans began to entertain a break with Spain and many wanted annexation to the United States in order to re-establish slavery in Cuba. As early as 1805, the United States held secret discussions with Cuban rebels about possible annexation as a Southern slave state. The major impetus for this discussion was primarily because of Spain's abolition of slavery and the Cuban sugar plantation owners desire to continue their repressive plantation economy.

However, the desire to become an American territory outlasted slavery which is why in 1898 the Americans backed Cuba's move for independence which began the Spanish American War which allowed Cuba to become a protectorate of the United States.

Cuba was granted independence in 1902. Independence was in name only and the US continued to govern Cuba as a puppet state. The UFC and other US corporations, business and the American Mafia controlled Cuba and her government. In 1940 the American puppet dictator, Fulgencio Batista, won election as president in a corrupt election that was contrived by the Americans.

In the 1920s, the American Mafia began operating in Cuba and smuggling liquor into the US during Prohibition. In the 1930s, they expanded their Cuban operations and soon controlled most of Havana. They controlled the drug, prostitution and the hotel, casinos and night club industries. In 1952 Eduardo Chibas, a Cuban progressive, was expected to easily win in the presidential election with his campaign to rid Cuba of corruption, the Mafia and American business influence. He very mysteriously "committed suicide" a few months before the election and Batista, with the support of the Americans, the CIA, and the Mafia, took over the Cuban government once again in a bloodless coup before the elections could take place.

Cuba, Before Castro Came to Power

> "One might best summarize the complex situation by saying that urban Cuba had come to resemble a Southern European country with a living standard as high or surpassing that of France, Spain, Portugal and Greece, while rural Cuba replicated the conditions of other plantation societies in Latin America and the Caribbean."—Mark Falcoff, American foreign policy analyst on pre-Castro Cuba.

The Americans painted a different picture of pre-Castro Cuba. Americans saw mostly Havana and assumed the best despite the corruption. And while Cuba's urban elite lived very well indeed, the majority of Cuba's population was rural and very poor. It was also divided by race as Whites lived much better than Cuba's poor Blacks.

Even the urban area was not as well off as Americans claimed. Valerie Ryan in an article for the *Seattle Times* described it as follows: "In pre-Castro Cuba, jointly run by dictator Fulgencio Batista and the Mafia, there is chicanery behind every important door. Casino lackeys carry suitcases of money to Miami every weekend; people are murdered, cut up and fed to the carnivores at the zoo. Night life is exotic, seedy, corrupt; more 'cabaret' than Las Vegas."

There were in reality two Cubas, one of luxury and massive money making enjoyed by mostly Americans and a few Cuban upper class urbanites, and a second very large group of rural poor. Americans including large corporations like the UFC, the Mafia, and wealthy Americans and the Cuban elite profited from the Cuban economy largely at the expense of everyone one else in Cuba who lived in third world poverty.

In the book *From Columbus to Castro: The History of the Caribbean 1492–1969*, Eric Williams wrote that pre-Castro Cuba was indeed a very poor third world country. Cuba then had a population of about five and a half million, of which over a million were totally illiterate. In rural areas forty-five percent were illiterate and forty-four percent never attended school. Twenty-five percent of urban children did not attend school, and the public school system was a national joke and anyone who could afford it sent their children to expensive private schools. Ninety-one percent of the population had no electricity. Eighty-five percent had no indoor water, and fifty percent had no toilets of any kind. Seventy percent of rural dwellings were huts made from palm fronds. A third of the rural population had intestinal parasites. There was only one doctor for every two thousand people.

The average Cuban diet was abysmal. Only four percent of Cubans could afford and ate meat regularly, only one percent ate fish, less than two percent had eggs, three percent bread, eleven percent milk, and green vegetables were not available. In 1956 the average peasant made ninety-one dollars a year and over a quarter were chronically unemployed. Most people living in pre-Castro Cuba were not living "a European lifestyle" as the American right and the upper class Cuban American exiles now claim. Most Cubans lived in dire poverty.

Fidel Castro

> "My idea, as the whole world knows, is that the capitalist system now doesn't work either for the United States or the world, driving it from crisis to crisis, which are each time more serious."—Fidel Castro

> "They talk about the failure of socialism but where is the success of capitalism in Africa, Asia and Latin America?"—Fidel Castro

> "For the thing we should never do in dealing with revolutionary countries, in which the world abounds, is to push them behind an iron curtain raised by ourselves."—Walter Lippmann, 1959

> "Castro couldn't even go to the bathroom unless the Soviet Union put the nickel in the toilet."—Richard Nixon

Fidel Castro was born in 1926, and was the illegitimate son of a sugar cane farmer. His father, Angel Castro, was Spanish and he took a Cuban woman, Lina Ruz Gonzalez, as a household servant. She eventually became his mistress, bore his children, and he later married her. Fidel was one of her seven children. Fidel was sent to private Catholic schools. He liked school and did well academically, but he really excelled in sports, particularly baseball, and was good enough to play in the US in the American minor leagues.

In 1945, he began to study law at the University of Havana. At the University he became interested in the student protest movement. He campaigned against poverty and he was passionate about opposing US imperialism and opposed US colonialism in the Caribbean and Latin America. At the University Castro became critical of the corruption and violence of Cuban President Ramon Grau's government and delivered a rousing public speech on the subject in November 1946 that earned him a place on the front page of several Cuban newspapers.

In 1947, Castro joined the Socialist Party of the Cuban People, founded by veteran politician Eduardo Chibás. A charismatic politician, Chibás ran for President advocating social justice, honest government, and political freedom. His socialist party began to expose corruption in Cuba's government and he demanded reform. Castro became an aide to Chibás. During the election Grau employed criminal gang leaders who he hired as police officers to enforce his will, and Castro was threatened with death unless he stopped his criticisms and left the university. He refused and began carrying a gun and surrounded himself with armed friends. Although Chibás lost the election, Castro remained committed to him and continued working on his behalf.

In 1947, Castro learned of a planned expedition to invade the Dominican Republic to overthrow the fascist military junta of Rafael Trujillo, a US CIA and UFC puppet. Castro joined the expedition which was to be launched from Cuba on July 29, 1947. The invasion consisted of about twelve hundred Dominican freedom fighters and some Cubans like Castro. However, the CIA knew of this attempt and had the Grau government arrest most of those involved before they could set sail. Castro was fortunate and successfully evaded arrest. Returning to Havana, Castro took a leading role in the student protest against the killing of a high school pupil by government thugs. During these protests Castro was detained and very badly beaten by the police, and according to many friends this was the incident that radicalized and moved Castro to the left.

In April 1948, Castro traveled to Bogota, Columbia, with a Cuban student group sponsored by President Juan Peron's Argentine government. While there the assassination of popular leftist leader led to widespread rioting and clashes between the fascist government backed by the army, and the popular leftists. Castro joined the leftist protests.

Castro returned to Havana and the University and married Mirta Diaz Balart, a university student from a wealthy family. The marriage was disapproved of by both families. It was through this marriage and his new in-laws that he was exposed to and revolted by the lifestyle of the Cuban upper class elite. Castro saw the urban elite, including his new in-laws, as parasites preying upon the majority of the Cuban people who lived in poverty.

In September 1949, Mirta gave birth to a son, and the couple moved to a larger Havana flat. Castro focused on his university studies, graduating with a Doctor of Law degree in September 1950. Castro co-founded a legal partnership that focused on helping poor Cubans assert their legal rights against the government and their employers. Although his legal practice was a financial failure Castro's reputation was greatly enhanced and he became very well-known as the people's champion. The practice failed because Castro cared very little for money and he took too many poor clients who had little or no hope of paying him any fees. As a result he didn't make enough to pay his bills. Eventually his furniture was repossessed and his utilities were cut off at his home, which caused severe marital discord with his wife Mirta.

Castro's hopes for Cuba were still centered upon his hero Chibás and the *Socialist Party*, and after Chibás' mysterious "suicide" in 1951, Castro saw himself as Chibás' heir to carry on the cause. Castro wanted to run for office in the June 1952 elections, but senior Socialist Party members feared that he was much too radical for most voters and they refused to nominate him. Instead he was nominated as a candidate for the House of Representatives by party members in Havana's poorest district where he had worked as a lawyer and was still considered their champion. Castro was expected to easily win.

In March 1952, a military coup took over the government just before the elections. They were assisted by the CIA. General Fulgencio Batista seized power and was declared president. He cancelled the elections, describing his dictatorship as "disciplined democracy." Castro publically called it for what it was, "a fascist dictatorship."

Many Cubans began to complain about Batista and as they did, he became more dictatorial and moved even further to the right. Batista solidified his ties with the wealthy Cuban elite, the UFC and the United States and he severed diplomatic relations with the Soviet Union. He also began to suppress the Cuban labor unions in favor of their large, mostly American employers, and he began arresting and persecuting the Cuban socialists. Castro brought several legal cases against the Batista government but these cases were ignored and dismissed by the Batista-controlled courts. Castro was also warned by the government that he was going too far. This forced Castro to begin thinking of alternate ways to combat the regime.

Castro formed "The Movement," a group consisting of both a civil and a military committee. After he was threatened by the police and Batista's thugs, Castro gave up on democratic reforms for Cuba and he became a revolutionary. However he avoided an alliance with the communists fearing it would frighten away Cuban political moderates. He kept in contact with the communists through his brother Raúl who was already an ardent communist. He later stated that later that he was already a communist but had to do it this way because the Movement's members were anti-Batista, but that very few had strong socialist or any political views. He also feared that aligning himself with the communists would bring a possible CIA or US military invasion.

Castro stockpiled weapons for a planned attack on a military garrison outside Santiago de Cuba. Castro's rebels intended to dress in army uniforms and arrive at the base on July 26, during the festival of St. James, when most of the officers would be away. The rebels would seize control, raid the armory and escape with the weapons before reinforcements arrived. With these weapons Castro intended to arm supporters and spark a revolution among the area's impoverished sugar cane cutters. The plan was to then seize control of a Santiago radio station and to begin broadcasting the Movement's manifesto, which would encourage and cause further uprisings. Castro's plan was a copy of the 19th century Cuban independence fighters who had successfully raided a Spanish barracks. Castro saw himself as the heir to the Cuban independence leader and national hero, Jose Marti.

Castro gathered a hundred and sixty-five revolutionaries for the mission and they set out in a convoy of about sixteen vehicles. The vehicles were old and three of them broke down along the way. When they reached the barracks they found the army had had been tipped off by an informer from their group. The army was ready for them and the surprise attack failed. Most of the Castro's rebels became pinned down by the army outside the base by heavy machine gun fire. A few rebels did make it inside the armory, but they faced heavy resistance inside. Four rebels were killed and the rest were pinned down by machine gun fire. Knowing the attack had failed, Castro ordered a retreat. In the aftermath two more rebels were killed while retreating. The rebels suffered a total of six dead and fifteen wounded. The Cuban Army had fared worse and had suffered nineteen dead and twenty-seven wounded.

The rebels then took over a civilian hospital. It was re-taken by the Army after a brief battle. As the rebels fled some were captured. They were all tortured and twenty-two were executed without a trial. Those few that had escaped, including Fidel and his brother Raul, assembled at their meeting place where some debated surrendering, while others fled to Havana. Castro and nineteen rebels decided to set out for the rugged Sierra Maestra Mountains several miles to the north, where they could establish a guerrilla base and live to fight another day.

Over the next few weeks Castro and all the rebels were captured by the Army. A trial was held in Havana. During the trial Castro defended himself and the other rebels stating that they cannot be accused of "organizing an uprising of armed persons against the Constitutional Powers of the State" because they had risen up against Batista, who had seized power in an unconstitutional military coup.

The press was present and during the trial it was revealed that the army had tortured many suspects and had castrated some. It was also divulged that the army had gouged the eyes out of some of the rebels. The judges promised that they would investigate these crimes. The army tried unsuccessfully to prevent Castro from testifying at the trial by claiming he had become ill and was too ill to leave his cell. The trial ended on October 5, with the acquittal of a few defendants. But fifty-five were sentenced to prison with terms of up to thirteen years. Castro was sentenced separately on October 16, and he was sentenced to fifteen years.

In prison Castro renamed his cause "The 26th of July Movement" after the date of the attack on the Armory. After a few months Castro was put into solitary confinement for the rest of his imprisonment because the prison officials were afraid he would cause a prison revolt. Meanwhile, Castro's wife Mirta obtained employment with the fascist government in the office of Batista's Ministry of the Interior. She had been encouraged to do so by her family, particularly her brother who was a friend and ally of Batista. This was kept a secret from Castro, but when he found out about it through a radio news broadcast that he overheard, he wrote to her that he would rather die "a thousand times than suffer impotently from such an insult." Fidel initiated divorce proceedings and Mirta agreed. The Batista-controlled court gave Mirta sole custody of their son.

Batista's government had come under international press scrutiny for his torture and abuse of the rebels. Even many in America began to complain about the dictator. Castro on the other hand was becoming well known and popular. He was already popular in Cuba for his former legal work defending the poor. Some Batista advisors and the Americans suggested to Batista that Castro's amnesty would be very good publicity and would help to cover up the torture of the captured rebels. They said it would show that the Batista was a generous man and would show that the Batista government was not as oppressive as the international press had claimed. Batista agreed. He was no longer concerned about Castro as he was now firmly in power with the full support of the US, the CIA, and the American Mafia, and they too all believed Castro was now an impotent political threat. On May 15, 1955, Castro and a few other rebel prisoners were released.

Shortly after he was released from prison, bombings and violent demonstrations led to another crackdown on dissenters. Batista decided he would re-arrest Castro and his brother Raul in retaliation for these uprisings. The two brothers were forced to flee the country. Castro sent a letter to the press, stating that he was "leaving Cuba because all doors of peaceful struggle have been closed to me. Six weeks after being released from prison I am convinced more than ever of the dictatorship's intention, masked in many ways, to remain in power for twenty years, ruling as now by the use of terror and crime and ignoring the patience of the Cuban people, which has its limits. As a follower of Marti, I believe the hour has come to take our rights and not beg for them, to fight instead of pleading for them."

He and Raul went into exile in Mexico. Raul befriended an Argentine doctor and Marxist-Leninist named Ernesto "Ché" Guevara, a proponent of guerilla warfare. Ché was anxious to join Cuba's Revolution. Fidel also liked him, later describing Ché as "a more advanced revolutionary than I was." Castro also befriended a knowledgeable leftist veteran of the Spanish Civil War, Alberto Bayo. Bayo agreed to teach Fidel's rebels the necessary skills to conduct guerrilla warfare and he began secretly training them.

Castro toured the US in search of wealthy sympathizers to fund his revolution, with some success, including the former Cuban President in exile, Carlos Prio, who contributed $100,000. In the US Castro was monitored closely by Batista's agents, the FBI and the CIA, who allegedly tried and failed to assassinate him. They also tried to bribe the Mexican government to assassinate the Castro brothers and bribed the Mexican police to arrest them, which they did. However, they were soon released by the Mexican courts as there was no cause or justification for the arrests.

Meanwhile in Cuba, Batista's heavy-handedness was allowing the now underground 26th of July Movement to recruit new members, and other anti-Batista groups began to flourish as well. One of the more powerful anti-Batista groups was the Revolutionary Directorate (DR), founded by the Federation of University Students and their President José Antonio. He wanted to join with the 26th of July Movement and traveled to Mexico to meet with Castro. The meeting didn't go well as they disagreed on tactics. Antonio was advocating large terroristic bombings and assassinations, and Castro strongly opposed this approach. Castro, already a victim of a failed assassination attempt, disliked assassinations and terroristic attacks, calling them "cowardly." He said he wanted a legitimate military victory by a people's army.

Purchasing a large decrepit yacht, the Granma, on November 25, 1956, Castro set sail from Mexico with eighty-one revolutionaries, armed with ninety rifles, three machine guns, about forty pistols and two anti-tank guns. The Cuban Revolution had begun. Form these meager beginnings it would take less than three years for this small ragtag poorly armed group of rebels to bring down the American supported Cuban government and their army.

About three years later when the US and the CIA realized that Batista would lose the war to Castro and the rebels, and fearing that Castro would displace US interests with socialist reforms, they decided to support Batista's removal in support of a another Fascist military junta, believing that Cuban General Eulogio Cantillo who was then commanding most of the country's armed forces should lead it.

Cantillo then secretly met with Castro, agreeing that the two would call a ceasefire, following which Batista would be apprehended and tried as a war criminal. Double crossing Castro, Cantillo warned Batista of the revolutionary's intentions and allowed Batista to resign and to flee Cuba to the US with over $300,000,000. Cantillo proclaimed the Cuban Supreme Court judge Carlos Piedra the new President and then his new junta began appointing new members of the government. It was another CIA rightwing military coup.

Castro was furious. He abruptly ended the ceasefire and started on the offensive. He put together a plan to oust Cantillo and Piedra and their military junta. He freed a high-ranking military officer, Colonel Ramon Barquín, from the Isle of Pines prison where he had been held captive for plotting to overthrow Batista and commanded him to fly to Havana to arrest Cantillo with the backing of his rebel army. On February 16, 1959, Castro was sworn in as the Prime Minister of Cuba accepting the position on the condition that the Prime Minister's powers were greatly increased. He then ruled over Cuba for forty-nine years until 2008 when he was succeeded by his brother Raul.

The Death of Dag Hammarskjöld

> "Pray that your loneliness may spur you into finding something to live for, great enough to die for."—Dag Hammarskjöld, United Nations Secretary General

The CIA and the American right have never liked the United Nations. The peacekeeping mission of the U.N. interferes with the mission of the CIA which is in the business of destabilizing socialist and other states to create rightwing revolutions to allow American corporate interests to colonize independent nations. In 1961, Dag Hammarskjöld, who is reputed to be the most respected and competent U.N. Secretary General, was very mysteriously killed in what was then called the Belgian Congo. Hammarskjöld was a fierce critic of the CIA and their clandestine wars for corporate colonization in other people's countries. He had made an enemy in the CIA by publicly chastising them for the coup in Guatemala and other actions.

At the time of Hammarskjöld's death, the CIA and Western intelligence agencies were heavily involved in the political situation in the Congo which culminated in the assassination of Congo Prime Minister Patrice Lumumba. According to Tim Weiner in *Legacy of Ashes*, Larry Devlin the CIA Station Chief in Brussels was sent to the Congo in 1960. He testified later under oath (declassified in 1998) that he was ordered to assassinate Congo Prime Minister Lumumba. He asked, "On whose orders were these instructions issued?" He was told "The President." President Eisenhower had ordered the assassination. Annie Jacobsen in her book *Operation Paperclip* documented that Sidney Gottlieb was originally given the job of assassinating Lumumba by putting poison in a tube of toothpaste. However Gottlieb's attempt failed. The CIA then supported a coup by Colonel Joseph Mobutu. According to John Prados in his book *Unsafe for Democracy: The Secret Wars of the CIA*, Lumumba was detained by Mobutu and was beaten and tortured by Belgian security forces before being shot. The assassination of Lumumba caused international outrage.

Belgium and the United Kingdom had a vested interest in maintaining their control over the country's copper industry. They worried about it because of the Congolese transition from Belgian colonialism to independence may cause the new country to nationalize their most profitable resource. The CIA and the President were also concerned about African communism and wanted to prevent the resources of the Congo from being exploited by the communist bloc. Concerns about the Congolese nationalization of the copper industry probably provided both a financial and political incentive to assassinate both Lumumba and United Nations Secretary Dag Hammarskjöld. It has long been suspected that Hammarskjöld was also assassinated for trying to bring about the independence of the Congo. The CIA, British and Belgian intelligence agencies greatly disliked Hammarskjöld's interference in the country's corporate matters and also saw him as an impediment to keeping the Congo in the Western sphere of influence. They were afraid that his policies would cause the copper and diamond mines to be nationalized.

On September 16, 1961, Hammarskjöld's plane went down in the Congo and he and all on board the plane were killed. Although the plane crashed only a very short distance from the airport the wreckage was supposedly not found for fifteen hours leading many to believe that a cover up took place. Witnesses at the time stated that they saw a bright flash of light that appeared to be a rocket fired at Hammarskjöld's plane. They reported sparks and flames as it hit. According to these witnesses this happened immediately after they saw that a second smaller aircraft was following Hammarskjöld's plane. Despite these eye witnesses accounts the crash was ruled an accident.

On September 9, 2013, the Associated Press article *U.N. Chief's '61 Death: A Cold War Mystery*, by Ralph Slater reported new evidence that may solve the mystery. When Hammarskjöld's plane mysteriously crashed in the Congo, it appears that the US National Security Agency, the NSA, was monitoring radio transmissions of Hammarskjöld's plane and the radio transmissions of another plane that was following it. Cmdr. Charles Southhall who was stationed at an NSA listening post at that time said that he heard an intercepted message from the plane that was pursuing Hammarskjöld's. The message was spoken in English and said, "I have hit it. There are flames. It's going down. It's crashing."

A U.N. commission is looking at the mystery again. Its chairman, Stephan Sedley, said, "The only dependable extant record of the radio traffic, if there is one, will so far as we know be the NSA's. If it exists, it will either confirm or rebut the claim that the DC-6 was fired on or threatened with attack immediately before its descent into the forest."

The U.N. commission has requested documents from George Washington University's NSA Archive. Sedley said, "Of the three documents or records which appear to respond to our request, two are classified top secret on National Security grounds."

The CIA and the American Right Overreacts to Cuba

> "The only way to Cuba is with the CIA."—Folk Singer Phil Ochs

> "Standing, as I believe the United States stands for humanity and civilization, we should exercise every influence of our great country to.... give to that island once more peace, liberty, and independence." —Senator Henry Cabot Lodge.

> "There's some new evidence that has just come out about the CIA planning terrorist attacks on US soil in the 1960s and how they were going to set up Castro for it in order to get America behind a war in Cuba."—Aaron McGruder, American writer commenting about CIA Operation NORTHWOODS

Immediately after Castro's revolution, the CIA went to work to overthrow the Cuban government. It is called Operation MONGOOSE. It was started and approved by Eisenhower and given to Kennedy when he took office. General Edward Lansdale who had defeated the Huks in the Philippines, and who had placed Diem in Vietnam led the operation. Samuel Halpern, a CIA co-organizer conveyed the breadth of involvement: "The CIA and the US Army and military forces and Department of Commerce, and Immigration, Treasury, God knows who else, everybody was in Mongoose. It was a government-wide operation run out of Bobby Kennedy's office with Ed Lansdale as the mastermind."

The Project's six-phase schedule was prepared by the Director of Plans at the CIA Richard Bissell, who had prepared the same unsuccessful plans for overthrowing Arbenz in Guatemala. Although Eisenhower had personally recommended that the new president go through with the invasion plans Kennedy had initially voiced grave reservations. Allen Dulles later said, "We made it very clear to the President that to call off the operation would have resulted in a very unpleasant situation." Later one Kennedy aide commented, "Allen and Dick [Richard Bissell] didn't just brief us on the Cuban operation, they sold us on it." They had threatened that if he cancelled it the Cubans involved would leak that he cancelled it and he would appear weak. The only adviser to Kennedy that raised any concern was Arthur Schlesinger Jr. who sent Kennedy a memo saying that the US and Kennedy would be blamed in any invasion of Cuba and that it would draw the criticism of millions around the world.

The concerned president was worried and he gave White House oversight for the project to his most trusted advisor, his brother, Attorney General Robert Kennedy. The final plans were presented by General Edward Lansdale to the president on February 20, 1962. President Kennedy was again briefed on the operation's guidelines on March 16, 1962. Lansdale outlined a coordinated program of political, psychological, military, sabotage, terrorism and intelligence operations as well as assassination attempts on key political leaders.

Kennedy was horrified. Part of this operation was called project NORTHWOODS according to David Ruppe of *ABC News* in a story, *US Military Wanted to Provoke War with Cuba*, May 1, 2001. Ruppe said that based upon recently discovered memos the CIA in 1962 proposed Operation NORTHWOODS. The operation's plan was then developed by the Joint Chiefs of Staff and signed by Chairman Lyman Lemnitzer and sent to the Secretary of Defense. Operation NORTHWOODS was part of the US government's highly secret anti-communist Cuban initiative and the plan received its authorization from the Joint Chiefs of Staff. The plan called for the CIA to plan terrorist attacks in US cities against innocent citizens to create a justification and sympathy for the Americans to attack Cuba. However when President Kennedy was told of the Operation he had it immediately cancelled.

A JCS/Pentagon document written by General Ed Lansdale dated 16 March 1962, titled *Meeting With The President, 16 March 1962*, confirms this. It reads: "General Lemnitzer commented that the military had contingency plans for US intervention. Also it had plans for creating plausible pretexts to use force, with the pretext either attacks on US aircraft or a Cuban action in Latin America for which we could retaliate. The President said bluntly that we were not discussing the use of military force."

NORTHWOODS called for the CIA, or their operatives, to commit acts of terrorism on US aircraft, in US cities and Latin America. These acts of terrorism were then to be blamed on Castro and Cuba in order to create public support for a war and invasion to oust Castro and install a new government. Operation NORTHWOODS proposals included hijackings and bombings followed by the introduction of phony evidence that would implicate the

Cuban government. The memo further stated: "The desired resultant from the execution of this plan would be to place the United States in the apparent position of suffering defensible grievances from a rash and irresponsible government of Cuba and to develop an international image of a Cuban threat to peace in the Western Hemisphere."

Operation NORTHWOODS also proposed to "develop a Communist Cuban terror campaign in the Miami area, in other Florida cities and in Washington." It called for terrorist attacks against various US military and civilian targets.

Journalist James Bamford wrote, "Operation NORTHWOODS, which had the written approval of the Chairman and every member of the Joint Chiefs of Staff, called for innocent people to be shot on American streets; for boats carrying refugees fleeing Cuba to be sunk on the high seas; for a wave of violent terrorism to be launched in Washington, D.C., Miami, and elsewhere. People would be framed for bombings they did not commit; planes would be hijacked. Using phony evidence, all of it would be blamed on Castro, thus giving Lemnitzer and his cabal the excuse, as well as the public and international backing, they needed to launch their war."

Kennedy cancelled Operation NORTHWOODS. When Kennedy stopped their phony terrorist attacks on the US and their planned war on Cuba, the CIA and the Joints Chiefs of Staff seethed with anger. Following presentation of the NORTHWOODS plan, Kennedy removed Lemnitzer as Chairman of the Joint Chiefs of Staff. The CIA, especially Dulles, Bissell, Ed Lansdale, and many senior American military leaders began to complain Kennedy was soft on Communism. The young President became increasingly unpopular with CIA and the military. The rift would later come to a head during the Cuban Missile Crisis when the Joint Chiefs advised Kennedy to invade Cuba again and some expressed a desire to launch a preemptive nuclear strike against the USSR.

Although the CIA had been stopped by the President from conducting acts of terror and from using US military to overthrow Cuba, these were still secret contingencies in their plans to overthrow Castro. Although the use of US military remained the key to overthrowing Castro they continued with their previous approved plans for the Bay of Pigs Operation anyway. They also continued to assure the president that odds of success were very good, even when they doubted it themselves.

At this time there were many other anti-Castro plans that were not known or approved by President Kennedy although the CIA later blamed the president and his brother for their creation and failure. Many of the covert plans devised by the CIA to were to assassinate or embarrass Castro. The assassination to kill Castro had been approved by Eisenhower according to Stephen Kinzer in *The Brothers*. It is likely that they continued these assassination plans without Kennedy's knowledge. They already felt they had presidential approval and why ask to continue if you didn't know what the new president would answer.

The CIA also devised plans to discredit Castro in the eyes of the Cuban public. One farfetched plan included contaminating his clothing with thallium salts that would make his trademark beard fall out. As incredibly silly as this may be the CIA believed that Castro's charisma and power came from his beard. They also sprayed a broadcasting studio with hallucinogens before Castro gave a televised speech to make him appear crazy, this too failed. One of the assassination plots included poisoning a box of Castro's favorite cigars with botulinus toxin, and another plan placed explosive seashells in his favorite diving spots. At one point the CIA hired his former mistress Marita Lorenz to kill him. All of their plots failed, so then they took out a contract with the Mafia to kill him. The hit on Castro was arranged through "Handsome" Johnny Roselli.

It was the most outrageous series of assassination attempts any government has ever made on a sitting head of state and the CIA lied to Congress and the American people about their complicity in these events for many years. The US Senate's Church Committee, in 1975, stated that it had confirmed at least eight separate CIA run plots to assassinate Castro. Fabian Escalante, who was Castro's personal security chief, contends that there have been 638 separate CIA assassination schemes or attempts on Castro's life.

The Bay of Pigs Invasion

> "So the reason that the Bay of Pigs failed was that the original promise made by Eisenhower was not kept by the subsequent Administration. It allowed hostile air to wipe out the approaching invasion force."—CIA Agent E. Howard Hunt

> "No doubt (Guatemala's Operation PBSUCCESS) left a positive impression on me, because I set up a project (the Bay of Pigs) similar to this."—Richard Bissell the CIA Deputy Director of Plans on the Plans

Planned and approved under President Eisenhower the CIA organized the Bay of Pigs invasion of Cuba to take place in 1961. It was a plan based upon their successful invasion of Guatemala. Just like Guatemala they planned that the US Air Force and US Marines would do the job after the "rebel" invasion had failed. There was one problem, unlike Eisenhower, Kennedy steadfastly refused to use US forces and said so from the beginning. The

CIA and the Joint Chiefs of Staff ignored him thinking that the young president would not refuse once the operation began. They were wrong.

Like Guatemala, the CIA recruited and trained a rebel army to invade Cuba, and planned to use this invasion, successful or not, as a pretext for involving the US Military. Recently declassified documents show that President Kennedy had officially denied the CIA and the Joint Chiefs the authorization to use the US military to invade Cuba. But the CIA and the Joint Chiefs were still sure that once the Bay of Pigs Invasion was launched that Kennedy would not let them fail. They thought that Kennedy as a politician would not suffer such political backlash that the failure would bring. They were sure he would relent and send in US forces. Unknown to the President, the Joint Chiefs had these forces already stationed and ready to go in Florida and at Guantanamo Bay in Cuba.

The CIA had also organized some rebel dissidents within Cuba, but only in the aftermath did they finally realize that most of this rebel support was not as strong or large as they had needed. They had fooled themselves. Some of this was due to the fact that they habitually lied to the President about the strength of these rebel forces and eventually came to believe some of their own lies. The Cuban rebel army were funded and armed by various sources, including the exiled Cuban community in Miami, the CIA, and the Fascist Dominican government of General Rafael Trujillo who had also been placed in power by the CIA.

The CIA's rebel dissidents within Cuba did engage in small terroristic attacks. On April 3, 1961, they delivered a bomb attack on a militia barracks in Bayamo which killed four soldiers and wounded eight more. On April 6 the Hershey Sugar factory in Matanzas was destroyed by sabotage. On April 14, 1961, a Cuban airliner was hijacked and flown to Jacksonville, Florida. This act spun off a group of Castro Cuban copycats that kidnapped American airliners and forced them to Cuba. The Cubans would then return the planes and passengers to America unharmed. The CIA also staged a phony defection of supposedly a Cuban aircraft and pilot at Miami on April 15, 1961, but the press discovered that it was a propaganda stunt.

Castro's government began a crackdown on this rebel dissident movement and arrested many suspects. Castro also infiltrated many of these dissident groups and frequently captured arms and money sent by the CIA that was meant for these rebels.

The CIA culture could not admit that Castro was popular with the Cuban people and contrary to the thoughts and plans of the CIA analysts, the majority of Cubans supported Castro. The CIA's wishful thinking about an enslaved Cuban population rising up once a revolution was started never happened. On the contrary they rallied to defend Cuba against the Americans and their rebel army.

Castro began redistributing Cuban wealth with the poor. He raised the level of quality in the public schools and brought free education and healthcare to all the Cuban people. He was viewed by most Cubans as fair. He had rejected the methods of physical torture which had been employed by Batista's regime. Castro was tough and ruthless on traitors. Dissidents caught in the act of sabotage or violence were imprisoned for long terms and some who had committed violence or murder were also executed.

Castro's Cuban government had ordered the country's oil refineries, then controlled by the US corporations Shell, Esso, and Standard Oil, to process all of Cuba's crude oil, including some purchased from the Soviet Union, but under the pressure from the US and the CIA these companies had refused. Castro had little choice and he then responded to their refusal by expropriating the refineries and nationalizing them under Cuban control. In retaliation, the US cancelled its import of Cuban sugar, which then provoked Castro to nationalize most other US owned assets on the island, including the Mafia's casinos and hotels, the American banks, sugar mills, and UFC plantations and property. Relations between Cuba and the US were further strained following the explosion and sinking of a French ship, Le Coubre, in Havana harbor in March 1960. It was carrying weapons Cuba had purchased from Belgium. The cause of the explosion was never determined, but Castro publicly stated that the CIA was guilty of the sabotage.

The Bay of Pigs Invasion was actually planned long before Castro appropriated the American properties. It was planned under Eisenhower with Vice President Richard Nixon as the administration's overseer. It was all planned and ready to go when it was presented to a reluctant John Kennedy. According to Col. L. Fletcher Prouty, who served as Chief of Special Operations for the Joint Chiefs of Staff under Kennedy, that at the end of the Eisenhower Administration when Kennedy was elected, the CIA decided that they would enlarge the operation and force it upon the new President as fait accompli. Kennedy was uncomfortable from the beginning and gave the oversight of the project to his brother Bobby so he could keep an eye on these planners.

According to Prouty Bobby Kennedy was equally uncomfortable, but he worked with General Edward Lansdale of the CIA to understand their plans. Lansdale's job as he saw it was to convince Bobby and the President to go ahead with the invasion and then to push them to bring US troops into the invasion when it began to fail.

George H.W. Bush and his Zapata Oil Company worked for the CIA and was active in the Bay of Pigs invasion. John Loftus, in his book *Secret War*, quotes former US intelligence officials saying that Allan Dulles (who was a friend and business partner of his father Prescott Bush) was the man who recruited George H.W. Bush's oil company, Zapata, as a cover company and a purchasing front for the CIA. Bush and Zapata also provided commercial supplies and transportation for the Bay of Pigs Invasion. In early November 1960, the CIA agreed to use Zapata Oil for the maritime component of the operation. Bush has steadfastly denied his involvement and refuses to speak to a large body of evidence as well as the many statements from former CIA agents that prove otherwise.

The proof is convincing the CIA codename for the invasion was "Operation ZAPATA" after Bush's oil company, and one of the ships carrying the invaders was the "Barbara J" named jointly after his wife and the San Jacinto, a ship he served on in World War II. (During the war Bush had knick-named the San Jacinto "Barbara.") Barbara J is likely a combination of their names Barbara and Jacinto. Another ship was the "Houston" named after his hometown. Through his work with Zapata Off-Shore during this time, Bush is alleged to also have worked with and had close contact with CIA agents: Felix Rodriguez, Barry Seal, Porter Goss, and E. Howard Hunt, who were all involved in the Bay of Pigs operation.

According to former OSS General Russell Bowen in his book, *The Immaculate Deception: Bush Crime Family Exposed*, "Bush, in fact, did work directly with the anti-Castro Cuban groups in Miami before and after the Bay of Pigs invasion, using his company Zapata Oil as a corporate cover for his activities on behalf of the agency. Records at the University of Miami, where the operations were based for several years, show George Bush was present during this time."

John Loftus, in his book *Secret War* quotes former US intelligence officials reporting the same story, "The Zapata-Permargo deal caught the eye of Allan Dulles, who the old spies report was the man who recruited Bush's oil company as a part time purchasing front for the CIA. Zapata provided commercial supplies for one of Dulles' most notorious operations: the Bay of Pigs Invasion."

Kevin Phillips in his book *American Dynasty*, notes an additional factor for Bush's involvement in the invasion. The Walker side of the family (who initially funded the Zapata Corporation) had apparently lost a large fortune when Fidel Castro nationalized their West Indies Sugar Co. This is something none of the Walker-Bush family has ever been willing to forget.

The invasion force included over 1,400 invaders divided into five infantry battalions and one paratrooper battalion. They assembled in Guatemala before setting out for Cuba by boats on April 13, 1961. On April 15, eight CIA supplied US Air Force bombers based in Florida and secretly piloted by former US Air Force pilots attacked Cuban air fields and then returned to Florida. They had unfortunately attacked a day too early and this warned Castro and gave him the time to prepare for the invasion. On the night of April 16, the main invasion landed at a beach in the Bay of Pigs.

It went bad from the beginning and steadily got worse. The plan called for the destruction of all ten of Castro's fighters by the Florida based bombers. The CIA knew that the fighters would doom the operation as the invasion would be defenseless against them. The CIA's covert air raid destroyed seven of the ten fighters the day before, but three were not where the CIA expected them to be. The three were scheduled to be destroyed in a second air raid before the landing, but the CIA inexplicably cancelled the second mission to destroy the fighters. This allowed these fighters to destroy the invasion by sinking the supply ships, downing some aircraft, and decimated the rebel troops on the beaches with their fire power. According to Tim Weiner, in *Legacy of Ashes*, it was CIA Deputy Director Richard Bissell who stopped the second airstrike to wipe out Castro's air force. However, this was later blamed on the Kennedys by those in the CIA.

It has been speculated that Bissell may have cancelled the flight in the mistaken belief that Kennedy would then relent and allow them to use US Forces to invade Cuba rather than letting the invasion force be slaughtered on the beaches. Whether this was a deliberate plan or just a mistake it was the Deputy Director of Plans Richard Bissell who owned it.

The massive Cuban rebel forces that the CIA had lied about to President Kennedy also never materialized. There was no nationwide upheaval as the CIA had dogmatically predicted. The invading force from the beginning was overwhelmed by the Cuban fighters and the local revolutionary militia who protected their homeland from what they saw as a foreign invasion.

With the invaders pinned down on the beach of the Bay of Pigs, Lansdale and Bissell again personally appealed to the President to use the US military to save the operation. Allen Dulles had conveniently left the country so as not to be blamed. The Joint Chief also weighed in and said they had the necessary force in standing by, but the president pointed out that National Security Memorandum 54-12 made this illegal as US military personnel in uniform were forbidden to be involved in any undercover operation since 1954. The President refused on these legal grounds and told them that he had warned them repeatedly from the beginning that US troops would not be involved in the covert invasion of Cuba.

In a second appeal to Kennedy they asked him to allow the Air Force to attack and provide the invaders with air cover saying he could tell the press and the public that it was a Cuban rebel air force. Again Kennedy turned them down saying that he had warned them that no US forces were to attack

Cuba and that he repeatedly told them that this Cuban rebel attack had to succeed on its own. These refusals by the President left a lasting bitterness between Kennedy, the NSA, Allen Dulles, Richard Bissell, Edward Lansdale and many CIA agents especially those involved in planning the Bay of Pigs invasion.

The Cuban Army's counter-offensive was led by Captain Jose Ramon Fernandez, before Castro decided to take personal control of the operation. After only four days, on April 20, 1961 the invaders finally surrendered and the invasion was over. After being publicly interrogated and imprisoned, the invaders were eventually sent back to the US by Castro in exchange for $53 million in food and medicine for the Cuban poor.

The failed invasion strengthened the position of Castro's administration with the Cuban people. Instead of weakening him as the CIA had planned the invasion made him even more popular in Cuba and Latin America. It also drove Castro further left and he now proceeded to openly proclaim his intention to adopt socialism and he began to strengthen Cuba's ties with the Soviet Union for their protection. This led eventually to the events of the Cuban Missile Crisis of 1962.

The failed invasion was a major embarrassment for US foreign policy and President Kennedy. The young president publically accepted responsibility for the disaster. He then ordered internal investigations concerning the CIA's incompetence. He wanted to know why the ten fighters had not been destroyed as per the plan and who had cancelled the second attack to destroy the remaining three.

Allen Dulles and Richard Bissell both later stated that the CIA planners had always discounted Kennedy's statements refusing to allow the US military to be involved in the invasion. They blindly believed that once the invasion forcers were on the ground, Kennedy would have no choice and that he would be forced to authorize US forces to intervene and prevent a failure, just as Eisenhower had done in PBSUCCESS in Guatemala in 1954. The CIA was positive that Kennedy would see a defeat like this as too politically embarrassing. Unlike the cancelled Operation NORTHWOODS, they believed that this time they had cornered Kennedy in a situation where he would be forced to commit US troops regardless of his wishes and reluctance and, apparently, the law.

They under-estimated his courage; Kennedy stood his ground and refused to commit US forces as he had warned them. When the whole invasion collapsed President Kennedy publicly took the blame. He was seething with anger at the CIA for their duplicity. He declared to his brother Bobby that he wanted "to splinter the CIA in a thousand pieces and scatter it to the winds." According to Col. Prouty, in the aftermath of the Bay of Pigs Kennedy told the Joint Chiefs of Staff that they would now be directly responsible "for all Cold War actions," implying that they, not the CIA would plan any future covert operations. Prouty said the Joint Chiefs understood these ramifications and were stunned by this directive. It was the CIA's turn to seethe with anger.

Kennedy's internal investigation into the Bay of Pigs failure showed gross incompetency by the CIA in the planning, reasoning and intelligence of the entire operation. It showed a complete failure in communications with the ten crucial fighters had not been destroyed and with a second attack cancelled by Bissell. He also realized in the aftermath that it was always the CIA's intention to force him into using the US military in the invasion. After Kennedy received the results of his investigation CIA Director Allen Dulles, CIA Deputy Director Charles Cabell, and CIA Deputy Director for Plans Richard Bissell were all forced by Kennedy to resign. General Ed Lansdale was demoted and reassigned to Vietnam. None of these men would ever forgive Kennedy for not using the US military to invade Cuba and for forcing their resignations. They also feared that in a second term Kennedy would make good on vow to dismantle the CIA and scatter its pieces into the winds.

As a result of the Bay of Pigs Invasion, the Cubans became even more paranoid about the United States intentions. Today, there are still yearly nationwide military drills in Cuba during the "Dia de la Defensa," (Defense Day) to prepare the Cuban population for an American invasion.

After the failed Bay of Pigs invasion the CIA still covertly continued to harass and plot against Cuba. The program was called Operation MONGOOSE, sometimes known as the Cuban Project. It too is widely acknowledged as a gross failure. It made matters worse and pushed Cuba further left. And it almost ended in a nuclear war during the Cuban Missile Crisis. According to Noam Chomsky in *Understanding Power*, Operation MONGOOSE "won the prize for the largest operation of international terrorism in the world." According to Chomsky MONGOOSE had a budget of fifty million dollars per year, employing 2,500 people including about 500 Americans, and it remained darkly kept secret for fourteen years, from 1961 to 1975.

The Cuban Missile Crisis

> "It was a perfectly beautiful night, as fall nights are in Washington. I walked out of the President's Oval Office, and as I walked out, I thought I might never live to see another Saturday night."—Secretary of Defense Robert McNamara, recalling the Cuban Missile Crisis

"We're eyeball to eyeball, and I think the other fellow just blinked."—Secretary of State Dean Rusk, during the Cuban Missile Crisis

In May, 1962, Soviet Premier Nikita Khrushchev was persuaded by his military to counter the United States' growing lead in developing and deploying strategic nuclear missiles by placing Soviet intermediate range nuclear missiles in Cuba. Despite the misgivings of the Soviet Ambassador in Havana who argued that Castro would not accept the deployment of these missiles, they went ahead. At this time the Soviets had only 20 missiles in the Soviet Union with the long range capabilities of reaching the United States and they were worried about being defenseless if the US launched preemptive strike against them. Khrushchev also thought that once the missiles were in place that he could possibly trade Cuban missiles for West Berlin, which the Soviets saw as a constant threat to their dominance of Eastern Europe.

The Soviet ambassador's concerns turned out to be correct. Castro objected to the deployment of Soviet missiles in Cuba saying that he didn't want them and that it would make him look like a Soviet puppet. In the end Castro was persuaded by the USSR that missiles bases would be in the best interests of Cuba, but Castro agreed only after he extracted the promise that the Soviet military would defend Cuba against any future American invasion. Castro later lamented that he only agreed to the missiles because of the constant military and invasion threats by the US and the economic pressure by the Soviets. The Soviets had a very large economic bargaining chip in these negotiations. A very large majority of Cuba's trade, particularly the sugar trade, was with the USSR after the American embargo was placed on any trade with Castro's Cuba. The Soviets also agreed to buy much more sugar and Castro reluctantly agreed to the Soviet Missiles in May of 1962.

In August of 1962, the U2 spy planes discovered and photographed the Soviets building the missile bases in Cuba. The first consignment of Soviet missiles arrived on the night of September 8, and on September 16, they were followed by a second group. On October 7, the Cuban President announced at the United Nations "If ... we are attacked, we will defend ourselves. I repeat we have sufficient means with which to defend ourselves; we have indeed our inevitable weapons, the weapons, which we would have preferred not to acquire, and which we do not wish to employ."

The Joint Chiefs of Staff and the CIA unanimously agreed that a full-scale attack and invasion of Cuba was the only solution and immediately and strongly advised Kennedy to do so. They also told Kennedy that the Soviets would back down and would not attempt to stop the US from conquering Cuba. After the Bay of Pigs Kennedy was very skeptical of their advice and said, "They, no more than we, can let these things go by without doing something. They can't, after all their statements, permit us to take out their missiles, kill a lot of Russians, and then do nothing. If they don't take action in Cuba, they certainly will in Berlin."

Kennedy met with his top advisers throughout October 21, and considered two options: an air strike primarily against the Cuban missile bases, or a naval blockade of Cuba. General Curtis LeMay the Chief of Staff of the US Air Force was strongly advocating for a total knock out strike against the USSR and the rest of the Joint Chiefs and the CIA were strongly advocating for a full Cuban invasion. Against all their advice Kennedy chose the blockade.

Even after the decision was made Le May continued to argue with Kennedy that he was ignoring sound and experienced military advice and insisted that the President authorize an immediate air strike to remove the threat.

Kennedy held his ground and at 3:00 pm EDT on October 22, President Kennedy formally established his command, the Executive Committee (EX-COMM) with National Security Action Memorandum (NSAM) 196. At 5:00 pm he met with Congressional leaders who had also been lobbied by Le May and the Joint Chiefs and they too contentiously opposed Kennedy's blockade. They forcefully demanded a full invasion of Cuba. Kennedy cautioned them that such an action could lead to a nuclear war. Kennedy again stood his ground.

The crisis deepened when the Soviets threatened to run through the American blockade. The USSR had shown no indication that they would back down and they made strong comments to the contrary. The US military began preparing for an invasion of Cuba as well as a possible nuclear first strike on the Soviet Union if they attempted to run through the blockade. Both the American military and the Soviet military were now advising Kennedy and Khrushchev respectively that military action was the only solution. Fortunately, neither Kennedy nor Khrushchev wanted war and both realized that a potential nuclear catastrophe could bring an end of humanity, and they began very secret negotiations.

In the end, the USSR agreed to remove their missiles from Cuba if the US removed their missiles from Turkey. They agreed. Khrushchev also told Kennedy of the Soviets' promise to Castro that the USSR would come to their aid in the event of a US invasion. He appealed to Kennedy and received a pledge from Kennedy that the US would not invade Cuba.

This pledge further angered the military and the CIA — they interpreted it as weak and traitorous. Both Kennedy and Khrushchev had ignored their military commanders and likely saved the world from nuclear war. They also agreed to install the "hot line" which would allow the President of the US and the Soviet Premier to communicate directly to avoid any further incidents.

Although Kennedy successfully resolved the Cuban Missile Crisis without conflict, the military and the CIA again were angry with his choices. They considered him weak. Le May publically called Kennedy's resolution of the Cuban Missile Crisis "the greatest defeat in our history." They hated Kennedy.

Lee Harvey Oswald

> "I don't know why you are treating me like this. The only thing I have done is carry a pistol into a movie. I don't see why you handcuffed me. Why should I hide my face? I haven't done anything to be ashamed of. . . I want a lawyer... I am not resisting arrest."—Lee Harvey Oswald upon his arrest in a Dallas movie theatre

> "When Lee got back from Russia, the way he talked about the Russian system, he didn't talk about it politically, in the sense that he was wrapped up in communism or Marxism. He was making fun of how inept they were, and he was making fun of them all the time. ... He wasn't political. He really wasn't.

> After Lee's return, approximately two weeks, in the latter part of June 1962, he gets a call from one of the FBI agents—I believe that was Mr. Fain—in wanting to have a meeting with him.....He went the following day, had the meeting. When I returned home from work that evening, I asked him about it, and he said, 'Well, everything went all right. They even asked me if I'd ever been an agent of the federal government or the CIA.' I said, 'What did you tell them?' He says, 'Well, don't you know?'"—Robert Oswald, Lee Harvey Oswald's brother in a PBS *Frontline* interview

On May 10, 1953, Lee Harvey Oswald was a fourteen year old boy living in the Bronx. It was Mother's Day and he would later claim to have received a pamphlet protesting the death sentence of the Julius and Ethel Rosenberg as Russian spies. Six years later he would tell the Russians that this event marked the beginning of his conversion to communism. It was a lie and a very good cover story. Lee Harvey Oswald was most likely a CIA agent and there is much evidence to support this.

Oswald was a former US Marine who defected to the Soviet Union in October 1959. He lived in the Soviet Union until June 1962, at which time he returned to the United States. The fact that he was allowed to return with his

Russian child and his Russian bride, a niece of a prominent KGB officer, is miraculous, unless of course Lee Harvey Oswald was an undercover CIA agent.

It is noteworthy that around this time the US Government was attempting to put Gus Hall of the CPUSA in prison again for just being a communist even though no one believed he was a spy or a traitor like Oswald. Hall was being prosecuted this time under the Internal Security Act of 1950, known as the McCarran Act which made being a communist a crime. Considering this extremely xenophobic anti-communist climate it is very unlikely that the State Department would then welcome back the traitor and supposedly avowed communist Lee Harvey Oswald who had formally renounced his US citizenship, declared himself a communist at an international press conference, who had committed treason by giving military secrets to the Russians, and who also insisted on bringing his Russian wife and child to the US. It is even less likely that the CIA and FBI would allow this supposed traitor to return without being arrested or even questioned after giving highly classified secrets to the Soviets, but they did. Incredibly the US government even paid for his family to return.

The Soviets, for their part always assumed Oswald was a CIA spy, but they allowed him to stay for propaganda purposes. It made for good press that a US Marine had renounced his US citizenship to be a communist and live in the USSR. When it was apparent that Oswald, the supposed hardcore Marxist, was getting nowhere in the USSR his mission was apparently aborted and he returned to the capitalist United States with his passage arranged and paid for by the US State Department.

Edward Voebel who the Warren Commission had established was Oswald's closest childhood friend said that reports that Oswald was studying communism as a teenager and the story about the Rosenbergs "were a lot of baloney." He and Oswald were in the Civil Air Patrol together and he told the Commission that all Oswald ever wanted to do was to join the Marines like his brother and be an American hero.

Oswald enlisted in the United States Marine Corps on in 1956 just after his seventeenth birthday. He joined because he idolized his older brother Robert who had also served in the Marines and he too wanted to serve his country. A photograph after his arrest for the Kennedy assassination by the Dallas police shows Oswald still proudly wearing his brother's Marine Corps ring. These acts are not congruent with what most communist traitors would do. And despite Oswald's claim that he was "a Marxist from the age of fourteen" we are then supposed to believe that the Marines had Oswald scrutinized and investigated and that he passed and was given a Secret Security Clearance placing him overseas in a sensitive radar installment and at a secret U2 base with access to classified materials despite freely admitting to being a communist. Oswald needed a secret security clearance because he worked with highly classified U2 and radar secrets. It was these secrets that Oswald gave to the Soviets to gain his Russian citizenship.

In December 1958, Oswald was stationed at El Toro Marine Air Station where his unit's function was to train both enlisted men and officers in radar operations for later assignments overseas. His commanding officer said that Oswald was a very competent crew chief. While in the Marines Oswald was also allowed and encouraged to learn Russian. In February 1959 he was given a Marine proficiency exam in written and spoken Russian. His level at the time was rated as poor but at the time he had only three months Russian language training from the Marines.

After studying more Russian and becoming fairly proficient in the language he received a hardship discharge from active service on September 11, 1959, under a false claim that his mother needed care. He was placed in the Marine reserves. In October 1959, just before turning twenty, Oswald sought and obtained a passport and a student visa from the US Government. Oswald spent two days with his mother in Fort Worth, Texas and then left by ship from New Orleans on September 20, for Le Havre, France. He then took the ferry to the United Kingdom from France. He arrived in Southampton where he told custom officials he planned to remain in the United Kingdom for one week before proceeding to a school in Switzerland. However, on that same day he then flew on to Finland, where he was quickly issued a Soviet visa. Oswald left Helsinki on the following day and arrived in Moscow on October 16, 1959. And all of this was supposedly planned and executed with precision timing by a twenty year old high school dropout with very limited resources and with little understanding of the world.

On October 31, 1959, Oswald appeared at the US Embassy in Moscow renouncing his US citizenship. The Associated Press ran a story of a defection to the Soviet Union by a US Marine who renounced his citizenship. It was reported on the front pages of most major US newspapers and in the international press.

Oswald was kept under constant surveillance in the USSR because they suspected he was a CIA plant. Oswald requested a job in intelligence or the military but the Russians gave him a job in a factory. However he was given very good housing and extra pay and he was used by the USSR for propaganda purposes to embarrass the United States.

Oswald received a dishonorable discharge because of his defection to the USSR and because he was a traitor who violated his oath of secrecy and revealed secret information to the Soviets. According to the *Warren Commission Report*, in an odd turnabout that occurred on September 13, 1960, Lee Harvey Oswald's Marine discharge was mysteriously changed from a "dishonorable" to an "undesirable" discharge. It is still unknown who initiated this action. If the original "dishonorable discharge" remained Oswald would have received a court-martial for treason and a prison sentence upon his return to the US. The mysterious reduction to an undesirable discharge meant that Oswald would not be tried in a military court for treason.

In Russia in March 1961, Oswald met Marina Prusakova, a nineteen year-old pharmacology student and they were married less than six weeks later in April. Marina was the niece of a high ranking KGB official. Oswald tried to use his wife's uncle to apply for an intelligence position with no success. Oswald's first child was born on February 15, 1962.

By May 24, 1962, Oswald had made no headway in Russia in obtaining a military or intelligence position and was still working in a factory. He decided to come back to the United States. He and Marina applied at the US Embassy in Moscow for documents and funds to enable both of them and their child to immigrate to the US. According to the Warren Report, on June 1, the US Embassy gave Oswald, the communist traitor, his full citizenship back without consequences and allowed him and his Soviet wife and child to travel to the US with a repatriation loan despite the fact that Oswald had committed treason and had given military secrets to the Russians. Oswald, Marina and their infant daughter left for the United States, where incredibly they received absolutely no attention from the either the government or the press. And more incredibly they were never interviewed or interrogated by the CIA or the FBI which was the law and standard operating procedure for any American who had been in the Soviet Union, let alone one who was a traitor and had given military secrets to the Russians. Oswald was never tried or punished for his traitorous acts.

There is no good reason why the CIA or FBI didn't interrogate and arrest him and put him on trial and send him to prison and even less reason for the State Department to give him his citizenship and pay for his and his Russian family's passage back to the United States. There is no apparent reason for his dishonorable discharge to be quietly changed to undesirable. There is only one likely reason they did these things. It was because Oswald was part of a failed CIA undercover mission.

There is much evidence to prove this. Oswald was stationed at Atsugi, Japan which was both a secret U-2 spy plane base and also hosted a CIA training school for spying on the Russians. Atsugi was only one station on Oswald's Far East intelligence route; he was also at the U-2 base at Subic Bay in the Philippines. (Among Oswald's possessions found and confiscated after his death was an undeveloped roll of film that was developed by Alan Weberman, researcher and author of the *Oswald Code*, under the Freedom of Information Act. It was a picture Oswald had taken in the Philippines of Gerald Patrick Hemming a Marine and CIA Agent posing with a dead communist guerilla that Hemming had just killed. It is another inexplicable thing for Oswald the supposed communist to do.

Oswald was also stationed for a short while at a base at Ping-Tung, Taiwan which is an intelligence center for spying on China. In May 1960, a U-2 was shot down over Russia and its pilot captured. The pilot, Francis Gary Powers, later angrily blamed his being shot down by the Russians on Lee Harvey Oswald and the classified information he gave to them.

In 1959, Oswald was transferred to the El Toro Marine Air Station as an instructor in radar surveillance, which required a Secret Security Clearance. His commanding officer had graduated from the Georgetown School of Foreign Service, which also has close CIA ties. It was while at this base that Oswald was given his Russian language training. Oswald clearly had the opportunity and proximity to be recruited and trained by the CIA both overseas and in the US.

When Lee and Marina Oswald arrived back in the US from the Soviet Union in June 1962, they moved to Ft. Worth, Texas where they were befriended by some three dozen anti-communist White Russians in the Dallas-Ft. Worth area. Many had jobs in the oil and defense industries. It was an improbable social set for a traitor and defector to the USSR and his Russian wife from Minsk. It is also another very odd thing for a supposed committed communist to do.

Oswald found a very unlikely friend and mentor in George de Mohrenschildt, a petroleum geologist and friend of George Herbert Walker Bush. In fact George H.W. Bush was also the roommate of de Mohrenschildt's nephew, Edward Hooker, at prep school in Massachusetts. De Mohrenschildt worked on many sensitive assignments for the US State Department and was a CIA asset who had worked with Bush, which made it more unlikely that he would befriend Oswald and Marina if Oswald really was a communist traitor. He and Oswald remained friends until Oswald's death. De Mohrenschildt adamantly stated that Oswald was not John Kennedy's assassin nor was he a communist. He was prepared to testify to Congress to these facts under oath. He was also writing a book about Oswald's innocence in the Kennedy assassination just before he died.

In another odd coincidence de Mohrenschildt was also a friend of the Bouvier family, including Jacqueline Bouvier Kennedy. His friendship with the family went as far back to when she was still a child. De Mohrenschildt was also a member of the rightwing Texas Crusade for Freedom and in addition to friendship with George H.W. Bush, he included among his friends the rightwing oil barons Clint Murchison and H.L. Hunt. Murchison was later tied to the Kennedy assassination by Lyndon Johnson's aide and mistress, Madeline Duncan Brown. De Mohrenschildt was an odd man to be affiliated with a communist traitor, unless of course Lee Harvey Oswald, like de Mohrenschildt, was also a CIA asset.

It was later learned during a trial, *Hunt v. Liberty Lobby*, that J. Lee Rankin, the Warren Commission's General Counsel, was told by a reliable source in January 1964 that it was common knowledge among journalists in Texas that Oswald had also received $200 per month from the FBI as an undercover agent for them. After Oswald's assassination, the name, address and private telephone number of an FBI agent was found among his papers according to research writer Mae Brussel.

In 1967, New Orleans District Attorney Jim Garrison interviewed George and Jeanne de Mohrenschildt as part of Garrison's ill-fated attempt to prosecute Clay Shaw in connection with the assassination of President Kennedy. Garrison said that both of the de Mohrenschildts insisted that Oswald had been "the scapegoat in the assassination of President Kennedy." These were the same words that Oswald had used while in detainment immediately after the death of Kennedy. Garrison concluded from his conversations with the couple that George de Mohrenschildt had been one of Oswald's CIA handlers, "baby-sitters ... assigned to protect or otherwise see to the general welfare" of Oswald after his failed Russian assignment.

In 1976, Congress formed the House Committee on Assassinations to look into the deaths of both Kennedys and Dr. King. George de Mohrenschildt was to be a key witness. During this time he became aware that all his phone conversations were being recorded and that he was under constant surveillance. He and his wife also felt threatened and his wife became very afraid. He wrote to his friend George Bush, who was then the Director of the CIA, asking for help as these harassments came from what he supposed were either the FBI or CIA and they were greatly disturbing his sick wife. Bush wrote back saying that he couldn't help.

Shortly thereafter de Mohrenschildt supposedly committed suicide while he was actively tape recording some soap operas for his wife who was out of the house at the time. A man committing suicide would not be in the middle of recording a soap opera. It is probable that he was killed before he could testify before the Committee to defend Oswald. His wife Jeanne de Mohrenschildt felt sure he was assassinated. She gave the House Committee on Assassinations Committee a copy of de Mohrenschildt's manuscript, *I Am a Patsy! I Am a Patsy!*, which he was writing to defend his friend Oswald.

The Committee released its conclusions in 1978. Some of the Committee's findings were disturbing: "Scientific acoustical evidence establishes a high probability that at least two gunmen fired at the President. Other scientific evidence does not preclude the possibility of two gunmen firing at the President. The committee believes, on the basis of the evidence available to it, that Kennedy was probably assassinated as a result of a conspiracy."

The Committee also felt that Oswald was a CIA Agent. The Committee heard from former CIA accountant James Wilcott, who testified that he had paid out money to an "Oswald project." The Committee also questioned why the US State Department paid for Oswald and Marina to return to the United States and why Oswald was never detained or arrested by the CIA or the FBI after his defection and treason as they normally would have done with any other defector, especially a defector who had prior military security clearance and who had given classified military secrets to the enemy.

In 2003, Robert Blakey, staff director and chief counsel for the Committee on Assassinations, issued a statement: "I no longer believe that we were able to conduct an appropriate investigation of the [Central Intelligence] Agency and its relationship to Oswald."

The Conspiracy

> "The committee believes, on the basis of the evidence available to it, that Kennedy was probably assassinated as a result of a conspiracy."—The Findings of the House Committee on Assignations 1978

The following statement is from the book *Plausible Denial, Was the CIA Involved in the Assassination of JFK?* It was written by the trial defense attorney Mark Lane. "In September 1963, the CIA, having planned to assassinate President Kennedy, established a false trail, a charade that would inexorably lead to Lee Harvey Oswald after the murder in Dallas. The plan was brilliantly conceived. Not only would it implicate an innocent man in the crime and thus spare the CIA from responsibility, but it would focus attention upon Oswald, a man with connections to the FBI. The FBI [connection] would freeze J. Edgar Hoover into inaction because of fear that his Bureau might be terminally embarrassed."

It would be easy to dismiss Lane and his work as another conspiracy book, except that Mark Lane is a highly respected lawyer and this book is about the classified documents, evidence, and sworn testimony of the CIA and government officials that Lane obtained during a 1983 libel trial in the US District Court of Miami involving E. Howard Hunt. It was called *Hunt v. Liberty Lobby*.

Hunt sued the *Liberty Lobby* magazine for libel after they wrote that he had been involved in the Kennedy assassination. Lane defended the magazine and won the case, showing that Hunt had indeed been involved in the Kennedy assassination, and in the process he uncovered a mountain of evidence showing that the CIA and the Mafia were also involved in the assassination.

Leslie Armstrong, the forewoman of the jury, said in conclusion, "Mr. Lane was asking us to do something very difficult. He was asking us to believe that John Kennedy had been killed by our own government. Yet when we examined the evidence, we were compelled to conclude that the CIA had indeed killed President Kennedy."

After Hunt's death his sons, Howard St. John Hunt and David Hunt, stated that before he died their father had tape recorded statements about himself and others who had been involved in the conspiracy to assassinate President John Kennedy. Hunt also wrote notes in addition to the audio recordings. In the April 5, 2007, issue of *Rolling Stone*, Howard St. John Hunt detailed a number of individuals purported to be implicated by his father in the Kennedy assassination including CIA agents Cord Meyer, David Phillips, Frank Sturgis, David Morales, William Harvey, and Lucien Sarti. He also said that Vice President Lyndon Johnson was involved. The two sons alleged that their father had cut the information from his previous memoirs to avoid lawsuits and possible perjury charges and harassment or assassination from the intelligence agencies. The audio tape of their father's deathbed confessions have been widely circulated on the internet.

Most of the CIA officers that Hunt named have also been named by others. Johnson, however, was a shock to some people. But, Johnson's longtime aide and mistress Madeleine Duncan Brown has also claimed this was true. Brown claimed to have been present at a party with Johnson at oil baron Clint Murchison's Dallas home on the evening prior to the assassination of Kennedy. She said those attending included J. Edgar Hoover, Richard Nixon, H.L. Hunt, George Brown and John Mc Cloy. According to Madeline Duncan Brown, Johnson met with several of the men in private after which he told her: "After tomorrow, those goddamn Kennedys will never embarrass me again. That's no threat. That's a promise." Brown said that Johnson later confirmed to her that there was a conspiracy to kill Kennedy, saying that those that plotted the assassination were "Texas oilmen and ... renegade intelligence bastards in Washington."

Another close friend of Johnson, Leo Janos, interviewed Johnson at his Texas ranch just before he died and in an article that appeared in *The Atlantic Monthly* in 1973, he said that Johnson had told him "that the assassination in Dallas had been part of a conspiracy."

Allen Dulles (who was fired by Kennedy as CIA Director after the Bay of Pigs fiasco) and John Mc Cloy were later appointed by Lyndon Johnson to the Warren Commission to investigate Kennedy's assassination. Dulles and

Mc Cloy insisted before any evidence was presented that it was Oswald and that he acted alone.

There are other statements that support the conspiracy and a cover up. Mob lawyer Frank Ragano in his 1994 memoir wrote that Tampa-based crime boss Santo Trafficante confessed to him in 1987 that he and Carlos Marcello, the mob boss of New Orleans, were also involved in the Kennedy assassination.

Col. L. Fletcher Prouty began his career in World War II as an intelligence officer and a pilot. He had several major assignments during the war, including being critically involved in the logistics and planning of both the top secret World War II high level allied conferences in Cairo and Tehran between Roosevelt, Churchill and Stalin. Col. Prouty also served as Chief of Special Operations for the Joint Chiefs of Staff under President Kennedy. In intelligence circles he was "a man in the know." Retiring as a Colonel in the US Air Force in 1964, he was then awarded one of the first three Joint Service Commendation Medals for his outstanding military and intelligence service. When he retired Prouty became a well-respected banker. L. Fletcher Prouty was a very knowledgeable about the CIA and was a very credible man. He was not a conspiracy theorist.

According to Prouty people within the intelligence and military establishment and other agencies of the United States government conspired to assassinate Kennedy. He maintained that their actions were a coup d'état to stop the President from taking actions against the CIA after the Bay of Pigs failure and because of Kennedy's firing of Allen Dulles and Richard Bissell. Prouty said the CIA was afraid that in Kennedy's second term that he would disband the CIA as he had threatened to do, and give intelligence back to the military. The previously mentioned Kennedy memo to the Joint Chiefs saying that the military would be responsible for Cold War operations confirmed their fears. J. Edgar Hoover had also learned from his illegal wiretapping of Kennedy's office that Kennedy also planned to replace him as Director of the FBI in his second term and Hoover passed on the conversation about the CIA with Kennedy's comments to "break the agency into a thousand pieces."

Prouty also claims that the CIA and Lansdale were furious over the Bay of Pigs Invasion. They and the Joint Chiefs of Staff were also angry that Kennedy had not invaded Cuba during the Cuban missile crisis. They considered Kennedy a weak link and a traitor in their war on communism. When Kennedy signed National Security Action Memorandum 263 ordering all American troops and CIA out of Vietnam within a year, it may have been the straw that broke the camel's back, according to Prouty. The CIA and military considered Kennedy to be weak and a Soviet appeaser for these actions.

Prouty stated that the assassination was ordered by Dulles and orchestrated by Edward Lansdale. In a review of photos taken during the assassination and shortly afterward both Prouty and General Victor Krulak, who both knew worked closely with Lansdale in the past have identified Lansdale in the infamous photographs of the supposed "three tramps" in front of the Dallas Book Depository at the time of the assassination. Two of the tramps in the photos have striking resemblances and were identified by a multiple people as CIA assets and future Nixon Watergate burglars, E. Howard Hunt and Frank Sturgis. Both Hunt on his death bed and Sturgis later confessed to being part of the plot to kill Kennedy. The third tramp is confused. He was identified by some as CIA man David Christ, but others have identified the third man as the mafia hit man Charles Harrelson, and some have identified him as Chauncey Holt another Mafia hit man. Harrelson admitted to being one of the tramps and being involved in the assassination but then later claimed that he was on drugs when he admitted it. His statements have led some to believe he recanted it out of fear of reprisal. Some have also claimed that there were actually six "tramps" in the area.

Marita Lorenz is a German woman who had a long affair with Fidel Castro. She was later recruited by the CIA to kill Castro. She testified in *Hunt v. Liberty Lobby* that she was a CIA asset and that she was part of group based in Miami that had various assignments dealing with the Cuba Project. She also had an affair with Frank Sturgis when they were both working for the CIA stationed in Miami. She testified in court that she was originally part of a team in November 1963 that included Sturgis and E. Howard Hunt that were sent to Dallas on a mission. She testified under oath that she did not know what the mission was until afterward as it was on a "need to know basis." She testified in court that they stayed at a Dallas hotel and that one of the people Sturgis and Hunt had met with at the hotel the night before the assassination was Jack Ruby (Rubenstein). She said she recognized Ruby afterward on television when he killed Oswald and knew he was the man who had met with Sturgis and Hunt.

While at the Dallas hotel she said she became spooked and didn't like hyper-secret atmosphere around the mission. She verbalized these reservations to Sturgis and Hunt and requested to return to Miami and she was allowed to do so. She flew back to Miami that night. The next day Kennedy was killed. Lorenz testified that when Sturgis returned to Miami that he told her "We killed Kennedy."

Jack Ruby (Rubenstein) was a small time mobster. He began working as a numbers runner for Al Capone in Chicago as a teen. He idolized mob boss Mickey Cohen and even dated Cohen's ex-girlfriend, Candy Barr, after Cohen was finished with her. In his memoir, *Bound by Honor*, Bill Bonanno, the son of New York Mafia boss Joseph Bonanno, said that he realized the Mafia was involved in the JFK assassination when Ruby appeared on television and killed Oswald. Bonanno knew Ruby as an associate of Chicago Mafia boss Sam Giancana and California mobster Mickey Cohen.

Mickey Cohen also owned an office building in California in 1946 where he gave free office space to a young lawyer running for Congress named Richard Nixon. One of Cohen's associates worked in the Nixon congressional campaign and helped Nixon with fundraising, particularly with Mob funding; he was Jack Rubenstein. Nixon has always claimed it was a different Jack Ruby.

The House Committee on Assassinations investigated Ruby and found that he "had a significant number of associations and direct and indirect contacts with underworld figures and the Dallas criminal element." It was also well known in Dallas that Ruby was the paymaster and managed a good number of corrupt Dallas police officers for organized crime, which is why he likely had access to kill Oswald in a place that was supposedly tightly secured away from the public by the Dallas Police.

A year after his conviction in March 1965 Ruby gave a brief televised news interview in which he stated: "Everything pertaining to what's happening has never come to the surface. The world will never know the true facts of what occurred, my motives. The people who had so much to gain, and had such an ulterior motive for putting me in the position I'm in, will never let the true facts come above board to the world."

Ruby had told Earl Warren, the Chair of the Warren Commission that he wanted to tell the truth but couldn't do it in Dallas. He begged him to go to Washington, DC, where he wanted to be protected by the government. According to Warren's investigator, Warren refused his request, saying he wouldn't likely be safe in Washington either.

Ruby was treated by the press as if he was crazy. According to an article in the *London Sunday Times* on August 24, 1974, not long before Ruby died, he told his psychiatrist Werner Teuter that the assassination was "an act of overthrowing the government." He also said that he knew "who had President Kennedy killed." He added: "I am doomed. I do not want to die. But I am not insane. I was framed to kill Oswald."

The man who forced Ruby to kill Oswald is most likely Carlos Marcello. He was the Mafia kingpin of Texas and Louisiana. In 2010, *Legacy of Secrecy* by Lamar Waldron, it was revealed that Carlos Marcello declared following about Kennedy's assassination, "Yeah, I had the son of a bitch killed. I'm glad I did. I'm sorry I couldn't have done it myself!"

Carlos Marcello lost a fortune in Cuba with Castro's revolution and was very involved with the CIA's Bay of Pigs Operation and CIA intelligence in Cuba. Some Cubans who remained in Cuba were still on his payrolls after the revolution and he had excellent intelligent sources inside Cuba. He also shared these resources with the CIA. It was Carlos Marcello with his Cuban contacts who was given a contract by the CIA to kill Castro. Marcello and Jack Ruby had also managed a gun running operation to Cuba for many years. Marcello blamed Castro for the loss of his lucrative gambling operations in Cuba and Kennedy for the failed Bay of Pigs invasion to take the country away from Castro. He also hated Attorney General Robert Kennedy for his aggressive prosecution of the Mafia and organized crime.

Senior CIA official Victor Marchetti would later tell Congress of the CIA-Mafia connections, "It goes all the way back to the predecessor organization OSS and its involvement with the Italian mafia, the Cosa Nostra in Sicily and Southern Italy." *Rolling Stone* investigative reporter Howard Kohn has also written about these connections and how the OSS/CIA and Mafia cooperation had started during World War II in Italy and on the docks of the East coast. In 1948, the newly created CIA partnered with the Unione Corse, the so-called French Mafia, operating in Marseille to break up a dockworker's strike because they thought it was communist inspired. The CIA would also later partner with the Unione Corse and the American Mafia in Southeast Asia in the drug trade to finance their secret war in Laos.

Before becoming governor of New York and a presidential candidate, Thomas Dewey was a US attorney and a district attorney in New York City where his biggest success as a prosecutor was putting Mafia chieftain Lucky Luciano behind bars. Luciano was Meyer Lansky's mentor. When Dewey was New York Governor during World War II, he was asked to make a deal on behalf of the US government and the OSS to grant a parole for Luciano in exchange for the Mafia's assistance to the OSS and Naval Intelligence in Italy. The assistance involved helping with the invasion of Sicily and Italy and also involved using the Mafia-controlled dock workers in New York and other east coast ports to guard against Nazi saboteurs. This was very beneficial to the Mafia because in gaining control of the docks it also allowed them to expand their growing drug smuggling trade with government impunity.

In another interesting reference to the Kennedy assassination President Nixon also referred to the Kennedy assassination in the Watergate Tapes and another clue to solving the assassination was provided when Nixon told his Chief of Staff Bob Haldeman to call the CIA and ask for help on Watergate. "When you get these people, say, 'Look, the problem is that this will open the whole Bay of Pigs thing...'" In his memoir, Haldeman wrote that he believed "Bay of Pigs thing" was Nixon's coded way of referring to the CIA's connection in the JFK assassination plot which Nixon believed would then get the CIA to help cover up Watergate.

Haldeman also said that Nixon told him that Kennedy was killed in a conspiracy and wrote in his book: "After Kennedy was killed, the CIA launched a fantastic cover-up. Many of the facts about Oswald unavoidably pointed to a Cuban connection......In a chilling parallel to their cover-up at Watergate the CIA literally erased any connection between Kennedy's assassination and the CIA."

President Lyndon Johnson

Lyndon Johnson was one of the shrewdest politicians in American history. The three things that Johnson loved the most were politics, power and gossip. He was the one politician that could hold his own with J. Edgar Hoover. Unlike the Kennedys, Johnson wanted Hoover to remain in power. The two men were neighbors in Washington for many years and they each cultivated the other's friendship. Johnson condoned and encouraged Hoover's spying on Congress and as long as Hoover shared the information allowing Johnson to use it to his political advantage. Neither man had many moral scruples when it came to illegal wire taps or blackmail. They used each other. Johnson encouraged and expanded Hoover's illegal wiretapping activities especially on Johnson's political enemies.

Hoover was glad to be rid of the Kennedys, particularly Bobby, who was the first Attorney General to actually give Hoover any oversight. He also was aware that JFK would have sought his removal in his second term. Johnson and Hoover both shared a mutual hatred of the Kennedys.

When Johnson became president Hoover fawned over him giving the president the dirt on everyone in Washington. In exchange Johnson pushed through a new law allowing Hoover to continue in office after the mandatory retirement age of 70. Johnson had Hoover spy on all his political enemies especially Bobby Kennedy. He also approved of Hoover's spying on Dr. King and the Civil Rights Movement. To his credit, while Johnson had many reservations about the Civil Rights Movement, he did support civil rights. Johnson was also responsible for Hoover and the FBI's campaign against the Ku Klux Klan. Hoover had previously told his agents to not bother with the Klan or their terrorism, but under Johnson this changed.

After the three civil rights workers, Schwerner, Goodman and Cheney were murdered in Mississippi Johnson came under enormous pressure to do something. He told Hoover he would rather have the FBI go to war with the Klan rather than the alternative which was to place a division of the Army in Mississippi to keep the peace. He ordered Hoover to take action saying, "I don't want these Klansmen to open their mouths without your knowing what they're saying......I want you to have the same kind of intelligence that you have on the communists." Hoover understood that Johnson was asking the FBI to declare war on the Klan. It was perhaps the most altruistic moment in the careers of both Johnson and Hoover.

The two men also shared some darkly undemocratic moments. Johnson was a war hawk and he was also concerned with the growing anti-war movement. He strongly encouraged Hoover and the FBI to harass, confuse, and destroy the movement and the individuals involved by all means necessary. These efforts became part of a covert FBI operation called COINTELPRO.

Johnson's War

Upon taking office Johnson immediately cancelled Kennedy's National Security Memorandum 263 which had ordered an end of American presence in Vietnam. Johnson began immediately sending American troops and the CIA back into Southeast Asia. He needed an incident to get congressional support for his buildup in Vietnam and he used a phony attack on the US Navy in the Gulf of Tonkin to get Congress to pass a resolution allowing him to greatly expand the conflict.

On August 2, 1964, a destroyer, the USS Maddox, deliberately sailed too close to North Vietnam and was greeted by three North Vietnamese Torpedo boats. The Maddox then fired more than 280 rounds at the three boats and US aircraft strafed the boats killing four North Vietnamese sailors and wounding six others. The North Vietnamese boats fled and did return some fire but, only one round hit the destroyer and there were no US casualties.

Two days later on August 4, the National Security Agency, NSA, alleged a second attack by North Vietnamese boats on the US Navy. In this alleged second and much larger attack the US Naval vessels were never hit, nor were any enemy ships ever actually seen, nor did they sink any ships in their horrific return fire during this supposed battle. Johnson would later privately joke about the Gulf of Tonkin attack and say for all he knew the US Navy had actually fired at "flying fish."

In a highly classified NSA document that has since been declassified, it has been revealed that the USS Maddox actually initiated the first battle by firing upon the North Vietnamese boats provoking the incident. The document also revealed that the second supposed naval battle was a hoax and that no Vietnamese vessels were involved. Johnson used these two supposed attacks to persuade Congress to declare war in Vietnam. In the wake of these alleged attacks Johnson's build up was rapid and by 1965 Johnson had about a half million US troops in Vietnam.

The Dominican Republic

A civil war also flared up in the Dominican Republic in 1965. A right-wing junta with support by the CIA overthrew the government of Juan Bosch, the first freely elected government of the Dominican Republic. However the junta's brutal tactics rallied the nation against them and it ignited the Dominican leftists. Johnson told the Congress and the press that it was a communist uprising and he claimed that the Soviets and the Cubans were behind the revolt and were pushing for a communist takeover. He told the Congress that did not want another Western hemisphere nation to go communist on his watch.

Bosch had fled to San Juan, Puerto Rico where he was immediately put under electronic surveillance by Hoover and the FBI. Bosch began to seek the help of any one, including some communists, to bring back his democratically elected government. Hoover relayed Bosch's efforts to Johnson.

It was also power play by Hoover. The CIA was still smarting over their failed intelligence in Cuba and elsewhere and Johnson was more than aware of their limitations. He trusted Hoover and the two men began to hatch a plot to take over the government of the Dominican Republic with the FBI in the lead role and the CIA as a junior partner.

Johnson told Hoover that the Dominican Republic was now his responsibility but warned that he had better make it a priority "unless you want to have another Castro." Hoover understood that if he was successful that he would become Johnson's intelligence czar, but he was also aware that if he failed Johnson would quickly blame him.

Hoover recruited Joaquín Balaguer who had served as the puppet President under the dictatorship of Rafael Trujillo. He persuaded Johnson that this was the perfect man to run the Dominican Republic. The State Department vetted him and Johnson approved. Johnson sent the Marines into the Dominican Republic under the guise of protecting Americans. Hoover and Johnson set up a "provisional government" saying that free elections would be held in a short time.

The election between Balaguer and Bosch was a fraud. Johnson ordered the CIA to provide enough cash and support, including black operations against the Bosch supporters, to assure Balaguer's election. The final result was 57 percent for Balaguer to 39 percent for Bosch. Johnson picked and Hoover vetted all of the people in Balaguer's government including his Supreme Court. Balaguer was another American supported dictator who would serve for the next twelve years.

Operation MOCKINGBIRD

> "We'll know our disinformation program is complete when everything the American public believes is false."—William Colby former CIA Director

> "Woe to that nation whose literature is cut short by the intrusion of force. This is not merely interference with freedom of the press but the sealing up of a nation's heart, the excision of its memory."—Aleksandr Solzhenitsyn

> "The press was to serve the governed, not the governors. The Government's power to censor the press was abolished so that the press would remain forever free to censure the Government. The press was protected so that it could bare the secrets of government and inform the people."—Supreme Court Justice Hugo Black

One of the supposed strengths of the American democracy is the free press, which as it turns out isn't that free. Operation MOCKINGBIRD was and is an on-going secret campaign by the CIA to influence or intimidate the media by placing false stories in the press, to discredit legitimate stories in the press, influence press and public opinions, and to blackmail and discredit journalists who don't cooperate. The operation also spread CIA lies and propaganda as the truth. It began in the 1950s. It was initially organized by Cord Meyer and Allen Dulles. It was later managed by Frank Wisner after Dulles became the head of the CIA. The Operation recruited many leading American journalists and cajoled, paid or bribed them into presenting the CIA's views, false stories and lies or prevented them from writing stories that the Agency did not want the public to see. The CIA has also funded many student and cultural organizations and magazines as fronts.

It is highly effective—as the quote by former CIA Director William Colby at the beginning of this topic indicates. The CIA also strongly influences the electronic media and the motion picture industry. As Operation MOCKINGBIRD developed, it also worked to influence the foreign media and eventually began to infiltrate and influence both foreign and domestic political campaigns. The assassination of uncooperative foreign press was also part of the operation. As we shall see, they have likely assassinated American journalists as well.

In 1953, Operation MOCKINGBIRD was known to have had a major influence over more than two dozen prominent newspapers and the wire services in the United States, according to Carl Bernstein in *Rolling Stone Magazine*. Their usual methodology was placing "stories or reports," true or not, with "their reporters" or to unwitting reporters. Those reports would then be repeated or cited by many other CIA-influenced newspapers and reporters, which in turn would then be cited throughout the media and wire services, making many things that were not true seem to be the truth because they were reported by so many media sources.

The CIA was also involved in the movies, influencing and changing manuscripts and films. In 1954, Wisner arranged for the complete funding of the Hollywood production of *Animal Farm*, the animated allegory based on the book written by George Orwell, as a propaganda tool to teach the American public about the horrors of communism. He actually changed Orwell's story to make communists the key culprit. The money Wisner used was secretly siphoned off and stolen from the Marshall Plan. The CIA also used other Marshall Plan monies to support the Gehlen Organization and black operations in Europe.

According to Alex Constantine in *Mockingbird: The Subversion Of The Free Press By The CIA*, "some 3,000 salaried and contract CIA employees in the press were eventually engaged." Details of Operation MOCKINGBIRD were revealed as a result of the Church Committee's investigations into the abuses of the CIA in 1975. The Church Committee said that "misinforming" the United States and the world was then costing the American taxpayers an estimated $265 million a year.

The extent of MOCKINGBIRD may never be known as the Ford Administration actively frustrated the Church Committee in their investigations. There were many other things that the CIA needed to hide from the Congress and the public. On January 16, 1975, President Gerald Ford hosted a luncheon at the White House for the senior editors and the publisher of the *New York Times*. His intention was to have the newspapers and the media back off from stories about the CIA's abuses that we coming to light from the Church Committee. He persuaded them that any investigation into the CIA could divulge things that would wreck the reputations of every president since Eisenhower. When an editor asked "Like what?" Ford replied. "Like assassinations."

Ford and his administration were determined to keep the Congress and the people from knowing the truth about the CIA. In a conversation with Donald Rumsfeld, his chief of staff, Ford said, "The question is how to plan to meet the investigation of the CIA?" Rumsfeld then pledged to the president that he would mount "a damage-limiting campaign for the President."

Vice President Rockefeller was then appointed by Ford and put in charge of a commission to look into CIA abuses and possible CIA links to the Kennedy assassination. The Commission's real purpose was to cover up CIA abuses and to whitewash them. It was also determined by Ford and his advisors that CIA Director William Colby was too soft and, according to Secretary of Defense James Schlesinger, he was being "too damn cooperative with the Congress." Colby was directed by the White House to keep his testimony to generalities and to avoid specifics. They told him that the future of the CIA was in his hands and to act accordingly. After this meeting Colby ordered the Agency to destroy all secret CIA files that could prove damaging to the Agency including MOCKINGBIRD and project MK-ULTRA, the mind control experiments.

Henry Kissinger and Donald Rumsfeld then drafted a memo to the Church Committee proposing to have Colby brief the Committee but not under oath—in other words, he would lie. The Committee refused this request. Colby was forced to testify under oath, but his testimony was rehearsed and practiced well in advance. These rehearsals were led by the White House staff, particularly Henry Kissinger and Donald Rumsfeld.

Despite his bland non-revealing testimony, Ford and his advisors were still not happy with Colby. He was shortly afterward replaced by George H.W. Bush, who Ford and the advisors felt would better keep secret the illegal activities of the CIA.

In February 1976, in response to the investigations by Congress and the Church Committee into Operation MOCKINGBIRD, George H.W. Bush, the recently appointed Director of the CIA, suddenly announced a new policy to head off the investigation and stated, "Effective immediately, the CIA will not enter into any paid or contract relationship with any full-time or part-time news correspondent accredited by any US news service, newspaper, periodical, radio or television network or station." However, Bush also ominously added that the CIA would continue to welcome the "voluntary unpaid cooperation of journalists" and the CIA's secret influence over the press, and Operation MOCKINGBIRD continued.

Operation MOCKINGBIRD has most likely changed names but it was never ended, and the illegal and immoral oversight and abuses of the press and media continues. The coercion, threats and intimidation of the press remained the same before and after the Church Committee.

The damage by Operation MOCKINGBIRD is on-going. The Operation was in full force in 1972, when the CIA was interfering with publishers and trying to stop the publication of a book, *The Politics of Heroin in Southeast Asia*, by Alfred McCoy. And Operation MOCKINGBIRD was still functioning in force in 1996, when Gary Webb was wrote his *Dark Alliance* series of articles for the *San Jose Mercury News* (later published as a book). In the three-part newspaper series Webb investigated Nicaraguans who were linked to the CIA and who were backed by the Contras that were smuggling cocaine into the US to pay for Contra operations — with the full knowledge of the CIA.

The drug smuggling and the sale of drugs in the US was encouraged and directly aided by the CIA. Their smuggled cocaine was mostly distributed as crack in California.

When Webb's series was published, the CIA harassed and intimidated the *San Jose Mercury News* who eventually fired Webb and then also backed away from his story, causing the entire media to doubt to the credibility of Webb's journalism and the story. The mainstream media wouldn't touch the story. The CIA then continued to destroy Webb's personal credibility and effectively ended his career as a mainstream media journalist. Webb became unemployable because of CIA lies, threats and intimidation.

In 2004, Webb was found dead from not one but two gunshot wounds to the face, which was suspiciously called a suicide. The suicide was even more suspicious because Webb was moving ahead with his life and was in the middle of moving into a new apartment when the alleged suicide occurred.

Just before his death he had told a friend that he knew some people were watching him. Some of his neighbors concurred and had also said that "government people" had been hanging around his apartment building the day of his suicide. It was all too suspicious. Who were these government people? A man in the middle of moving is not likely to commit suicide. People don't commit suicide by shooting themselves in the face, and twice in the face is incredibly unbelievable.

Although Webb's "Dark Alliance" series was criticized and his journalism questioned, Webb and his reporting were eventually vindicated and all his findings have since been validated by other journalists and government sources. Since his death, both the *Los Angeles Times* and the *Chicago Tribune* have strongly defended the *Dark Alliance* series and Webb's journalism. The CIA and the US government eventually admitted to even more horrors and drug running than Gary Webb had attributed to them in his articles.

The CIA inspector general released a report where the investigative team admitted that CIA assets had indeed smuggled, sold and traded in cocaine and crack and that the CIA had also pressured the Department of Justice and other agencies such as the DEA and FBI to drop or suspend their own drug-related investigations into their drug smuggling and sales. They also admitted that all of these drug sales were to fund illegal CIA operations in Latin America, particularly the Contras, as previously reported by Webb.

One of the areas hardest hit by this cocaine epidemic was Los Angeles, which prompted Congresswoman Maxine Waters to tell the *Los Angeles Times* in 1997, "It doesn't matter whether the CIA delivered the kilo of cocaine themselves or turned their back on it to let somebody else do it. They're guilty just the same."

In the entry of the CIA Headquarters at Langley, Virginia, is a quote that greets all visitors: "And ye shall know the truth and the truth shall set you free." It is another CIA lie. Unfortunately, the CIA shows very little regard for the truth or freedoms, especially freedom of the press.

The Civil Rights Movement

> "The way Martin Luther King was hounded and harassed is a disgrace to every American."—Vice President Walter Mondale

> "Half a century ago, the amazing courage of Rosa Parks, the visionary leadership of Martin Luther King, and the inspirational actions of the civil rights movement led politicians to write equality into the law and make real the promise of America for all her citizens."—David Cameron, British Prime Minister

The modern civil rights movement started on May 17, 1954, when the Supreme Court handed down its decision *Brown v. Board of Education of Topeka, Kansas* in which they concluded that the education of Black children in separate public schools from their White counterparts was unconstitutional. The Court then ordered segregation to be phased out over time "with all deliberate speed."

Greensboro, North Carolina, became the first city in the South to publicly announce that it would abide by the Supreme Court's *Brown v. Board of Education* ruling on May 18, 1954. Greensboro School Board Superintendent Benjamin Smith said, "It is unthinkable that we will try to ignore the laws of the United States."

Unfortunately, others were not as lawful. In many Southern states like Alabama, Arkansas, Mississippi, Georgia and Virginia there was massive resistance. In Virginia, some counties closed their public schools rather than integrate, and many Christian private schools were opened to accommodate White students who used to attend public schools across the South. This bigotry became the foundation for the "school choice" and "charter school" movements that have been pushed by the American right and the Republicans.

After the *Brown v. Board of Education* decision the Southern states either refused to integrate or put impediments in the way of school desegregation. In 1957, these issues came to a head in Little Rock, Arkansas when nine exceptional Black students were chosen to attend the all-White public Central High School. They were chosen because of their excellent grades and good conduct. The vehemence of the White community in Little Rock against these children was so hateful and violent that President Eisenhower had to deploy the 101st Airborne Division to Little Rock to protect the nine students. Little Rock then closed its public school system completely rather than continue to integrate. Other school systems across the South followed suit.

Although President Eisenhower backed the Supreme Court he was a reluctant participant in desegregation. While the Brown decision was pending he defended White Southerners and said to Supreme Court Justice Earl Warren, "These are not bad people they just want to see that their little White girls are not required to sit in school alongside some big Black bucks." Eisenhower, a Texan, was also against inter-racial dating and marriage.

On December 1, 1955, Rosa Parks refused to give up her seat on a public bus in Montgomery, Alabama to a white man. Parks was secretary of the Montgomery NAACP chapter and had recently returned from a meeting in Tennessee where nonviolent civil disobedience as a strategy had been discussed. Parks was arrested, tried, and convicted for disorderly conduct and violating a local ordinance. After word of this incident reached the black community, fifty African-American leaders gathered and organized the Montgomery Bus Boycott to demand that the public bus system treat their passengers equally.

Dr. Martin Luther King Jr., a young Baptist minister, was the president of the Montgomery Improvement Association, the organization that directed the boycott. The lengthy protest eventually forced the City of Montgomery to give into their demands when it became apparent that the bus system would collapse without the support and fares of Black riders. The bus boycott attracted national attention for King. His eloquent speeches and appeals for Christian brotherhood and American idealism and his nonviolent methods created a positive impression with Blacks and Whites, and King soon found himself the national leader of the modern civil rights movement.

King's civil rights movement began to use a variety of nonviolent methods of confrontation, including sit-ins, kneel-ins at local churches, and marching en masse to the county courthouse to mark the beginning of a drive to register voters. The city of Montgomery obtained a local court injunction barring all of these types of protests. King said that the court order was unconstitutional and that it violated their freedoms of speech and assembly. King and his followers defied it and prepared for their inevitable mass arrests. King was arrested in a protest on April 12, 1963. The local authorities feared King. While in jail, King wrote his famous *Letter from a Birmingham Jail* on the margins of a newspaper because he was not allowed any writing paper while he was held in solitary confinement in the jail. Civil rights leaders and supporters across the nation appealed his incarceration to the Kennedy administration. The President and his brother Bobby, the Attorney General, intervened to obtain King's release and on April 19 he was released.

In 1960, United States Supreme Court decision *Boynton v. Virginia* ruled that segregation was unconstitutional for passengers engaged in interstate travel. In response to the ruling a protest called the Freedom Riders emerged. Freedom Rides were journeys taken by Civil Rights activists on interstate buses into the segregated South to test the new law. The first Freedom Ride of the 1960s left Washington D.C. on May 4, 1961, and was scheduled to arrive on May 17, in New Orleans.

In Birmingham, Alabama, an FBI informant reported that Public Safety Commissioner Eugene "Bull" Connor told Klan members he would give the Klan fifteen minutes to attack an incoming group of Freedom Riders before he would allow the police to intervene. The riders were very severely beaten. James Peck, a White rider, was beaten so badly that he required fifty stitches to his head. Kenneth O'Reilly, in his book *Racial Matters: The FBI's Secret File on Black America, 1960–1972*, wrote, "Aware of the planned violence weeks in advance, the FBI did nothing to stop it and had actually given the Birmingham police the details regarding the Freedom Rider's schedule, knowing full well that at least one law enforcement officer relayed everything to the Klan."

J. Edgar Hoover was a racist bigot. He greatly disliked the civil rights movement and insisted until he died that it was communist inspired. Anthony Summers in his biography of Hoover, *Official and Confidential*, wrote, "In the FBI's oppression of civil rights activists and liberals, Hoover's personal venom comes into focus. His rage over the award of the Nobel Peace Prize to Martin Luther King Jr., was the greater because for years previously, he had indulged the conceit that he himself deserved the Prize."

In 1963, when *Time* magazine named King the "Man of the Year," Hoover was furious and wrote, "They had to dig deep in the garbage to come up with this one."

Despite never finding any evidence to support his bias, Hoover continued to insist that King was a communist and that the civil rights movement was a Soviet inspired communist plot. And he insisted forcefully that his subordinates and agents never contradict him on the subject by word or report. He also persistently insisted that his agents uncover the communist plot and to find the communist connections. Summers wrote of one of these attempts, "When Edgar refused to accept solid research showing the Civil Rights movement was not, as he had insisted, Communist-inspired, an Assistant Director simply admitted humbly that his report had been 'wrong.'"

J. Edgar Hoover and COINTELPRO

"COINTELPRO was a program of subversion carried out not by a couple of petty crooks but by the national political police, the FBI, under four administrations... It was aimed at

the entire new left, at the women's movement, at the whole
Black movement, it was extremely broad. Its actions went as
far as political assassination."—Noam Chomsky

The CIA wasn't the only intelligence agency with rightwing and fascist tendencies. It also wasn't the only agency that violated American's constitutional rights or controlled the media. COINTELPRO was an FBI acronym for a counterintelligence program operating from 1956 to 1971. This is the program that expanded and enlarged Hoover's illegal Responsibilities Program that operated from 1951 to 1955. It was a series of covert and illegal projects conducted by the FBI aimed at surveying, infiltrating, discrediting, and disrupting domestic political organizations. It was a war against the left. FBI records show that COINTELPRO resources targeted all groups and individuals that Hoover deemed "subversive," which included organizations and individuals associated with: the Civil Rights Movement and Dr. King, the Southern Christian Leadership Conference, the NAACP, and the Congress of Racial Equality, the Black Power Movement, the Farm Workers and Latino movements, the American Indian Movement, the Gay Rights and Women's Movements, and all groups, especially university and college groups, protesting the Vietnam War and atomic weapons, which Hoover said were all communists.

On February 28, 1955, J. Edgar Hoover sent a report to President Eisenhower warning of an eminent communist attack by communists within the United States. He said these attacks would involve the assassination of civilian, military and political leaders as well as attacks from "biological, chemical and radiological warfare." It was reminiscent of Hoover's failed May Day prediction and fiasco during the Red Scare in the 1920s. In the report Hoover told the president that the FBI had already made plans for this eventuality by making a list of 26,500 dangerous suspected leftists and communists who could be immediately arrested upon the president's command.

The list shamefully included the American prisoners of war from the Korean Conflict. Hoover told the president that many of these prisoners were likely brainwashed by the Chinese and were possibly Manchurian candidates ready to betray the country. Much of Hoover's information about this eminent communist attack came from Harvey Matusow, an FBI informant who had claimed to have infiltrated the top ranks of the communists and the KGB in America. Matusow testified in court and before Congress that the communists had infiltrated every corner of American society and were preparing for an attack. It was all false. He was later given forty-four months for perjury and wrote a book, *False Witness* about his perjured testimony on behalf of the FBI.

After delivering his report about the eminent attack Hoover told the President Eisenhower and the Attorney General that the FBI would now fight this communist menace on their dirty terms. His answer was COINTELPRO. According to Anthony Weiner in *Enemies*, President Eisenhower and Attorney General Herbert Brownell knew that it was illegal but they covertly approved of it and then to turn a blind eye to the operation.

In the initial startup of COINTELPRO Hoover issued personal directives beginning in 1956, which ordered FBI agents to do whatever was required to "expose, disrupt, misdirect, discredit, or otherwise neutralize" the activities of the left and these black-listed political movements and their leaders. It became standard procedure for FBI infiltrators to commit, encourage and push the organizations and targeted individuals into committing crimes or violence by their example. They also began planting false evidence claiming these groups had or planned to commit violence. In addition to inciting violence the FBI agents committed many other crimes, including jury tampering, planting incriminating evidence including weapons and drugs on innocent victims, as well as hiding and destroying any evidence that would prove the innocence of those deemed by Hoover and the FBI to be subversives.

In the Wounded Knee siege and the subsequent trial against the American Indian Movement the judge found the FBI's actions so egregious and illegal that he dismissed all charges. The presiding Judge Fred J. Nichols of the Federal District Court of South Dakota criticized the FBI and the prosecutors of being "more interested in convictions than in justice." He also said, "It is hard for me to believe that the FBI that I have revered so long, has stooped so low."

According to Ward Churchill in *The COINTELPRO Papers: Documents from the FBI's Secret Wars Against Dissent in the United States*, the FBI and local police departments at the FBI's specific encouragement, used a variety of illegal acts to undermine what they considered to be leftist movements. The FBI, like the CIA, had a media control and a press suppression campaign that also planted false media stories and published bogus leaflets and other publications in the name of the targeted groups. They forged correspondence and signatures, sent anonymous letters, and made anonymous telephone calls to discredit the leaders and the organizations. They spread misinformation about meetings and events. They set up pseudo movement groups run by FBI agents to recruit, manipulate, and destroy people attracted these causes. They also encouraged, manipulated, threatened and strong-armed parents, spouses, employers, landlords, public schools, colleges and university officials to discipline and rein in the activists.

The FBI and the local police at FBI encouragement abused the legal system to harass dissidents and make them appear to be criminals. They drugged people without their knowledge and placed them in sexual and other compromising positions. They planted false evidence, weapons and drugs on people to make it appear they were dealing drugs or committing other crimes. On many occasions the FBI agents and cooperating local police officers gave perjured testimony and presented fabricated evidence for false arrests and wrongful imprisonments. These actions were, as many leftist critics claimed at the time, "very Gestapo like."

The FBI also involved the IRS to discriminatorily enforce tax laws on individuals and organizations targeted by the Bureau for being "leftist" and they also used other government regulatory agencies against these activists and their organizations. They intimidated or recruited friends and relatives to act against or inform on the targeted individuals. They used trumped up local laws like fire and building codes and zoning laws to harass them. They used conspicuous surveillance to cause stress on their targets and they harassed these individuals and their families and friends with what they called "investigative interviews." They used grand jury subpoenas to intimidate and scare activists and their families and to silence their supporters. They also conducted illegal break-ins in order to search dissident homes and committed vandalism to their properties and encouraged local police officers to assault, beat and even assassinate their targets.

The program was successfully kept a secret until 1971, when a group of citizen activists broke into an FBI field office in Pennsylvania and took their records and several dossiers. They then exposed the illegal program by giving this information to the news agencies.

In 1975, the Church Committee investigated the FBI and COINTELPRO. A partial summary of their findings is as follows: "Many of the techniques used would be intolerable in a democratic society even if all of the targets had been involved in violent activity, but COINTELPRO went far beyond that...the Bureau conducted a sophisticated vigilante operation aimed squarely at preventing the exercise of First Amendment rights of speech and association, on the theory that preventing the growth of dangerous groups and the propagation of dangerous ideas would protect the national security and deter violence."

The Church Committee found many COINTELPRO documents concerning numerous cases of the FBI preventing and disrupting protests against the Vietnam War. They uncovered many crimes and the illegal techniques that the agents and local police had committed against innocent individuals on behalf of the FBI. These illegal methods included: using undercover agents to create violent splits and fights among antiwar groups, creating phony counter demonstrations, and committing violence and encouraging violent confrontations by others, and by using the local police to commit violence and to disrupt peaceful demonstrations.

The Committee concluded: "The Constitutional system of checks and balances has not adequately controlled intelligence activities. Until recently the Executive branch has neither delineated the scope of permissible activities nor established procedures for supervising intelligence agencies. Congress has failed to exercise sufficient oversight, seldom questioning the use to which its appropriations were being put."

CHAPTER 10. THE 1960S, ASSASSINATING THE NEW LEFT

> "The ultimate measure of a man is not where he stands in moments of comfort and convenience, but where he stands at times of challenge and controversy."—Dr. Martin Luther King Jr.

> "Without censorship, things can get terribly confused in the public mind."—General William Westmoreland the US Commander in Vietnam speaking about the Vietnam War

> "The real 1960s began on the afternoon of November 22, 1963. It came to seem that Kennedy's murder opened some malign trap door in American culture, and the wild bats flapped out."—Lance Morrow *Time* Magazine

> "Fascism is capitalism plus murder."—Upton Sinclair

Hoover started COINTELPRO in 1954 because of his opposition to the Civil Rights Movement and his disdain for the American left. As the 1960s emerged, Hoover became more concerned about a variety of new "leftist" and protest movements that began to arise. Hoover greatly disliked how America was changing.

The dissatisfaction with American norms among the new left started with Jack Kerouac and the Beat writers in the 1950s and the Beatniks. Kerouac's book *Dharma Bums* was the work that most inspired this movement. The counterculture evolved into the 1960s Hippie movement. As American mainstream society became more rightwing and conformist in their views, a small section of the populace and many young people began to question those norms. They questioned societal racial prejudice, sexual and drug taboos, war and peace issues, American imperialism, the divide between poverty and wealth, and they even questioned America's strongest cultural truisms, Christianity and capitalism. They looked at Eastern philosophy as an alternative to Western religion. They championed communalism over individualism and people over materialism. This questioning by the young and this "new left" encouraged every group that was not receiving their fair and equitable share of American liberty and prosperity to begin to question why, and these groups then began to organize and demand fair treatment.

The Black civil rights movement gave birth to Native American, Latino, and Asian-American civil rights movements. Women's rights came to the fore, especially after July 25, 1968, when Pope Paul VI issued a Papal encyclical, Humanae Vitae, against family planning and banned birth control and abortions. Pollution and the growing concern about the deteriorating natural environment caused by man and his machines gave birth to the green and ecology movement.

The Johnson and Nixon administrations and the FBI and the American right fought to suppress these new movements, but these movements began to find support among the young and what little remained of the American left. However, the issue that gave the most strength to the new American left in the 1960s was the anti-war movement against the Vietnam War.

Most Americans were never really sure why we were at war in Vietnam. President Eisenhower told the nation that it was like dominoes. He said that if Vietnam fell to communism, then all of Southeast Asia would fall. Many Americans, even those that believed in this domino theory, wondered why they should care anyway. Vietnam was far away and presented no threat.

Television didn't help the government's case. Viewers watched young American soldiers being killed on their television sets during the dinner time news in an ill-defined war and they were appalled. They also saw Buddhist monks immolating themselves, protesting the repressive and dictatorial government that America was supporting, and wondered why? They saw a little naked girl crying and running down a road from napalm bombs made by American factories that were being dropped by American planes. They saw a South Vietnamese police chief executing a defenseless man by shooting him in the head on a Saigon street and they watched in horror in their living rooms as the blood spurted from his head onto the pavement. They heard the young boys that were drafted and sent to Vietnam saying that the vast majority of Vietnamese didn't support or want them there. They watched tons of bombs falling on North Vietnam, killing tens of thousands of people, with an American General, Curtis Le May saying that "We will bomb them into the stone age."

Americans heard stories of horrific acts and atrocities committed by Americans, like My Lai and Operation Phoenix where women and children were indiscriminately killed and tortured. And these things made Americans question the validity of the war and the intentions of their government. Americans also began to see that their government was lying to them about the war, its purpose, and its likelihood of success. In the end it had all been for nothing. The service of the hundreds of thousands of young men who were forced to go to war was for nothing. All the deaths and casualties on both sides were also for nothing. Vietnam moved in the same direction that it would have had the US not made war there.

1968: The Death of the New Left

> "The American Dream has run out of gas. The car has stopped. It no longer supplies the world with its images, its dreams, its fantasies. No more. It's over. It supplies the world with its nightmares now: the Kennedy assassination, Watergate, Vietnam."—J.G. Ballard, English writer

> "The accumulation of all powers, legislative, executive, and judiciary, in the same hands ... is the definition of tyranny."—James Madison

> "A nation with the strength and determination to rise and demand an investigation into the Death of President Kennedy — as well as the deaths of Robert Kennedy and Martin Luther King – will have the strength to survive and prosper."—Col. L. Fletcher Prouty

Nineteen sixty-eight was a pivotal year in American history. The Vietnam War was at its peak, as was the anti-war movement. Senator Eugene McCarthy, an anti-war Senator from Minnesota, had almost beaten President Johnson in the New Hampshire Democratic Presidential Primary. President Johnson sensed his time was over and was worried he would be embarrassed in an election. He unexpectedly announced that he would not seek a second term in office. After Johnson's announcement Robert Kennedy and Hubert Humphrey decided to run for the Democratic nomination for president in addition to McCarthy. In the Republican race Nixon, Reagan, Rockefeller and George Romney decided to run. Rightwing assassinations and treason would determine the outcome.

On January 21, the battle for Khe Sanh, one of the most publicized and controversial battles of the Vietnam War, began and didn't end until April 8. This battle, along with the Tet Offensive, destroyed any notion that America was winning the Vietnam War. The Tet Offensive began on January 30, and the US Embassy in Saigon, which was thought to be safe and secure, was attacked on the last day of January. Recovering the lost ground from the Tet Offensive cost the US military a year of bloody combat. Americans began to think that there was no end to this confusing conflict. The Tet Offensive raised grave doubts about the war with a majority of Americans and this majority began to doubt the truthfulness of their government and its military leaders. It was called the "credibility gap."

On January 22, North Korea seized an American vessel, the USS Pueblo, claiming the ship had violated its territorial waters while spying. In truth the North Koreans were testing to see if the US, now bogged down heavily in Vietnam, would respond to North Korean aggression and defend the South. The US responded with Operation Combat Fox, adding more than 38,000 troops to its existing forces in South Korea in a very short period of time. This dissuaded the North Koreans from further aggression. America told the North Koreans they would defend the South and retaliate in kind.

Although President Johnson edged out antiwar candidate Eugene McCarthy on March 12, in the New Hampshire Democratic Primary, he knew it was the end of his presidency. On March 31, he announced that he would not seek a second term.

The My Lai massacre occurred on March 16, and American troops killed scores of old men, women and young children for no apparent reason. However, this incident would be covered up by the Army and would not become public knowledge until November 1969.

All through April and May, university students staged sit-ins and takeovers of university administration offices in protest of the Vietnam War. In May, a Selective Service office in Maryland was vandalized and protestors took dozens of draft records and burned them with napalm to protest against the Vietnam War.

The United States Defense Department announced on October 14 that the US Army and the Marines would send about 24,000 troops back to Vietnam for involuntary second tours. The CIA's Operation Phoenix, which had actually been operating covertly for some time, was "officially" established on July 1, in Vietnam. A joint CIA and US Army operation, Operation Phoenix was responsible for killing and torturing hundreds of thousands of Vietnamese men, women and children. The covert counterinsurgency program that had been operating since 1965 was folded into it.

In other events:

- On February 8, a civil rights protest at a Whites-only bowling alley in South Carolina was broken up by highway patrolmen and three college students were killed.

- Dr. Martin Luther King Jr. was assassinated on April 4 at the Lorraine Hotel in Memphis, Tennessee. Riots erupted in many major cities and even in some military units, lasting for several days.

- A shootout between the Black Panthers and the Oakland Police occurred on April 6, and resulted in arrests and several deaths, including a sixteen-year-old boy who was unarmed and in police custody.

- On April 11, President Johnson signed the Civil Rights Act of 1968.

- On June 5, US presidential candidate Robert Kennedy was assassinated just after giving a victory speech in Los Angeles, California. The California victory and the projected victory in his then home state of New York likely would have assured him of the Democratic nomination for president. Kennedy died the next day.

- Pope Paul VI issued a Papal encyclical on July 25, 1968, *Humanae Vitae*, banning birth control and abortions and splitting Catholics and giving urgency to the Women's movement.

- The Republican National Convention was held August 5–8, at Miami Beach, Florida. They nominated Richard Nixon for President with Spiro Agnew as his Vice President.

- Bloody riots occurred August 22 through 30 at the Democratic Convention; this was later determined to be a police riot. The Democrats nominated Hubert H. Humphrey for President and Edmund Muskie as Vice President. The police riot and Humphrey's support of the Vietnam War greatly hurt his chances of becoming president.

Citing progress in the Paris Peace Talks, President Johnson announced to the nation that he had ordered a complete cessation of "all air, naval, and artillery bombardment of North Vietnam" effective November 1, 1968. Many Americans were skeptical because this was proposed right before the presidential elections.

The King Assassination

> "For those of you who are Black and are tempted to be filled with hatred and mistrust of the injustice of such an act against all White people, I would only say that I can also feel in my own heart the same kind of feeling. I had a member of my family killed, but he was also killed by a White man."— Robert Kennedy on the Death of Martin Luther King.

According to Anthony Weiner in *Enemies*, just before Dr. Martin Luther King Jr. was assassinated J. Edgar Hoover wrote the following to his field agents: "The negro youth and moderates must be made to understand that if they succumb to revolutionary teaching, they will be dead revolutionaries." Dr. King was assassinated the next day on April 4, at the Lorraine Hotel in Memphis, Tennessee, at the age of thirty-nine. We are supposed to believe that James Earl Ray, an incompetent and ne'er-do-well petty thief was the lone assassin that plotted King's assassination. We are then asked to believe that this semi-literate man planned his own dramatic escape across the globe with forged passports. We are asked to believe that this devious master plan came from a man with very little education or ambition, and who lacked the where-with-all to accomplish this. The King family and a jury do not believe that Ray was the killer, and with good cause.

James Earl Ray was born to a poor family in Alton, Illinois. He was a poor student and quit school at fifteen and was at best semi-literate. He joined the Army at sixteen and served at the end of World War II. After the war Ray became an unsuccessful petty thief. He was not very bright and not an accomplished criminal. In 1949, he was convicted of bungled burglary and sent to jail. In 1952, he served two years in prison for the badly bungled armed robbery of a taxi driver. In 1955, he stole some money orders and stupidly attempted to cash them in his own name and went to prison for theft and mail fraud. In 1959, he robbed a Kroger Store of a paltry $120 and was convicted and sent to prison for twenty years. Ray was a not a very bright or successful petty thief. He was not a sophisticated killer who could plot jail breaks, a big time assassination, forge passports and plan a global getaway. This was a man who couldn't even successfully rob a cab driver.

In 1967, Ray supposedly cleverly escaped from prison in a prison bakery truck. Ray then moved from place to place settling in Alabama where the ne'er-do-well unsuccessful petty thief somehow obtained enough money to buy a new Ford Mustang and obtain a false driver's license. Ray claimed a man by the name of Raul, who he thought was a "government man," had helped him do all this. Ray claims he was taken by Raul to Los Angeles and was then paid by Raul to work volunteering at the "George Wallace for President" campaign headquarters in North Hollywood. On March 5, 1968, Ray somehow raised a significant amount of money and had a plastic surgeon perform rhinoplasty in secret to change his face. According to Ray, this was also arranged and paid for by Raul. On March 18, 1968, Ray left Los Angeles and began a cross-country drive to Atlanta, Georgia, where Raul told him to buy a map and get familiar with the city.

Then at Raul's instruction Ray drove his Ford Mustang to Birmingham, Alabama. On March 30, 1968, he said he was told by Raul to buy a hunting rifle and a box of 20 cartridges. On Raul's instruction he also bought a scope, which he had mounted on the rifle. He told the store clerks that he was going on a hunting trip with his brother. Ray had been using the name Galt, but when he made this purchase, he gave his name as Harvey Lowmeyer. He then returned to Atlanta. On April 2, 1968, Ray was told to pack a bag and drive to Memphis. King was assassinated there two days later.

After the assassination Ray fled north to Toronto, Canada, where he stayed for a month and then somehow acquired two forged Canadian passports, one under the false name of Ramon George Sneyd. At the airport check-in, the ticket agent noticed that the name on his passport, Sneyd, was on the Royal Canadian Mounted Police (RCMP) watch list and reported it to the RCMP. The RCMP still mysteriously allowed Ray to board the plane and flee. Ray then flew to Lisbon, Portugal and from there he flew on to London. At the airport in London immigration officials found that Ray was carrying another passport under a second name and he was detained. He was then identified by British authorities as James Earl Ray and shortly afterward he was extradited to the United States for the murder of Dr. King.

Ray confessed to the crime on March 10, 1969, and after pleading guilty was sentenced to 99 years in prison. Later Ray protested his guilty plea, claiming he only confessed under duress, and for several reasons. First, he said he was told by FBI agents that if he didn't confess that they would have his father and brother tried and convicted with him as accessories to the King murder. Second, the FBI told him that if he didn't confess he would be given a jury trial and if he was convicted he would be sentenced to death. Third, the FBI agents reasoned to Ray that he was facing a very long prison sentence for escaping from prison anyway, said if he confessed that they would help him get better treatment in prison. With this coercion Ray confessed.

Three days later he recanted his confession, but the Court had already entered a guilty plea on the advice of his attorney Percy Foreman, and they refused to reconsider. Ray later said that Foreman had also threatened that if he didn't confess, he would get the death penalty. Ray came to believe that Foreman was working "with the government." He fired Foreman as his attorney and thereafter derisively called him "Percy Four-flusher." Ray later became convinced that Foreman was working directly with the FBI. Ray claimed that he had been used as a patsy by the FBI, saying he did not "personally shoot Dr. King," but may have been "partially responsible without knowing it." Ray believed it was Raul and the FBI that killed King. Ray spent the remainder of his life unsuccessfully attempting to withdraw his guilty plea and to have a trial.

In 1997, King's son Dexter met with Ray and publicly supported his efforts to obtain a retrial. In 1998 the King family filed a wrongful death lawsuit against Lloyd Jowers and "other unknown co-conspirators" for the murder of Dr. King. In December 1993, Jowers, a Memphis restaurant owner, appeared on the ABC news show *Prime Time Live* and related the details of an alleged conspiracy involving the Mafia and the FBI to kill King. According to Jowers, Ray was a scapegoat, and not involved in the assassination. Jowers believed that Lieutenant Earl Clark, a Memphis police officer, fired the rifle that killed King. A Memphis jury found Jowers responsible for the death of King and on December 8, 1999, and the jury also found that the assassination plot also involved "governmental agencies." The King family accepted $100 in restitution, an amount they chose to show that they were not pursuing the case for any financial gain.

At a press conference in 1999, following the verdict, Coretta Scott King stated that "There is abundant evidence of a major high level conspiracy in the assassination of my husband, Martin Luther King, Jr... the conspiracy of the Mafia, local, state and federal government agencies, were deeply involved in the assassination of my husband. The jury also affirmed overwhelming evidence that identified someone else, not James Earl Ray, as the shooter, and that Mr. Ray was set up to take the blame."

Author and theologian Jim Douglass attended the trial and said afterward, "This historic trial was so ignored by the media and that apart from the courtroom participants I was the only person who attended it from beginning to end."

Ray died in prison on April 23, 1998, at the age of seventy. He was a very bitter man. He complained that the US government had lied and framed him. His brother Jerry Ray told CNN that James Earl Ray did not want to be buried in the United States because of "the way the government has treated him." Ray was cremated and his ashes were flown to Ireland, the home of his family's ancestors.

Considering what we now know about COINTELPRO and Hoover's blind hatred of King it is likely and perhaps probable that the FBI was involved in the King assassination. It is likely that the Mafia and local police were also involved. Hoover had personal connections to the Mafia that were revealed in Anthony Summer's biography of Hoover, *Official and Confidential.* Ray's story, Jowers' confessions and trial, and the King family's beliefs that the FBI, Mafia and the local police killed Dr. King are plausible. It has to be considered more likely in the light of the *New York Times* story and the re-printed letter in November 2014, revealing that the FBI had tried to blackmail King by threatening to reveal his sexual affairs to his wife and the public unless he committed suicide. It is apparent that Hoover and the FBI had sought King's death.

Dr. Martin Luther King Jr. gave rise to the Civil Rights Movement and inspired the American Indian Movement, the Women's Movement, the Latino and Asian rights movements, and the anti-War movement. He had just begun his campaign against poverty, and at the age of thirty-nine he was just entering his prime as a force in America. King's death was a rightwing assassination.

The Robert Kennedy Assassination

> "Anybody here seen my old friend Bobby?
> Can you tell me where he's gone?
> I thought I saw him walk up over the hill,
> With Abraham, Martin and John."

—Lyrics from the song *Abraham, Martin and John* written by Richard Holler, performed by Dion

Abraham Lincoln was the first American president assassinated in a rightwing plot and it is perhaps fitting that Richard Holler included him in his song *Abraham, Martin, and John* about the 1960s rightwing assassinations of JFK, MLK, and RFK. America has a long and sad history of rightwing assassins.

On June 5, Robert Kennedy was assassinated just after giving a victory speech in the California Democratic primary. The win likely assured him the Democratic nomination for president. Kennedy died the next day. In the aftermath of Bobby Kennedy's assassination J. Edgar Hoover wrote in a memo to his men that Kennedy's election would have been the end of Hoover's power.

The fatal bullet that killed Kennedy was to the back of the head, and Sirhan Sirhan who was supposedly the only gunman involved in the assassination was in front of him according to every witness. Cyril Wecht is a renowned forensic pathologist and one of two independent physicians who examined Kennedy's body. Wecht said the coroner in the RFK case gave "unchallenged, unequivocal" testimony to the grand jury that Kennedy had also been "shot from behind at close range." Every witness put Sirhan in front of Kennedy. The official record of events also contradicts the eyewitnesses' accounts of the assassination. The official record also deliberately and arbitrarily changed some of the witness' sworn statements.

In 2011, Sirhan's defense attorneys filed motions for a new trial, arguing he "should be freed from prison or granted a new trial based on 'formidable evidence,' asserting his innocence and 'horrendous violations' of his rights." At his parole hearing, on March 2, 2011, after forty-two years in prison, Sirhan testified that he continues to have absolutely no memory of the assassination or any memory of his 1969 trial and his confession. His attorneys and his psychiatrist claimed, as Sirhan's lawyers had claimed in the past, that Sirhan's mind was "programmed" and then "wiped" by an unknown conspiracy behind the assassination, which is why Sirhan still has no memory of the murder or of the aftermath even under deep hypnosis. His parole was again denied on the grounds that Sirhan still "does not understand the full ramifications of his crime."

On April 30, 2012, CNN ran a story, *Witness Claims Second Shooter*. They reported: "A key witness to the 1968 assassination of Robert F. Kennedy has retracted her official statements in the case and now claims that convicted assassin Sirhan Sirhan did not act alone."

Nina Rhodes-Hughes, told CNN that the FBI "twisted" her original statements to authorities. She said they deliberately changed her statements. "What has to come out is that there was another shooter to my right. The truth has got to be told. No more cover-ups." Rhodes said to CNN.

Rhodes says that her original FBI statement is not true that she only heard eight gunshots at the time, and the statement makes no mention of a second shooter that she had told the FBI and the police about. Rhodes, who was just feet away from Kennedy said, "I never said eight shots, I never, never said it. There were more than eight shots. There were at least twelve or maybe fourteen. And I know there were because I heard the rhythm in my head." Rhodes believes that she was never called as a witness during the trial because she told the FBI that there were more than twelve shots and a second shooter. Sirhan's pistol had a capacity of only eight bullets. The pieces of walls and door that would have proved how many bullets were fired were taken from the hotel as evidence and were then "accidently destroyed" according to the Los Angeles Police Department (LAPD).

A Kennedy campaign worker, Sandy Serrano, reported seeing a girl in a polka dot dress running from the scene with a man accompanying her and claimed that the girl exclaimed, "We shot him! We shot him!" When asked to whom the girl was referring, Serrano reported that the girl said, "We shot Senator Kennedy!" Another witness, Evan Freed, also saw the girl in the polka dot dress. There were also reports by other witnesses that a girl wearing a polka dot dress was seen with Sirhan at various times during the evening prior to the assassination, including in the kitchen where the assassination took place.

Serrano was adamant that what she saw and heard was true. Serrano stated that LAPD SGT Hank Hernandez bullied her into recanting her account. An audio of the thirty-eight minute interview between Hernandez and Serrano justified her assertion that she was pushed and bullied into withdrawing her account at the time.

What has now become known as the Pruszynski recording was uncovered in 2004 by CNN's Brad Johnson, who had the recording independently examined and authenticated by two audio analysts, Spence Whitehead in

Atlanta, Georgia, and Philip Van Praag in Tucson, Arizona. The Pruszynski recording "clearly showed that 13 shots were fired in the pantry, and Sirhan's gun had only eight shots, so it definitely means there was a second shooter," according to William Pepper Sirhan's attorney.

Paul Schrade was a Kennedy friend who was shot in the forehead while standing immediately behind Robert Kennedy in the pantry. In 2008, Schrade told CNN that he believes new evidence clearly shows Sirhan was not the only person who fired shots in that assassination. "We have proof that the second shooter was behind us and off to our right. Sirhan was off to the left and in front of us."

In November 2006, the BBC's *Newsnight* program presented research by filmmaker Shane O'Sullivan alleging that several CIA officers were present on the night of the assassination. Three men who appear in video and photographs from the night of the assassination were positively identified by their former CIA colleagues and associates as former senior CIA officers who had worked together in 1963 at the CIA's main anti-Castro station based in Miami. The Operation was called JMWAVE. The three were identified as JMWAVE Chief of Operations David Sanchez Morales, Chief of Maritime Operations Gordon Campbell and the Chief of Psychological Warfare Operations George Joannides.

David Morales' friend Ruben Carbajal claimed that in 1973, Morales opened up about his involvement in assassinations and stated that "Kennedy was responsible for me having to watch all the men I recruited and trained get wiped out." Carbajal claims that Morales added, "Well, we took care of that SOB, didn't we?"

In 1963, numerous employees of New Orleans taverns testified that they saw Lee Harvey Oswald frequently in the company of a man matching the exact appearance of Morales prior to the Kennedy assassination. The employees identified the man with Oswald from photos of Morales.

A BBC *Newsnight* program also featured an interview with Morales's former attorney Robert Walton, who quoted Morales as having said, "I was in Dallas when we got the son of a bitch and I was in Los Angeles when we got the little bastard." The program reported that the CIA declined to comment on these issues or about these agents.

Morales was also identified by E. Howard Hunt as an accomplice in the assassination of JFK in Hunt's death bed confession.

Morales died of a mysterious heart attack in 1978. Ruben Carbajal thought he was poisoned before he could testify before the House of Representatives Select Committee on Assassinations (HSCA). He says that Morales declined rapidly in his visit to Washington and complained he felt "strange." Morales was hospitalized shortly after these complaints. Carbajal went to visit Morales in the hospital but was stopped by sheriff's deputies who were guarding Morales' room and not allowing any visitors. Morales died the next day.

He died before he could testify. Morales would have been interviewed by the House Select Committee on Assassinations, HSCA, much earlier, but when HSCA staff interviewed the CIA's David Atlee Phillips, he lied and told them Morales was unimportant to their investigations and that he was unavailable because he had died of alcoholism. When the Committee found out this wasn't true, they summoned Morales to testify which may have led to his mysterious death.

In addition to Morales' death and there is the mysterious suicide of George de Mohrenschildt while he was recording his wife's soap operas. He was another HSCA witnesses who also met with a mysterious fate. Another fatality was the Mafia's "Handsome" Johnny Roselli, who also had CIA connections. He was to be one of the first people to be interviewed by the HSCA but he went missing in July 1976. His body was later discovered at the bottom of the Florida Intracoastal Waterway cut up in pieces hidden in an oil drum near Miami. Another Mafioso with CIA connections, Sam Giancana, was another witness called before the HSCA to testify about the death of President Kennedy. He was given a police detail to guard his house in Oak Park, Illinois. On June 19, 1975, an unknown someone recalled the police detail that was guarding his house. Shortly after the police guard left Giancana was shot multiple times and died. Another witness William Pawley also mysteriously committed suicide in 1977, when he was asked to appear before the HSCA.

Sirhan Sirhan, a Manchurian Candidate?

> "We have proof that the second shooter was behind us and off to our right. Sirhan was off to the left and in front of us."—Paul Schrade, a Kennedy supporter who was also shot during the assassination

He was born in Jerusalem and emigrated with his family to the United States when he was twelve. His family was Christian. He attended Eliot Junior High School in Altadena, California and John Muir High School. Sirhan was a good student and had many friends. At John Muir High School, he studied two difficult languages, German and Russian, and joined the California Cadets, a high school ROTC. In 1963, Sirhan Sirhan enrolled in Pasadena City College, but he quit in early 1965 when his sister Aida, to whom he was very close, died from leukemia. Sirhan became depressed after the death of his sister and began to get regular mental health treatments, including hypnosis. This was the same time that the CIA was conducting MK-ULTRA mind control experiments on patients with depression in California.

Sirhan loved horses and he wanted very badly to become a jockey. Although his small physical stature was ideal, he was a passive person and lacked the confidence to be a jockey according to acquaintances. After a horse-riding accident which sent him to the hospital, his dreams of being a jockey ended. He received a $1,700 settlement check after falling off the horse and injuring himself. His depression then deepened and he received more intensive mental health treatments.

Dr. Bernard L. Diamond, a psychoanalyst, and professor of law, psychiatry and criminology at the University of California at Berkeley, was a witness for Sirhan's defense. His testimony was added to the diagnoses of five other experts that Sirhan was afflicted with paranoia and schizophrenia. He confirmed that Sirhan has no recollection of shooting Kennedy. Diamond testified that the murder was committed in a complete trance that suggests it was an external command planted in his mind by others using mind control techniques. It was clear to him that Sirhan lacked both the will and the motive to commit the crime. It was his firm opinion that Sirhan had been controlled by an external source.

Daniel Brown, an associate clinical professor in psychology at Harvard Medical School, interviewed Sirhan for sixty hours over a three-year period. Brown's report confirms Sirhan's complete loss of his memory, including in the day of the shooting and significant parts of his life in the year prior to the Kennedy slaying which are totally erased from his mind. Witnesses of the assassination also testified that Sirhan acted as if he were unaware of his surroundings and was in a deep trance.

If there were any doubts that the CIA has the ability to create these Manchurian candidates it has since been removed. Annie Jacobsen in her book *Operation Paperclip* uncovered memos that the CIA had these abilities since 1952. They initially used these methods on suspected Soviet Agents. Their memos show that "light doses of drugs were coupled with hypnosis to induce a complete hypnotic trance. The trance was held for one hour and forty minutes of interrogation with a subsequent total amnesia produced." The subjects could be programmed to do anything in these altered states. Other victims of the MK-ULTRA Program have also been found.

A Rightwing Coup-de-tat

> "Hoover lied his eyes out to the Commission, on Oswald, on Ruby, on their friends, the bullets, the guns, you name it."—Congressman Hale Boggs, House Majority Leader and

Warren Commission Member who was mysteriously killed in a plane crash in Alaska

"We have not been told the truth about Oswald."—Senator Richard Russell, Warren Commission Member

"On what basis is it claimed that two shots caused all the wounds?...It seemed to me that Governor Connally's statement negates such a conclusion. I could not agree with this statement."—Senator John Sherman Cooper, Warren Commission Member

"I think the [Warren] report, to those who have studied it closely, has collapsed like a house of cards.....the fatal mistake the Warren Commission made was not to use its own investigators, but instead to rely on the CIA and FBI personnel, which played directly into the hands of senior intelligence officials who directed the cover-up."—Senator Richard Schweiker, Church Committee Member

Most Americans would rather accept a comfortable lie rather than face a painful depressing truth. It is easier to believe that three lone crazed gunmen coincidentally killed the Kennedys and King rather than suspect rightwing assassins and plots by the American government. It is easier and less painful to say it is all coincidental and to dismiss anyone suspecting the truth of being a "conspiracy nut."

Despite knowing that the evidence shows that the CIA and FBI committed multiple illegal activities and other murders and assassinations of political leaders during this time, Americans do not want to believe that these dangerous organizations killed these three particular men. Americans don't want to believe they were killed because two of them, the Kennedys, wanted to end their power and reign of terror, and the third was murdered because of his rejection of leadership against the status quo that kept many Americans as second class citizens. Americans don't want to believe it could be a rightwing plot. They don't believe it even though there is a mountain of evidence that the CIA and the Mafia conspired to kill many other people. They don't want to believe that both the CIA and J. Edgar Hoover were also heavily involved with the Mafia and had committed many crimes and murders. It is too painful for Americans and they still don't want to believe that men in their government caused these three deaths.

The Kennedys wanted to end the CIA and dismiss FBI Director J. Edgar Hoover, but Americans do not want to believe the obvious. They don't want to believe the FBI and Hoover killed King even though Hoover was so filled with envy and hatred of King that he regularly demoted agents who were assigned to find fault with King and failed to do so. They don't want to believe even after it was known that Hoover and the FBI attempted to blackmail King into committing suicide. Hoover ominously tipped off King's death in a memo to his agents the day before King was killed saying that, "The Negro youth and moderates must be made to understand that if they succumb to revolutionary teaching, they will be dead revolutionaries."

Even after some of these men have later admitted their guilt, many Americans still refuse to hear the truth. Even after Congress found there was a conspiracy, many Americans still refuse to believe. It is a slumber of self-inflicted ignorance.

In the end does it make any difference which assassin actually fired the bullets that killed John and Robert Kennedy and Dr. King? Whoever fired the bullets the effect was the same. All three were assassinated so that America would move politically further to the right without the potent interference from these three popular political figures. Had they lived American politics and history would have taken far different course.

They were assassinated in a rightwing coup-de-tat. And instead of anger Americans are in disbelief and this is the reason the country continues to slide ever further to the right. Americans are dumbfounded on how a civilized country like Germany could slide into barbaric Nazism, but like the Germans, Americans fail to see and understand their own decline into a rightwing immoral abyss. Americans like the Germans do not want to know.

Vietnam, the CIA and Drugs

"It goes all the way back to the predecessor organization OSS and its involvement with the Italian Mafia, the Cosa Nostra in Sicily and Southern Italy. Later on when they were fighting communists in France they got in tight with the Corsican brotherhood. The Corsican brotherhood of course were big dope dealers. As things changed in the world the CIA got involved with the Kuomintang types in Burma who were drug runners because they were resisting the drift towards communism there. The same thing happened in Southeast Asia, later in Latin America. Some of the very people who are the best sources of information, who are capable of accomplishing things and the like happen to be the criminal element."—Victor Marchetti, Central Intelligence Agency

"I was on the airstrip that was my job, to move in and about and to go from place to place and my people were in charge of dispatching aircraft. I was in the areas where opium was transhipped. I personally was a witness to opium being placed on aircraft, American aircraft. I witnessed it being taken off smaller aircraft that were coming in from out-

lying sites"—Ron Rickenbach, US Agency for International
Development

The CIA, starting in the 1950s and through to the present, is a rightwing lawless group. They ran operations with or without government approval or oversight. They set up dummy corporations or formed partnerships with corporations Like George H.W. Bush's Zapata Oil to make money and provide cover for their operations. In addition they also began to trade in drugs. In his book *The Politics of Heroin in Southeast Asia*, Alfred McCoy states the CIA and the US military were heavily involved in drugs and drug running in Vietnam. It started with turning a blind eye and eventually became a major money making operation for the CIA linking them once again with organized crime. The CIA is a criminal organization.

After Mao consolidated China, a group of approximately twelve thousand Kuomintang soldiers who had been loyal to Chiang Kai-shek escaped to an area that became known as "the Golden Triangle" and continued launching guerrilla attacks into southern China. During the 1950s and 1960s the CIA secretly supported and supplied this army with reinforcements and arms at various times. The Kuomintang began to grow opium to support their efforts and the drug trade became their main source of revenue to finance their army and it eventually became their primary business. The French crime organization, the Unione Corse, operated the drug trade in Southeast Asia when they were French controlled colonies. They operated what was called "Air Opium" flying the opium to the Southeast Asian markets for the Kuomintang and other opium producing tribes like the Hmong.

General Ed Lansdale, the CIA chief in Vietnam, and his old friend Lt. Col. Lucien Conein, the CIA agent who had helped engineer President Diem's overthrow for the CIA in 1963, came to an agreement with the Unione Corse. As a former OSS liaison officer with the French Resistance during World War II, Conein had worked with the Unione Corse in breaking up the dockworkers strike in Marseille in 1948. He knew many of Saigon's Corsican gangsters and persuaded Lansdale that they had been good allies and could be allies in Vietnam. He saw them as a good source of intelligence and financing for CIA covert activities such as the secret war in Laos.

Soon the CIA and the Unione Corse were operating cooperatively in the drug trade. Air America, a private air company owned and operated by the CIA, became the drug transportation system after the French Air Opium was shut down according to Alexander Cockburn and Jeffrey St. Clair in their book, *Whiteout: The CIA, Drugs and the Press*.

General Vang Pao and the Hmong armies in Laos were backed by the CIA and were also supporting themselves with the drug trade. The CIA created Hmong (sometimes called Meo) mercenary army which supported themselves by manufacturing of heroin. Their heroin was then shipped by the CIA for sale in South Vietnam. A significant amount of this drug trade was going to young American military personnel. At this same time the US State Department had adopted a policy of also providing support for corrupt local and state governments in the area that were openly engaged in the drug traffic as long as they were pro-American and anti-communist.

According to Cockburn and St. Clair, the American Mafia was at the time also looking for financial opportunities and they saw Vietnam as very fertile ground. They began sending younger members of their crime families to Saigon. The most significant of these Mafioso was Frank Carmen Furci, a young Mafioso from Tampa, Florida who was the son of Capo Dominick Furci in the crime family of Santo Trafficante the Mafia boss of Tampa. The CIA and the Mafia in Florida already had deep ties and connections from World War II and in their Cuban efforts. Furci arrived in Vietnam in 1965, with solid financial backing from the crime families and soon became a key figure in the systematic graft and corruption that began to plague US military clubs and supply bases in Vietnam as hundreds of thousands of GIs poured into the war zone.

A lengthy US Senate investigation later exposed the network of graft, bribes, and kickbacks that Furci and his fellow profiteers employed to cheat military clubs and their GI customers out of millions of dollars and to rob US supply bases to sell American goods on the black market, including weapons that found their way to the Viet Cong.

Furci and the Mafia also got into the drug trade with the CIA and the Unione Corse and began buying from them to sell to American soldiers and Marines in Vietnam. They also began to export these drugs to the United States. One of their alleged smuggling methods was to smuggle the drugs into the US in the body bags of dead soldiers according to Mike Levine a former DEA agent who claims to have witnessed this. Levine was also a radio talk show host in New York and has since become a journalist and has written on this subject. An Air Force Chief Master Sergeant Bob Kirkconnell also claimed to have witnessed this method of using body bags of dead soldiers as part of a military heroin investigation he participated in while in Vietnam in 1972. Levine and Kirkconnell had a radio interview on New York's WBAI on June 21, 2004, titled *"The Vietnam Body Bag Case,"* talking about their experiences and findings.

In late 1960s, new heroin laboratories sprang up in the tri-border area where Burma, Thailand, and Laos converge, and suddenly unprecedented quantities of heroin started flooding the troops in Vietnam and began to be smuggled into the United States by the Mafia. Fueled by these seemingly limitless supplies of heroin, America's total number of addicts skyrocketed.

Heroin and many other drugs were a large part of Vietnam and the American soldiers, airmen, sailors and marines experience in Vietnam. Drug addiction became an epidemic among them. Many of these young veterans came home with their addictions and many more were recreational users, and they both added to the growing drug culture of the 1960s and early seventies in the US upon their return.

Later Victor Marchetti of the CIA would testify to Congress about the CIA drug dealing in Vietnam, "I doubt that they had any strong deep understanding of what they were allowing to happen by turning their heads the other way and letting Vang Pao ship his dope out which was made into heroin which was going to our troops, which was corrupting people throughout Southeast Asia and back here, the effect it had on crime, I doubt that any one of them really thought in those terms at the time." He was mistaken, the CIA knew what they were doing and why, it was a planned operation, not passive, and not a matter of just "turning their heads" to allow it to occur. This was how they financed their dark and dirty secret wars and it would later come to light.

CHAPTER 11. THE 1970S, NIXON, FORD AND CARTER

Richard Milhous Nixon

> "When the President does it that means that it's not illegal."—
> Richard Nixon

> "I'm glad I'm not Brezhnev. Being the Russian leader in the
> Kremlin you never know if someone's tape recording what you
> say."—Richard Nixon

> "Nixon's offences had been so long in the past, so much part of
> a different era that he now seemed like some lovable but bigoted
> uncle you tolerated at Christmas and Thanksgiving."—Jacob M.
> Appel, American writer and critic on Nixon's resurgence during
> the Reagan years

Richard Nixon in many ways was a primary beneficiary of the rightwing
coups that killed John and Robert Kennedy. Saying that Nixon was an odd man
is a vast understatement. He was a complex, paranoid, angry and sometimes a
depressed man. He was self-serving and immoral, but he was also intelligent and
crafty and he was a good politician. He was a man who would use any means to
get what he wanted, and did.

According to John Loftus when Richard Nixon was a Navy Officer at the end
of World War II he found himself in a position to promote himself by cooperating with Allen Dulles and others in helping to sanitize Nazi war criminals for
the then OSS, who wanted to use the Nazis for their knowledge in torture, mind
control, spying, biological weapons and rocketry. Nixon was happy to oblige, es-

pecially when Dulles suggested that a young lawyer like Nixon could find a career in politics after the war if he knew the right people. Allen Dulles and his business partners, especially Prescott Bush, were the right kind of people.

Richard Nixon was very intelligent. He graduated third in his high school class despite having to work almost fulltime in this father's grocery store. He was offered a scholarship to Harvard, but his family needed him to work in the store, so Nixon stayed home and attended Whittier College. Nixon became an excellent debater in college. He graduated with very good grades and was offered and accepted a scholarship to Duke University School of Law.

After graduating from Duke, Nixon initially hoped to join the FBI. When he received no response to his letter of application he gave up this idea. He learned years later from J. Edgar Hoover that he had been hired, but his appointment had been canceled at the last minute due to budget cuts. However Hoover was also known to lie to please superiors.

Nixon returned to California, and after passing his bar examination, he began practicing with a small law firm in Whittier. He worked primarily in commercial litigation representing local petroleum companies and other corporations, as well as well as in estate planning and wills. His firm wanted him to practice family law, but Nixon was reluctant to work on divorce cases. He was extremely uncomfortable about sexual issues and women.

There are a few Nixon biographers who believe Nixon was gay, and he seemed to have had a spousal like relationship with his very close friend Bebe Rebozo. Rebozo was with Nixon for many years and was at Nixon's side when he died. In the biography *Nixon's Darkest Secrets: The Inside Story of America's Most Troubled President*, former United Press International Washington Bureau Chief and White House correspondent Don Fulsom cited numerous sources and incidents that suggest Nixon had a romantic gay relationship with Rebozo. Some of these incidents include: that Rebozo and Nixon were caught holding hands under the table at a White House dinner; that they frequently vacationed alone together and booked a single hotel room together; and statements from a Nixon aide who said that he had to coach Nixon on how to kiss Mrs. Nixon so that they would come across as a loving couple. Another Washington reporter told Fulsom that he once spotted Nixon drunk and hugging and nuzzling Rebozo "the way you'd cuddle your senior prom date." The rumors about Nixon and Rebozo were fairly common in White House inner circles, according to Fulsom.

Nixon was a tortured man and being found gay during this time period would have been political suicide. This fear of discovery could have also aggravated Nixon's growing paranoia and added to his constant quest for secrecy and fear of press leaks.

In addition to possibly being Nixon's lover, Rebozo was a banker who laundered money for the Mafia. According to Fulsom, Nixon and Rebozo also obtained bargain real estate prices and financing on their adjoining Key Biscayne, Florida homes from Donald Berg, a Mafia associate. The Secret Service strongly advised Nixon to stop associating with Berg because of his many Mafia ties.

A lender for another of Nixon's properties was Arthur Dresser. He was another mob financier who did business with Teamsters President Jimmy Hoffa and mob boss Meyer Lansky. Nixon and Rebozo were also close friends with James Crosby, the chairman of a company repeatedly associated with the Mafia. Rebozo's Key Biscayne Bank was long suspected of money laundering for the mob and it was also a pipeline for Mafia money to and from Crosby's casino in the Bahamas. By the 1960s, FBI agents monitoring the Mafia had identified Rebozo as a "non-member associate of organized crime figures." In their words he was not a "made" Mafia member but rather a Mafia associate. He was their banker.

Nixon had many other Mafia ties. In *Hollywood's Celebrity Gangster, The Incredible Life and Times of Mickey Cohen*, Brad Lewis wrote that Nixon was indebted to the mob and particularly mob boss Mickey Cohen. Cohen gave Nixon free office space for his first congressional campaign in one of the buildings he owned. Lewis also contends that Nixon was well financed by the Mafia in both his House and Senate elections. In Nixon's 1950 Senate race, Mickey Cohen held a fundraiser for him in the Banquet room of the Hollywood Knickerbocker Hotel. It was attended by Mafia leaders and hundreds of US bookies, and Las Vegas gamblers, all giving envelopes of cash to Nixon for his campaign. Cohen's close associate, Jack Ruby (Rubenstein) also assisted Nixon in fundraising. It was the same Jack Ruby who later killed Oswald.

Columnist Drew Pearson described Nixon's Senate race as "One of the most skillful and cut-throat campaigns I have ever seen." Nixon ran a dirty campaign against Congresswoman Helen Gahagen who he called "the pink lady." He was fed private information about her by J. Edgar Hoover and Nixon spread malicious gossip and half-truths that she was a socialist. He was also better financed with the mob's money and won the election.

According to Rolling Stone investigative reporter Howard Kohn, the CIA through Dulles, and the Mafia through Lansky, funneled money and valuable information into Nixon's political campaigns. However the primary source of campaign information came from J. Edgar Hoover. After observing his first congressional race Hoover saw Nixon as a potential leader in the anti-communist movement and decided to befriend this young man.

The friendship between Richard Nixon and J. Edgar Hoover began in the late 1940s, when young Congressman Richard M. Nixon was working on the Alger Hiss trial. Nixon first gained national attention and ingratiated himself to Hoover in 1948 when his investigation, as a member of the House Un-American Activities Committee (HUAC), broke the Alger Hiss spy case. While many doubted Whittaker Chambers' allegations that Hiss, a former State Department official, had been a Soviet spy, Nixon at the urging of Hoover alleged them to be true and pressed hard for the committee to continue its investigation. Hiss was later convicted of perjury but his conviction is still dubious. Nixon was given considerable credit for the Hiss perjury conviction.

A newly assembled collection of Nixon–Hoover conversations secretly captured on the Nixon taping system demonstrates that Nixon and Hoover were more than simply colleagues. They were good friends and co-conspirators against the American left. They were both paranoid. They agreed on most things and their temperaments and their approaches to controversial issues and their methods, including using illegal operations to accomplish their means, were also similar. It is also probable that each may have also known about the other's secret gay life.

General Dwight D. Eisenhower was nominated for president by the Republicans in 1952. He was somewhat indifferent on a selection for vice presidential candidate and left that decision to party officials. Prescott Bush and the Dulles brothers and others on the right pushed for Nixon. They strongly recommended him to Eisenhower who then agreed to the senator's selection. Nixon's youth complimented the older Eisenhower. His strong stance against communism and his political base in California, which had just become the largest state, were also appealing to Eisenhower and together the older extremely popular World War II General with young Nixon as his running mate easily won the election. Nixon allowed Eisenhower to stay above the political fight as Nixon served as the attack dog during the election. This was very suitable to the easygoing Eisenhower and he liked the fact that he didn't have to dirty himself in the political fray.

In mid-September of 1952, Nixon caused an election crisis in the Eisenhower campaign when the media reported that Nixon had a secret political fund donated by private backers which reimbursed him for all his political expenses. The fund was very questionable but legal. However it was unprecedented and it exposed Nixon to allegations of conflicts of interest. The nation wondered to whom Nixon was indebted to and why? With growing pressure building for Eisenhower to demand Nixon's resignation from the ticket, Nixon went on television to deliver an address to the nation on September 23, 1952. It was possibly Nixon's best speech. The address, later termed "The Checkers speech," was heard by sixty million Americans which was the largest television audience at the time. An emotional Nixon defended himself, stating that the fund was not secret nor had donors received special favors. He painted himself as a family man of very modest means saying his wife didn't have a mink coat and said she wore a "respectable Republican cloth coat." The speech would be remembered for one of the gifts that Nixon had received, but which he refused to give back saying, "a little cocker spaniel dog ... sent all the way from Texas. And our little girl Tricia, the six year old, named it Checkers." Nixon hid behind his wife, children and their dog as an "average Joe," and it was emotional and effective and he remained on the ticket.

Eisenhower was a military man and unlike previous presidents he delegated most duties to others. He included Nixon in decisions and delegated meaningful tasks to him. One task was overseeing the planning for the Bay of Pigs Invasion, which Vice President Nixon later passed on to the incoming President Kennedy as a fait accompli when Kennedy took office in 1961, after he narrowly defeated Nixon. It was a defeat Nixon took with some bitterness. Nixon was envious of the charismatic Kennedy who the ever bitter Nixon thought of as a "spoiled rich boy." He was also extremely jealous of Kennedy's Harvard education, an education he was forced to turn down because he was needed to work in his family's store. He truly disliked Kennedy.

After his defeat to Kennedy in 1960, Nixon returned home to California. Local and national Republican leaders then encouraged Nixon to challenge the incumbent Pat Brown for election as the California Governor in 1962. The campaign was clouded by the voter's and the press' suspicion that Nixon was just using the governor's office as a stepping-stone for another presidential run, which was true. When he lost the election to Brown, the ever paranoid Nixon blamed his loss completely on the press. Nixon delivered a speech on television in what should have been a death blow to any future political ambitions. In fact it was widely thought to be the end of Nixon's political career at the time.

In an unrehearsed and unplanned concession speech the morning after the election a visibly angry and out of control Nixon blamed the media for favoring his opponent, saying, "You won't have Nixon to kick around anymore because, gentlemen, this is my last press conference." The California defeat and speech was highlighted in the November 11, 1962, episode of the ABC network program *Howard K. Smith: News and Comment* and was called, *The Political Obituary of Richard M. Nixon*. On the program Smith also interviewed the controversial Alger Hiss who Nixon helped convict for perjury. Many members of the political right complained that it was unseemly to allow "a convicted spy" air time to attack a former vice president. The Smith–Hiss interview helped to create strong rightwing sympathy for Nixon which would later help him launch a successful comeback.

In 1964, Nixon actively supported the rightwing conservative Arizona Senator Barry Goldwater for the Republican nomination for president. He campaigned for him vigorously and when Goldwater won the nomination Nixon was selected to give the speech introducing the nominee to the convention on national television. Although he thought Goldwater would not win against Johnson, Nixon actively campaigned for him. In the process he won back many Republican supporters and won the gratitude and admiration from the Republican rightwing. In the 1966, congressional elections he also campaigned across the nation for many Republicans who were seeking to regain seats lost in the Johnson landslide of 1964, and Nixon received much of the credit for helping the Republicans make major gains in the midterm election. The winners and even the losers of these campaigns felt indebted to Nixon and this allowed Nixon to build very solid support for his comeback in 1968 to defeat Reagan, Rockefeller and George Romney to win the Republican nomination and to then narrowly win the election over Humphrey.

Incredibly in 1968, Nixon ran as a peace candidate only becoming extremely hawkish after his election. Nixon benefited by the extraordinary events of 1968 especially the assassination of Robert Kennedy. He also won because Nixon "the peace candidate" committed treason by secretly destroying the Vietnam peace talks.

After a narrow win in New Hampshire over the anti-war candidate Senator Eugene McCarthy, President Johnson bowed out after realizing his unpopularity with voters angry over Vietnam. Johnson did not want an embarrassing loss and he saw that his defeat was likely. The assassination of Dr. King disrupted Democratic support in the 1968 election with a large voting block of African-Americans deciding to not participate in the election because of their grief driven hopelessness over King's death. The riots after King's death also hurt Democrats with White voters because Alabama Governor George Wallace and the Republicans began to accuse the Democrats, and supporters of civil rights of being "soft on crime," implying they somehow caused or condoned racial riots and unrest.

The Democratic Party was in turmoil and every time it seemed they were about to unite tragedy struck. As the nation's most popular politician, Robert Kennedy won the California primary and with it the likely Democratic nomination, he was then assassinated. Just as the Democrats began forming around Hubert Humphrey a police riot in Chicago during their convention destroyed their unity. It was made worse for Democrats when Alabama Governor George Wallace ran on the American Independent Party ticket taking away the once solid South from the Democrats as well as some White blue collar workers in the Northeast and Midwest.

Nixon's biggest fear was that Johnson would spring an "October Surprise" and broker a peace agreement before the election and destroy any chance "the peace candidate" had on winning the presidency. In fact Johnson's negotiators were about to reach a truce in Vietnam prior to the election. In his 1984 book *The Price of Power*, Seymour Hersh revealed that the double-crossing Henry Kissinger, then LBJ's adviser on the Vietnam peace talks, secretly leaked to Nixon's staff that a cease-fire was looming. According to a BBC news report called, *LBJ Tapes: Nixon Sabotaged Vietnam Peace Talks*, by James Joyner, on March 17, 2013, Nixon and his campaign were in regular contact with Anna Chennault the widow of World War II hero Lt. General Claire Lee Chennault. She was also a rightwing anti-communist and a long standing member of the China Lobby.

Chennault was told by Nixon to advise South Vietnamese President Nguyễn Văn Thiệu to not to go to Paris to join Johnson's peace talks and that in exchange Nixon would give him a much better support when he was elected. Chennault met with Thiệu and gave him the message and strongly urged him to not attend the peace talks.

Johnson became aware of what was going on because he had secretly and illegally bugged the telephones and offices both Chennault and the South Vietnamese ambassador to Washington. He was enraged by what he considered a treasonous attempt by Nixon to undermine US foreign policy for his own selfish political purposes.

On October 31, with no agreement from South Vietnam Johnson still announced a unilateral halt to the bombing anyway, and stated that peace negotiations would start in Paris on November 6, the day after Election Day. However four days before the election on November 2, after speaking with Chennault again, Thiệu then scuttled the peace talks by publically refusing to go to Paris. Johnson was angry and telephoned Republican Senator Everett Dirksen to complain about what he called "Nixon's treason."

After Johnson and Dirksen had their conversation, Nixon, who was tipped off by Dirksen, became worried about Johnson filing treason charges and he called Johnson and lied and denied any involvement. But Johnson knew from his illegal wire taps that Nixon was lying to him. However, Johnson also felt he could not publicly mention Nixon's treasonous act because he too had broken the law as his information had been obtained by illegal wiretapping. Johnson did tell Vice President Humphrey who also chose not to use the information because he feared any charges of political corruption and wiretapping against Johnson would also taint his campaign. These events were confirmed in a three page memo from Walt W. Rostow on May 14, 1973, that has been recently released from the LBJ library revealing Nixon's and Kissinger's conspiracy and treason that sabotaged the Paris peace talks.

Despite his illegal wiretapping Johnson was going to go public in 1968 with Nixon's treason. But Clark Clifford, one of the creators of the CIA and a Washington insider, dissuaded him in a taped conversation. Clifford told LBJ that "some elements of the story are so shocking in their nature that I'm wondering whether it would be good for the country to disclose the story and then possibly have a certain individual (Nixon) elected. It could cast his whole administration under such doubt that I think it would be inimical to our country's interests."

During Nixon's first term in office more than twenty thousand US troops died in Vietnam, more than a hundred thousand were wounded and more than a million Vietnamese were killed. In one of the most bizarre twists of history Henry Kissinger was awarded the Nobel Peace Prize in 1973 for negotiating the very same peace settlement that he illegally helped Nixon to sabotage in 1968. Like Nixon, Kissinger is an immoral charlatan and a hypocrite. Kissinger also promoted and championed the infamous Operation PHOENIX, a CIA and US Army program of killing and torture.

Operation PHOENIX was a secret CIA counterinsurgency program to identify and destroy the Viet Cong. CIA operatives along with U.S. Army Special Forces and trusted South Vietnamese army personnel set out to destroy the Viet Cong "by any means possible." The CIA described Operation PHOENIX as "a set of programs that sought to attack and destroy the political infrastructure of the Viet Cong." The major two components of the program were Provincial Reconnaissance Units (PRUs), a sort of political police, and the regional interrogation centers (RICs) which were torture prisons.

PRUs were primarily made up of American Army and trusted South Vietnamese Army personnel under CIA or US Army Special Forces guidance. They would kill or capture any suspected Viet Cong or any civilians they thought that may have any information about the Viet Cong, or antigovernment activities which included many Buddhists who were opposed to the Catholic dominated government. Those captured included women and children. Many were taken into custody without any real connection to the Viet Cong. If a soldier desired a Vietnamese girl he would use the program to have his way with her. Many others were taken in because they had angered their neighbors or had angered the Americans or South Vietnamese officials.

These prisoners were then taken to the RICs where they were tortured in an attempt to gain intelligence on Viet Cong and anti-government activities. Every form of torture was used including rape and gang rape of both male and female prisoners. It was here that the CIA began to use their infamous waterboarding techniques. The CIA also began medical experiments to gain mind control over these prisoners. Prisoners were also forced to give the names of others and most did, many of them innocent, in order to save themselves from further torture.

Much of this torture was pointless and used for the sadistic enjoyment of the soldiers and CIA operatives. Prisoners were sometimes forced to fight another prisoner to the death with the promise that the victor could go free. These fights included women and children. Children were tortured in front of parents. Husbands and wives were forced to watch as their spouse was tortured or raped. A favorite torture of the Americans was what they laughingly referred to as the "Bell telephone hour," where violent electric shocks were applied to men's testicles and into women's vaginas to shock them into submission. Prisoners were paraded naked and forced into humiliating sexual positions. Other techniques used were starvation in small cages and being mauled by dogs. All forms of torture were used and perfected. These perfected torture techniques were later used by the US Army and the CIA in Iraq and the War on Terror.

One army veteran of Operation PHOENIX later admitted that at night they would knock on the door of a suspect's house and to whoever answered the door, man woman or a child they would say "April fool motherfucker" and shoot them dead. Some of these troops cut off and collected the ears of their victims to prove how many they killed.

The program was not effective as it made more enemies for the South Vietnamese government and US forces and encouraged more recruits for the Viet Cong. The program operated from 1968 to 1972, but similar programs operated before and after. The U.S. officially lists about 82,000 torture victims of Operation PHOENIX with over 40,000 killed, but the Vietnamese give a number almost double this.

The program came to light when some of the returning soldiers began openly talking about the program. In 1971, a Congressional Hearing uncovered these horrors. In response to the inquiry from Congress the military command in Vietnam issued a directive that reiterated that they had based the anti-Viet Cong Phoenix Program on South Vietnamese law and lied and said that the program was in compliance with the laws of land warfare. CIA Director William Colby insisted that the program was effective, but admitted that some field commanders had "committed some abuses." He destroyed of most of the CIA files on Operation PHOENIX before Congress could investigate the program. This destruction was ordered by Henry Kissinger.

In April of 1975, when Saigon began to fall Henry Kissinger said, "I think we owe—it is our duty—to get the people who believed in us out.....We have to take out these people who participated in the PHOENIX Program."

Kissinger was referring to the South Vietnamese who assisted in these campaigns of torture and murder who were then allowed to come to the United States rather than face war criminal trials in Vietnam.

In 2001, English journalist Christopher Hitchens claimed to have amassed more than sufficient evidence to secure prosecutions for "war crimes, for crimes against humanity, and for offences against common or customary or international law, including conspiracy to commit murder, kidnap, and torture" against Kissinger.

Kissinger and the CIA also orchestrated the coup against the elected president of Chile, Salvador Allende and plotted his murder in 1973, and placed into power the fascist General Augusto Pinochet and his tortuous fascist regime. Kissinger called the General "his good friend." This has made the travels of Kissinger very risky as he is wanted for trial as a war criminal in several countries by victims of the Pinochet regime.

The war crimes charge sheet against Kissinger is extremely long, even considering the eight long tumultuous years Kissinger was running US foreign policy for Nixon and Ford. In addition to Operation PHOENIX and the Chilean Coup, he and Nixon invaded neutral Cambodia in 1970, where they indiscriminately bombed civilians. They planned and gave support to the Indonesians and their brutal repression in East Timor. Kissinger also allowed the Kurds to be attacked by chemical weapons at the hands of Saddam Hussein in Iraq without complaint and some thought at his encouragement. Add the charge of treason for scuttling Johnson's Vietnam Peace Plan and Kissinger's crimes against humanity are many.

In 1968, after committing treason and destroying Johnson's peace talks, Nixon just barely won with about forty-four percent of the votes, Humphrey had about forty-three percent, and Wallace had more than thirteen percent of the votes. At Nixon's inauguration Pat Nixon made a great show of holding the family Bible open to a passage in a great show of false piety which read, "They shall beat their swords into plowshares, and their spears into pruning hooks." In his inaugural address Nixon stated that "the greatest honor history can bestow is the title of peacemaker."

Nixon also had the audacity of having the phrase: "the greatest honor history can bestow is the title of peacemaker" placed on his gravestone when he died. This from a man who scuttled Johnson's peace talks for political purposes and deliberately prolonged a useless war for seven more years, long after the majority of the American people had stopped supporting it. This was a man who conducted a secret war in Laos and Cambodia and lied to the American people about it. This was a man who plotted with the CIA in the overthrow of Guatemala, the assassination attempts against Castro, and the man who destroyed the democratic government of Chile. This was a man who ruthlessly pursued anti-war groups and activists and ordered aides to break into and burglarize Daniel Ellsberg's psychiatrist's offices. Nixon made up an enemies list, with many anti-war activists on it and throughout his presidency he used any all methods, including using illegal means, to discredit and do them harm. Richard Nixon was a traitor, a liar, unequivocally immoral and as his tombstone shows a remorseless hypocrite. He was not a peacemaker.

Nixon coveted the Wallace voters and in 1972 his aides Patrick Buchannan and Kevin Phillips devised the Republican Party's Southern Strategy which decided to end the Republican Party's support of civil rights in order to court the bigoted Southern conservatives switch to the Republican Party. These efforts were greatly aided on May 15, 1972, when Governor Wallace was shot four times in Maryland while campaigning for the presidency. Although Wallace survived, his campaign for president was ended and into this breech stepped Richard Nixon and the Republican Party who began to campaign using Wallace's political rhetoric and States' Rights themes. Nixon also then declared he was against school busing for desegregation.

In the 1972 election Nixon won every state in the Union except Massachusetts and won more than seventy percent of the popular vote in most of the Deep South in the states of Alabama, Georgia, Florida, Mississippi, and South Carolina. He won over sixty-five percent of the votes in the other states of the former Confederacy as opposed to only sixty-one percent of the nationwide vote. It was a pivotal election and thanks to the Southern Strategy the South now belonged to the Republicans. And while these Southern votes sustained the Republican Party through the remainder of the twentieth century and even into the first two presidential terms of the twenty-first century its continued legacy may ultimately be the death of Republican Party's presidential ambitions. The Republicans have now become the party of Southern and rural White people and they have alienated most minority groups to their demise as America is becoming a minority majority. It was Nixon's shameful Southern strategy that has ultimately led to this decline.

The 1972 election was a disaster for the Democrats from the start. The frontrunner and a candidate that stood a good chance of beating Nixon, Senator Ted Kennedy was horribly tarnished with the Chappaquiddick scandal. It occurred when a young woman aide he was having an affair with was killed when Kennedy drove his car off a bridge and she drowned. Kennedy made matters initially worse by trying to get a cousin to take the blame before confessing.

Senator Edmund Muskie was in contention as well, but he was sabotaged by Nixon's men with a forged letter where he supposedly insulted French-Americans with a derogatory term costing him votes in New England. After winning the California Primary in June, the anti-war candidate George Mc-Govern finally wrapped up the Democratic nomination. Nixon substantially led McGovern in the polls from the very beginning and McGovern's campaign became even more difficult when it was revealed that his Vice Presidential choice, Senator Tom Eagleton, had been treated for depression. This raised questions about his fitness to serve as President should he be required to do so. Initially McGovern stood by Eagleton but when public opinion began to weigh heavily against him, McGovern changed his mind and abandoned Eagleton picking the Kennedy brother-in-law Sergeant Shriver as his running mate. This created an impression of both indecisiveness and weakness. Nixon exploited the matter and his campaign and began to make assertions that McGovern's anti-war stance was also out of weakness. McGovern campaigned on ending the war, granting amnesty to draft evaders. He was for civil rights and women's rights including abortion. Nixon successfully campaigned against all these issues.

The rightwing Nixon posed himself as a moderate compared to McGovern. He was even able to appear moderate to most Americans on civil rights because in his Southern strategy Nixon referred to civil rights and integration through vague references to states' rights and busing, so that Southern bigots would understand his meaning, while northerners and others wouldn't realize Nixon's opposition to civil rights. This tactic was later described as "dog whistle politics."

Many of McGovern's most vocal supporters also hurt him and made him appear to be radical compared to Nixon. There were many young McGovern supporters who were openly engaged in the drug culture and the Hippie Counterculture and these anti-establishment supporters were very visible at every McGovern political event. The television news teams were also guilty of exploiting these pictures. Very few people in business suits were ever filmed at McGovern events, but long-haired, bell-bottom wearing, Hippie looking young people loudly protesting the war were filmed in abundance. These pictures scandalized many mainstream Americans and created a concern about declining morals and law and order issues which Nixon also shamelessly exploited.

Nixon's re-election was never in doubt which is why the Watergate scandal is so puzzling. It was totally unnecessary. Nixon was going to win big anyway, so why burglarize the offices of the Democratic National Committee and commit other illegal acts?

The Watergate scandal exposed many clandestine and illegal activities that were undertaken by members of the Nixon administration. Those activities included what the Nixon campaign internally called "the dirty tricks division" which used illegal activities such as break-ins and bugging the offices of political opponents and other people of whom Nixon or his advisors disliked. Nixon and his aides also ordered the harassment of activist groups and political figures, using the FBI, CIA, and the IRS as their accomplices.

The whole of these illegal acts became slowly known after five men, who were former FBI and CIA agents, were caught burglarizing the Democratic Party headquarters in Washington, D.C. on June 17, 1972, in the Watergate Complex. These men were known in the Nixon White House as "the Plumbers," they had been dubbed this by Nixon aides because one of their early jobs was to find and stop press leaks in the Nixon Administration. This team of criminals had brazenly been given actual offices in the Nixon White House.

In the wake of the Watergate Scandal it became clear that Nixon aides had committed many crimes in their attempts to sabotage the Democrats and other "Nixon enemies" and later lied about it committing perjury. Nixon's most senior aides, Chief of Staff H.R. Haldeman and White House Counsel John Dean, faced prosecution for their participation, and when it was over both men along with a total of forty-six Nixon aides were convicted of crimes. Nixon faced impeachment and probable prosecution as well. He was forced to resign to avoid this. As part of the bargain for him to resign Nixon was guaranteed that he would not face prosecution. On September 8, 1974, his successor, Gerald Ford, granted Nixon a "full, free, and absolute pardon," which ended any possibility of an indictment or prosecution. It was a very unpopular decision. Ford later paid the price for this in the 1976 election and lost to Jimmy Carter.

Surprisingly Nixon made another comeback. Nixon supported Ronald Reagan for president in 1980 making television appearances portraying himself in biographer Stephen Ambrose's words, "as the senior statesman above the fray." He wrote guest articles for many publications both during and after the campaign and played the role of elder statesman after Reagan's victory.

Gerald Ford the Interim President

> "My fellow Americans, our long national nightmare is over."—President Gerald Ford

Gerald Ford was an accident. He has the distinction of being the first person appointed to the Vice Presidency under the 25th Amendment of the Constitution when Nixon's Vice President Spiro Agnew resigned due to corruption and taking bribes while he was governor of Maryland. Ford then became Vice President when Nixon resigned to avoid impeachment and possible prosecution. He is the first person and only person to be both Vice President and President without ever being elected. He was a caretaker in both offices.

After serving in the Navy in World War II, Ford returned home to Grand Rapids, Michigan and ran for Congress where he served until Nixon appointed him Vice President. While Ford was a competent man, he gained the unfortunate reputation of being a clumsy oaf, which was unjust as Ford was actually an excellent athlete and a talented football player at Michigan. He turned down professional contract offers from both the Detroit Lions and Green Bay Packers professional football teams to go to law school.

Ford did not distinguish himself in Congress and was known as something of a plodder. He was very average and did not stand out in any way. He was thought to be somewhat slow and in this regard Lyndon Johnson joked about Ford that, "He played football for too long without a helmet." But Ford had a reputation as a "team player" which is why Johnson also chose him to serve on the Warren Commission to investigate the death of John Kennedy. He was appointed by Johnson at the request of J. Edgar Hoover. Anthony Weiner in *Enemies* wrote that Congressman Ford was Hoover's informant on the Warren Commission and provided him with intelligence. He was also there to make sure the FBI was not implicated. Hoover distrusted Earl Warren the committee's chair.

When Nixon resigned on August 9, 1974, Ford assumed the presidency. On August 20, Ford nominated former New York Governor Nelson Rockefeller to fill the vice presidency he had vacated. Ford had also considered George H.W. Bush for Vice President, but instead selected as him as the Chief of the US Liaison Office to China in 1974, and then he appointed him in 1975 to head the CIA during the Church Committee hearings. Many thought that Ford made these appointments to head off Bush as a possible political rival for the presidency in 1976. However it has since been revealed that Kissinger and other aides were worried that William Colby was not stout enough to stand up to the Congressional inquiries into the CIA and they felt that Bush was better able to keep these secrets.

When Rockefeller appeared before Congress for his confirmation the hearings he became an embarrassment to both Ford and the Republicans when it was revealed that Rockefeller had given expensive gifts to Ford's senior aides in the process of securing the Vice Presidential nomination from Ford and again in gaining the confirmation from the Senate. Some of these questionable gifts from Rockefeller came by way of his former aide Henry Kissinger. There were charges that Rockefeller and Kissinger had bought the Vice Presidency.

Interestingly, one person who was pleased that Rockefeller had become Vice President was Hillary Rodham Clinton. She had been a volunteer for him and was a Rockefeller supporter attending the 1968 Republican Convention on his behalf.

Ford was a caretaker for the Neo-conservatives (Neo-cons) and his presidency was run largely by his Chief of Staffs, Donald Rumsfeld and Dick Cheney. Kissinger was his National Security Advisor and controlled all foreign policy matters and all intelligence including the CIA. He was later replaced by Brent Scowcroft when Kissinger decided to retire. Ford continued most of the policies of Nixon especially on foreign affairs. He was always on a short leash as president.

In deference to the rightwing Neo-cons Ford supported "a federal constitutional amendment that would permit each one of the 50 States to make the choice" on abortion. This had also been his position as House Minority Leader in response to the 1973 Supreme Court case of Roe v. Wade which he opposed. But Ford also came under much criticism from the Neo-cons for a 60 Minutes interview his wife Betty gave in 1975, in which she stated that Roe v. Wade was a "great, great decision." Many on the right wondered if Ford was a "true" conservative.

In 1976, former California Governor Ronald Reagan ran against Ford for the Republican nomination. Reagan personally disliked Ford. Reagan faulted Ford for allowing South Vietnam to fall. Reagan had previously said, "We should declare war on North Vietnam. We could pave the whole country and put parking strips on it, and still be home by Christmas."

Reagan also disliked Ford for signing the Helsinki Accords in which the US and Europe agreed to recognize the legitimacy of the Communist Bloc to improve East-West relations. Reagan and the rightwing were also angry at Ford for negotiating to cede the Panama Canal to Panama. These negotiations for the canal were continued under President Carter who eventually signed the treaty and has since been solely blamed for it by the Republicans.

Reagan launched a campaign in autumn of 1975 and won several primaries before being persuaded to withdraw from the 1976 presidential race at the Republican Convention for fear of splitting the Party. But in 1976 Ford dropped Vice President Nelson Rockefeller who supported abortion rights in favor of Senator Bob Dole.

The Democratic nominee, former Georgia Governor Jimmy Carter, campaigned as a Washington outsider and reformer. He gained support from voters dismayed by the Watergate scandal and Ford's pardoning of Nixon. After the Democratic National Convention, Carter held a significant lead over Ford in the polls. However the race tightened and by election day the polls showed the race to be very close.

In a stunning reversal of the 1964, 1968 and 1972 presidential elections, the Southerner Jimmy Carter won the Southern vote for the Democrats and carried all the Southern States except Virginia. He also carried the northern Democratic areas as well and won in Massachusetts, Rhode Island, New

York, Ohio, Pennsylvania, Wisconsin, Minnesota, and Missouri. The total popular vote was close but Carter won with about 50 percent against Ford with 48 percent.

Operation Condor

Beginning in the 1950s the CIA began overthrowing democratic governments in Latin America in favor of rightwing military dictatorships. By the mid-1970s the US and the CIA were supporting some very strong dictatorships in South America including the fascist governments of Argentina, Bolivia, Brazil, Chile, Paraguay and Uruguay. In 1975, these governments and the CIA began Operation Condor to destroy all leftists in South America along with any opposition to these fascist states by any means possible including torture, kidnappings, and murder. The US through the CIA gave technical and military aid to support the operation. Two of the creators of this Operation were Secretary of State Henry Kissinger and the CIA Director George H.W. Bush.

Victor Flores Olea in *Editoriales Operacion Condor* and J. Patrice McSherry in *Tracking the Origins of a State Terror Network: Operation Condor* estimate that over 60,000 people were killed as part of Operation Condor. The American people became aware of Operation Condor when Orlando Letelier the former Ambassador to Chile under the democratically elected government of Salvador Allende was killed by a car bomb in Washington, DC. His American aid Ronni Moffitt was also killed in the assassination. Under Operation Condor the Chilean dictator Augusto Pinochet employed anti-Castro Cubans and an American soldier of fortune, Michael Townley, to build and plant the bomb.

Operation Condor was supported by the CIA until President Carter was elected and stopped US involvement. Support for the operation resumed when Reagan became president.

Jimmy Carter

> "It is difficult for the common good to prevail against the intense concentration of those who have a special interest, especially if the decisions are made behind locked doors."— Jimmy Carter

> "I'll never tell a lie. I'll never make a misleading statement. I'll never betray the confidence that any of you had in me. And I'll never avoid a controversial issue."—Jimmy Carter

> "The truth is that male religious leaders have had, and still have, an option to interpret holy teachings to exalt or

to subjugate women. They have, for their own selfish ends, overwhelmingly chosen the latter. Their continuing choice provides the foundation or justification for much of the pervasive persecution and abuse of women throughout the world."—Jimmy Carter

Carter attended the Naval Academy graduating in the top ninety percent of his class. After serving as an officer in both the Atlantic and Pacific submarine fleets he went to graduate school attaining a master's degree in nuclear physics. In December 1952, the first major nuclear accident occurred in Canada when a nuclear reactor melted down. Carter was given command of the rescue team and was sent to Canada to remedy a dangerous situation, which he did successfully.

Carter had planned on making the Navy his career when his father unexpectedly died in 1953 and Carter was urgently needed to run his father's large agri-business company. Returning to business in Georgia, he also became active in local politics; in the 1960s he was elected to two terms in the Georgia Senate.

In 1966, Carter ran for Governor of Georgia, ultimately losing to Lester Maddox.

He ran again four years later. In the 1970 gubernatorial campaign, Carter ran as a populist in the Democratic primary against the former governor Carl Sanders. He courted the Georgia Black vote very successfully. Carter was a civil libertarian and was never a segregationist. He had refused to join the popular White Citizen's Council which caused an expensive boycott of his peanut warehouse and his business. His family was also one of only two in their congregation to vote to admit blacks to the Plains Baptist Church. The Black community strongly backed Carter because of his civil rights advocacy.

After winning his gubernatorial election Carter announced, "I've traveled the state more than any other person in history and I say to you quite frankly that the time for racial discrimination is over. Never again should a Black child be deprived of an equal right to health care, education, or the other privileges of society." He was the first statewide office holder in the Deep South to be openly against segregation. He went on to become the most progressive Governor in Georgia history.

When Carter entered the Democratic Party presidential primaries in 1976, he was considered to have little chance against nationally better-known politicians. He became quickly known as "Jimmy Who?" Despite very little national name recognition in most early polls Carter outworked his better known opponents, including Congressman Mo Udall of Arizona, Governor Jerry Brown of California, Senators Henry Jackson of Washington and Fred Harris of Oklahoma, and the right-wing Governor George Wallace of Alabama. He won the nomination and he picked the liberal Senator Walter Mondale of Minnesota as his running mate. He then ran a successful campaign as a reformer and a Washington outsider and won. Initially America loved his honesty, humility and especially loved the fact that he was an outsider and not a Washington politician.

Early in the Carter administration it became more than apparent that Carter had won because of Watergate and the disgrace of Nixon. And while being a Washington outsider was a great advantage in the 1976 election, it was also a disadvantage during his presidency. Carter never really had his own constituency or even any real support within the Democratic Party. Carter had no national political base. His support in his own party remained very weak throughout his presidency.

As a Southerner and a very open "born-again Christian" Carter was stereo-typed by Republicans and Democrats alike as some kind of Southern "Bubba." There were times when they even questioned Carter's superior intellect. Carter was actually one of the more intelligent of the presidents, certainly much more intelligent than his predecessor Ford or his successor Reagan.

Carter's presidency was tumultuous. His administration faced continuing inflation and recession brought on by the Johnson and Nixon Administration's extraordinary Vietnam expenditures and their refusal to raise taxes to cover those expenses. Carter would pay for their errors with inflation and recession during his entire presidency. To make matters worse in 1977 the country was also had an energy crisis and an oil shortage.

Carter was the first president whose foreign policy was built upon human rights. Prior to Carter the US and the CIA had supported the White supremacy governments of South Africa and Rhodesia. Carter changed this policy and he began supporting the Black freedom movements. The CIA and many in the State Department thought that Carter's foreign policy based upon human rights was naïve and ill-advised, but Carter persisted. He also refused to send the US Olympic Team to the Soviet Union for the Summer Games because of the Soviet invasion of Afghanistan.

There were other catastrophic events. The Mariel Boat Lift was initially a popular humanitarian effort where Castro allowed any Cubans who wanted to leave the country to go to the United States. It became a fiasco because Castro also then emptied his prisons placed among the refugees some hardened criminals. This was not discovered until they had gained entry into the US.

In the final year of Carter's presidency Iran had a revolution against the dictatorial Shah of Iran who had been installed in a coup d'état and supported by the Dulles Brothers through the CIA. The CIA was caught totally unaware of the uprising and the Iranian Revolutionary Guard took American hostages. The military attempted a hostage rescue but they bungled it very badly and Carter was blamed. The Iranian Hostage Crisis and the bungled attempt by the military were devastating to Carter's chances of winning re-election. Night after night television news showed Iranians burning American flags as television networks kept a running count and reported how many days the hostages had been in captivity.

Carter began his term with a sixty-six percent approval rating which dropped to thirty-four percent approval by the time he left office. In the 1980 election, Carter was fighting against his own party as well as the Republicans. The Democrats still saw Carter as a political outsider and seemed as eager to defeat Carter as the Republicans. Both Senator Edward Kennedy and California Governor Jerry Brown campaigned against Carter reminiscent of the Gene McCarthy challenge to Johnson. Most liberals in the Democratic Party disliked Carter although there never was a cogent argument as to why they should as Carter was very progressive. There were even editorial cartoons showing Carter-Mondale headquarters with Carter in very small letters and Mondale in very large letters expressing some views of the Democratic Party at the time.

As a Carter delegate to the National Democratic Convention in New York in 1980, I can attest to the hate on the part of some liberal Democrats at the time against Carter. It divided the convention. Carter won twenty-four of thirty-four primaries and the President entered the party's convention with sixty percent of the delegates pledged to him on the first ballot. Despite this, Ted Kennedy refused to drop out leading to a fight and a split at the New York City convention.

At a pre-convention event for all the delegates at Radio City Music Hall, New York Governor Hugh Carey was to give a "welcome to New York" speech to the delegates; instead, he began a plea to have an "open convention" where the elected Carter delegates could feel free to abandon their election commitments and switch to Kennedy. The audience, the majority of whom were Carter delegates, proceeded to boo the Governor. Carey tried for twenty minutes to finish his plea for Kennedy but was met with louder boos and jeers and finally left the stage.

After the convention nominated Carter, Ted Kennedy at first refused appear on stage or to shake hands and endorse Carter, but Speaker of the House Thomas "Tip" O'Neal warned Kennedy that he would burn his bridges with the Party if he didn't endorse, shake hands, and appear on stage with Carter at the end of the convention. Kennedy did but then stayed to one side of the stage visibly pouting. In the general election many of the Kennedy supporters voted for Republican Congressman John Anderson, who ran as an independent. Some Democrats even defected to Reagan.

In 1980, the election results showed fifty percent for Reagan, forty-one percent for Carter, with the remaining going to the third-party candidate Anderson and others. Unrecognized were Carter's achievements. His administration oversaw one of the largest reorganizations of the federal government. Americans overlooked his administration's promotion of human rights which he continued to champion after he left office. Carter also created an Energy Department and a national energy strategy which was later scuttled by Reagan at the request of the oil and energy companies. Carter's efforts at Camp David brought peace between Israel and Egypt and brought the only meaningful peace to the Middle East in recent history. Carter is also the most highly praised president outside of the United States. In 2002, President Carter received the Nobel Peace Prize for his lifetime work "to find peaceful solutions to international conflicts, to advance democracy and human rights, and to promote economic and social development."

Unlike most Presidential libraries which are shrines to their namesakes, the Carter Center is an active place promoting human rights, global health care initiatives, conflict resolution and fair elections. And Carter's reputation with the American people has finally improved to the point where he is the most popular ex-president. Carter's approval rating was at thirty-four percent just prior to the 1980 election, in early 2009 his approval rating was at a whopping sixty-four percent. In retrospect most historians agree Carter had been a good president.

Reagan and Bush Commit Treason to Prolong the Hostage Crisis

> "They made a deal with Reagan that the hostages should not be released until after Reagan became president. So, then in return, Reagan would give them arms. We have published documents which show that US arms were shipped, via Israel, in March, about two months after Reagan became president."—
> Former Iranian President Abolhassan Banisadr in 1993

In a shameful and treasonous act similar to the one Nixon committed to defeat Humphrey, Reagan and Bush made certain that the Iranian Hostage Crisis would not end before Reagan came to office, to assure Carter's defeat.

One of the most emotional issues during the 1980 election was the release of the fifty-two Americans being held hostage in Iran since November 4, 1979. Reagan won the election because many voters were angry at the inability of the Carter Administration to obtain their release. On the day of Reagan's inauguration, about twenty minutes after he concluded his inaugural address, Iran suddenly announced the release of the hostages. It was no coincidence. Former Iranian President Abolhassan Banisadr in a 1993 letter to Congress and in subsequent interviews says that Reagan's people scuttled a deal that Carter was negotiating with Iran for a promise that Reagan would trade arms to Iran through Israel in exchange for Iran keeping the hostages until Reagan was in office.

A quote from Banisadr is above. Banisadr also said that the Carter Administration's proposal for Iran to release the hostages was going to be accepted, but the Ayatollah Khomeini decided to take Reagan's deal because it gave Iran much needed arms.

Former Naval intelligence officer and National Security Council member Gary Sick, and former Reagan-Bush campaign and White House staffer Barbara Honegger, have also confirmed that Reagan and Bush, through William Casey, made this deal with the Iranians to keep the hostages until Reagan had won the election. Reagan was in fact so petty about it that he insisted that the hostages be kept not until he won election, but until he was sworn into office, so that Carter would not have the satisfaction of having the crisis resolved during his presidency.

Gary Sick authored a book recently on US–Iran relations, *All Fall Down*. Sick wrote that in October 1980 officials in Ronald Reagan's presidential campaign including future CIA Director William Casey made a secret deal with Iran to delay the release of the hostages until after the election. In return for this the United States arranged for Israel to ship American weapons to Iran. President Carter has stated since that he believes Donald Gregg, a National Security Council official in his administration, had leaked the classified information about the hostage negotiations to Bush during the campaign. Bush had previously been Gregg's boss at the CIA.

On September 23, 1988, Richard Brenneke, an arms dealer from Portland, Oregon, voluntarily testified at a sentencing hearing of Heinrich Rupp for misuse of government funds related to this incident. In his deposition, Brenneke testified that on the night of October 18, 1980, Rupp had flown Reagan–Bush campaign director William Casey and others from Washington's National Airport to the Le Bourget Airfield north of Paris for a series of secret meetings. According to Brenneke it was at these meetings on October 19 and 20, at the Waldorf Florida and Crillon hotels, that members of the Reagan–Bush campaign secretly negotiated with the representatives of the Ayatollah Khomeini. The agreement was to give arms to Iran in exchange for Iran keeping the American hostages prisoners until Reagan was sworn into office. Also in attendance at the meeting, according to Brenneke, was Donald Gregg, a CIA liaison to President Carter's National Security Council.

Because of his testimony at the Rupp trial, Republicans accused Brenneke of perjury and he was then tried for perjury on five counts. On May 4, 1991, after deliberation, the jury found Brenneke "not guilty" on all five counts. Following the trial jury foreman Mark Kristoff stated, "We were convinced that, yes, there was a meeting, and he was there and the other people listed in the indictment were there.... There never was a guilty vote.... It was 100 percent."

Brenneke also testified that others had also seen George H.W. Bush at the meetings in Paris. In 2001, the PBS investigative news program *Frontline* aired a show about the Bin Laden family. They revealed a French intelligence report which claimed that Salem Bin Laden, Osama Bin Laden's oldest brother, who was a close friend of the royal Saudi family as well as a close friend of the Bush family, had started these negotiations. Salem Bin Laden frequently worked on secret and sensitive matters for the Saudi family and he was also one of those involved in the secret Paris meetings between Reagan and Iranian emissaries. *Frontline* concluded, "Rumors of these meetings have been called the 'October Surprise' and some have speculated that in these meetings, George H. W. Bush negotiated a delay to the release of the US hostages in Iran, thus helping Ronald Reagan and Bush win the 1980 Presidential election. All of this is highly speculative, but if the French report is correct, it points to a long-standing connection of highly improper behavior between the Bush and Bin Laden families."

Barbara Honegger was a member of the 1980 Reagan–Bush campaign team and later served as a Reagan White House policy analyst. In 1995, she became the Senior Military Affairs Journalist at the Naval Postgraduate School. While working in the Reagan White House she discovered information that proved to her that George Bush and William Casey had conspired to assure that Iran would not free the US hostages until Jimmy Carter had been defeated in the 1980 presidential election and until Regan was sworn into office. She says that arms sales to Iran were a definite part of that bargain. She resigned from the Reagan administration shortly after her discovery. In 1989, she wrote a book about it called, *October Surprise*.

Luxembourg banker Ernest Backes has also verified this story and stated that he was in charge of the transfer of $7 million from the Chase Manhattan Bank and Citibank on January 16, 1980, which was then used in the Reagan–Iran deal to pay for the liberation of the hostages. He said he gave copies of these files to the National French Assembly.

Former Nixon aide Kevin Phillips also believes that Reagan and George Bush were involved in the hostage delay for weapons deal and wrote about it in his book about the Bush family entitled *American Dynasty*.

In reward for their traitorous acts, William Casey became Director of the CIA under Reagan, and Donald Gregg, the man who betrayed President Carter and broke several National Security laws leaking the information to Reagan and Bush, became National Security Advisor to Vice President George H.W. Bush.

More proof that the American press is still controlled through Operation MOCKINGBIRD can be found in this event as the mainstream media has ignored this story. The CIA has continued to apply pressure to newspaper editors, some publishers and others to disavow this event. This included planting false stories to discredit it. This was sometimes done in very clever ways so as to appear to prove this story only to be revealed the information is horribly false and thereby discrediting all of it as conspiracy theory. One of the ways in which this was done was to have conspiracy theorist Lyndon LaRouche make outlandish statements about the event that are not true so that anyone believing any part of the arms-for-hostage deal looks as nutty as LaRouche. It is not clear whether LaRouche did this on behalf of the CIA or that the CIA planted stories and used LaRouche, but the effect is the same.

According to several CIA officials LaRouche also independently worked with and supplied information to the CIA on a regular basis. There is a lot of evidence for this assumption. Former Deputy Director of the CIA Bobby Ray Inman has admitted to frequent meetings with LaRouche. The CIA has also admitted that LaRouche also met with Former Deputy Director John Mc-Mahon in 1983, when William Casey was CIA Director at the time. The fact that LaRouche met with Deputy Directors of the CIA from time to time suggests LaRouche was very important to them and the relationship was not as casual as some have been led to believe.

It is apparent from the Iran Hostage incident that the Reagan–Bush Administrations were as corrupt as the Nixon White House, but they didn't get caught. It also appears that the rightwing CIA was promoting and protecting Reagan and their former Director George Herbert Walker Bush.

This was not the only illegal deal by the Reagan Administration with Iran. The Reagan–Bush administrations would later use these Iranian connections for even more illegal trading in the Iran–Contra scandal, only this time some of their cronies would be caught in the act.

CHAPTER 12. REAGAN AND BUSH, AND THE RIGHTWING DOMINATED 1980S

"Ronald Reagan wasn't qualified to be governor, let alone president. I was Vice President of the Screen Actors Guild when he was its president. Ronnie never had an original thought. We had to tell him what to say. That's no way to run a union, let alone a country."—Actor James Gardner

"Bush is functioning much like a co-president. George is involved in all the national security stuff because of his special background as CIA Director."—White House Press Secretary James Brady, March 1981

"Well, I learned a lot....I went down to (Latin America) to find out from them and (learn) their views. You'd be surprised. They're all individual countries"—Ronald Reagan

"My name is Ronald Reagan. What's yours?" Reagan introduced himself after delivering a prep school commencement address in his second term. The person responded, "I'm your son, Mike," to which Reagan replied, "Oh, I didn't recognize you."

Nixon was a bad president because he was caught committing crimes. Reagan was supposedly a good president because he wasn't caught, even though quite a few members of his administration were caught in illegal dealings including the drug trade.

Nixon was paranoid but very bright. Reagan was not a particularly bright or educated man. He frustrated his staff by reading trite magazine articles and then getting excited about them and insisting on national policy changes based upon these articles until his staff patiently talked him out of whatever he was proposing. We also now know that in his second term that he was already suffering from dementia. Reagan was an actor playing president while the rightwing Neo-cons, particularly George Herbert Walker Bush, ran the Executive Branch.

Reagan was another politician that was cultivated by J. Edgar Hoover. According to Tim Weiner in *Enemies,* Reagan began working in 1947 as an FBI informer for Hoover. He was a professional tattletale who gossiped about and spied on supposed communists and other leftists in Hollywood. Regan was one of those responsible for the McCarthy firings in Hollywood. He destroyed the reputations of many actors, writers and producers during Joe McCarthy's communist witch hunts.

Reagan likened himself to John Wayne. He always kept a nice smile and was usually ready with a humorous homespun cowboy homily written by someone else. Ronald Reagan was scripted. He had good writers. Reagan the politician was an act as phony as the color of his hair. Reagan was a very vain man and he practiced being presidential in a mirror. He was a very shallow man and politician and was a totally disengaged and detached president even in the best of times. The great Ronald Reagan is a national myth.

The "Great Communicator" was a dullard. He had little interest or appetite for policy or intellectual matters. After the Iran-Contra Scandal his own self-appointed Tower Commission in their report held Reagan accountable "for a lax managerial style and aloofness from policy detail." It was polite political speak for an absentee president who had no clue as to what was happening in his administration. George Bush and Reagan's rightwing aides ran the country while Reagan attended state dinners, entertained the masses and remained his jolly old self. Jim Cannon, an aide to Howard Baker, would later talk about what Reagan's staff had told him, "They told stories about how inattentive and inept the President was.... They said he wouldn't come to work, all he wanted to do was to watch movies and television at the residence."

It wasn't that Reagan faded over time. He was never attentive or cognizant of his duties from the very beginning. When he assumed office in January 1981, Anthony Quainton, the US counterterrorism coordinator, was asked to brief the President and other officials on significant emerging threats and the likelihood of possible terrorist attacks. He recalled this important briefing as follows: "I gave that briefing to the President, who was joined by the Vice President, the head of the CIA, the head of the FBI, and a number of National Security Council members. After a couple of jelly beans, the President dozed off. That in itself was quite unnerving."

Reagan in a candid interview with Barbara Walters admitted that in his academic life, "I never knew anything above Cs." Even his allies and supporters were frequently astounded by how little he knew. Peter Jenkins in his book, *Mrs. Thatcher's Revolution*, quotes Margaret Thatcher talking to her aides about Reagan and saying, "Poor dear, there's nothing between his ears."

Reagan's rightwing quotes are some of the more astounding things said by any public official. These are remarks that wouldn't have been tolerated by the American people or the press with any other President. He said the following: "Unemployment insurance is a pre-paid vacation for freeloaders." On another occasion, "We think there is a parallel between federal involvement in education and the decline in profit over recent years." and "We were told four years ago that seventeen million people went to bed hungry every night. Well, that was probably true. They were all on a diet." And another, "Fascism was really the basis for the New Deal." And he also called Medicaid recipients, "a faceless mass, waiting for handouts." He also thought that pollution was caused by plants and made numerous moronic statements in that regard, such as, "Trees cause more pollution than automobiles." In a tightly scripted speech, he failed to quote John Adams and said, "Facts are stupid things." Adams' actual quote is "Facts are stubborn things."

In addition to being intellectually dull, Reagan was horribly superstitious. Astrologer Joan Quigley had given advice to Ron and Nancy Regan before his presidency, and when he decided to run for president in 1980, they again asked for her advice. She studied his horoscope and gave them the go-ahead, and she volunteered her services to the Reagan campaign. After he was elected she provided advice on a regular basis to President Reagan on a variety of issues. Former White House Chief of Staff Donald Regan, in his book, *For the Record*, told of what he called "the most closely guarded domestic secret of the Reagan White House." He wrote, "Virtually every major move and decision the Reagans made during my time as White House Chief of Staff was cleared in advance with a woman in San Francisco (Joan Quigley) who drew up horoscopes to make certain that the planets were in a favorable alignment for the enterprise."

Reagan's opponent in the 1984 presidential election was former Vice President Walter Mondale. With questions about Reagan's age and a weak performance in the first presidential debate his ability to perform the duties of president for another term was seriously questioned. His apparent confused and forgetful behavior was becoming more evident to his aides and supporters. He sometimes didn't recognize his family members like his son Mike in the quote at the beginning of this chapter, or his close aides and cabinet members.

During a White House reception for mayors he once said in a confused state, "How are you, Mr. Mayor? I'm glad to meet you. How are things in your city?" Reagan was greeting Samuel Pierce, his secretary of Housing and Urban Development who he was friends with and who he had personally asked to attend the event. Rumors began to circulate that he had Alzheimer's disease which was later confirmed.

Reagan rebounded in his second debate with Mondale and even made a joke about his age, albeit written by others. Despite the fact he couldn't actually fulfill the duties as president, Reagan was re-elected in a lop-sided victory. Mondale carried only his home state of Minnesota and the District of Columbia. Reagan won and received over fifty-eight percent of the total popular vote with Mondale winning forty percent.

Reagan's economic policies resulted in huge budget deficits because of tax cuts to the rich. The gap between the rich and poor grew enormously during his presidency and since, and his economic policies hurt the middle class. His references to "welfare queens" denigrated the poor and helpless and contained hidden racial overtones. The denigration of "welfare queens" was pure and simple dog whistle politics to appeal to working class White bigoted voters. Reagan also derided the homeless whose population doubled during his time in office due to his callous policies of cutting off funds and closing federally supported mental health hospitals.

He also denigrated the presidency. The illegal actions of his staff in the Iran-Contra affair lowered American credibility around the world and provided another low point in the history of the American Presidency. His supporters say he defeated the Communists and brought about the demise of the Soviet Union which didn't actual end until after his presidency in 1991. It is a hollow boast. The USSR fell under the enormous cost of supporting its vast military and it had nothing to do with Regan. Despite the glowing almost saint like obituaries about Reagan from the American right, he was indeed a very poor president.

El Salvador

El Salvador was another fascist regime supported by the United States and the CIA during the Reagan administration. During this US supported reign of terror death squads killed approximately 65,000 civilians including priests, nuns, church officials, labor leaders, students, and anyone showing the slightest disagreement with the US supported regime. Shortly after Regan won the 1980 election four American Catholic women, three nuns and a lay person, who were working with the poor in El Salvador and advocating on their behalf, were kidnapped, raped and murdered by the rightwing Junta in El Salvador. Their kidnapping and murder was ordered by General Carlos Eugenio Vides Casanova a man supported by the CIA.

Americans and the Catholic Church were outraged. The FBI was asked to investigate. The investigating officer Agent Stanley Pimentel was eventually able to find and to bring about the conviction of four members of the El Salvador Army. Pimentel was also able to prove that it was General Casanova who had given the orders, but the Reagan administration hid this information from the public and covered up his involvement in the kidnapping, rapes and murders.

The Reagan administration was an impediment during Pimentel's investigation including having the FBI working at cross purposes. At one point Secretary of State Al Haig lied and suggested that the four women victims were working with left-wing communist guerillas and were somehow deserving of their fate.

During the investigation the Reagan administration strongly supported the fascist regime in El Salvador especially General Casanova. They said Casanova was a hero in the fight against communism. The General was later given the Legion of Merit Award by President Reagan along with a Green Card allowing him to eventually move to and retire in Florida in 1988.

As part of their support for El Salvador the administration had the FBI investigate hundreds of church and student groups that were protesting the killing of the Catholic women along with anyone protesting the Administration's support of the fascist government in El Salvador. Hundreds of people had their lives disrupted by wiretaps, were subjected to brutally harsh interrogations and were generally harassed similar to what the FBI had done during COINTELPRO. Regan revived the use of the FBI and CIA as weapons to be used against the American left and his other domestic and international enemies.

Iran-Contra, the Reagan-Bush Administration and the CIA Run Amok

"I was provided with additional input that was radically different from the truth. I assisted in furthering that version."—Lt. Col. Oliver North explaining his participation and why he had lied in the Iran-Contra scandal

"I have put thousands of Americans away for tens of thousands of years for less evidence for conspiracy with less evidence than is available against Ollie North and the CIA people. . . . I personally was involved in a deep-cover case that went to the top of the drug world in three countries.

The CIA killed it."—Former DEA Agent Michael Levine on
CNBC-TV, October 8, 1996

In 1984, Congress passed three pieces of legislation which have become
collectively known as the Boland Amendment which severely restricted the
CIA, NSA and Department of Defense operations in Nicaragua, specifically
against any support of the rightwing fascist Contras. In 1985 while Iran and
Iraq were at war, Iran made a secret request to buy more weapons from the
United States. The CIA Director William Casey who had been the point person in the arms for delay of the release of the hostages in 1980 was interested
and thought he could do business with the Iranians once again.

National Security Advisor Robert McFarlane gave his approval despite
a Congressional embargo against selling arms to Iran which made these negotiations and these transactions illegal. McFarlane later justified the illegal
sale by saying that although it was illegal, that the sale of arms would not
only improve US relations with Iran, but it could buy the release of the seven
American hostages being held by Iranian terrorists in Lebanon.

Shipping arms to Iran violated the Congressional embargo and it was
highly illegal. Negotiating with and rewarding terrorists also violated Reagan's personal 1980 campaign promise to the American people to never do so.
It was also an act which also made Americans unsafe and vulnerable to more
taking of hostages and kidnapping for arms or ransom by other terrorists.

It was a fiasco from the outset and by the time the sales were discovered
by the public more than 1,500 missiles had been shipped to Iran. In exchange
only three hostages were released and were then replaced by the Iranian terrorists capturing and imprisoning three more American hostages. Secretary
of State George Shultz later called this disaster "a hostage bazaar."

When conservative Republican Senator Barry Goldwater, the Chairman
of the Intelligence Committee, became suspicious of the Reagan Administration's Iran- Contra dealings and he began to raise concerns in Congress
about the CIA and the Contras. The Administration and the top CIA officials then attacked and defamed Goldwater by characterizing him to many
in Congress and the press as "a confused old drunk."

In November 1986, the Lebanese newspaper *Al-Shiraa* printed an exposé
on the arms for hostages deal. Reagan responded by going on television and
in a statement to the American people he vehemently denied that any such
operation had occurred. The president was forced to retract the statement
a week later, but he again insisted that there were no sales of weapons to
Iran. He said forcefully that it had not been "an arms for hostages deal." It
was another lie.

Shortly after Reagan's second lie, it was proven that the US had sold
weapons to Iran through Israel. After this finding Attorney General Edwin

Meese also made a discovery that the Reagan administration could account for only $12 million of the $30 million that the Iranians had paid for the weapons. Eighteen million dollars had just completely disappeared. It was later discovered that Lieutenant Colonel Oliver North of the National Security Council had diverted these funds from the arms sales to the Nicaraguan Contras in violation of Congressional action and US law, at the request of and with the full knowledge of the CIA, the NSA and National Security Adviser Admiral John Poindexter.

Poindexter was forced to resign and North was fired, but the Iran-Contra story was not finished. The press finally began to investigate. In defense of himself Reagan ordered his own investigation, the Tower Commission, which eventually concluded that there was no evidence linking the President to the deal, but in their report they held Reagan accountable and blamed him "for a lax managerial style and aloofness from policy detail." In plain words, he had no idea what was happening in the day to day events of his administration. He had no idea about his administration's policies or their development and he made no effort to find out.

An Independent Counsel, Lawrence Walsh, was appointed and investigated the affair which he did for the next eight years as a massive cover-up took place within the White House and in the intelligence community. Although President Reagan and Vice President Bush were never charged, fourteen of their aides were charged for either participating in the crimes or in the cover-up of the crimes. However, Oliver North's conviction was later overturned on a legal technicality.

When George Herbert Walker Bush became President he issued six presidential pardons, including one to Robert McFarlane who had already been convicted and one to Secretary of Defense Casper Weinberger even before he stood trial. Bush publically denied any involvement and insisted that he was completely "out of the loop" on Iran-Contra. However, this too was a lie according to government records. In *The Iran-Contra Affair 20 Years On*, National Security Archive Electronic Briefing Book 210, Bush's own diaries from that time stated, "I'm one of the few people that know fully the details."

While it is likely that the absentee president Ronald Reagan sat in total ignorance, Bush and Reagan's aides were heavily involved. They were given regular briefings about the progress of the Contras and their illegal financing by Felix Rodriquez a CIA officer who had worked for the Vice President's National Security Advisor Donald Gregg in the CIA in Vietnam. He had also worked with Bush in the Bay of Pigs Invasion. His regular briefings on these illegal dealings to Bush were such a concern that in September 1986 General John K. Singlaub wrote to Oliver North expressing his concern about Felix Rodriguez's daily contacts with the Vice President's office. He warned of probable damage to Vice President Bush, President Reagan and the Republican Party.

In the Independent Counsel's Final Report, (*The Walsh Report*) it said that Rodriguez also met briefed and spoke repeatedly with Bush's National Security advisor Donald Gregg and his deputy Col. Samuel J. Watson III on numerous occasions. A single chapter in the *Walsh Report* titled "Donald P. Gregg" contains 329 references to Rodriguez. Donald Gregg was also the CIA officer that President Carter believes to have leaked the details of the hostage negotiation to the Reagan campaign in 1980 and then assisted them in the treasonous deal for arms to delay the Iranian hostage's release.

It should be noted that it was during the Reagan Administration's illegal funding of the Contras that the CIA also began transporting cocaine and crack into the United States and supporting and protecting drug gangs in California with the proceeds from the sale of these drugs also going to finance the rightwing Contras in Nicaragua. This was the story that was first exposed by the journalist Gary Webb.

Apparently there is no crime too big or horrific that the CIA will not use to further their self-chosen rightwing covert operations. There appears to be very little difference between the CIA and organized crime when these covert operations have come to light. In fact, as previously explained, the CIA works in partnership with organized crime in many operations.

George Herbert Walker Bush was involved in many of these operations. In *Defrauding America*, by Rodney Stich, he cites Michael Maholy who claimed that George H.W. Bush's Zapata Off-Shore was used as part of a CIA drug-smuggling ring to pay for arming Nicaraguan Contras from 1986 to 1988. Maholy is not without knowledge as he worked for Naval Intelligence, the US State Department and the CIA for two decades. He is not alone in these assertions. Others have also made the same claims. Maholy also claimed Zapata's oil rigs were used as staging bases for drug shipments to the US, an operation he claims was named by the CIA "Operation WHALE WATCH."

Chapter 13. The 1990s, More Bush and Clinton

> "George Bush was born on third base and thought he had hit a triple."—Jim Hightower, Texas journalist and politician

> "I'm going to be so much better a president for having been at the CIA that you're not going to believe it."—George H.W. Bush

> "The family's ties to oil date back to Ohio steelmaker Samuel Bush's relationship to Standard Oil a century ago, while its ultimately dynastic connection to Enron spanned the first national Bush administration, the six years of George W. Bush's governorship of Texas, and the first year of his Washington incumbency.... No other presidential family has made such prolonged efforts on behalf of a single corporation."—Kevin Phillips

George H.W. Bush had been planning his presidential run long before 1980, when he entered the Republican primaries and lost to Reagan. In his second attempt he entered the Republican race for President of the United States in October 1987. His challengers for the Republican presidential nomination included US Senator Bob Dole and US Representative Jack Kemp of New York, and conservative Christian televangelist Pat Robertson. As Vice President Bush was considered the early frontrunner for the nomination but flubbed his debut by coming in third in the Iowa caucus behind Dole and Pat Robertson. However after this early scare Bush then rebounded and went on to easily win the Republican nomination. At that time there was much speculation as to Bush's choice of a running mate. Dole, Kemp and many other well-known names were speculated about in the media. Bush surprised many when he chose a mostly unknown and undistinguished US Senator Dan Quayle from Indiana.

Quayle was the favorite choice of the rightwing branch of the Party. The Republicans thought he would appeal to women voters. He was young and good-looking and was compared in looks to John Kennedy. Quayle loved the comparison and began to frequently compare himself to Kennedy. It irritated the Democrats. It prompted Senator Lloyd Bentsen the Democratic nominee for Vice President to quip during the Vice Presidential debate, "I served with Jack Kennedy. I knew Jack Kennedy. Jack Kennedy was a friend of mine. Senator, you're no Jack Kennedy."

It turned out that Quayle was less Kennedy-like and more a Reagan-like choice in that he was dogmatically right-wing and like Reagan he wasn't very bright. He was easily controlled by Bush and the rightwing of the party. He later embarrassed himself in front of the nation with the inability to spell the word potato at a spelling bee photo-op. Like Reagan he also said many stupid things. He said in a 1988 press conference, "The Holocaust was an obscene period in our nation's history." When the reporters asked in a follow up if he thought America caused the Holocaust he became confused and responded, "No, not our nation's, but in World War II. I mean, we all lived in this century. I didn't live in this century, but in this century's history."

In a very insulting speech with racial overtones the oblivious Quayle said to a group of American Samoans, "You all look like happy campers to me. Happy campers you are, happy campers you have been, and, as far as I am concerned, happy campers you will always be."

In Hawaii he became confused and awkwardly stated, "Hawaii has always been a very pivotal role in the Pacific. It is in the Pacific. It is a part of the United States that is an island that is right here."

In a speech before the United Negro College Fund, he managed to mangle their slogan, "A mind is a terrible thing to waste," by saying, "What a waste it is to lose one's mind, or not to have a mind is being very wasteful, how true that is."

And about exploring Mars he perhaps showed just how ignorant he truly was when he said, "Mars is essentially in the same orbit.... Mars is somewhat the same distance from the Sun, which is very important. We have seen pictures where there are canals, we believe, and water. If there is water, that means there is oxygen. If oxygen, that means we can breathe."

Because of his frequent uneducated remarks Quayle became a national joke, with Senator Kerry saying in jest of the Vice President, "If something happens to President Bush, the Secret Service has orders to shoot Dan Quayle." And others joked that Bush had chosen Quayle as his Vice President to insure he would never be assassinated.

In his acceptance speech at the Republican Convention in 1988, Bush demonstrated his rightwing credentials by endorsing the Pledge of Allegiance with the phrase "one nation under god," and also strongly endorsed Christian prayer in public schools, capital punishment, gun rights, and promised that he would make all abortions illegal. The speech also included Bush's famous pledge: "Read my lips, no new taxes!" a quote that would come back to haunt him.

The general election campaign that Bush conducted has been described as one of the nastiest in modern times. Bush knowingly and falsely accused Michael Dukakis of polluting the Boston Harbor as the Massachusetts governor. In a show of false piety he drummed up the fervor of the religious right in the campaign by continually pointing out that Dukakis was opposed to the law that would require all students to say the Pledge of Allegiance with the phrase "one nation under god" and also pointed out that Dukakis was against mandatory school prayer.

Dukakis's unconditional opposition to capital punishment led to one of the most unfair questions ever asked during the presidential debates. The conservative moderator Bernard Shaw asked hypothetically if Dukakis would support the death penalty if his wife Kitty were raped and murdered. Many critics have questioned this highly inflammatory, unwarranted and biased question at a presidential debate, and it is largely suspected that Shaw's question was planted by the Republicans. Bernard Shaw was known to have a rightwing bias in his reporting and he has since gone to work for the rightwing biased Fox News. When Dukakis' responded "No," it then gave Bush an opening in the debate to attack Dukakis as too weak to even defend his wife from rape and murder. Bush then took further unfair advantage of this situation with his dishonorable "Willie Horton" campaign ads. The ads were false and also smacked of racism and more dog whistle politics.

Willie Horton was an African-American felon who was given a weekend furlough because of good behavior as part of a long standing Massachusetts prisoner reform program. While on furlough Horton escaped and raped a White woman after pistol-whipping, knifing, binding, and gagging her fiancé. He was later shot and captured and returned to prison. The incident occurred while Dukakis was Governor.

The incident had little to do with Dukakis. The Massachusetts inmate furlough program was actually signed into law by a Republican Governor Francis Sargent. The furlough program had operated since 1972. The program was actually abolished during Dukakis' final term of office on April 28, 1988. But the Bush campaign ad blamed the Willie Horton rape incident directly on Dukakis.

The ads shamelessly ran nationwide and were particularly effective with White working class racist voters. Bush had aired the Willie Horton ads with Horton's mug shot to show that he was Black. The strategy was to use Black on White rape as a way of triggering racial prejudice to sway the election. The ad was run as an "independent expenditure" through a political action committee to give cover and to separate it from the Bush campaign to avoid criticism. It allowed Bush to deceptively claim he and his campaign had no role in its production. It was a lie. The ad was made at the direction of Lee Atwater who was Bush's campaign manager. It was Atwater's decision to deliberately use a mug shot of Horton in the ad to show that he was Black and to play upon White racial fears. Playing on White racial fears was a common strategy for Republicans after Nixon devised his Southern Strategy.

Atwater was a promoter of the Republican Party's Southern Strategy and knew the power of using racial fear and prejudice in a campaign. On November 13, 2012, *The Nation* magazine released the audio of a full interview where Atwater said the following about the Southern Strategy he used in the Bush and other Republican campaigns: "You start out in 1954 by saying, 'Nigger, nigger, nigger.' By 1968 you can't say 'nigger,' that hurts you, backfires. So you say stuff like forced busing, states' rights, and all that stuff. You're getting so abstract now you're talking about cutting taxes and all these things you're talking about are totally economic things and a byproduct of them is Blacks get hurt worse than Whites. And subconsciously maybe that is part of it. I'm not saying that. But I'm saying that if it is getting that abstract and that coded, that we are doing away with the racial problem one way or the other. You follow me, because obviously sitting around saying, 'We want to cut this,' is much more abstract than even the busing thing, and a hell of a lot more abstract than 'nigger, nigger.'"

Atwater at the behest of Bush was not above using other dirty tricks. During the election a number of allegations were made in the media about Dukakis's personal life, including more false claims that his wife Kitty had burned an American flag to protest the Vietnam War. This rumor was also traced back to Atwater.

Another grossly false rumor from the Bush campaign was that Dukakis had been treated for a mental illness and was unfit to be president. In the film *Boogie Man: The Lee Atwater Story*, conservative columnist Robert Novak revealed that Atwater had personally tried to get him and others in the press to spread these false mental health rumors about Dukakis.

In the nationwide popular vote Bush took about fifty-three percent of the ballots cast while Dukakis received about forty-six percent. Bush was inaugurated on January 20, 1989. It was a smooth transition as he had been working as the de facto president the previous eight years and now he was succeeding the absentee president Ronald Reagan.

The collapse of Soviets came early in the Bush presidency. It was a shock to everyone as the CIA and American intelligence had no clue. The uprisings in Eastern Europe and the fall of the Berlin Wall in 1989 signaled the end of the Soviet Union, who Reagan had labeled "the Evil Empire." The USSR formally ceased to exist in 1991. Although it happened during the Bush presidency Regan was credited with the demise of the Soviet Union adding to his rightwing mythical status. Neither man actually had anything to do with the collapse. They were caught completely unaware. In truth the Soviet Union had been a paper tiger for some years sacrificing everything to keep their military dictatorship strong enough to control their Eastern European satellites as well as their Soviet Republics. They were fast running out of resources and their economy was in shambles. It was just a matter of time that they would have eventually collapsed and neither Reagan nor Bush can legitimately claim credit for this event.

Early in his term Bush faced the problem of what to do with huge deficits spawned by the Reagan tax cuts. The deficit reached $220 billion in 1990 and had grown to three times its size since Reagan took office in 1980. Bush realized that taxes, not just spending cuts, were needed to curb the fast growing deficit. He raised tax revenues and as a result many Republicans felt betrayed because of Bush's pledge of "no new taxes" in his 1988 campaign. It was the Republicans in Congress that defeated Bush's tax proposal which would have enacted tax increases and would have reduced the deficit by $500 billion over five years. Eventually Bush and congressional members reached a grudging compromise on a budget package that increased the marginal tax rate and phased out exemptions for high income taxpayers, but because of this increase Bush's popularity fell with Republicans and conservatives.

At this time the country also entered into a recession. As the unemployment rate edged upward in 1991, Bush signed a bill providing additional benefits for unemployed workers to keep the economy and consumer spending from contracting. This was also very unpopular with rightwing Republicans. In his second year in office Bush was told by his Chicago School economic advisors to stop regulating the economy and to let the free market take over. His political advisors also said that he had already done everything necessary to ensure his reelection. By 1992 interest and inflation rates were the lowest in years, but by midyear the unemployment rate had reached almost eight percent the highest since Regan's recession in 1984.

The economy would be his undoing in attempting to win a second term. Bush also gave the impression that he was not really engaged in economics and appeared aloof and detached from the concerns of the average American. At one point he appeared at a political photo-op at a supermarket checkout and admitted he didn't know what a grocery scanner was or how it worked. It was obvious to the American public that Bush hadn't actually been at a supermarket checkout for many years making him seem like the rich man he was and he appeared even more detached from the average American and their economic concerns.

Panama and Noriega

> "And there is a question of a news blackout. Neither Americans, nor anyone else, saw the ravages of the first night bombing or the dead or the wounded in the first days of the invasion. The US managed to block such pictures or news reports by frustrating news coverage."—Helen Thomas UPI White House Correspondent

> "Thousands of Panamanians were killed or wounded during the invasion. The bulk of these casualties were civilians. Estimates of the numbers killed range from over 1,000 to as many as 4,000. A precise figure is hard to arrive at because the US Government has carried out a deliberate and systematic cover-up of the numbers killed."—The Independent Commission of Inquiry on the US Invasion of Panama 1991

Although the relationship did not become contractual until 1967, Manuel Noriega worked with the CIA from the late 1950s until the 1980s. He was their man and he was heavily involved in the CIA drug sales program and was also involved in the Iran-Contra scandal. He was also making himself a wealthy man with this drug and arms trade. Perhaps the CIA grew tired of him or perhaps they believed he had become uncontrollable. Some have suggested that Bush went after Noriega to hide his own connections to Iran-Contra. However for whatever reason Bush attacked Panama and went after Noriega and captured him during the US invasion. In the aftermath grand juries in Tampa and Miami indicted Noriega on US federal drug charges.

In 1988, the Senate Subcommittee on Terrorism, Narcotics and International Operations said of him, "The saga of Panama's General Manuel Antonio Noriega represents one of the most serious foreign policy failures for the United States. Throughout the 1970s and the 1980s, Noriega was able to manipulate US policy toward his country, while skillfully accumulating near-absolute power in Panama. It is clear that each US government agency which had a relationship with Noriega turned a blind eye to his corruption and drug dealing, even as he was emerging as a key player on behalf of the Medellin Cartel."

The Committee went on to say that Noriega was allowed to establish "the hemisphere's first narcoleptocracy" with the support, encouragement and cooperation of the CIA and other US agencies.

Bush launched the US invasion of Panama on December 20, 1989. Losses on the US side were limited to twenty-three military and three civilian casualties. On December 29, the General Assembly of the United Nations voted seventy-five to twenty with forty abstentions to condemn the US invasion as a flagrant violation of international law. There were also many accusations of unwarranted use of force and unnecessary civilian deaths. The US buried of thousands of innocent civilians in mass graves during and immediately after the invasion. All these atrocities were later confirmed by the Independent Commission of Inquiry on the US Invasion of Panama. A press blackout at the time prevented any accurate accounts of the invasion and casualties. Records from hospitals and mortuaries were then destroyed by the US forces to prevent any accurate picture.

In April 1992, Noriega went on trial in Miami. At his trial Noriega intended to defend himself by claiming that his alleged crimes were approved by the CIA and Reagan, Bush and their administrations, which was likely true. The US government objected to any disclosure of the purposes for which the United States had paid Noriega or that the Reagan and Bush Administrations had cooperated with him because they said that this information was classified and that its disclosure went against the interests of the United States.

Noriega insisted that the CIA paid him $10,000,000, and that he should be allowed to disclose the duties he had performed for the CIA and the Reagan and Bush administrations. The district court held that the "information about the content of the discrete operations in which Noriega had engaged in exchange for the alleged payments was irrelevant to his defense." The court said that the introduction of evidence about Noriega's role with the CIA and the two administrations would "confuse the jury" and it wasn't allowed.

Noriega was convicted and on September 16, 1992. He was sentenced to forty years in prison, later reduced to thirty years. After a while Noriega's prison sentence was reduced from thirty years to seventeen years for good behavior. After serving the seventeen years in detention and imprisonment he was released on September 9, 2007. On April 26, 2010, Noriega was extradited to France. On July 7, 2010, Noriega was convicted of drug smuggling by the French and sentenced to seven years in jail. Panama asked France to extradite Noriega so he could face trial for human rights violations there. He was extradited to Panama on December 11 and incarcerated at El Renacer prison, and he is still serving time for crimes he committed during his rule of

Panama. It is apparent Noriega was a bad man, but it was equally apparent was that he had been the CIA's and the Regan and Bush administration's bad man. He was punished while they were not.

The Gulf War

"The Gulf War was like teenage sex. We got in too soon and out too soon."—Senator Tom Harkin

On August 2, 1990, Iraq invaded Kuwait their oil-rich neighbor to the south. Bush who is well connected with the region's oil sheiks strongly condemned the invasion. Secretary of Defense Dick Cheney traveled to Saudi Arabia to meet with King Fahd. Fahd requested a US military response to the invasion saying he also feared a possible invasion of his country as well. The US military buildup in Saudi Arabia and the Mideast began immediately.

Early on the morning of January 17, 1991, the US and allied forces launched the first attack. It was a quick and devastating defeat. Bush made the decision to stop the offensive after a mere one hundred hours. Some critics labeled this decision premature as hundreds of Iraqi forces were then able to escape sure destruction. Bush responded by saying that he wanted to minimize US casualties. Opponents further charged that Bush should have continued the attack, pushing Hussein's army back to Baghdad and then removing him from power. The truth was that the Bush administration and the military still wanted Iraq to be a military counterweight to Iran in the region, which was why Bush had the war stopped once Kuwait was liberated.

The 1992 Election

"In the New Hampshire primary in 1992, she (Hillary Clinton) knowingly lied about her husband's uncontainable sex life and put him eternally in her debt."—Christopher Hitchens

"When I was in England I experimented with marijuana a time or two, and I didn't like it. I didn't inhale."—Bill Clinton

"I am in support of the NRA position on gun control."—Bill Clinton selling himself out to the NRA

"I think it's wrong to demonstrate against your own country or organize demonstrations against your own country in foreign soil. I just think it's wrong. Maybe, they say, well, it was a youthful indiscretion. I was 19 or 20, flying off an aircraft carrier, and that shaped me to be Commander in Chief of the Armed Forces. And I'm sorry, but demonstrating – it's not a question of patriotism. It's a question of character and judgment."—George H.W. Bush to Bill Clinton during the 1988 Presidential debates.

Bush announced his reelection bid in early 1992. His victory in the Persian Gulf War gave him extremely high approval ratings and his reelection looked certain. Bush's approval ratings were unbelievably high at 89 percent. This approval rating was actually much higher than the sainted Ronald Reagan's had ever been. As a result many Democrats who would have been formidable candidates like New York Governor Mario Cuomo and Senator Al Gore thought his re-election was inevitable and they declined to seek the Democratic Party's presidential nomination.

Conservative political columnist and the former architect of Nixon's Southern Strategy, rightwing commentator Pat Buchanan, challenged Bush for the Republican nomination and shocked political pundits by finishing a strong second in New Hampshire, but it was a momentary blip and Bush easily went on to win the nomination.

Among the Democrats US Senator Tom Harkin of Iowa ran as a populist liberal with labor union support and as expected won the first Democratic contest in Iowa. Then Senator Paul Tsongas of Massachusetts won the Democratic primary in his backyard of New Hampshire. California Governor Jerry Brown won the Maine Democratic caucus, and Senator Bob Kerry of Nebraska won in South Dakota. Tsongas won the Utah and Maryland primaries and a caucus in Washington. Harkin won caucuses in Idaho and Minnesota, and Jerry Brown won Colorado. It looked like the Democrats would have a brokered convention with no candidate getting the required votes to win the party's nomination.

The only Southerner in the race was Arkansas Governor Bill Clinton who won Georgia and then went on to win the big Super Tuesday primaries in the South. Suddenly Clinton had a commanding lead that he never surrendered. After winning the nomination, Clinton chose Al Gore to be his running mate. Choosing a fellow Southerner went against the popular strategy of balancing a Southern candidate with a Northerner on the ticket, but the idea of two Southerners on the ticket allowed Clinton to take Southern states that were not available to other Democrats. Clinton was a "Bubba," a native-born working-class White Southerner rather than a transplanted Yankee like Bush. Gore was also a Southerner, but he balanced the ticket in other key ways. Gore was strong on women's, family and environmental issues, while Clinton was not. Gore appealed to the liberals. He was also a Vietnam veteran.

Bush was also damaged by the independent candidacy of rightwing conservative billionaire Ross Perot of Texas. Perot's volunteers succeeded in collecting enough signatures to get his name on the ballot in all fifty states. Incredibly by June of 1992, Perot led all the presidential candidates in the national public opinion polls with support from thirty-nine percent of the voters polled versus thirty-one percent for Bush, with Clinton in last place with just a meager twenty-five percent. The remaining five percent were undecided.

Clinton had major character flaws that should have been fatal to his candidacy. Many character issues were raised during the campaign including allegations that Clinton had dodged the draft during the Vietnam War which was true. He was pardoned by Carter's blanket pardoning of the Vietnam War draft dodgers in 1977. He was also accused of using marijuana, to which Clinton lamely said he had only pretended to smoke but "didn't inhale." Bush also unfairly accused Clinton of meeting with communists on a trip to Russia that he took as a student. It was a clearly deceptive accusation since anyone you would meet on a student trip to Russia was most likely a communist.

Clinton was rightly accused by many political opponents, both Republicans and Democrats of being a womanizer and a sexual predator. He had a well-deserved reputation of being predatory when it came to women. There were many allegations about Clinton having sex with young campaign aides. During the campaign a story came out that Clinton had also engaged in a long-term extramarital affair with a woman named Gennifer Flowers. Clinton lied and denied ever having an affair with Flowers on the television news program *60 Minutes*. He was also accompanied on the *60 Minutes* interview by Hillary Clinton and she too forcefully denied the affairs, which gave credence to his adamant denials. In retrospect, it is almost certain that Hillary knew he was lying and had also lied.

After the Clintons' denial on television, Flowers held a press conference in which she played tape recordings she had secretly made of her private phone calls with Clinton. Bill and Hillary again lied to the public, saying that these recordings were fakes and not the voice of Bill Clinton. In a 1998 deposition made while Clinton was fighting another sexual accusation against him, he finally admitted that he had had a sexual relationship with Flowers and that the voice on her recordings was his. It was also apparent that Hillary had also known and had lied.

On November 3, Bill Clinton won the election, receiving a paltry forty-three percent of the total popular vote against Bush's thirty-seven percent and Perot's nineteen percent. It was the first time since the Nixon, Humphrey, and Wallace election of 1968 that a candidate had won the White House with under half of the popular vote. Clinton's home state of Arkansas was the only state to give any of the three candidates a statewide majority. In all the remaining states the winner received less than fifty percent. It was a deeply divided election where none of the three were the choice of a majority of Americans. The right-wing conservative independent Perot had certainly cost Bush the election.

William Jefferson "Bill" Clinton, the Chameleon Democrat

"What does a Clinton really believe in? You might as well ask a chameleon to tell you its favorite color."—Historian Joseph Sobran

"During the 1992 election I concluded as early as my first visit to New Hampshire that Bill Clinton was hateful in his behavior to women, pathological as a liar, and deeply suspect when it came to money in politics."—Christopher Hitchens

"Bill Clinton is probably about as religious as I am, meaning zero, but his managers made a point of making sure that every Sunday morning he was in the Baptist church singing hymns."—Noam Chomsky

In 1992, Bill Clinton had the ability to make a person believe that he was of whatever political bent they were. Conservatives thought he was conservative, moderates thought he was moderate, liberals thought he was liberal, civil rights advocates believed he was a civil rights advocate, Southerners believed he was a traditional Southerner. In truth Bill Clinton lacks a political ideology other than to get himself elected or to enhance his own power or wealth. His wife is a willing partner in these pursuits. Both are political panderers with no real core beliefs and few morals. They are both more than willing to lie and deceive when it suits their needs.

Clinton was inaugurated as the 42nd President of the United States on January 20, 1993. On May 19, 1993, Clinton fired seven employees of the White House Travel Office causing a major controversy. Although the Travel Office staff serves at the pleasure of the President who may dismiss them without cause, they were nonpolitical employees and this traditionally was not done. Clinton aides claimed the firings were done because of financial improprieties that had been revealed by a brief FBI investigation. It was later revealed that the Clintons' had forced the FBI to investigate the Travel Office to justify their firings. It has since been revealed that the firings had been done to allow some close Arkansas friends and supporters of the Clintons to take over the very lucrative White House travel business. Later evidence has shown that Hillary was the instigator of the firings in favor of her friends. It was the first of a number of shady business dealings by the president and his wife.

Clinton was also greatly dissatisfied that the FBI was not working enthusiastically on his behalf. So he appointed Louis Freeh a former FBI Agent and a New York District Court Judge as Director of the FBI on September 1, 1993. Freeh was a loyal supporter of Clintons and Clinton expected unquestioned loyalty from Freeh as the FBI Director. It was not to be.

Shortly after Freeh was appointed he was asked to look at Travel Office firings and the apparent suicide of Deputy White House Council Vince Foster, a former law partner of Hillary Clinton at the Rose Law Firm and his connection to the Whitewater scandal. As the FBI began their inquiries it was apparent that Freeh would allow them to conduct a fair and unbiased investigation. Despite his loyalty to the Clintons he would not let the investigation be influenced by the Clintons and he protected his agents from the administration during the investigation. As a result the Clintons rarely spoke to Freeh thereafter. FBI directors had been close advisors to the presidents since Roosevelt, but according to Tim Weiner in *Enemies*, when Freeh began his unbiased investigation, Bill Clinton quit communicating altogether with Freeh and it remained that way for the remainder of his presidency. FBI Director Freeh was frozen out of the Clinton administration.

In November 1993, David Hale was sentenced to two years and four months in prison for fraud. He was a former Arkansas municipal judge and former Arkansas banker who had done business with the Clintons. During his testimony he made criminal allegations against Bill and Hillary Clinton in the Whitewater Real Estate controversy. He alleged that the Clintons, while Bill was Governor of Arkansas, pressured him to provide an illegal $300,000 loan to Susan McDougal, Clinton's partner in the Whitewater land deal.

A US Securities and Exchange investigation began, and it resulted in convictions against McDougal and her husband for their illegal dealings in the Whitewater project. In the Whitewater Real Estate projects Susan and Jim McDougal were partners with Bill and Hillary Clinton. Hillary was also their legal counsel. The McDougals were also very close friends of the Clintons.

Despite being full partners of the McDougals in Whitewater and Hillary being their legal counsel, the Clintons were never charged. Despite their close business ties and their close friendship with the McDougals, the Clintons incredibly claimed that they were totally unaware of any details of Whitewater. They still maintain their innocence in the affair.

Susan McDougal and Jim served prison time as a result of Whitewater along with fifteen individuals who were also close to the Clintons and who were also convicted of various federal charges in these illegal business activities. The fifteen included Webster Hubbell who was appointed Associate

Attorney General by Clinton and who had been a partner of Hillary Clinton's at the Rose Law Firm. Hubbell was formally nominated on April 2, 1993, as Clinton's choice for Attorney General but his nomination was immediately attacked in the Senate and the press because his close financial and business ties to the Clintons. His nomination was then withdrawn and he was later quietly appointed by Clinton to Associate Attorney General, the number three position at the Department of Justice.

Another of the thirteen convicted in the Whitewater scandal was Arkansas Governor Jim Guy Tucker who was a supporter and partner of Clinton's and also served as Bill Clinton's Lt. Governor succeeding him as the governor when Bill left to be president. Both Hubbell and Tucker served time in prison for their role in the Whitewater fraud. Jim Guy Tucker refused to testify or answer questions about either Bill or Hillary Clinton's involvement in Whitewater. It is not a coincidence that he received a full presidential pardon for his crimes from Bill Clinton at the end of his presidency.

One of the primary reasons the Clintons were never charged was that Susan McDougal took the fall and also refused to answer grand jury questions about Bill or Hillary Clinton's involvement or knowledge of Whitewater. She steadfastly refused to answer questions as to whether President Clinton lied in his testimony during her Whitewater trial. Her refusal to answer these questions resulted in a jail sentence of eighteen months just for contempt of court and for refusing to answer these questions about the Clintons. The two years she spent in incarceration was mostly due to her refusal to answer the prosecutors and the grand jury's questions about Bill and Hillary Clinton's involvement. McDougal also received a full Presidential pardon for all her crimes from outgoing President Clinton in the final hours of his presidency in 2001. McDougal is currently serving as Chaplain at the University of Arkansas for Medical Sciences. Her two brothers are active in politics and have received the Clintons' lucrative support. A 2011 book, *The Death of American Virtue*, by law professor Ken Gormley, also claims that Bill Clinton had a long term and on-going extramarital affair with Susan McDougal.

Stories of Bill Clinton's unsavory sexual behavior never went away. After the Flowers incident, other women began to come forward with claims about Clinton's predatory sexual behavior. In December of 1993, two Arkansas State Troopers, Larry Patterson and Roger Perry, claimed that as governor Bill had used them to prey on women and cover up his affairs. This scandal became known as "Troopergate."

The two officers stated that as State Troopers assigned to the Governor they were required by Governor Clinton to arrange sexual liaisons for him on numerous occasions. The press coverage of these allegations began to mention that one of the women was named "Paula," which was later discovered to be Paula Jones. Jones sued Clinton for sexual harassment. Clinton settled with Jones for $850,000, the entire amount of her claim, in exchange for her agreement to drop her lawsuit so that he would not have to testify publicly and under oath about his affairs and other allegations of sexual harassment.

In 1998 Kathleen Wiley also alleged that Clinton had physically assaulted and groped her in a hallway in 1993. Also in 1998, Juanita Broaddrick alleged Clinton had raped her in 1978. In another 1998 event, Elizabeth Ward Gracen recanted a six-year-old denial of an affair with Clinton and admitted that she had "a one night stand" with Clinton in 1982.

In 1995, Monica Lewinsky was a twenty-two-year-old recent college graduate. She was hired to work as an intern at the White House during Clinton's first term. She began a sexual relationship with him. After her first sexual encounter with Clinton, she was promoted from being a volunteer intern to a paid intern.

She confided the details of the affair to her friend Linda Tripp, a Defense Department worker. Tripp was appalled by the president's behavior with the young intern and began to secretly record their telephone conversations. When Tripp discovered in January 1998, that Lewinsky had lied for Clinton and had signed an affidavit in the Paula Jones lawsuit that denied she ever had a relationship with Clinton, Tripp became angry and delivered the tapes to Kenneth Starr the Independent Counsel who was investigating Clinton's misogynous behavior.

Lewinsky eventually admitted to having nine sexual encounters with Bill Clinton from November 1995 to March 1997. According to Kate Anderson Bower in her book *The Residence: Inside the Private World of the White House*, White House staffers confirmed that the Lewinsky affair was common knowledge and that the staff even kept track of "Lewinsky sightings." The staff also said that Hillary knew about Lewinsky long before it became public and that she only became upset when the affair was discovered by the press. They said that Hillary only got angry at Bill because of the political feeding frenzy that followed the media's discovery of his affair.

Despite the swift and forceful lies and denials from both Bill and Hillary Clinton and their aides about Lewinsky, the clamor for answers about the president's sexual relationship with the young intern grew louder. On January 26, President Clinton, standing once again with Hillary at his side for support, spoke at a White House press conference and issued another forceful denial. In part he said, "I want to say one thing to the American people. I want you to listen to me. I'm going to say this again: I did not have sexual relations with that woman, Miss Lewinsky. I never told anybody to lie, not a single time, never. These allegations are false." It was another Clinton lie, another lie in which Hillary knowingly and willingly participated.

Hillary Clinton claimed that the Lewinsky charges were the result of a "vast rightwing conspiracy." She forcefully characterized the charges as the latest in a long organized collaborative series of false sexual charges against Bill Clinton by his political enemies and not any wrongdoing by her husband. When they were both finally caught in these lies Hillary again lied and claimed that she had been misled by her husband's initial claims that no affairs had taken place.

Lewinsky was unwilling to discuss the affair or testify about it. On July 28, 1998 Lewinsky received immunity in exchange for grand jury testimony concerning her sexual relationship with Clinton. She was ordered to cooperate or be sent to jail for contempt of court. She then began to tell the truth and turned over a blue dress stained with Bill Clinton's semen to Kenneth Starr and the investigators. This provided conclusive DNA evidence that proved there was a sexual relationship despite Clinton's public denials. After this Clinton then admitted in a taped grand jury testimony on August 17, 1998, that he had indeed lied to the American public and the court. He admitted that he had an "improper physical relationship" with Lewinsky. That evening Clinton went on nationally television to make a statement admitting to a relationship with Lewinsky which he downplayed as "not appropriate."

In the aftermath Bill Clinton was held in civil contempt of court for his perjury by Judge Susan Webber Wright. He was disbarred and his license to practice law was suspended in Arkansas for five years. His law license was also suspended by the United States Supreme Court. He was also fined $90,000 for lying under oath and giving false testimony.

While it may seem cruel to place any of Bill's misogynous behavior on Hillary Clinton, it is very difficult to believe in her advocacy of feminist causes while she ignores her misogynist husband's behavior and defends him on every occasion, including lying for him. This goes beyond any "stand by your man" behavior as she also appears at times to make light of his behavior. She has frequently made light-hearted jokes about his womanizing. She was also not above making harsh derogatory remarks about Bill's female victims. She was especially harsh and cruel to Lewinsky and blamed the young intern for Bill's actions. She has also done this with Bill's other women victims. It appears that Hillary is willing to put up with this behavior, and to lie and defend him and then blame these women for his behavior, in order to protect and have an equal share in his power and influence.

It is difficult to believe Hillary's feminist credentials are genuine. During the presidential campaign, after she accompanied Bill on the 60 Minutes interview where he lied about and she knew he was lying about his affair with Gennifer Flowers, Hillary Clinton later made very odd, insensitive and belittling remarks about Tammy Wynette and the "stand by your man" sentiments of some women. It was also about this time that she made disparaging remarks about stay at home mothers and what Hillary derisively called, "women staying home and baking cookies and having teas." When she realized that her anti-housewife remarks had caused an outrage among women, she only half-apologized and downplayed these remarks by saying that they may have been "ill-considered."

As a politician, Bill Clinton wanted to please everybody. In his policies he tried to please both the left and right. He initiated "Don't Ask, Don't Tell," which was a weak solution and never really resolved the issue of Gays serving in the military to anyone's satisfaction. This policy almost caused a rift with his Vice President, Al Gore, who thought that Clinton should have had the courage to order that Gays be allowed to serve in the military. He told Clinton that he should be brave and act like Truman did when he gave the executive order that allowed Blacks to serve in the military.

Clinton was also trying to ingratiate himself with the right. On September 21, 1996, he shamefully signed into law the Defense of Marriage Act (DOMA), which defines marriage for federal purposes as the legal union of one man and one woman and allows states the right to refuse or recognize gay marriages that are performed in other states. Both Bill and Hillary Clinton publically and strongly defended DOMA and state's rights on this issue. Hillary Clinton remained weak on gay rights and marriage, and only announced her support for gay marriage in late 2013 when all the national polls showed that a growing solid majority of Americans finally approved of it. She did this in preparation for her second possible run for the Presidency.

Bill Clinton did cut taxes for fifteen million low-income families, but then he also cut America's safety net for poor children by endorsing the Personal Responsibility and Work Opportunity Reconciliation Act (PRWORA) and signed it into law on August 22, 1996. It fulfilled the Republicans' rightwing election promise to "end welfare as we have come to know it." The program replaced the Aid to Families with Dependent Children (AFDC) program which had been in effect since Roosevelt's New Deal in 1935. It was the safety net for America's poor children and the Clintons ended it with little remorse and to great rightwing fanfare. It was also dog whistle politics. The Clintons also knew that ending AFDC would ingratiate them with working class Whites who believed in the racist Reagan mantra that most AFDC recipients were "Black welfare queens."

As odd as it may seem, both Bill and Hillary Clinton are mostly apolitical in their views. They are neither left or right nor even moderate. They are the consummate panderers who do anything for power, personal popularity and self-gain. It is why he was liberal in his first term as governor and then after losing his second election he became conservative to successfully regain the governorship. The Clintons play both sides, which is why they at-tempted to be liberal with things like Hillary's failed healthcare initiative in his first term, and then became conservative and destroyed Aid to Families with Dependent Children in his second term. The Clintons have no political core or principles. They are poll watchers who use popular political trends to advance themselves. The Clintons crave power and wealth and little else. It is why Hillary who was a conservative Republican became a Democrat in the first place.

Hillary Rodham Clinton, "Co-president"

"Those of us who follow politics seriously rather than view it as a game show do not look at Hillary Clinton and simply think 'first woman president.' We think, for exam-ple, 'first ex-co-president' or 'first wife of a disbarred lawyer and impeached former incumbent' or 'first person to use her daughter as photo-op protection during her husband's per-jury rap."—Christopher Hitchens

"She's the most unbelievable actress I have ever met.... She has this unbelievable ability to be a liar. She is soulless."—Edward Klein quoting a Hillary Clinton staff member in his book *The Truth About Hillary.*

"She is one of the most ruthless people we have ever seen in politics."—Dick Morris, former Bill Clinton Advisor

"Without nepotism, Hillary would be running for presi-dent of Vassar."—Maureen Dowd, journalist

Hillary Rodham Clinton is the only First Lady to have been subpoe-naed. She was forced to testify before a federal grand jury in 1996 due to the Whitewater Scandal as she, like Bill was a full partner with Susan and Jim McDougal in the scandal-tainted real estate development. She was also their attorney. However she incredibly claimed that she knew no details of her investment and was never charged with wrongdoing in this or indeed in several other investigations in the many scandals during the Clinton Presi-dency. She was never charged in Whitewater because of lack of evidence due to her "lost" legal records and also because Susan McDougal served eigh-teen months for contempt of court for refusing to testify about the Clintons' knowledge and role in the scandal.

Hillary, very much like Bill, is a blatant opportunist. Her father was a hardcore anti-communist and she was raised in a very conservative Republican family. At age thirteen Hillary helped her father and the Republicans canvass Chicago's Southside following the 1960 presidential election hoping to find fraud committed by the Kennedy campaign. Four years later she was a campaign volunteer for Republican candidate Barry Goldwater in the 1964 Presidential Election.

In 1965, Hillary enrolled at Wellesley College where she majored in political science. She served as President of the Wellesley Young Republicans. She has since claimed that during this time she was an anti-war activist, but this too is a fabrication. In reality she was well known for her activities in preventing campus anti-war demonstrations at Wellesley that were common on other college campuses at the time.

At Wellesley she also volunteered in the elections of New York Republican Mayor John Lindsay and Massachusetts Republican Senator Edmund Brooke. In her junior year she interned at the House Republican Conference. Hillary was invited to New York by Republican Congressman Charles Goodell to work in Governor Nelson Rockefeller's late-entry campaign for the Republican presidential nomination in 1968, and she attended the 1968 Republican National Convention in Miami as a Rockefeller supporter. She was a Republican and had very large political ambitions.

Hillary's senior college thesis was a severe criticism of the left and liberal community organizer Saul Alinsky, a hero in liberal and community organizing and development circles. He was also the inspiration for President Barack Obama's life in public service. This rightwing thesis belittling Alinsky could have been damaging to her newly found Democratic image when the Clintons were in the White House and because of this the access to her college thesis was very unusually restricted by the college at the request of the White House. This restriction continued during the entire Clinton Presidency.

After she graduated from Wellesley, Hillary attended Yale Law School where she met Bill Clinton who also had very large political ambitions. Bill was a Southern Democrat and she conveniently became a Democrat after they started living together and he convinced her that as a woman she would have more political opportunities if she were also a Democrat. Hillary the former Republican then inexplicably campaigned in Texas for George McGovern in the 1972 presidential election with Bill. Although they both would later admit that they already knew his was a failed campaign they openly admitted that they only did it to make Democratic Party connections that would help them later.

Hillary received her law degree the following year. In 1974, she served as staff to the House Committee on the Judiciary during the Watergate scandal. Hillary disliked Nixon going back to her 1968 support for Rockefeller when he failed in presidential bid against Nixon. She helped the Committee's senior counsel research procedures of impeachment and the historical grounds and standards for impeachment. This knowledge would later become very useful in her husband's administration.

Bill had repeatedly asked her to marry him, but she was politically ambitious and told him that she would rather have a career in Washington than marry. However when she failed the bar exam in Washington, DC it was a major setback and she reconsidered.

On Bill's advice she then tried and passed the bar exam in Arkansas and went with Bill to Arkansas where he was running for a seat in the US Congress in 1974. Bill Clinton lost his congressional race, but in the end it was close. In September of 1974 he was losing badly. Clinton had only 23 percent to his opponent John Paul Hammerschmidt's 59 percent. When Gerald Ford pardoned Nixon the polls shifted in his favor dramatically. The general dissatisfaction with Ford and the Republicans because of the pardon caused Bill's numbers to shoot up dramatically but he still lost by four points. However the close race gave him a reputation in Arkansas as a politician on the rise.

Hillary agreed to marry him in 1975, but she strongly insisted on keeping her name and she remained Hillary Rodham. In November 1976, Bill ran and was elected as the Arkansas Attorney General. They moved to Little Rock and Hillary joined the Rose Law Firm. Hillary also used Bill's newly elected position to get appointed to the board of directors of the Legal Services Corporation and she served in that capacity from 1978 until the end of 1981.

In November 1978 Bill was elected as Governor of Arkansas and took office in January 1979. However in Bill's two years as Arkansas Governor many voters began to feel that he was too Liberal and he lost his re-election in 1980. It was a major setback to both of their political ambitions.

The Clintons became more conservative overnight. One of the more visible of these conservative changes was that Hillary who had insisted on keeping her maiden name of Rodham suddenly changed it and asked to be called "Mrs. Clinton" or "Hillary Clinton." Bill then ran to the right and won the gubernatorial election in 1982. He served as the Governor for the next ten years until he ran for President in 1992.

During 1978 and 1979 while Hillary was looking to supplement their income, it was Hillary who began their ill-fated investment in the Whitewater Development Corporation with their close friends Jim and Susan McDougal.

Hillary continued to work at the Rose Law firm where she was considered "a rainmaker" because of all the work she brought to the firm from the governor's office and because of her husband's lucrative connections. In 1986 the Clintons were accused of conflict of interest because the Rose Law Firm was financially benefiting from an unusually large amount of State of Arkansas business that came directly from the Governor's office. The Clintons lied and denied that they profited by this even though Hillary made over $200,000 in her final year at the Rose Firm despite working very limited hours and not billing anywhere near as many hours as other attorneys at the firm who earned less.

When Bill became president, many critics called it inappropriate for the First Lady to play a central role in matters of public policy. Bill Clinton's campaign reference to Hillary was "two for the price of one" and his wife's constant influence in his presidency led his opponents to derisively refer to the Clintons as the "co-presidents." This was a role and a title that the ever ambitious Hillary openly embraced. She had so aggrandized her role as co-president that Bob Woodward would later write that Hillary bizarrely began to walk around the White House having imaginary conversations with Eleanor Roosevelt about presidential affairs.

Hillary was also important in improving Bill's conservative credentials. When they first came to Washington, she used her previous Republican connections to join a conservative prayer group, The Fellowship, where she could socialize with many wives of the conservative Republican Washington notables. As she and Bill climbed the political ladder, she also changed her appearance which had evolved over time from what her critics had described as "total boyish inattention" into very fashionable and much more feminine. However, she hated dresses and began to wear pantsuits.

In her first big foray into presidential politics the "co-president" took on healthcare reform. She saw healthcare as a platform that would one day launch her own presidential ambitions. She bungled the issue very badly. Her approval ratings, which had generally been in the high fifty percent range during the Clintons' first year in office, fell to forty-four percent in April of 1994 and tumbled to thirty-five percent by September 1994. The Republicans made Hillary Clinton's healthcare plan a major campaign issue in the 1994 midterm elections; the Republicans gained fifty-three seats in the House and seven in the Senate and won control of both houses of Congress for the first time in many years. Most analysts and pollsters found that Hillary and her healthcare plan were the major factor in the Democrats' defeat and their loss of the Congress. It was a devastating setback to her ambitions.

According to White House chronicler Bob Woodward, Hillary was mean, self-centered and had a very aggressive bad temper. She frequently reduced her personal travelling aide to tears when she failed to produce something that Hillary wanted. Her friend Mary "Mel" French recalled, "One time, Hillary said: 'Mel, your problem is you just aren't mean enough.' I couldn't work for her and keep our friendship. She is too dogmatic. She gets so into it that she ends up being mean. That is why she has to have such a young staff. They take it and they bow and scrape."

Kate Anderson Bower in her book *The Residence: Inside the Private World of the White House* also claimed that Hillary was extremely mean and foul-mouthed. She quotes a white house staffer who said that in a fit of temper Hillary once threw a White House table lamp at Bill while screaming loud obscenities at him.

She was also rude, mean and condescending to Secret Service agents who she considered to be her servants. According to now-retired Secret Service Agent Dan Emmett in his book *Within Arm's Length: The Extraordinary Life and Career of a Special Agent in the United States Secret Service,* Hillary regularly ridiculed Secret Service Agents with gross profanity and treated them as subhuman servants. Emmitt said that in one angry episode Hillary threw a book hitting the back of the head of a Secret Service agent who was driving her in the Presidential limo accusing him of eavesdropping. In another event Hillary screamed, "Stay the fuck away from me! Just fucking do as I say!" at a Secret Service agent who had politely refused to carry her luggage after he pointed out to her that it is not the job of the Secret Service to carry luggage because it would greatly interfere with his job of protecting her.

If Hillary is sometimes credited with "standing by her man," then Bill should be credited with standing by his woman. Hillary had her own baggage and plenty of allegations of illegal activities, suspicious business dealings and scandals that also followed her.

There have also been rumors for years that Hillary puts up with Bill's peccadilloes because they have an open marriage and that she is bi-sexual and has had numerous affairs of her own. There have been so many accusations of lesbian affairs that Hillary has had to publically deny them. Recently Gennifer Flowers re-asserted her previous claims in the *London Daily Mail* about conversations she had with Bill Clinton that were also revealed in a 1995 book, where she said that Bill Clinton told her that they had an open marriage and had also told Flowers that his wife was bisexual. She said Bill crudely revealed to her with delight and graphic language that Hillary had more oral sex with women than he ever had.

The Whitewater scandal was more Hillary's than Bill's. Jim and Susan McDougal, their close friends and partners in Whitewater, also operated a savings and loan called Madison Guaranty. The McDougals retained the legal services of Hillary at the Rose Law Firm for Madison Guaranty. It was later discovered that this S&L was improperly subsidizing the Whitewater losses of Bill and Hillary Clinton while Hillary was their legal counsel.

Madison Guaranty later failed and Hillary's work at the Rose Firm was also criticized as a conflict of interest in representing the financial institution before the state regulators that her husband as Governor had appointed.

There were many questions about the subsidy by Madison Guaranty for Hillary and Bill's Whitewater losses. Hillary incredibly claimed to the regulators that although Madison Guaranty was her client that she personally had done only "minimal work" for the S&L and was unaware of all these issues. A Special Counsel subpoenaed Clinton's legal records, but she lied and claimed she did not know where her personal records were located. The Rose Law Firms records of these issues were also suspiciously missing from their offices. Some of the missing records were later found stored in the First Lady's White House book room after a two-year search. These records also appeared to have been altered and changed during this time.

Vince Foster, Hillary's close friend and her former partner at the Rose Law Firm, who was then Deputy White House Counsel, committed suicide at this time and suspicions grew that his suicide was connected to the growing scandal about Whitewater and the McDougal's failed S&L. Before Foster died he had told his wife he wanted to resign from the White house and go back to Arkansas because he felt under enormous pressure to do things he "wasn't comfortable with for Hillary Clinton." Allegations were made that Hillary Clinton had ordered Foster hide her records and then to remove and destroy all potentially damaging legal files related to Whitewater and the Madison Guaranty S & L. It was alleged that these records were actually in Foster's office for the two years when she was telling prosecutors that she couldn't find them. It has been also alleged that some of these files were also destroyed on the night of his suicide. A ripped up letter of resignation by Foster was also found in his office.

During the incident Hillary rather infamously said, "I'm not going to have some reporters pawing through our papers. We are the President."

According to the *New York Times* within hours after the death of Vince Foster in July 1993, Chief White House Counsel Bernard Nussbaum also removed documents, some of them concerning Whitewater, from Foster's office and gave them directly to Margaret Williams, Hillary's Chief of Staff. These documents were never seen again.

This two year gap in finding her missing legal files and the Foster suicide created many doubts and suspicions. The two year gap gave the investigators and the court the impression that this was done to allow ample time for Hillary to clean up, hide, change, or delete and destroy any evidence that would prove damaging. The final report didn't exonerate Hillary as she would later boldly claim. It was issued in 2000, and it stated that it was "inconclusive" and further stated that there was "now insufficient evidence" that she had engaged in criminal wrongdoing. The implication in the report was that the incriminating files had been destroyed.

In May 1993, the firings of the White House Travel Office employees, the affair that became known as "Travelgate," began with charges that the White House had used audited financial irregularities in the Travel Office operation as an excuse to replace the staff with Clinton friends from Arkansas. In 1996 the discovery the of a two year old White House memo caused a new investigation to focus on whether Hillary Clinton had personally orchestrated these firings and whether the statements she made originally to investigators about her role in the firings were false and misleading. The 2000 final Independent Counsel Report concluded she was indeed involved in the firings and that she had also lied and made "factually false" statements and that Hillary had "committed perjury" to cover-up the incident. However as she was then the outgoing First Lady, the Independent Counsel did not want to charge her with perjury as she should have been.

Another outgrowth of the Travelgate investigation was in June 1996, when the investigators also discovered improper White House access to hundreds of FBI background reports about former Republican White House employees. This scandal became known as "Filegate." Accusations were made that Hillary Clinton had personally requested these files. In 2000, the Independent Counsel issued the final report on Filegate ambiguously stating that there was "no credible evidence of any criminal activity" by her, however a separate civil lawsuit on the matter was filed and lingered on for years until was finally dismissed by a federal judge in 2010 as too much time had passed.

In March 1994, the New York Times revealed that Hillary had invested a thousand dollars in cattle futures trading, a business where she had no knowledge or experience but in which surprisingly resulted in a large profit of over a hundred thousand dollars from a few weeks of speculation. This occurred in 1978 and 1979, while Bill was Governor. Allegations were made in the New York Times about conflicts of interest and bribery in Hillary's futures trading and her records were analyzed, but as this was a very old case, many of the records were again missing or unavailable. Because of the missing records the investigation could not proceed and she was never charged with any wrongdoing.

It was in the Clintons' early days in Arkansas as they moved up the political ladder that they needed additional income to support their expensive public lifestyle. Hillary began to earn considerable income from her seat on the rightwing, anti-labor, corporate board of Wal-Mart and she also began serving other similar corporate boards. These appointments seemed to come very easy to the Governor's wife whose husband could be of use to these corporations. In six years as a member of the Wal-Mart Board of Directors between 1986 and 1992, Hillary Clinton remained silent as the world's largest retailer waged a major war against labor unions seeking to represent Wal-Mart workers. Hillary the self-proclaimed feminist was also silent during this time when Wal-Mart was also found to have had discriminated against women in pay and promotions and had for many years also forced many of their workers to work illegally for no pay "off the clock." As a board member she was directly responsible for these policies.

As a politician she has always been for sale. In 2013, when Hillary Clinton was raising funds for her 2016 Democratic presidential run she delivered a paid speech to a trade association, the National Association of Convenience Stores, who are strongly opposed the Affordable Care Act. Hillary who is supposedly a strong supporter of this law is not above being swayed by money. Her speech and her question and answer session to this group was "private" and was not allowed to be recorded.

In 1998, when New York's longest serving Senator, Daniel Patrick Moynihan, announced his retirement in November, Hillary saw a political opportunity. In a calculated move to get Hillary eligible for the Senate race in New York the Clintons made a sudden purchase of a home in Chappaqua, New York in September 1999.

In another stroke of luck, Clinton had expected a very difficult senate race against Rudi Giuliani the popular Mayor of New York City as her Republican opponent in the election. However, Giuliani withdrew from the race in May 2000, after being diagnosed with cancer. Rick Lazio a Republican member of the United States House of Representatives was then nominated by the Republicans. He was a weak candidate. The contest drew national attention and Lazio stupidly blundered during a September debate by seeming to man-handle and bully Clinton by invading her space in trying to get her to sign a fundraising agreement. It was a rude performance and it was seen by many women as a man trying to physically assert his will on a woman. Hillary played the victim and it cost Lazio considerable support.

Throughout the campaign opponents accused Hillary Clinton of being a carpetbagger. It was justified as she had never been a New York resident until this time and had never participated in the state's politics other than her brief volunteer work in college as a Young Republican. The Clinton money machine went to work and the campaigns of Clinton and Lazio spent a record combined $90 million on the race. There were charges that she was buying the election. Clinton won the election on November 7, 2000 with fifty-five percent of the vote to Lazio's forty-three percent.

In the Senate Clinton was initially differential to her colleagues and was careful to build relationships with senators from both parties. She remained politically ambitious and was still working to shore up her support among conservatives and forged alliances with religiously conservative senators and became a regular participant in the conservative Senate Prayer Breakfast whose participants were mostly of the religious right.

She added to her conservative credentials by supporting and voting for the Patriot Act in October 2001. Hillary also wanted to shore up her foreign policy and military credentials and she became a war hawk and strongly supported the US military action in Afghanistan saying it was a chance to combat terrorism. She tried to ease this decision with women voters who were largely unsupportive of the war by claiming that the war would improve the lives of Afghan women who suffered under the Taliban government.

She voted for and was a strong advocate of the October 2002 Iraq War Resolution which authorized George Bush to use military force to invade Iraq. Support for the War in Iraq significantly dropped off when it was discovered that there were no weapons of mass destruction there, and suddenly Hillary reversed herself and said she had been wrong to support it.

In 2006, she was elected for a second Senate term. Clinton spent $36 million for her reelection, more than any other candidate for Senate in the 2006 elections against a very weak opponent. Many Democrats criticized her for spending too much in a very one-sided contest, but Hillary wanted to run up her numbers in the senate election in anticipation of her 2008 run for the presidency.

The Aftermath of the Clinton Co-Presidency

> "He is the Willy Loman of Generation X, a travelling salesman who has the loyalty of a lizard with his tail broken off and the midnight taste of a man who'd double date with the Rev. Jimmy Swaggart."—Hunter S. Thompson about Bill Clinton

> "I have never lied about my relationship with Bill Clinton. The only proven liar, at this point, and the only admitted liar, is Bill Clinton; not Gennifer Flowers, not Kathleen Willey, not Paula Jones and not Monica Lewinsky, at this point he is the only proven liar."—Gennifer Flowers

In 1998, the House voted to impeach Bill Clinton, based on acts of perjury and obstruction of justice related to the Lewinsky scandal making Clinton only the second US president to be impeached, the other was Andrew Johnson. After the Independent Counsel's report was submitted to the House providing what it termed "substantial and credible information that President Clinton Committed Acts that may constitute grounds for an impeachment," the House began impeachment hearings against Clinton. As the House Judiciary Committee's hearings ended there was lively debate on the House floor. The two charges passed in the House mostly with Republican support, however a number of Democrats also felt the charges were justified and they too voted against Clinton. The Senate finished a twenty-one-day trial on February 12, 1999, with the vote of 55 Not Guilty to 45 Guilty on the perjury charge, and 50 Not Guilty to 50 Guilty on the obstruction of justice charge. The final vote was generally along party lines, with no Democrats voting him guilty. It was a hung jury as Impeachment requires a two-thirds vote in the affirmative and the disgraced Clinton continued in office.

On his last day in office, January 20, 2001, Clinton created a large controversy in granting 141 pardons and 36 commutations. Most of the controversy was the pardoning of the McDougals and his other Whitewater conspirators. Another controversy arose with the pardon of Marc Rich. There were allegations that Hillary Clinton's brother, Hugh Rodham, had accepted large payments in return for Bill Clinton's pardoning Marc Rich and in the granting of some other pardons. Marc Rich was best known for founding the commodities company Glencore and for being indicted on federal charges of tax evasion and illegally making oil deals with Iran during the Iran Hostage crisis. At the time of his pardon he was hiding from US authorities in Switzerland. He had remained there in hiding after his indictment and had never returned to the US to face trial.

When Bill Clinton left office, a *CNN/US TODAY/Gallup poll* revealed that sixty-eight percent thought he would be remembered for his "involvement in personal scandal," and fifty-eight percent answered "No" to the question "Do you generally think Bill Clinton is honest and trustworthy?" Ironically almost half of those polled said they had been at one time Clinton supporters. In 2006, a Quinnipiac University Poll asked respondents to name the worst president since World War II, and Bill Clinton came in at number three behind only Richard Nixon and George W. Bush. Opponents sometimes referred to him as "Slick Willie," a nickname first applied to Clinton when he was governor of Arkansas and which has lasted throughout his presidency and his retirement. This title has come back to haunt him in the controversy surrounding the Clinton Foundation and its fundraising.

CHAPTER 14. SON OF BUSH

"You can fool some of the people all the time, and those are the ones you want to concentrate on."—George W. Bush

"The media are desperately afraid of being accused of bias. And that's partly because there's a whole machine out there, an organized attempt to accuse them of bias whenever they say anything that the Right doesn't like. So rather than really try to report things objectively, they settle for being even-handed, which is not the same thing. One of my lines in a column—in which a number of people thought I was insulting them personally—was that if Bush said the Earth was flat, the mainstream media would have stories with the headline: 'Shape of Earth—Views Differ.' Then they'd quote some Democrats saying that it was round."—Paul Krugman

"He's a man who is lucky to be governor of Texas. He is a man who is unusually incurious, abnormally unintelligent, amazingly inarticulate, fantastically uncultured, extraordinarily uneducated, and apparently quite proud of all these things."—Christopher Hitchens about George W. Bush

George W. Bush took the country further to the right. While he was still in office, even before the American economy crashed on his watch, he was voted the second worst president since World War II in a 2006 Quinnipiac University Poll. He finished only behind the disgraced Richard Nixon and just ahead of the impeached Bill Clinton.

He is the product of two giants of the American right. He is the grandson of Prescott Bush and the son of George H.W. Bush. He went to Texas public school in his elementary years and was then sent to a private boarding school in Massachusetts. He was a poor student but was the head cheerleader and liked to party. One of the things that Bush was noted for as a student was the large confederate flag that he hung on the wall of his room.

Despite his poor academic record Bush was allowed to enroll and attended Yale University from 1964 to 1968 graduating with a B.A. in history. He was also a cheerleader at Yale and also became a member of the infamous secret society "Skull and Bones" like his father and grandfather. Skull and Bones and Yale alumnae are so prominent in CIA circles that the CIA headquarters at Langley are jokingly called "the campus" referring to all the Yale and Ivy League grads employed by the agency. Despite less than average grades he was still admitted to Harvard because of his family connections. He received an MBA at Harvard where by his own admission he was a less than average student.

Bush had multiple episodes of alcohol abuse. In one instance, on September 4, 1976, he was arrested near his family's summer home in Kennebunkport, Maine for driving under the influence of alcohol. He pleaded guilty and was fined $150 and had his driver's license suspended for two years. It had been widely alleged that Bush has also had an illegal drug problem. When asked about past illicit drug use Bush has consistently refused to answer. He has defended his refusal to answer in a publicized conversation with a friend saying that he feared setting a bad example for the younger generation. He has also called these problems "youthful indiscretions" although they occurred until he was forty. Bush gives credit to his wife Laura for his 1986 decision to give up substance abuse.

In 1978, Bush ran for Congress and lost. He returned to the oil industry and began a series of small independent oil exploration companies which were mostly unsuccessful. He was investigated for possible insider trading by the Securities and Exchange Commission (SEC), but the investigation concluded that while Bush had been given highly improper information at the time of his stock sale that there was not sufficient enough evidence to convict him of insider trading. After this Bush moved his family to Washington, D.C. and in 1988 he went to work on his father's campaign for the US presidency.

In April of 1989, Bush assembled a group of investors from his father's close friends and a fellow fraternity brother. The group bought an 86 percent share of the Texas Rangers baseball team for $75 million. Bush received just a 2% share by investing $606,302 of which $500,000 was from a bank loan. Against the advice of his legal counsel, Bush repaid the loan by selling $848,000 worth of stock in Harken Energy and was once again investigated for insider trading. The subsequent SEC investigation ended in 1992 with a memo stating "it appears that Bush did not engage in illegal insider trading." However the memo further noted that this ruling "must in no way be construed as indicating that the party has been exonerated or that no action may ultimately result."

In 1994, Bush ran for Governor of Texas. After easily winning the Republican primary he faced off against a popular Texas governor in Ann Richards. His campaign advisors were Karl Rove, Joe Albaugh and Karen Hughes. Just like his father's campaigns, Bush's campaign immediately resorted to dirty tricks. According to *The Atlantic Monthly* a wide-spread rumor began to surface that Ann Richards was a lesbian. A regional chairman of the Bush campaign allowed himself to be quoted criticizing Richards for "appointing homosexual activists to state jobs." *The Atlantic Monthly* and others connected all the lesbian rumors to Karl Rove, but Rove lied and denied any involvement which then allowed Bush to also say he had no knowledge of this.

The National Rifle Association (NRA) also played a key role in Bush's victory over Richards. The NRA portrayed Richards as anti-gun for vetoing a bill allowing permits to carry concealed weapons in Texas. Bush campaigned saying he would sign the bill and the NRA provided money and volunteers and campaigned heartily for Bush. He won the general election with about fifty-three percent with Richards at about forty-six percent.

As governor Bush used a large budget surplus to push through the largest tax-cut in Texas history, about $2 billion. At the behest of the chemical and oil industries Bush came out strongly against environmental regulations saying they were unnecessary impediments to business. During Bush's time as governor the state of Texas became a haven for industrial polluters because of the relatively few environmental regulations and during his governorship Texas became ranked near the bottom in almost every environmental evaluation.

In 1998, Bush won re-election with a record sixty-nine percent of the vote. In his second term Bush began to wear his born-again Christianity on his sleeve and strongly promoted faith-based organizations and campaigned on bringing faith back into the government. He enjoyed very high approval ratings particularly among the Christian Right. In a move to please the religious right he issued a gubernatorial proclamation declaring June 10, 2000, to be "Jesus Day" in Texas.

Although Bush was a rightwing Christian politician, much of this campaign proselytizing was part of a very calculated plan by Karl Rove and others to cater to the fast growing Christian Right in the Republican Party and to assure Bush the nomination for president in 2000. Rove became known as "Bush's brain." For his part the low-brow Bush jokingly referred to Rove as "Fart Blossom."

When Bush announced his candidacy for president in June 1999, he entered a crowded field with no front runner. The field of candidates for the Republican Party presidential nomination consisted of John McCain, Steve Forbes, Orrin Hatch, Gary Bauer, Elizabeth Dole, Dan Quayle, Alan Keyes, Pat Buchanan, Lamar Alexander, Herman Cain, John Kasich, and Robert Smith.

After securing support from old line conservatives, mostly friends of his father, Bush won the Iowa caucuses and became the front runner. Although he was expected to win New Hampshire he lost big to McCain. The Bush campaign then got nasty and decided to use some of the same dirty tactics against McCain that they had used in his race for governor against Ann Richards.

Bush soundly defeated McCain in South Carolina using very dirty racial politics. Bush's campaign used push-polling, faxes, e-mails, flyers, and audience plants to that imply that McCain's adopted Bangladeshi-born daughter was really an African-American child that McCain had fathered out of wedlock. They also accused McCain of being "a closet gay" and also claimed McCain's wife was a drug addict. They turned his military service into a liability by saying that McCain was a communist, "a Manchurian Candidate brainwashed by the communists while he was a prisoner in Vietnam" and that he was a traitor. They also shamelessly claimed he was angry and mentally very unstable from his North Vietnam POW days and therefore mentally unfit to be president.

George Bush strongly denied that he or his campaign was involved in all these grossly unfair and false attacks. And when McCain accused the Bush campaign of lying, the Bush campaign claimed that it was McCain that was running a smear campaign. It was disgusting by all accounts and the *New York Times* called the Bush campaign "a painful symbol of the brutality of American politics."

Unfortunately many in the electorate are gullible, and it worked. Bush won the primary with fifty-three percent to McCain's forty-two percent. In response to Bush's dirty tricks McCain said, "I believe that there is a special place in hell for people like those." Bush then went on to easily win the Republican nomination.

Vice President Al Gore easily won the Democratic nomination. Bill Clinton's impeachment and his Whitewater and sex scandals were still very fresh in the minds of the American electorate and they cast a dark shadows on Gore's campaign. Although Gore's behavior was impeccable, he bore the brunt of this animus as Clinton's former vice president. Bush and the Republicans strongly denounced "the Clinton-Gore administration" scandals and called them "years of scandal" and implied that Gore was part of these scandals. Bush repeatedly promised to restore "honor and dignity" to the White House, and it became the centerpiece of his campaign as he pushed his Christianity to the forefront in order to prove his integrity. Gore ignored the Bush campaign's rhetoric about the Clinton Whitewater and sex scandals and he steadfastly refused to criticize Clinton even when his campaign staff begged him to do so.

One of the most significant misquotes in presidential politics was used successfully by the Bush campaign against Gore. Even the media began to believe this misquote and used it to discredit Gore. Gore made one comment that he was part of the original committee that funded the research that created the internet, which was true. But Gore was deliberately misquoted by the Bush campaign who claimed that Gore said "he had invented the internet." This misquote gave the impression that Gore was exaggerating his personal accomplishments and it discredited him with the voters.

In the general election Gore received over a half million votes more than Bush. The popular vote showed Gore with 48.4 percent, Bush with 47.9 percent with the remainder going to third party candidates. However the final Electoral College count was 271 for Bush and 266 for Gore. Florida was the tipping point. It was a controversial call with many challenged ballots and many accusations that George Bush's brother, Florida Governor Jeb Bush, and the Republican Secretary of State had rigged the election for his brother. The results were challenged and there were recounts, but it was confusing because no one was using the same methodology. The ballots in Democratic South Florida were made so deliberately confusing that many voters thinking they had voted for Gore had inadvertently voted for third party conservative candidate Patrick Buchanan.

In the aftermath an unbiased media consortium was hired by the National Opinion Research Center at the University of Chicago to examine the ballots. They concluded that if the disputes over the validity of all the ballots statewide in question had been consistently resolved and if a uniform standard had been applied that the electoral result would have been reversed and Gore would have won by 107 to 115 votes if only two of the three coders had to agree on the ballot. When counting ballots wherein all three coders agreed Gore would have won the most restrictive scenario by 127 votes. Gore was the actual winner of the election both nationally and in Florida.

However after a lower court stopped the recount of Florida's disputed ballots the US Supreme Court inappropriately intervened and in a highly controversial and in a sharply divided and very partisan political decision they voted 5 to 4 to declare George W. Bush as the President of the United States. Many Americans viewed this as a stolen election. The US Supreme

Court permanently tarnished their image in making this disgracefully biased political decision. The right had stolen the election.

Bush, the Budget, Deficits, and Outcomes

> "Reagan proved deficits don't matter."—Vice President Dick Cheney

> "For the last four years, our Federal Government has produced the four biggest deficits in history, and the estimated 2006 deficit of $423 billion is projected to be the largest of all."—Congresswoman Melissa Bean commenting on Bush's first term

> "If there were such a thing as Chapter 11 for politicians, the Republican push to extend the unaffordable Bush tax cuts would amount to a bankruptcy filing. The nation's public debt... will soon reach $18 trillion... but the nation's wealthiest taxpayers (will) be spared even a three-percentage-point rate increase."—David Stockton, Reagan's OMB Director

When Bush took office the US government had a large surplus. In fiscal year 2000 the surplus was $237 billion. It was quickly squandered by his administration. Bush actually argued against the surplus saying that unspent government funds should be returned to the taxpayers. "The surplus is not the government's money. The surplus is the people's money." He proudly said and he then hypocritically proceeded to not return a penny and to spend it all.

On June 7, 2001, Bush signed a $1.35 trillion tax cut into law. It was an economic disaster. During the eight years of George W. Bush's presidency revenues rose by only thirty-five percent while spending increased by sixty-five percent when cyclically adjusted. Despite his anti-government spending rhetoric the Bush administration increased federal government spending from $1.789 trillion to $2.983 trillion. By October 2008, due to increases in spending, the National Debt rose to $11.3 trillion. This was an increase of over one hundred percent from 2000 when the National Debt was only $5.6 trillion.

Even before the economic meltdown of 2007 caused by Bush and Alan Greenspan's policies there were significant other failures. Adjusted for inflation, the median household income dropped by $1,175 between the years 2000 and 2007. Bush's policies hurt the poor. The poverty rate increased from 11.3 percent in 2000 to 12.3 percent in 2006 casting millions of families into poverty. Poverty also rapidly increased in the aftermath of Bush's 2007 financial crisis and because of this it rose dramatically to 18.4 percent by 2012 according to the Economic Policy Institute.

Bush did have some unplanned tragedies to contend with like hurricane Katrina. However Katrina was very badly bungled and mismanaged and left the administration with a permanent black-eye as they were slow and incompetent in their response. Despite the growing catastrophe and the government's failure to respond, FEMA Director Michael Brown said on Sept. 1, 2005, "Considering the dire circumstances that we have in New Orleans, virtually a city that has been destroyed, things are going relatively well."

Bush then appeared on *Good Morning America* that same day. And despite repeated warnings from experts about the frailties of the levies and the scope of damage expected from Hurricane Katrina, he lied and said, "I don't think anybody anticipated the breach of the levees." When things got worse, Bush notoriously said to his inept FEMA director Michael Brown while touring hurricane-ravaged Mississippi on Sept. 2, 2005, "Brownie, you're doing a heck of a job."

Bush and the Bush family also seemed detached and unsympathetic to the misery caused by Katrina. While touring the disaster Bush joked, "We've got a lot of rebuilding to do ... The good news is, and it's hard for some to see it now, that out of this chaos is going to come a fantastic Gulf Coast, like it was before. Out of the rubble of (Senator) Trent Lott's house, he's lost his entire house, there's going to be a fantastic house. And I'm looking forward to sitting on the porch."

His mother, Barbara Bush, didn't help. The former first lady laughed and made disparaging comments about poor Black victims that were aired on *Marketplace* a Public Radio show broadcast nationwide. She callously said, "What I'm hearing, which is sort of scary, is they [Katrina's poor Black victims] all want to stay in Texas. And so many of the people in the arena here, [laughing] you know, were underprivileged anyway, so this is working very well for them." Many took her uncaring remarks to be both classist and racist.

Christian Fundamentalism Replaces Science

> "This is the dysfunctions and motivations of the Bush administration laid bare."—US Congressman Ed Markey, on former EPA advisor Jason Burnett's claim that the Bush administration ordered portions of Congressional testimony regarding the public health effects of global warming deleted.

Perhaps one of the most significant legacies of the Bush Presidency is his anti-intellectualism, anti-science, anti-climate change and the reliance on faith-based ideology. These traits have now become part of the core beliefs of the American right. In 2003, the US Justice Department at the direction of Attorney General John Ashcroft, the Bush White House began an investigation of Professor Michael Dini, a biology professor at Texas Tech University. It was alleged by the Liberty Legal Institute, a group of fundamentalist Christian lawyers, that Dr. Dini was violating the civil rights of his students. His crime was that he required any of his students who wished a letter of recommendation from him for a career in biology or to enter medical school to have a basic knowledge of and belief in the principle of evolution.

In 2000, an environmental dispute occurred in Oregon where farmers use of irrigation water from rivers and streams had severely damaged Salmon breeding areas and also adversely impacted Native American fishing grounds. A sarcastic Bush dismissed the Native claims and the Salmon breeding problems saying, "I know the human being and the fish can coexist peacefully."

President Clinton signed the Kyoto Protocols, an international treaty that set binding obligations on industrialized countries to reduce emissions of greenhouse gases. However it remained only a symbolic act and was never submitted to the Senate for ratification. Bush falsely claimed that he took climate change seriously but then he obliged corporate interests and openly and strongly opposed the Kyoto protocols and the treaty as anti-business. Over 192 parties signed the agreement, including the European Union and all the UN members and except Andorra, South Sudan and the United States. Canada has since stopped following the Kyoto Protocols following Bush's lead. The US accounts for well over a third of all greenhouse emissions.

Bush's attitudes toward global warming and climate change are now part of Republican and the American right's philosophy. In 2010, Sara Palin the former Alaskan Governor and 2008 Republican Vice presidential nominee said, "These global warming studies [are] a bunch of snake oil science." In 2009, the conservative columnist George Will wrote in the *Washington Post* that, "According to the University of Illinois Arctic Climate Research Center, global sea ice levels now equal those of 1979." Will's statement was a lie. The Arctic Climate Research Center doesn't exist and the scientists who do climate research at the University of Illinois said that Will and the *Washington Post* should apologize and that he should be reprimanded for this deliberate blatant lie.

In 2008, Congresswoman Michele Bachmann who ran for President in 2012 said, "(Nancy Pelosi) is committed to her global warming fanaticism to the point where she has said she's just trying to save the planet. We all know that someone did that over 2,000 years ago, he saved the planet, we didn't need Nancy Pelosi to do that."

The Big Lie and the War in Iraq

> "I said that a solution to the problems right now, I told Bush, is a Marshall Plan. He got angry. He said the Marshall Plan is a crazy idea of the Democrats. He said the best way to revitalize the economy is war and that the United States has grown stronger with war.... Those were his exact words.... The Democrats had been wrong. All of the economic growth of the United States has been encouraged by wars. He said it very clearly."—Argentina's President Néstor Kirchner

In 1954, President Dwight Eisenhower set the American policy in the Mideast when he told the Dulles brothers that in order to get the Muslim countries to fight the Soviet Union and the communists "We should do everything possible to stress the holy war aspect!" This policy would eventually come back to severely hurt the US. Unfortunately this "holy war aspect" eventually caused many in the Muslim world to also view the US as infidel invaders in the holy war.

George W. Bush has been harshly criticized internationally for his Middle Eastern policies and his wars. In general his administration's foreign policies were protested around the world. However a majority of Americans in the wake of the September 11, attacks believed him when he said that Iraq had weapons of mass destruction and the nation rallied to his call for war.

In the international community and among foreign diplomatic corps the opinions of Bush were much more negative than those of most previous American Presidents. Bush was privately criticized even by close allies. They abhorred his biased Christian views about Muslim and other non-Christian nations and his concept of "nation building" whereby foreign governments should be persuaded or forced to adopt the Chicago School's economic policies and form non-regulated free market capitalist governments that favored American corporations. It was however Bush's war in Iraq that brought the most criticism, even eventually from the self-centric Americans.

Bush, Vice President Cheney, Secretary of Defense Rumsfeld and Under Secretary Paul Wolfowitz were dubbed "the Chicken Hawks" by critics. When they were young men and it was compulsory to serve in the American military during Vietnam and the Cold War. However Bush, Cheney, Rumsfeld and Wolfowitz were all able to gain exceptions from that duty and did not serve. Although Bush was briefly in the Air Reserves, most of his time was spent assisting in a Republican senatorial campaign in Alabama. There were also allegations that he was given preferential treatment and that he rarely showed up for any reserve duty.

These were men were who were unwilling to serve, but were more than willing to send young men and women to die in Iraq and Afghanistan. These are men who then lied to the American people to gain their support for war by saying that there were imminent threats from weapons of mass destruction in Iraq and that America needed to go to war to protect it from this growing menace. They also implied that Iraq was somehow related to the September 11 attacks.

This is what they said: Vice President Dick Cheney said on August 26, 2002, "Simply stated, there is no doubt that Saddam Hussein now has weapons of mass destruction." President George W. Bush said on September 12, 2002, "Right now, Iraq is expanding and improving facilities that were used for the production of biological weapons." And on March 18, 2003, "Intelligence gathered by this and other governments leaves no doubt that the Iraq regime continues to possess and conceal some of the most lethal weapons ever devised." Secretary of Defense Donald Rumsfeld said on March 30, 2003, "We know where they are. They are in the area around Tikrit and Baghdad." They were all lies. These were not intelligence failures but rather a giant deliberate deception by the Bush administration.

The Center for Public Integrity examined every public pronouncement by President Bush and seven of the Administration's top officials on the existence of weapons of mass destruction in Iraq and on the links between Iraq and Al Qaeda. Bush and his top advisers made 935 false statements from September 11, 2001, to September 11, 2003. President Bush personally made 232 false statements about weapons of mass destruction in Iraq and 28 false statements about Iraq's connections with Al Qaeda. He did most of this knowing that he was lying to the American people.

Bush and his aides also persuaded and coerced American Generals to repeat their lies. General Colin Powell made 244 false statements about weapons of mass destruction and 10 about Al Qaeda links. Powell said on February 5, 2003, "We know that Saddam Hussein is determined to keep his weapons of mass destruction, is determined to make more." And General Tommy Franks said on March 22, 2003, "There is no doubt that the regime of Saddam Hussein possesses weapons of mass destruction. As this operation continues, those weapons will be identified, found, along with the people who have produced them and who guard them."

There were no weapons of mass destruction ever found because there were none. The Administration also knew there were none. A glimmer into why the administration lied was made in a statement by Deputy Secretary of Defense Paul Wolfowitz on May 28, 2003, for the justification for invading Iraq he said, "For bureaucratic reasons, we settled on one issue, weapons of mass destruction because it was the one reason everyone could agree on."

Most US polls showed that immediately before and after the 2003 Iraqi invasion, a substantial majority of the American population supported the war because they believed the Bush lies that Iraq had and was developing these weapons. However by December 2004, when no weapons of mass destruction were found and it was apparent that the administration lied, the polls then began to consistently show that a solid majority of Americans thought the Iraq invasion was a very bad mistake and many were very angry.

Their Revenge for Revealing Their Lies

> "I did not believe that the President was in any way directly involved in the leaking of her [Valerie Plame's] identity, but that was a very disillusioning moment for me when I found out when it initially hit the press, and I was in North Carolina, if I remember correctly, and a reporter shouted out to the President, 'Is it true that you authorized the secret leaking of this classified information?' We walked onto Air Force One, and the President asks, 'What was the reporter asking?', and I said, 'He asserted that you were the one who authorized Scooter Libby leaking this information,' and he said, 'Yeah, I did."—Bush Press Secretary Scott McClellan, on the illegal revealing of Valarie Plame as a CIA agent, MS-NBC May 29, 2008, *Countdown with Keith Olbermann*

The Bush Administration also raised fears of nuclear weaponry and falsely claimed that Iraq was trying to buy uranium in Africa to build a nuclear bomb. And when former Ambassador Joseph C. Wilson stated his opinion in various interviews and in his 2004 memoir *The Politics of Truth* that rumors of Iraq buying uranium was blatantly false, angry members of the Bush administration revealed that Ambassador Wilson's wife, Valarie Plame, was a covert CIA agent. The exposure wrecked her CIA cover and her CIA career and in the revealing it also destroyed Wilson's diplomatic career. Bush and his cronies did it out of revenge for Wilson's public statements and his op-ed titled *What I Didn't Find in Africa*, published in *New York Times* on July 6, 2003, which exposed the Bush Administration lies.

Because publicly outing a CIA agent is a felony, Scooter Libby, a senior aide to Vice President Cheney, was convicted for this act and also for perjury because he had lied in testimony under oath about these events to cover up his illegal actions. He was sentenced to prison. But his two and a half year prison sentence was commuted by George W. Bush, and later Virginia Gov. Republican Bob McDonnell very quietly pardoned him restoring his voting rights allowing him to participate in Republican politics again. Bush who admitted that he was the one who had initiated this illegal action was never punished.

The Election of 2004

> "I don't know what it is that all these Republicans who didn't serve in Vietnam are fighting a war against those of us who did."—Senator John Kerry

> "For Saxby Chambliss, who got out of going to Vietnam because of a trick knee, to attack John Kerry as weak on the defense of our nation is like a mackerel in the moonlight that both shines and stinks."—Senator Max Cleland

At the beginning of 2004, the Democratic race for the presidential nomination looked interesting as there was a crowded field. However four candidates stood out in terms of support and money, Senator John Kerry, former House Majority Leader Dick Gephart, former Governor Howard Dean, and Senator John Edwards. However most of the opposition dropped out between January and March and endorsed Kerry.

Kerry selected John Edwards as his running mate and they were nominated in August at the Democratic Convention in Boston. Kerry made his Vietnam War experience the prominent theme of the convention. In accepting the nomination, he began his speech with, "I'm John Kerry and I'm reporting for duty." It was effective and the Bush campaign was worried that the decorated war hero would attract many independent voters in what looked like a tight election, so once again Bush and his team resorted to their dirty tricks.

The Swift Boat Veterans for Truth (SBVT) was supposedly an independent political group of veterans and former POWs of the Vietnam War that was formed during the 2004 presidential campaign for the purpose of opposing John Kerry as president. They made accusations (all of which later proved to be grossly false) and ran ads questioning his loyalty, patriotism and honesty. The SBVT was never an independent veterans' group as they claimed. The people who financed SBVT were prominent players in the Republican Party and included many of George W. Bush's largest campaign donors. According to information released by the IRS on February 22, 2005, more than half of the SBVT's reported contributions came from just three sources, all prominent wealthy Texas Republicans and George W. Bush donors and backers. Bob J. Perry, a longtime supporter of Bush, donated $4.45 million; Harold Simmons, another close supporter, donated $3 million; and rightwing oilman T. Boone Pickens Jr. donated $2 million. More than another million dollars came from just five other Bush donors.

There were other connections. John E. O'Neill, the primary author of *Unfit for Command* the SBVT book that was used to discredit Kerry, and who was responsible for the formation of SBVT, also personally donated over

$14,000 to Republican candidates that year. He has long ties to the Republicans including that he seconded Nixon's nomination at the 1972 Republican National Convention. The SBVT postal address was registered to Susan Arceneaux, the treasurer of a PAC closely tied to the former Republican Congressional leader Dick Armey also of Texas. Republican activist Sam Fox donated $50,000 to SBVT during the 2004 campaign which caused a controversy when Bush nominated him to the position of ambassador to Belgium. It appeared to be a political payback and Bush quickly withdrew the nomination when the Senate grumbled. Later Bush very quietly appointed Fox as the Ambassador to Belgium anyway while Congress was in recess. SBVT was neither independent nor was it a veteran's group. It was another big lie.

Former POW Senator John McCain condemned the SBVT ads and said, "I hope that the president will also condemn it." The Bush campaign did not condemn SBVT or their ads.

Kerry received a Silver Star, a Bronze Star, and two Purple Hearts while serving in Vietnam as a Swift Boat Commander. When he returned home he became an anti-war activist, saying that Vietnam was a mistake. SBVT used his anti-war activities to paint Kerry as a traitor and coward. They also falsely claimed that the four medals were dishonestly earned. They claimed that Kerry had embellished his war record. They blatantly lied and claimed that a picture of Kerry hung in the War Remnants Museum in Ho Chi Minh City as a gesture of honor by the communists for Kerry's contribution to their victory over the United States because of his anti-War activities.

The SBVT allegations were all lies. The real Swift Boat veterans who served alongside Kerry and those under his command refuted these allegations and criticisms. They supported Kerry's version of events and they also supported his presidential campaign. The picture in Hanoi that the SBVT claimed was a tribute for helping communists win their victory against the Americans was actually a 1993 photo of Kerry as part of a delegation sent to Vietnam by President Clinton to improve ties with the nation. It was not a mistake by the SBVT, they knew they were lying.

The Navy Inspector General, in September 2004, completed a review of Kerry's combat medals after a public demand was made from the rightwing conservative group Judicial Watch which also supported SBVT. The Inspector General said, "Our examination found that existing documentation regarding the Silver Star, Bronze Star and Purple Heart medals indicates the awards approval process was properly followed. I have determined that Senator Kerry's awards were properly approved and will take no further action in this matter."

More recently an early member SBVT, Steve Hayes, stated that he came to see that the group was deliberately lying and twisting Kerry's record and he broke with the group and in the end voted for Kerry. Hayes told the *New York Times*, "It became clear to me that it was morphing from an organization to set the record straight into a highly political vendetta. They knew it was not the truth."

The Federal Elections Commission also found that the SBVT failed to register and file disclosure reports as a federal political committee. SBVT had also accepted contributions in violation of federal limits and source prohibitions. After the election the Commission determined that SBVT was not an independent political group, that they had accepted illegal campaign donations, and had made illegal campaign expenditures. They were fined $299,500 and forced to disband and donate their remaining funds to a charity. However all this was too late and after the election.

The Bush White House refused to release records detailing any Bush administration contacts with prominent individuals associated with SBVT. On August 25, 2004, Benjamin Ginsberg the top election lawyer to the Bush campaign on campaign financing law was forced to resign after it was learned that SBVT was one of his clients. Kenneth Cordier a former vice-chair of Veterans for Bush/Cheney in 2000 and a volunteer member of the Bush campaign veteran's steering committee had to resign when it was discovered that he had appeared in the second SBVT anti-Kerry television advertisement.

In January 2005, the President's brother, Florida Governor Jeb Bush, who was also chairman for his 2004 Florida campaign sent a letter to SBVT member Bud Day thanking him for his "personal support of my brother in his re-election." He also said of the SBVT, "As someone who truly understands the risk of standing up for something, I simply cannot express in words how much I value their willingness to stand up against John Kerry."

There is nothing more shamefully dishonest as someone who had the choice and didn't serve his country criticizing and questioning by cowardly proxy the service and the medals of a political opponent who did. And George W. Bush did this to both John McCain and John Kerry.

These lies were effective. *Time* magazine conducted a poll in late August of 2004, showing that about one-third of the viewers of these SBVT political ads believed there was "some truth" to the allegations. Even more damaging, among independent swing voters in the election about one-fourth felt there some truth to the SBVT ads. The dirty tricks were again effective in a close election. Bush won the election with about fifty percent of the vote to Kerry's forty-eight percent. The SBVT lies had made a difference.

The Department of (No) Justice

> "We're talking about the lawyers for the United States of America. And I think it's very, very important that the lawyers be comfortable being very candid and open about their views on very sensitive issues affecting the United States."— Attorney General Alberto Gonzalez on why he needed to know the political views of DOJ lawyers.

During Bush's second term, a controversy arose over the Department of Justice (DOJ) dismissal of seven United States Attorneys. In an order dated March 1, 2006, which was not published in the *Federal Register* as is required, Attorney General Gonzales formally delegated the authority to hire and dismiss "political appointees and some civil service positions" to his two senior DOJ staff. This unpublished order delegating this authority violated civil service laws and federal regulations. After being granted this illegal authority his staff then fired seven US attorneys because of their politics.

These fired attorneys either held "leftist" political views not in sync with the Bush administration politics or had prior ties to the Democratic Party. As the scandal unfolded investigators discovered other illegalities most notably that all the hiring at the US Department of Justice was done on the basis of political affiliation. They also found that rightwing political litmus tests were applied to all new DOJ hires. The subsequent investigation into these matters also exposed many E-mail illegalities in the Bush White House and uncovered illegal politically motivated prosecutions by US Attorneys in several states.

When the Congressional investigations began they focused on whether the Bush Administration was using the US Attorney positions for political purposes. During these investigations the Senate became aware of little-noticed provision hidden by the Bush Administration in the re-authorization of the Patriot Act in 2006 to eliminate the 120 day term limit on interim appointments of US Attorneys made by the Attorney General to fill vacancies. The new previously unknown provision also permitted the Attorney General to appoint interim US Attorneys without any term limit in office and thus avoided a confirming vote by the Senate, which would have to be done if the President was making the appointment under normal procedures. This illegal provision gave the Attorney General more power than the President or the Congress. The Attorney General then began using this illegal power to politicize these positions and to illegally use the prosecution powers of the office against Bush's political opponents.

In addition to the firing of the seven attorneys Congress discovered that two other attorneys were previously dismissed for political reasons in 2005 and 2006, and that an additional twenty-six US Attorneys were under consideration for dismissal because of their politics by the Bush Administration.

Attorney General Alberto Gonzalez stated the Bush administration's position was that the US Attorneys all "serve at the pleasure of the president." He then lied and said that the dismissals were not political, but that they all have been dismissed for poor job performance. Gonzalez publicly called the Congressional investigations "an overblown personnel matter."

By mid-September in 2007, as the investigation made progress nine of the highest-level officers of the Department of Justice associated with the controversy were forced to resign in the growing scandal including Attorney General Alberto Gonzalez. A subsequent report by the Justice Department Inspector General in October 2008, found that the process used to fire the first seven attorneys and two others dismissed around the same time was "arbitrary," and "fundamentally flawed," and that it "raised doubts about the integrity of Department prosecution decisions." In July 2010, the Department of Justice prosecutors closed the investigation determining that the firings were inappropriately political. Members of Congress investigating the dismissals found that the sworn testimony from the Attorney General and other DOJ officials was false and was contradicted by their internal Department memoranda, e-mails and other evidence. They concluded that Congress had been deliberately lied to and misled by the Attorney General and his staff as they attempted to cover up their illegal political activities.

The Bush White House Email Scandal

> "The high rank of the White House officials involved, and the large quantity of missing emails, the potential violation of the Presidential Records Act may be extensive."—House Oversight Committee Report June 18, 2007

According to the Hatch Act and the Presidential Act of 1978 all White House and Executive Branch emails must be sent on an email server controlled and hosted by the federal government. During the DOJ investigation it was discovered not all emails requested by the Congressional inquiry were available to federal investigators because the Bush White house was illegally using a server hosted by the Republican National Committee (RNC) to hide their political and illegal communications from the Congress and others. Congressman Henry Waxman who was the Chair of the investigating committee said "White House officials were using nongovernmental accounts specifically to avoid creating a record of the communications." The Congress sent a formal directive to the RNC advising them to retain copies of all emails sent by White House employees. Even though the RNC's own policy since 2004 had been to save and retain all emails of White House staff with RNC accounts, the RNC then claimed that they had already erased the emails and said they were unavailable for the Congressional investigators. It was another cover-up.

According to the House Oversight Committee report released on June 18, 2007, in an effort to cover up the growing scandal, White House spokesperson Dana Perino in March 2007, lied and said that the RNC email accounts were granted to "just a handful" of people in the administration. When it was discovered that this wasn't true, her estimate was then upwardly revised to "about fifty." It was later discovered during the investigation that eighty-eight of Bush's White House officials used these illegal email accounts to cover-up their activities. The senior administration officials with these accounts included, Karl Rove the President's senior advisor; Andrew Card the former White House Chief of Staff; and Ken Mehlman the former White House Director of Political Affairs. Of the eighty-eight White House officials who used RNC email accounts, the RNC had claimed to have saved no emails for fifty-one of these officials, including Karl Rove who had 140,216 emails destroyed by the RNC.

The Committee report concluded, "The evidence obtained by the Committee indicates that White House officials deliberately used their RNC email accounts in a manner that circumvented these requirements. At this point in the investigation it is not possible to determine precisely how many presidential records may have been destroyed by the RNC. Given the heavy reliance by White House officials on RNC email accounts, the high rank of the White House officials involved, and the large quantity of missing emails, the potential violation of the Presidential Records Act may be extensive." The Bush White House had a lot to hide.

Bush Promotes and Condones Torture

> "And yes, I'm aware our national security team met on this issue. And I approved.... I told the country we did that. And I also told them it was legal. We had legal opinions that enabled us to do it."—George W. Bush regarding his awareness that he and his top national security advisors had discussed and approved the use of torture

The Bush administration called it "enhanced interrogation techniques," but it was by any definition torture. The most common torture methods used were hypothermia to make a victim feel they would freeze to death, forced stress positions to produce prolonged and agonizing pain and permanent joint damage, and waterboarding where a person feels as if they will drown. They also used sexual humiliation where the victims would be subjected to such treatments as being paraded naked in front of male and female interrogators who taunted them about their sexual anatomy. They were also placed in sexually humiliating positions while nude and had photos taken of them. The victims were subjected to prolonged loud and unpleasant sounds and had bright lights shined upon them twenty-four hours a day bombarding their senses. They were deprived of sleep and were subjected to long periods of isolation. There were also reports of rape. And when these victims went on hunger strikes to protest these conditions they were brutally force-fed.

According to *A Question of Torture: CIA Interrogation, from the Cold War to the War on Terror* by Alfred McCoy, the CIA and the Defense Department employed these methods at Bagram in Afghanistan and in numerous black sites and secret prisons in the Mideast, Thailand, Eastern Europe, at Guantanamo Bay and at Abu Ghraib prison in Iraq. They used them on untold thousands of prisoners and they justified this torture in the name of the September 11, 2001, attacks although most of these prisoners had nothing to do with these attacks and their interrogators knew this.

According to Tim Weiner in *Enemies*, the FBI agents who had initially participated in terrorist interviews at these CIA black sites reported these abuses to their superiors at the FBI and refused to participate. Some agents also resigned because of the use of torture by CIA agents during the joint interrogation of suspected terrorists.

Debates arose over the legality of the techniques and whether or not they had violated US and international laws. Congress began to ask questions. The Washington Post reported that in 2005, the CIA destroyed many video tapes depicting prisoners being interrogated while being tortured. They destroyed them for fear that these videos would be turned over to Congress. The tapes had been stored in a CIA black site in Thailand. The CIA Chief of the Directorate of Operations Jose A, Rodriquez Jr. sent a cable to the CIA's Bangkok station ordering the destruction of the tapes on November 8, 2004. An internal justification of their destruction was that what they showed was so horrific that they would be permanently "devastating to the CIA," and that "the heat from destroying them is nothing compared to what it would be if the tapes ever got into the public domain." Rodriguez was never reprimanded by anyone for the destruction of the video tapes.

A nonpartisan independent review of the CIA and military interrogation and detention programs concluded that "It is indisputable that the United States engaged in the practice of torture" and that "the nation's highest officials bore ultimate responsibility for it." American and European officials including former CIA Director Leon Panetta, many former CIA officers, a Guantanamo prosecutor, a military tribunal judge, and former POW and Republican Senator John McCain have called "enhanced interrogation" a euphemism for torture.

On March 8, 2008, Bush vetoed H.R. 2082. It was a bill that would have expanded congressional oversight over the intelligence community and which would have also banned the use of water boarding as well as other forms of "enhanced interrogation." Bush said at the time of his veto that "the bill Congress sent me would take away one of the most valuable tools in the War on Terror." After leaving office President Bush and Vice President Cheney continue to condone and defend the use of torture during their administration.

In 2009, both President Obama and Attorney General Eric Holder stated the techniques used by the military and CIA during the Bush Administration were torture and they repudiated their use. They ended their practice. However, they also declined to prosecute the CIA personnel and the military personnel who committed these tortures or the Bush administration officials who authorized the illegal torture program.

Problems with the CIA's torture program and their cover-up continued well into Obama's second term as president. On July 31, 2014, CIA Director John Brennan was forced to apologize for the CIA hacking the computers of the Senate Intelligence Committee during a Senate investigation into the CIA's torture and interrogation techniques. The CIA tried to steal documents from the Senate Committee and also tried have Senate Committee staff prosecuted for their role in the investigation by making it appear that they had obtained classified documents illegally. Senate Intelligence Committee Chair Diane Feinstein said, "The investigation confirmed what I said on the Senate floor in March—CIA personnel inappropriately searched Senate Intelligence Committee computers in violation of an agreement we had reached and, I believe, in violation of the constitutional separation of powers."

In response to Senator Feinstein's accusations in March, at a Council of Foreign Relations event CIA Director Brennan adamantly told Andrea Mitchell of NBC News that the CIA "wouldn't do that." Brennan also said in March, "As far as the allegations of CIA hacking into Senate computers, nothing could be further from the truth. I mean, we wouldn't do that. I mean, that's—that's just beyond the scope of reason in terms of what we would do."

Senator Ron Wyden, who is also on the Intelligence Committee, said, "The CIA Inspector General has confirmed what senators have been saying all along: The CIA conducted an unauthorized search of Senate files and attempted to have Senate staff prosecuted for doing their jobs. Director Brennan's claims to the contrary were simply not true." Brennan had lied to the press and the Congress.

On December 9, 2014, the Senate Intelligence Committee released an executive summary of the years-long investigation into the CIA's torture program approved by President George W. Bush. The revelations were astonishing and revealed new forms of torture that were used by the CIA and military. In addition to the previously mentioned methods of torture the CIA's torture program also included "rectal feeding" where agents used force to shove water and pureed items up the rectums of their victims, causing hemorrhoids, anal fissures and rectal prolapses where the lower end of the colon becomes stretched out and protrudes out of the anus causing anal leakage. Victims were forced into ice water baths for prolonged periods and multiple times until they were at the very edge of death from hypothermia. Victims were subjected to long periods of standing sleep deprivation, similar to the medical experiments done by the Nazis in the concentration camps. It was also reported that these "enhanced interrogation" techniques were so horrific that even seasoned CIA agents cried upon seeing them in practice.

The CIA agents also threatened their victim's children, spouses and parents with bodily harm, death, sexual abuse and rape.

Most of the CIA agents involved in the torture programs reported to the CIA leadership that "enhanced interrogation" was not working or producing any usable results. Although the CIA knew that the torture wasn't working they continued torturing and hid these reports and their lack of results from Congress. The Report also showed that the CIA and the Bush Administration lied many times to the Congress about the torture program. The Bush Justice Department lied to the Congress claiming that the "dirty bomber" Jose Padilla was captured because of information that was obtained by torture. Padilla was actually caught by an FBI informer. The CIA lied to Congress in its claims that torture was only used if the detainee refused to cooperate. The report shows that detainees were often tortured before they were determined to guilty of terrorism and before the CIA determined if they would cooperate. Victims were also routinely tortured for complaining about conditions or any medical problems and for very minor offenses including not calling their torturers "sir."

Bankrupting the World Economy

> "We're now in the 'middle innings' of the current economic expansion, and the next economic recession is not yet in sight."—David Seiders, Chief Economist, National Association of Home Builders, January 2006

> "The idea that we're going to see a collapse in the housing market seems to me improbable."—John Snow, Secretary of the Treasury

"When I hear (about a housing bubble) I get the sense that people aren't connecting the dots."—James Glassman, Author of *Dow 36,000*

In 2007, the US housing market collapsed causing the near collapse of the American and world economies. It was proof certain that the Chicago School's "free market capitalism" was not workable. Markets did not and could not regulate themselves.

In the wake of the global market crash Bush summed up the risk to the global economy and what would happen if Congress failed to approve Treasury Secretary Henry Paulson's $700 billion financial bailout plan saying on September 26, 2008: "If money isn't loosened up, this sucker [the US economy] could go down." He was desperate, his credibility was at an all-time low and he needed to persuade the doubters in his own party and the Democrats on the need of bailing out the quickly failing American economy.

When Bush first took office there was an economic recession caused by the bursting of the Dot-com bubble. At this time Bush and his administration were also rapidly spending the surplus revenues left by Clinton and they were rapidly increasing the National Debt. Although he also faced congressional opposition, Bush held town hall style meetings across the US in order to increase his public support for a plan for a $1.35 trillion tax cut. It was the largest tax cut in US history which benefited mostly the richest people in America. Bush and his Chicago School economic advisors claimed the tax cut would stimulate the economy.

Initially The Chairman of the Federal Reserve Allan Greenspan opposed the tax cuts stating that they would contribute to budget deficits and undermine Social Security but his remarks fell on deaf ears. Greenspan also opposed these cuts because he doubted their affordability with the Dot-com recession. But the ever dogmatic Bush and his Chicago School free market advocates insisted that the tax cuts would stimulate the economy and would create more jobs. Bush insisted that Greenspan get behind his decision. It then became Greenspan's job to find a way to rev up the economy to pay for this.

Long before Greenspan became the Chairman of the Federal Reserve he was intrigued with using real estate to stimulate the economy. Before he became Chairman of the Federal Reserve Greenspan wrote an essay on economics where he noted how home equity borrowing had fueled consumer spending had pumped money into the economy in the mid-1970s and prevented further financial turmoil. Greenspan's conclusion was that American's home equity was like a giant piggy bank that could be used to rev up the economy with consumer spending. He also speculated that mortgage lending and new home purchases would also rev up the economy. The American economy is at least 80% consumer driven, and Greenspan realized that if American homeowners could be persuaded to spend their home equity and to buy more expensive homes, the economy would boom. It proved to be true in the short run, but it carried with it dire consequences.

In July of 2003, Greenspan cut the overnight bank interest rate to one percent and sent strong signals that home mortgage lending of any type including home equity loans was strongly encouraged. Bush did his part before the Association of Home Builders in Columbus, Ohio, on October 2, 2004, he said, "We're creating... an ownership society in this country, where more Americans than ever will be able to open up their door where they live and say, welcome to my house, welcome to my piece of property... I'm asking Congress to pass my Zero Down Payment Initiative. We should remove the three percent down payment rule for first time home buyers with FHA-insured mortgages."

Bush used the September 11, 2001, attacks to say that in the wake of the attack it was "patriotic" to spend and show the terrorists that the American economy was healthy.

Fannie Mae and Freddie Mac, the secondary markets for mortgages were told to buy and keep buying from the banks and mortgage companies. American mortgage debt went from about $4.9 billion to over $10 billion, a whopping increase of 102 percent in just six years.

It was not sustainable. To reach these numbers the banks and mortgage lenders began creating exotic mortgages with zero down payments, interest only loans for five years, and the fraudulent stated income loans, which were better known in the trade as "liar loans" because the borrowers were encouraged to lie about their income to get loans they couldn't afford.

The lenders encouraged their borrowers to take out these exotic and stated income loans telling and many times even persuading the borrowers to do this, claiming that the market would continually go up and that if they got in trouble they could easily sell for more than they paid. The lenders didn't care whether their borrowers could repay because they were selling these mortgages to the secondary markets without recourse, meaning they had no responsibility after the loan was sold. They made their money up front without consequences. The secondary markets began to sell some of these exotic mortgages in the market which were then divided into derivative investments based on problematic mathematical models that promised false security with high returns for investors. It was a giant pyramid scheme and destined to fail.

The Washington Post reported a study by the Mortgage Asset Research Institute that showed that ninety percent of the liar loan borrowers greatly exaggerated their household income and that sixty percent had exaggerated their total income by more than fifty percent. The people making these false stated incomes were frequently encouraged to do so by their lenders who had unrealistic quotas to fill from their lending institutions and were paid large bonuses for exceeding these quotas by any means possible. CNN reported that there were $60 billion in liar loans in 2003, but just three years later the number had sky-rocketed to $386 billion and these loans peaked at about $100 million per quarter in 2006, a year before the market crashed.

Three of the largest lenders of the liar loans were IndyMac Bankcorp, Countrywide Financial, and Washington Mutual. IndyMac failed in 2008, and was the fourth largest bank failure in US history. Countrywide then collapsed and was bought for pennies on the dollar by Bank of America at the urging of the federal regulators. And Washington Mutual also collapsed in 2008, making it the largest bank failure in US history.

By the spring of 2009, the F.D.I.C. reported that forty six banks failed costing the American taxpayers well over $20 billion. But American banks and financial markets were only part of the growing problem. The derivatives of these highly toxic mortgages were sold to foreign markets and when the American housing market collapsed so did the global economy. After the bubble burst in 2007, the FBI investigated 800 cases of massive corporate mortgage fraud, and by 2008, the number of cases of massive large institutional fraud had sky-rocketed to 1200. In the unregulated free market Wall Street, the banks and other mortgage lenders had taken advantage of the unregulated climate and caused the catastrophic greed-driven financial collapse.

Greenspan's defense was that like the Chicago School and Milton Friedman, he too personally believed that free markets could regulate themselves. The country and Congress were angry and Greenspan was asked to explain his actions in the wake of this economic disaster. In testimony before Congress on October 23, 2008, Congressman Henry Waxman asked if Greenspan still believed that the markets could regulate themselves as he, the Chicago School and the Bush administration had claimed. Greenspan responded, "Those of us who have looked at the self-interest of financial institutions to protect shareholders equity, myself especially, are in a state of shocked disbelief."

When Waxman pressed him further Greenspan said of his Chicago School laze faire free market economic policy beliefs, "I have found a flaw. I don't know how significant or permanent it is. But I have been very distressed by that fact."

Exiting in Disgrace

George W. Bush was a failed president. His presidency was marred with torture, scandal, and lies. His presidency had nearly destroyed the US and world economies. In 2006, 744 professional historians were surveyed by Siena College and asked to look at the Bush presidency in total. They rated Bush's presidency as follows: Great: two percent; Near Great: five percent; Average: eleven percent; Below Average: twenty-four percent; and Failure: fifty-eight percent.

CHAPTER 15. BARACK OBAMA

"There is not a liberal America and a conservative America there is the United States of America. There is not a Black America and a White America and Latino America and Asian America. There's the United States of America."—Barack Obama

"It was the labor movement that helped secure so much of what we take for granted today. The 40-hour work week, the minimum wage, family leave, health insurance, Social Security, Medicare, retirement plans. The cornerstones of the middle-class security all bear the union label."—Barack Obama

"It's not surprising, then, they get bitter, they cling to guns or religion or antipathy to people who aren't like them or anti-immigrant sentiment or anti-trade sentiment as a way to explain their frustrations."—Barack Obama

The right considers Obama as a leftist. Perhaps comparing him to the presidents since Nixon it would appear to be so. But Barack Obama is a moderate, a Christian, a capitalist, and concerning economics he is a very traditional and cautious politician. This isn't to say he won't take a political risk, as he clearly did that in the killing of Osama Bin Laden by ordering a commando raid into Pakistan which could have backfired on him in a hundred different ways. He also took a risk by promoting gay rights before a majority in the nation supported their civil liberties. He also took on healthcare reform which had previously humbled and defeated the Clintons. He passed the Affordable Care Act despite strong opposition and maintained it despite many continuous attempts by rightwing Republicans to destroy it. His bailout of the auto industry was at considerable political risk and saved the industry. Obama also clearly took political risks early in his career vaulting up the political ladder at an incredibly fast pace. But when it comes to economics and capitalism Obama is a very cautious and conservative man.

In 1991, Obama accepted a two-year position as Visiting Law and Government Fellow at the University of Chicago Law School to work on his first book. He then taught at the Law School for twelve years, as a Lecturer from 1992 to 1996, and as a Senior Lecturer from 1996 to 2004. He taught constitutional law.

In 1993, he joined Davis, Miner, Barnhill & Galland, a medium sized law firm specializing in civil rights litigation and neighborhood economic development. He was an associate at the law firm for three years from 1993 to 1996, and then of counsel from 1996 to 2004. In 1996 he was elected to the Illinois Senate. He was reelected in 1998. In 2000 he ran for Congress in the Democratic primary but lost.

In the March 2004 Illinois Democratic US Senate primary election Obama won in an unexpected landslide which made him a rising national star within the Democratic Party. In July 2004, Obama delivered the keynote address at the 2004 Democratic National Convention and was seen by 9.1 million viewers. It was this event that started speculation about a possible presidential future. In the 2004 US Senate election, Obama won with seventy percent of the vote and won all but ten counties in Illinois. It was an impressive win for a young rising new political star.

After just a little over two and a half years in the Senate on February 10, 2007, Obama announced his candidacy for President of the United States. A large number of candidates entered the Democratic primaries but the overwhelming favorite was Hillary Clinton. Clinton entered the race with a sense of entitlement. She felt "it was her turn." Clinton and her campaign strategists had mapped a victory scenario that envisioned the former first lady wrapping up the Democratic presidential nomination by Super Tuesday in February. They all believed it was a fait accompli, but Obama upset Clinton in the Iowa caucuses and suddenly Hillary Clinton, the unbeatable candidate, was in a close race.

Clinton managed to just barely eke out a win over Obama in New Hampshire by a two percent margin and the race between the two remained very close up until the spring of 2008. The primaries were heated between the two campaigns and Hillary and Bill Clinton began tacking to the right to attract mostly older and rural White voters. The Clintons were at times very dismissive of Obama which angered the African-American community and some claimed it was race based. The Clintons then resorted to dog whistle politics to attract the White blue collar voters.

Hillary Clinton further angered African Americans with the comment, "Dr. King's dream began to be realized when President Lyndon Johnson passed the Civil Rights Act of 1964. It took a president to get it done." Many saw that as a dig against Obama for his race and they believed that she was saying a Black man couldn't possibly do what she could do as a powerful White person. Obama said at the time that Clinton's words about Dr. King "offended some folks who felt that [her remarks] somehow diminished King's role in bringing about the Civil Rights Act."

Many people became aware that divisive racial politics was becoming a deliberate Clinton campaign strategy to win White blue collar workers in both the North and South. And it worked as Obama struggled with the rural and blue collar White vote. However Obama was still winning because of record turnout of Blacks and other minorities, women and young people. His popularity and the very large turnouts at his events infuriated the Clintons. Hillary was angry at the turnout at her events compared to Obama and let her advance staff know of her dissatisfaction.

Bill Clinton responded to a reporter's question about Obama's expected victory in the South Carolina primary by noting that Jesse Jackson had won the state in 1984 and 1988. It was an obvious attempt to marginalize Obama's win because Jackson did not win the nomination and was thought by many at the time to be "just a marginal Black candidate." Blacks and other minority voters noticed and took offense to his remarks too.

The Clinton strategy has always been to lie, deflect and blame someone else for their short-comings and after they were criticized in the press for their race-baiting dog whistle politics they began to claim that it was Obama who was playing racial politics. Hillary Clinton said, "I think it [racial politics] clearly came from Senator Obama's campaign and I don't think it was the kind of debate we should be having in this campaign." When Blacks and Obama supporters became angry about her remarks, Bill Clinton complained again in a radio interview that Obama had "played the race card on me," which further enraged Blacks and most Obama supporters. It became apparent to most that it was the Clinton's strategy to make race an issue and to minimize Obama as a marginal Black candidate with no chance of actually winning a general presidential election. They emphasized over and over again that only Clinton could carry the White working class voters.

Many Whites also took issue with the Clintons' remarks and tactics. Even some longtime Clinton political supporters disavowed them. Congressman James E. Clyburn, the South Carolina Democrat who is the highest ranking African-American in Congress and who was a friend and a former staunch Clinton supporter, was among many who expressed disappointment in the Clintons.

The Clintons kept insisting that it was Obama who was playing racial politics and not them. They used Congressman Clyburn's expressed disappointment in the Clintons to say that this was proof of Obama's racial politics. Bill Burton, a spokesman for the Obama campaign, said that voters were offended by the Clintons' accusations that it was Obama who was using race in the campaign, saying, "I think that Congressman Clyburn and other leaders across the country would take great offense at the suggestion that their response [to Bill Clinton's remarks] was somehow engineered by this campaign."

The truth has always been a limited commodity in Clinton campaigns. Hillary Clinton began to dismiss Obama as unqualified on international issues and began to tout herself as the "foreign policy and military expert" in the campaign. She attempted to demonstrate her toughness as a future commander in chief when she falsely said of a visit to Bosnia in 1996 as First Lady, "I remember landing under sniper fire. There was supposed to be some kind of a greeting ceremony at the airport, but instead we just ran with our heads down to get into the vehicles to get to our base."

It was a gross lie. It was not a slip of the tongue or poor memory, as she told this tale on more than one occasion on the campaign trail and to different audiences. It contradicted all other accounts, including a previous account of the event in her own book where she wrote that there was no threat of gunfire. And when a film of the actual event surfaced showing Clinton arriving to a peaceful day and being greeted by a little girl who gave her flowers, she was caught in her ridiculous lie. Clinton later tried to dismiss and to smooth this over, saying that she "misspoke," which is a Clinton euphemism for lie. She was forced to eventually admit that, "On a couple of occasions in the last weeks I just said some things that weren't in keeping with what I knew to be the case and what I had written about in my book. And you know I'm embarrassed by it. I'm very sorry I said it. I have said that, you know, it just didn't jive with what I had written about and knew to be the truth."

In another weird pandering episode, Hillary, who grew up in Illinois and was educated in the East, was caught on video tape faking a very bad and heavy Southern drawl while touting her "Southern background" when speaking at a church in the South.

In another incident she laughed off a question from a voter who asked Clinton what qualified her to deal with leaders from countries such as Iran and North Korea. She once again made light of Bill's misogynous behavior with women and said, "The question is, we face a lot of dangers in the world and, in the gentleman's words, we face a lot of evil men. And what in my background equips me to deal with evil and bad men?" Then she and her audience had a good laugh about her predatory husband's misogynous and sexist behavior.

On another occasion she also said of her husband, "If I didn't kick his ass every day, he wouldn't be worth anything." And of his affairs and misogyny she joked and laughed again, "In the Bible, it says they asked Jesus how many times you should forgive and he said seventy times seven. Well, I want you all to know that I'm keeping a chart."

These statements making light of Bill's long term predatory behavior with women only served to distance her from many in the Women's movement. It reveals that she is unconcerned with her husband's misogyny. It makes her promotion of women's rights seem hollow and phony.

Obama became the clear frontrunner, and toward the end of spring Hillary became more of an angry spoiler than a viable candidate. She tried to demean Obama by saying petulantly, "I have a lifetime of experience that I will bring to the White House. I know Senator McCain has a lifetime of experience that he will bring to the White House. And Senator Obama has a speech he gave in 2002."

After being asked by George Stephanopoulos about Rush Limbaugh's encouraging Republicans to vote for Clinton in hopes of dividing the Democratic Party, she joked "He's always had a crush on me."

As the campaign wore on, she got more hostile and angry. She was greatly bothered by Obama's popularity and his ability to draw much larger crowds almost anywhere. She whined and pouted that the press liked Obama more than her. During a television debate with Barack Obama, she got mean and said patronizingly, "Maybe we should ask Barack if he's comfortable or needs another pillow." When a reporter asked why people seemed to like Obama more, she whined and said, "Well, that hurts my feelings."

Lies and miscues fell from the mouths of the Clintons as easily as eloquence did from Obama. Rather than owning their mistakes and their lies, the Clintons became angry with Obama and remained so throughout the primaries. In June after the last of the primaries had taken place and Obama secured enough delegates to win the Democratic nomination for President, Clinton was so angry and indignant about her loss to him that for several days she refused to concede the race even though she had already signaled that her presidential campaign was ending in a speech on June 3, in New York.

The Clintons were told by their senior staff that if either one of them wanted a future role in Democratic Party politics, they would need to get over their personal animosity and graciously endorse and support Obama or risk alienating the Democratic Party. Hillary finally conceded the nomination to Obama on June 7, and she grudgingly pledged her support. Always the pragmatist, Obama on his part was magnanimous, and it paid political dividends down the road.

The American right took the meaning of the Obama win over Clinton in the Democratic Party as a left-wing victory and incredibly saw Obama as a left-wing socialist threat. It was never a rational thought. It was pure unreasonable emotionalism with a good deal of closet racism. It was rightwing xenophobia as they saw Obama as a Black man with an odd name and a Kenyan father and said he was "one of the others" and not "one of us." Immediately they spread rumors that he was a Muslim or an Arab and that he was not born in the United States. The rightwing began to say that it was not legal for him to be president. It spurred a whole rightwing movement called "the Birthers" who were determined to make a case that Obama was a foreigner, a socialist, a Muslim, and a Manchurian Candidate who was out to destroy Christian America. Much of this was just pure racism.

Some of these rightwing extremists eventually started calling themselves the "Tea Party" after the Boston Tea Party tax protest in the Revolutionary War era. They attended rallies and demonstrations holding up rightwing, xenophobic and racist signs and Confederate flags protesting anything Obama. It has been learned since that the rightwing Koch brothers financed the Tea Party Movement and encouraged its lies and excesses.

The Republicans chose Senator John McCain for their candidate. He wasn't a rightwing zealot like many in his party, but he was a conservative and is still the nation's biggest war hawk. McCain wanted to occupy Iraq and Afghanistan for the far distant future and was a strong advocate for the use of strong military force against possible threats in North Korea, Iran and other parts of the Mideast. He would later loudly advocate for US military action in Libya, Egypt, and Syria. With McCain it wasn't saber rattling as much as it was the steady beat of constant war drums. He is a true believer in the use of American military power to cure all the world's ills. McCain promotes the idea of a world dominated by an American military empire.

Among the Republicans, Governor Mitt Romney and New York Mayor Rudy Giuliani had been early frontrunners and Mike Huckabee was an early favorite of the religious right. Huckabee won the Iowa caucuses, but it was short-lived. McCain won the New Hampshire primary and with this win he began to solidify his frontrunner status. In the Super Tuesday contests in February, Romney won seven states as did McCain, but McCain won twice as many delegates as Romney. Shortly afterward Romney dropped out of the race and endorsed McCain. McCain then went on to easily win the nomination.

In his search for a Vice President McCain had favored his close friend Democratic Senator Joe Lieberman who was also a war hawk and an apologist for Israel. Lieberman had shared the ticket with Gore in 2000, but in 2008 he endorsed McCain's presidential bid greatly angering most Democrats. However the opposition to Lieberman from conservatives and the rightwing of the Republican Party was too strong and McCain was told that a Lieberman pick would cause a floor fight and divide the upcoming convention. McCain then decided to go with someone that would reaffirm his independent maverick status and made the unfortunate choice of selecting the rightwing Republican Governor of Alaska, Sara Palin.

Palin quickly endeared herself to the far rightwing of the party. She also gave McCain a temporary bounce in the polls as American voters were attracted to something new and different. After announcing Palin as the presumptive vice-presidential nominee the McCain campaign received $7 million in contributions in a single day mostly from the far right. According to a *Washington Post/ABC News Survey* published on September 9, 2008, John McCain had also gained huge support among white women voters because of his pick of Palin. McCain also took a lead of five percentage points over Obama in the Gallup polls.

It was short lived. Palin was also dogmatic, unprepared and was obviously intellectually unfit for the office. During the campaign she demonstrated a complete lack of understanding of basic issues and at one point referred to Africa as a country and was surprised to learn it was a continent. She also thought the Mideast was a country instead of a region. She was asked in a television interview what she read. She seemed puzzled by the question and it became apparent that she did not read anything. She replied that she read newspapers and magazines and when asked to name them, a confused Palin clumsily replied "all of them."

When asked about her lack of foreign policy, she claimed she had some experience because "Russia is close to Alaska," which was soon parodied on the television show *Saturday Night Live*, with Tina Fey playing Palin and saying, "I can see Russia from my house." In the Vice Presidential debate prep, she could not remember Joe Biden's last name or that he was a Senator, so her aides told her to just call him "Joe" during the debate. And they also told her to ask at the first chance, "May I call you Joe?" which she did.

It also came out during the campaign that her husband was one of the leaders of a radical rightwing movement that wished to have Alaska declare independence and break away from the United States. Also while Palin was touting moral Christian family values, it was revealed that her young daughter was pregnant out of wedlock, and this unfortunately and unfairly brought the poor young girl into the national spotlight. There were also bizarre stories about Palin's belief in witches and witch-hunting and that people could be possessed by devils and demons. Palin was a political train wreck.

During a week in which the Republicans were trying to highlight its connection to the common American and were trotting out their newest campaign symbol, an average White working class man called "Joe the Plumber," Palin had a wardrobe malfunction of sorts. The press reported that Palin's fashion budget for the past several weeks was worth more than the median salary of an American plumber for four years. It was reported that the Republican National Committee had spent more on Palin's clothes in one month than the average American household spends on clothes in eighty years. It got worse.

Politico reported that the RNC's monthly financial disclosure reports revealed that the Republican National Committee had spent many thousands of dollars on the vice presidential candidate's wardrobe and accessories since Palin was nominated, including $150,000 in September alone. Palin's clothes came from high dollar retailers such as Saks Fifth Avenue, Macy's, Bloomingdales, Neiman Marcus and Barneys New York and these expenses included nearly $5,000 for hair and makeup. In the aftermath it was revealed that the RNC had spent over $180,000 on Palin's clothes for the campaign and that some of this was spent on her family. Palin became the butt of jokes and late night television comedians as she began to come across as something of a not-so-bright aging beauty queen.

Once they realized just how unprepared she was to be a vice presidential candidate the McCain campaign developed a strategy of sheltering Palin from unscripted encounters with the press, but it was too late.

In the election Obama won by almost ten million votes winning about fifty-three percent of the total votes to McCain's almost forty-six percent. Obama won twenty-eight states and the District of Columbia to McCain's twenty-two. McCain's wins were confined to Alaska, the South and the Rocky Mountain west. Obama had won in some normally Republican states such as Indiana, the Southern states of Virginia, North Carolina and Florida, and the Rocky Mountain states of Colorado and New Mexico. It was a decisive win.

A Fast Start

> President Obama inherited a broken country mired in two wars, a financial crisis, a mortgage mess and more than we all probably even know about and has in my opinion brought us back from the brink."—Don Cheadle, actor and political activist

"There is much to dislike about President Obama's approach to the financial crisis. But opposition, it seems, will have to come from somewhere other than conservatism. The party out of power is also a party out of touch."—Thomas Frank, political analyst and columnist

In a peace-making gesture Obama appointed Hillary Clinton as Secretary of State, a move that ensured the Clintons' support during his presidency. On January 20, 2009, in his first few days in office, Obama issued executive orders and presidential memoranda directing the US military to expand their plans to withdraw troops from Iraq. He ordered the closing of the Guantanamo Bay Detention Camp, but Congress prevented the closure by refusing to appropriate the required funds and they also prevented moving any Guantanamo detainees into the US or to other countries.

Obama reduced the secrecy given to presidential records. He also revoked the Bush policies of prohibiting federal aid to international family planning organizations that perform or provide counseling about abortion. The first bill signed into law by Obama was the Lilly Ledbetter Fair Pay Act, relaxing the statute of limitations for equal-pay lawsuits. Five days later, he signed the reauthorization of the State Children's Health Insurance Program (SCHIP) to cover an additional four million uninsured children. In March 2009, Obama reversed a Bush-era policy which had limited funding of embryonic stem cell research.

But the crumbling economy prevented Obama from achieving many of his ambitions. Obama is a moderate and a capitalist and his appointments of Wall Street insider Timothy Geithner, as Treasury Secretary and his appointment of economist Lawrence Summers as the Director of the National Economic Council showed his conservative economic outlook. In these two positions Geithner and Summers emerged as the key economic decision makers in the Obama administration and they signaled his intentions of staying with a conservative capitalist free market course on economic issues. They were odd choices because like Greenspan they were also responsible for the collapse of the world economy.

In 1999, Summers endorsed and recommended the Gramm-Leach-Bliley Act to Clinton which removed the separation between investment and commercial banks, saying "With this bill, the American financial system takes a major step forward towards the 21st Century." The Act greatly allowed the rampant greed and speculation into housing that caused the economic catastrophe to occur.

It was also Geithner and Summers, along with Chairman Allan Greenspan and Clinton's Treasury Secretary Robert Rubin, that that prevented regulations and oversight on the derivatives market that had been proposed by Brooksley Born in the Clinton administration. Born was the Chair of the

Commodities Future Trading Commission (CFTC) under Clinton and she had warned Congress and the Clinton Administration that the little understood and fast growing derivative market was ripe for abuse, She said that it was a calamity waiting to occur. She warned that the derivative market was so large that a failure could bring down the entire US economy. She rightly proposed new regulations to oversee these markets in her role as the Chair of the CFTC.

Greenspan, Rubin, and Summers all strongly testified to Congress that her regulation was unnecessary and would cause unneeded restrictions of the "free market." They were adamant to the point of insulting in their opposition to Born's proposed derivative market regulations. They were sexist and dismissive of Born and they prevailed with Clinton and the Congress who sided with them. Born then resigned.

Born didn't have long to wait to be proven right. In 1998, a trillion dollar hedge fund called Long Term Capital Management (LTCM) collapsed. LTCM was investing the monies of fifteen of Wall Street's largest financial institutions in derivatives. The unregulated derivative transactions failed dramatically and in September 1998 the entire American economy hung in the balance. It was saved only after intervention by the Federal Reserve and it was only this very costly and expensive bailout by the American taxpayer that the crisis was averted, but even in the aftermath of the LTCM crisis the derivative market still remained unregulated at the insistence of these men. Had they allowed Born to do her job and regulate the derivative market the 1998 bailout and the 2007 world economic crisis would likely have been avoided.

In 2009, Born was awarded the John F. Kennedy Profiles in Courage Award in recognition of the "political courage she demonstrated in sounding early warnings about conditions that contributed to the current global financial crisis." In 2009, the PBS investigative news show *Frontline* aired a documentary called *The Warning* about Brooksley Born and her attempts to prevent the US economy from collapse.

Obama is a capitalist and a free market moderate and he chose these Wall Street free market capitalist insiders to find the solution even though they had been the cause of the problem. He did this rather than finding someone like Brooksley Born to fix these problems.

With the economy still in deep recession, on February 17, 2009, Obama signed the American Recovery and Reinvestment Act of 2009, a $787 billion stimulus package aimed at helping the economy recover and preventing further collapse. In March Treasury Secretary Geithner took further steps to manage the crisis, including buying up to two trillion dollars in greatly depreciated real estate assets. This move was highly controversial in that it had mostly saved the large banks and investment firms whose reckless speculation had caused the collapse. The bailout was expensive and controversial but it did save the failing US economy, but at an enormous cost to US taxpayers.

In March 2009, Obama took a major political risk and intervened in the automotive industry which was collapsing and made loans to General Motors and Chrysler to continue manufacturing while reorganizing. Over the following months the White House set terms for both bankruptcies which included the sale of Chrysler to Fiat, and a bailout and reorganization of General Motors in which the US government took a temporary sixty percent equity stake in the company with the Canadian government taking a twelve percent ownership.

The bailout of the auto industry was comically decried as socialism by the right. Mitt Romney ran against Obama in 2012 claiming the "nationalization of the auto industry" was a step toward socialism. His claims proved wholly ineffective with most voters as they realized that the car industry in the United States was only saved through Obama's efforts. It likely cost Romney his home state of Michigan in the election.

In 2010, Obama passed the Tax Relief, Unemployment Insurance Reauthorization, and Job Creation Act of 2010. The act extended the Bush payroll tax cuts of 2001 and also included several other measures which were intended to have a stimulatory effect on the economy. Mostly notably was a federal extension of unemployment benefits and a one-year reduction in the FICA payroll tax. This act was done in a very rare compromise agreement between Obama and Congressional Republicans.

After the Republicans and the right came into control of the House in 2010, they began to refuse any compromise with Obama and they became obstructionists on all legislation for fear that Obama would receive the credit. They wanted to destroy his presidency.

The Patient Protection and Affordable Care Act also called the Affordable Care Act (ACA) or what is derisively called "Obamacare" by the right, was signed into law on March 23, 2010. Together with the Health Care Reconciliation Act it represents the most significant regulatory overhaul of the American health care system in a half century. After winning a majority in the House the Republicans and the American right then tried to end ACA. There were over forty attempts by the Congress to end the ACA. They shut down the federal government and tried to blackmail Obama by threatening to not authorize an extension of the debt limit unless Obama ended the ACA, thereby throwing the country and the world into economic chaos. Obama stood his ground and in the end the Republicans had to surrender in defeat at the last minute angering everyone including many of their rightwing supporters.

Obama also enacted the Don't Ask Don't Tell Repeal Act of 2010 making it legal for gays to serve openly in the military. In May 2012, he became the first US president to publicly support same sex marriage and in 2013 his administration filed briefs which urged the Supreme Court to strike down the Defense of Marriage Act of 1996 that had been signed into law by Bill Clinton, as well as California's Proposition 8 as unconstitutional. The public began to support Obama's efforts and it turned the tide of gay rights in the United States and one by one the states began to legalize gay marriage, and in 2015 the Supreme Court also approved gay marriage.

In foreign policy Obama ended US military involvement in Iraq, but increased troop levels in Afghanistan with an end date. He signed a new START arms control treaty with Russia, but Russia's incursion into the Crimea and the Ukraine in 2014 brought an end to Obama's cooperation with Russia. He also began the normalization of diplomatic relations with Cuba, much to the consternation of the right.

In other military actions he ordered US Military involvement in Libya, ordered the military operation that resulted in the death of Osama Bin Laden, challenged Syria on biological weapons and began negotiations with Iran. On October 9, 2009, the Nobel Committee announced that Obama had won the 2009 Nobel Peace Prize "for his extraordinary efforts to strengthen international diplomacy and cooperation between peoples." Obama accepted this award in Oslo, Norway on December 10, 2009. The award drew a mixture of praise and criticism.

2012 Election

> "There are forty-seven percent of the people who are dependent upon government, who believe that they are victims, who believe the government has a responsibility to care for them, who believe that they are entitled to health care, to food, to housing, to you-name-it. That that's an entitlement, and the government should give it to them...These are people who pay no income tax. My job is not to worry about those people. I'll never convince them they should take personal responsibility and care for their lives."—Mitt Romney

> "I am just mystified by these people telling me I would think Obama was doing a great job if his skin contained less melanin."—Rightwing commentator Jonah Goldberg

Barack Obama secured the Democratic nomination with no serious opposition. The Republican Party was more fractured, but this turned into an advantage for Mitt Romney who was consistently competitive in the

polls, but also faced challenges from a number of more rightwing challengers whose popularity was frequently greater than his. Romney's Republican
opponents' popularity fluctuated wildly, many times besting Romney's, but
none of these opponents popularity lasted long enough to build momentum
and win significant delegates. While Romney was considered to be the likely nominee by the Republican establishment, a large segment of the party's
hard rightwing found him to be too moderate. In their search for a more
rightwing candidate they kept shifting their support from candidate to candidate in each primary and caucus thereby strengthening Romney and he
eventually secured the nomination.

Congresswoman Michele Bachmann was an early rightwing and religious right favorite. The first major event of the campaign was the Ames
Straw Poll in Iowa which took place on August 13, 2011. Michele Bachmann
won the straw poll causing Minnesota's Republican Governor Tim Pawlenty
to withdraw from the presidential race when his poor showing in the straw
poll in his neighboring state caused his support and money to dry up.

Because she had won the Ames Straw Poll Bachmann was then expected
to win in the Iowa Caucuses, but she lost to former Senator Rick Santorum,
another religious right candidate. Former Speaker of the House Newt Gingrich, also of the right, won South Carolina, and Romney won New Hampshire, making it the only time in Republican politics that the first four contests had been won by four different people.

A number of potential other rightwing "anti-Romney" candidates were
put forward, including Donald Trump who shamelessly campaigned on the
"Birther" issue claiming that Obama was not really an American citizen and
was born in Kenya. The intellectually vacant Sara Palin was briefly considered by the right and the equally intellectually vacant Texas Governor Rick
Perry became an early favorite but destroyed himself with his poor debate
performances.

After his win in Iowa, Rick Santorum unexpectedly carried three states
in a row in February and overtook Romney in nationwide opinion polls. He
became the only candidate in the race to effectively challenge the notion that
Romney was the inevitable nominee. However Romney was able to come
back in the Super Tuesday Primaries in March. Romney won six states, Santorum won three, and former Speaker of the House Newt Gingrich won in
his home state of Georgia. Santorum and Gingrich effectively cancelled each
other out in most of these primaries allowing Romney to win.

In April Santorum suspended his campaign due to his daughter's health
and because he was trailing Romney by enough in the delegate count that
it would be unlikely he could catch up. This left Mitt Romney as the undisputed front-runner. Romney was nominated in August by the Republican

Party and in a nod to the unhappy rightwing of his party he chose the rightwing Congressman Paul Ryan as his running mate. Like Greenspan, Ryan was a follower of Ayn Rand and was a Chicago School free market zealot. Unlike Greenspan, he had learned nothing in the economic collapse and he remained an unblinking free market capitalist zealot.

There were three televised presidential debates during the campaign. Obama seemed unconcerned and uncaring in the first debate. He didn't take the Romney challenge seriously. His supporters felt that he didn't want to participate, a charge to which Obama admitted to later. He seemed unprepared and distant. After being criticized by many in his party after the first debate Obama then became engaged and won the last two.

Romney made some major gaffes during the campaign. Romney claimed that he had been a "severely conservative Republican governor." A phrase which both the rightwing of the Republican Party and the Democrats poked fun at, both claiming that the chameleon-like Romney was changing the past to suit the present. In the second television debate Romney, when asked if he had considered appointing any women to public office when he was the Massachusetts governor, replied that he had consulted "binders full of women." This phrase was clumsy and it made many women believe Romney was not serious about appointing women. In another gaffe he appeared out of touch with the financial condition of most Americans when he referred to the high cost of education and student loans and suggested that children should borrow the money from their parents to go to college. He didn't understand that most parents don't have this money to lend.

But the most costly gaffe occurred when he was caught on video tape speaking to a group of rightwing funders and said that that forty-seven percent of the American people would vote for Barack Obama no matter what Romney said or did because those people "are dependent upon government." The "forty-seven percent" incident haunted Romney throughout the election, making him appear to be the uncaring and distant rich man that he was.

In the end Obama beat Romney by about five million votes. He won fifty-one percent to Romney's forty-seven percent. Obama won most of the states he had in is 2008 win, having lost only two states he had won in 2008. Obama lost the traditionally Republican states of Indiana and North Carolina to Romney and the Republicans, but North Carolina was only lost by a very thin margin.

In an election night comedy, the right was so emotionally sure of a Romney win that when Obama was declared the election winner after winning the State of Ohio, Karl Rove and a few others on the right had an election night meltdown on FOX Television as they challenged the truthfulness of the results that Fox News was reporting. The rightwing Fox News found they were in the strange position of defending their reporting to Karl Rove's on-air challenge. He insisted that they were wrong. In an odd and demented melodrama Rove continued to argue that Romney was the winner as the television showed the victory celebrations in the Obama camp.

Chapter 16. The Hard Right, Oil Money and the Tea Party

> "A democracy cannot function effectively when its constituent members believe laws are being bought and sold."—Supreme Court Justice John Paul Stevens

> "The ruling will, to a significant degree, give control of the political process in the United States to the wealthiest and most powerful institutions in the world and the candidates who support their agenda. Instead of democracy being about one-person one-vote, it will now be about the size of a company's bank account."—Senator Bernie Sanders on the Supreme Court decision about Citizens United

During the 2004 presidential campaign a rightwing organization called Citizens United filed a complaint before the Federal Election Commission (FEC) charging that advertisements for documentary film maker Michael Moore's movie *Fahrenheit 9/11*, a documentary critical of the Bush administration's response to the attacks on September 11, 2001, constituted political advertising and said these could not be aired within the 30 days before a primary election or 60 days before a general election. The FEC dismissed the complaint after finding no evidence that the broadcasts for the movie violated the acts. The FEC later dismissed a second complaint from the rightwing Citizens United which argued that the movie itself constituted illegal corporate spending advocating the election or defeat of a candidate, which they claimed was illegal under the Taft Hartley Act and the Federal Election Campaign Act Amendments of 1974.

In the wake of the court decisions against them, Citizens United then sought to establish that they were bona fide commercial film makers and produced several documentary films between 2005 and 2007. By early 2008 they sought to run television commercials to promote their latest political documentary *Hillary, The Movie*. The movie was highly critical of Senator Hillary Clinton. The District Court described the movie as a longer version of a negative campaign advertisement. In January 2008 the US District Court for the District of Columbia ruled that the television advertisements for *Hillary: The Movie* violated federal election law. Citizens United claimed that the film was nonpartisan, however, it was obvious it was not and the lower court found that the film had no purpose other than to discredit Clinton's candidacy for president.

The Supreme Court docketed the case *Citizen's United v. Federal Election Commission* on August 18, 2008, and heard oral arguments on March 24, 2009. In a five to four political decision along strict partisan lines, the Court held that portions of US election laws violated the First Amendment.

The Supreme Court reversed the lower court's decision and then in an amazingly brazen rightwing political act they also struck down those provisions of the law that prohibited corporations from making independent expenditures and political ads. It meant that billionaires and corporations could now spend and contribute as much as they wanted to any candidate and to buy or influence any election. Since this disastrous decision sixteen states have called for an amendment to reverse the Supreme Court's decision.

Justice John Paul Stevens wrote the dissenting opinion and said that the Court's ruling, "threatens to undermine the integrity of elected institutions across the nation. The path it has taken to reach its outcome will, I fear, do damage to this institution.... A democracy cannot function effectively when its constituent members believe laws are being bought and sold."

The wealthy and powerful can now legally buy elections. An Arlington, Virginia conservative group, whose existence until now was unknown to almost everyone, raised and spent $250 million in 2012 to shape national and local politics and policies promoting a rightwing agenda. The group is Freedom Partners and its president Marc Short serves as an outlet for the rightwing ideas and millions of dollars in campaign financing from rightwing billionaires, especially the Koch brothers. The Koch brothers have cut checks as large as $63 million to groups promoting their rightwing causes according to IRS documents. One of the groups they support is Citizens United. According to *Dark Money: Bombshell Report Exposes the Koch Brothers' "Secret Bank"* at *Billmoyers.com*, the thirty-eight page IRS filing amounts to "the Rosetta Stone" of the vast web of the rightwing conservatives who spend time, money and resources to influence public debate. According to the website they have been particularly active in discrediting the Affordable Care Act, which they have labeled as "Obamacare."

Freedom Partners has about 200 rightwing donors, each paying at least $100,000 in annual dues. Created in November of 2011, they raised $256 million in 2012. They in turn made grants of $236 million to various rightwing political causes and groups. This little known group was the largest contributor for conservative and the rightwing agenda in the last election, second in total spending only to Karl Rove's rightwing American Crossroads and Crossroads GPS, the two of which spent about $300 million to influence the elections. The American rightwing is now effectively spending a half a billion dollars per year buying elections and funding ads to shape American opinion. Many of their ads are not known for their accuracy or truthfulness.

Senator Bernie Sanders of Vermont said that the spending of billionaires like the Koch brother's demonstrates that we are no longer a nation of the people. He said, "When one wealthy family spends more money than was raised altogether by the last Republican presidential candidate, it tells us that we are no longer a country of the people, by the people and for the people. We are becoming a country of the rich, by the rich and for the rich."

The Koch brothers (pronounced like coke) are billionaire oilmen who control Koch Industries, which owns and operates oil refineries and other industries. Koch Industries is the second-largest privately owned company in the United States. The family business was started by Fred Koch. Two of his sons, David and Charles Koch, still manage Koch Industries and own 84 percent of the company in addition to a vast fortune their father left them. They also control the lucrative Koch Family Foundations and give generously to rightwing causes and organizations. Annual revenues for Koch Industries have been estimated to be about a hundred billion dollars per year according to Jane Mayer in a 2011 article in *The New Yorker*.

Their father, Fred Koch, was a very hardcore right-winger and was a founding member of the far right John Birch Society. There are many other rightwing groups created by the Koch brothers that are influencing American politics.

The Cato Institute is a large well-funded rightwing think tank headquartered in Washington, D.C. It was created by Charles Koch, the chairman of the board and chief executive officer of Koch Industries and was funded by the Charles Koch Foundation in 1974. The mission of the Cato Institute "is to originate, disseminate, and increase understanding of public policies based on the principles of individual liberty, limited government and unregulated capitalist free markets."

Specific policy proposals advanced by Cato scholars include such measures as abolishing the minimum wage and abolishing affirmative action and in general abolishing industry and environmental regulations. As they are funded by the Koch oil refineries, the Cato Institute has a rightwing view of ecology and denies global warming. They are against the Kyoto Protocols and three out of five *"Doubters of Global Warming"* interviewed by the PBS show *Frontline* were funded by or had some other institutional connection with the Koch funded Cato Institute.

American for Prosperity (AFP) is another Virginia based rightwing political advocacy group that was funded by the Koch brothers. AFP's stated mission is "educating citizens about economic policy and mobilizing citizens as advocates in the public policy process." The group played a major role in the 2010 Republican takeover of the House of Representatives. David Koch is the chairman of the AFP Foundation. AFP was founded with the support of both David and Charles Koch and Koch Industries. It was originally part of another Koch financed rightwing nonprofit, Citizen's for a Sound Economy.

FreedomWorks is yet another Koch financed nonprofit that split off of Citizen's for a Sound Economy. FreedomWorks trains volunteers, assists in campaigns and encourages them to mobilize, influencing both citizens and their political representatives. According to a 2010 article in the *New York Times*, FreedomWorks "has done more than any other organization to build the Tea Party Movement." It is alleged that FreedomWorks created and runs the Tea Party. FreedomWorks found, endorsed, financed and managed rightwing political candidates. These candidates include: Marco Rubio, Pat Toomey, Mike Lee, Rand Paul, Don Stenberg, Jeff Flake, Richard Mourdock, and Ted Cruz. These were the men behind the shut down the federal government on October 1, 2013. They tried to blackmail the US Senate and President Obama into canceling the Affordable Care Act, or what they derisively called "Obamacare." They said they would close down the US Government by refusing to pass a funding bill to keep the government operating. Then they doubled down by also threatening to not extend the US debt limit which would have caused the government to default on its debts unless Obamacare was ended. The operation ended in defeat when Obama refused to be blackmailed and public opinion turned against them.

FreedomWorks is also against Social Security, Medicare and is for school choice as they are against public schools. They have also run political-type campaigns to fire any corporate CEOs who they believe have a progressive agenda or who are not a supporter of the Chicago School's free market philosophy.

After the Tea Party supported Senator Ted Cruz to shut down the government and brought the nation to the fiscal cliff, Senator Cruz, Sara Palin, and Larry Klayman, along with others from the Tea Party and FreedomWorks held a "veterans protest" in Washington, DC on October 14, 2013, where they hypocritically protested the government shutdown they had caused. They complained that the veterans were not getting their benefits caused by the shutdown crisis they created.

Larry Klayman is the creator of Freedom Watch and was also the founder and the former chairman of Judicial Watch. He said to the veterans and the Tea Party protesters at the event, "I call upon all of you to wage a second American nonviolent revolution, to use civil disobedience and to demand that this president leave town, to get up, to put the Quran down, to get up off his knees, and to figuratively come out with his hands up."

These references about Obama being Muslim, which Klayman knows to be untrue, are used to inflame racial and religious tensions among the religious right and the less educated working class Whites. It is a disinformation campaign for their uneducated followers in order to rouse xenophobic fears that Obama is a Kenyan and a radical Muslim who is out to destroy the United States. During the protest, Rebel flags were waived in front of the White House as a blatant racial taunt to the nation's first Black president. These acts caused considerable indignation from African-Americans and many other Americans.

The Koch brothers are also behind the denials about global warming and climate change. Their oil refineries and other businesses would be greatly impacted by environmental regulation and they oppose all of it and sponsor groups like the Cato Institute to promote the idea that global warming and climate change is a leftwing hoax. They are not above unfairly influencing local officials in these pursuits. In 2015, *The Daily Kos* reported that the Koch brothers and former Florida governors Jeb Bush and Rick Scott have been exposed in a Florida pipeline scandal. In 2003 Governor Jeb Bush and his cabinet approved an illegal pipeline for Georgia Pacific, a Koch Brother's company, over the legal objections of the Florida Attorney General Charlie Christ. The pipeline allows Georgia Pacific to dump toxic waste from the Palatka paper mill into the pristine St. Johns River, a protected American Heritage River. The permit was done with a public notice that environmental groups call "grossly misleading" to give the appearance that the permit was legal and would not cause any environmental damage.

Rightwing Authoritarianism

Why would the average German support Hitler? Why do average Americans support billionaires like the Koch brothers and rightwing politics that are not in their own self-interest? Why would they believe that rightwing rich men have their best interests at heart? The answer lies in a psychological condition known as rightwing authoritarianism.

In 1950, at the University of California Berkeley four psychologists, Theodor Adorno, Nevitt Sanford, Else Frenkel-Brunswik, and Daniel Levinson developed a theory called Authoritarian Personality Disorder in part to explain the rise of fascism in the 1930s, World War II and the Holocaust.

Another psychologist Robert Altemeyer expanded on this theory after his extensive study of authoritarians and their followers. He developed the theory of Rightwing Authoritarianism (RWA). After extensive questionnaire research and statistical analysis, Altemeyer found that there are three traits that identify someone who is susceptible to Rightwing Authoritarianism. They are: 1. Authoritarian Submission, which is a high degree of submissiveness to the authorities who are perceived to be the established and legitimate controllers in the society in which we live. 2. Authoritarian Aggression, caused by a general aggressiveness directed against deviants, other groups or minorities and other people that are perceived to be different according to established authorities. 3. Conventionalism, caused by a high degree of adherence to the traditions and social norms that are perceived to be endorsed by society and its established authorities and a belief that all others in the society should also be required to adhere to these exact same norms.

Susceptibility to Rightwing Authoritarianism is measured by the RWA scale which is a simple scale from minus four to plus four, with minus four meaning total disagreement with a question to plus four meaning total agreement. The first scored question on the scale asks, "Our country desperately needs a mighty leader who will do what has to be done to destroy the radical new ways and sinfulness that are ruining us." People who strongly agree with this are showing susceptibility toward authoritarian submission. They believe that the "country desperately needs a mighty leader." They desire to see a leader who will do whatever is necessary to destroy the enemy. They want a leader who supports norms and is opposed to the radical new ways and sinfulness which they believe are "ruining us." A current version of the RWA is 22 questions long and can be found online. You can take this test to see how susceptible to Rightwing Authoritarianism you may be.

Another reason that may also explain why the average German supported Hitler and why some Americans support billionaires like the Koch brothers and their rightwing politics that are not in their own self-interest may be due to another psychological condition called cognitive dissonance. This condition is the excessive mental stress and discomfort experienced by an individual whose core beliefs, ideas, or values are challenged or refuted by the facts, science or experience. This mental stress and discomfort may frequently cause an individual with cognitive dissonance to totally and illogically reject and even disdain something that is obviously true to others. It is a disorder that afflicts many with fervent radical religious and rightwing political views. It is why some may discount scientific facts about global warming or evolution, and to believe that poor people deserve to be poor because it is god's will.

CHAPTER 17. BIG BROTHER

"We don't hold data on US citizens."—Keith Alexander the Director of the National Security Agency lying to Congress in July 2012.

"No, sir."—James Clapper the Director of National Intelligence lying to the Congress in a public hearing in March 2013, when asked, "Does the NSA collect any type of data at all on millions or hundreds of millions of Americans?"

"I responded in what I thought was the most truthful, or least untruthful manner by saying 'no'."—James Clapper, Director of National Intelligence about why he lied in March 2013, to the Congress about NSA spying on the American people

"I think it's important to understand that you can't have one hundred percent security and then have one hundred percent privacy and zero inconvenience. We're going to have to make some choices as a society."—Barack Obama

"Those who surrender freedom for security will not have, nor do they deserve, either one."—Benjamin Franklin

There is something wrong with a people who willingly surrender their liberties every time a national threat emerges. Americans ignored and forgot the constitutional rights and guarantees of the unionists and anarchists at the turn of the century. They did again with the communists and socialists during the first Red

Scare in the Wilson Administration. They ignored the Constitution with the Japanese internments of World War II and again with the communists and socialists during the Cold War. They ignored the Constitution with their illegal actions against civil rights leaders in the 1950s and 1960s and with anti-war activists during the Vietnam War. And we are ignoring the Constitution and allowing our freedoms to be undermined once again in the wake of the September 11, terrorist attacks. America has become so rightwing paranoid about threats by unnamed others that the nation is now willing to allow the government to spy, read everyone's email, mail and telegrams and to listen to our phone calls as they please.

Most Americans are unaware that this spying has been done by the government on American citizens since World War II. In the modern electronic era the government has greatly expanded and continues to spy on hundreds of millions of Americans. The spying includes: internet searches, emails, text messages and cell phone calls, Facebook, Twitter, Linked-In, etc. and likely other untold methods of monitoring supposedly free American citizens.

Contrary to what most Americans believe the majority of this spying is not done by permission of the courts or Congress and it is done without court warrants. It is wholesale random spying and surveillance on virtually every American. Big brother is constantly watching you on video cameras, listening to your phone calls, sometimes bugging your home or business, monitoring your computers, reading your Facebook posts, telegrams and emails, your twitters, looking at what you search for on the internet and what you read, write and think. All these illegal acts are done to supposedly to prevent terrorism and to keep America "safe." These are acts that by their very nature threaten Americans privacy, security and freedoms.

This wholesale spying started just after World War II, it was called Project SHAMROCK. It started with the Armed Forces Security Agency and continued when that agency was reorganized as the National Security Agency (NSA) in 1952. Project SHAMROCK was a top secret espionage exercise on the American people that was started in August 1945, and involved the accumulation of all telegrams entering into or exiting from the United States. The Armed Forces Security Agency and its successor the NSA were given direct access to daily microfilm copies of all incoming, outgoing, and transiting telegrams. The NSA sorted the information and if this information was of interest to other intelligence or government agencies the material was then passed on to them. Intercepted messages were disseminated to the CIA, FBI, the Secret Service, the Bureau of Narcotics and Dangerous Drugs, the IRS and the Department of Defense. It was illegal as no court ever authorized the operation and there were no court warrants.

In 1975, Project SHAMROCK was discovered by Congress during the Church Committee inquiries. In a CIA historical document, *Recollections from the Church Committee's Investigation of NSA* by L. Britt Snider, Snider documents how it came to be discovered, "The Committee received from the Rockefeller Commission a copy of the 'family jewels,' the name given to a roughly 800-page compilation of the recollections of CIA employees who had previously been directed by then DCI James Schlesinger to identify all past abuses or improprieties in which CIA may have been involved. Buried within this infamous tome were two references to the NSA. The first was a reference to an office in New York that CIA had provided NSA for the purpose of copying telegrams. The other disclosed that CIA had asked NSA to monitor the communications of certain US citizens active in the antiwar movement."

In May 1975, Congressional critics began to investigate and expose the entire program. The Senate Intelligence Committee Chairman Senator Frank Church concluded that the unauthorized and illegal Project SHAMROCK was "probably the largest government interception program affecting Americans ever undertaken." The result of these investigations was the creation of the Foreign Intelligence Surveillance Act (FISA) in 1978, which supposedly limited the powers of the National Security Agency and put in place a process of warrants and judicial review before any data could be collected on any American citizen.

As a result of FISA, the NSA Director Lew Allen publicly terminated SHAMROCK. But like many terminated illegal CIA and NSA projects, the NSA secretly replaced it with another top secret program that was even more invasive.

Project MINARET was a sister project to Project SHAMROCK and was operated by the NSA from 1967 to 1973. It spied upon predesignated US citizens. These were mostly individuals who were on "watch lists" of American citizens, generated by the Executive Branch and many of these persons were dissidents designated by Johnson and those on the Nixon "Enemies List." The spying and surveillance came from law enforcement and intelligence agencies which allowed wholesale unauthorized illegal spying and telephone tapping on the American left, anti-war and civil rights leaders, as well as Native-American, Latino and women's rights advocates and organizations. There was never any judicial oversight and the project had no warrants for their telephone wiretapping, mail reading and other surveillance. NSA Director Lew Allen testified before the Senate Intelligence Committee in 1975 that the NSA had issued well over 3,900 reports on the "watch-listed Americans" that went just to the Nixon White House.

"Watch-listed Americans" included some interesting people such as civil rights leaders like Martin Luther King Jr. and Whitney Young, athletes like

Mohammad Ali, newspaper reporters like Tom Wicker and Art Buchwald, and even US Senators like Frank Church a Democrat and Howard Baker a Republican who were at the time investigating the NSA.

Another NSA spy program, Project ECHELON, has been in existence since at least the mid-1970s. In a 1999 article entitled, *ECHELON was My Baby*, former NSA employee Margaret Newsham claims that she worked on the configuration and installation of software that makes up the ECHELON system while employed at Lockheed Martin for whom she worked from 1974 to 1984. It is similar to SHAMROCK, but it is an expanded version working globally and apparently in cooperation with the United Kingdom and the Commonwealth countries of Canada, Australia and New Zealand. The project's capabilities and political implications were investigated by a committee of the European Parliament during 2000 and 2001. The European Parliament stated in its report that the term ECHELON is used in a number of contexts, but that the evidence presented indicates that it was the name for a signals intelligence collection system. The report concludes that based upon their investigation that ECHELON was capable of interception and content inspection of telephone calls, fax, e-mail and other data traffic globally through the interception of communication bearers including satellite transmission, public telephone networks and microwave links.

In 2013, it was revealed that the NSA secretly monitored European leaders from a spying hub in the United States German Embassy. German Chancellor Angela Merkel was so distressed by the US spying on her and her government that even after President Obama personally apologized to her for this spying that she called for an end to European cooperation with the US intelligence agencies.

The Europeans have also asserted that the United States is also exploiting ECHELON traffic for industrial spying on the behalf of US corporations and stealing technology from other nation's industries as well as military, political and diplomatic spying. An article in the *Guardian* in May, 2001, warned that if Echelon were to continue unchecked it could become a "cyber secret police, without courts, juries, or the right to a defense." ECHELON is not just a foreign surveillance operation. It also spies on Americans. It is the greatly improved replacement for SHAMROCK.

ThinThread was a program in the 1990s that involved massive wiretapping and spying with sophisticated analysis of the resulting data. The program was discontinued three weeks before the September 11, 2001, attacks due to the changes in priorities and the consolidation of US intelligence authority according to the *Baltimore Sun*. The change in priority was a decision made by the director of NSA General Michael V. Hayden to go with a new project called Trailblazer.

ThinThread had privacy protections for US citizens built into it. Despite the fact that ThinThread was a working prototype that protected some privacy of US citizens the NSA decided to replace it with the Trailblazer Project which has the exact same capabilities of ThinThread but it has no privacy protections to protect Americans. ThinThread had been designed very carefully from a legal point of view so that even in wartime the NSA could do surveillance quasi-legitimately and with some judicial oversight. The NSA wanted to operate without these privacy limitations and without judicial oversight and so Trailblazer was created.

A consortium led by Science Applications International Corporations was awarded a $280 million contract to develop Trailblazer without the privacy protections. A group of whistleblowers including former NSA staff Kirk Wiebe, William Binney, Ed Loomis, and Thomas A. Drake, along with a House Intelligence Committee staffer Diane Roark (an expert on the NSA budget) complained that ThinThread was a better system and that it was a huge waste of money to design another program, especially one that was only being created to avoid the privacy protections and the courts.

In response to these whistleblowers the FBI raided their homes in 2007. One of the Trailblazer whistleblowers who assisted with the Inspector General report, Thomas A. Drake was later charged under the Espionage Act of 1917 for allegedly retaining documents in his home. Two of those documents were about Project Turbulence a new electronic surveillance program that replaced Trailblazer. His defense lawyers pointed out that one of these documents was clearly marked "UNCLASSIFIED" and the other was declassified very shortly afterward. Despite this he was found guilty. To avoid more serious charges and a jail sentence Drake was forced plead guilty to a misdemeanor count of unauthorized use of a computer on June 10, 2011. The court realized that the charges were mostly harassment and were made only to silence his whistleblowing and he was sentenced to one year probation.

President Bush and his administration began to crackdown heavily on whistleblowers and leaks after the *New York Times* disclosed another NSA warrantless spy program. According to intelligence officials quoted in the *Baltimore Sun*, The privacy protections that had been offered by ThinThread were permanently abandoned in the post-9/11 push by the Bush administration to create a more intrusive national spy system. The NSA then disabled all privacy safeguards and also stopped seeking court approvals. President Bush then personally gave the go-ahead for the NSA to secretly gather and analyze all American phone and computer records.

NSA Director Air Force Gen. Michael V. Hayden admitted in a speech that the warrantless surveillance program was "not limited to al-Qaida communications," but he lied at the time saying that it had been "carefully implemented with an eye toward preserving the Constitution and rights of Americans." There were no such protections. When General Hayden left the NSA, he was rewarded and was appointed by President Bush as the Director of the CIA from 2006 to 2009.

Trailblazer was cancelled by Congress in 2006 and the NSA replaced it with Project Turbulence. It also included the same invasive capabilities as Trailblazer, but also contained new offensive cyber-warfare capabilities like injecting malware into the remote computers that it was monitoring. It was designed without privacy protections and court oversight. When Congress became aware of some of this in 2007 they criticized the NSA for ignoring the law and Congressional directives as they had done with the Trailblazer Project. They insisted on installing privacy protections and provisions for judicial oversight. The NSA told the Congress what it wanted to hear and then continued as they had been and ignored their directives.

STELLARWIND is the code name of a secret security compartment for information collected under the President's Surveillance Program (PSP). This was another massive electronic surveillance project conducted by the NSA during the Bush administration. One of the known uses of this data was the creation of suspicious activity reports, or "SARS." It was illegal government wiretapping. Some of these SARS reports were used for political purposes. One SARS was used to reveal that former New York Governor Eliot Spitzer had hired prostitutes. This event showed Congress that the program was being used by the Bush Administration for illegal domestic political spying and that the White House and NSA spying was not limited to "terrorist threats" as had been publicly claimed by the Bush administration and the NSA.

Congress demanded that the STELLARWIND program be stopped. It did not stop. In March 2012 *Wired* magazine published: *NSA Is Building the Country's Biggest Spy Center (Watch What You Say)* which stated, "For the first time, a former NSA official has gone on the record to describe the program, codenamed STELLARWIND, in detail." The article quoted William Binney a former NSA code breaker. Binney said that the NSA had highly secured rooms that tap into major switches and satellite communications at both AT&T and Verizon. The article alleged that although many including Congress had been told that STELLARWIND had ended that it was still a very active program.

In June 2013, the *Washington Post* and the *Guardian* published an Office of the Inspector General Draft Report dated March 2009 which was leaked to the press by former CIA and NSA employee Edward Snowden detailing the STELLARWIND program. He also leaked the details of PRISM, a clandestine mass electronic surveillance data mining operation program operated by the NSA since 2007. Documents indicate that the previously unknown PRISM program is primary source of raw intelligence used for NSA analytic reports and that it accounts for ninety-one percent of the NSA's Internet traffic spying.

The leaked information came to light one day after the revelation that a FISA Court had ordered a subsidiary of the telecommunications company Verizon Communications to turn over to the court the NSA logs tracking all of its customers' telephone calls on an ongoing daily basis. The information had been leaked by NSA contractor Edward Snowden who warned the press that the extent of mass data collection was by far greater than the public knew and included what he characterized as "dangerous" and "criminal" activities. The disclosures were published by *The Guardian* and *The Washington Post* on June 6, 2013.

On June 11, 2013, a *New York Times* article said the following: "The surreptitious collection of 'metadata'—every bit of information about every phone call except the word-by-word content of conversations—fundamentally alters the relationship between individuals and their government.... The government's capacity to build extensive, secret digital dossiers on such a mass scale is totally at odds with the vision and intention of the nation's framers who crafted the Fourth Amendment precisely to outlaw indiscriminate searches that cast a wide net to see what can be caught."

The NSA's relationship with the large corporations is also disturbing as they too are part of this spying effort. According to Craig Timberg at the Washington Post, the government threatened to fine Yahoo $250,000 a day in 2008 if it failed to comply with their demands to hand over all their user data. The company believed this order was unconstitutional and had initially refused to comply according to court documents unsealed in 2014. The documents illuminate how federal intelligence officials forced American tech companies to participate in the NSA's controversial PRISM program. These companies were also told that any individual leaking the existence of this data collection would be subject to long prison terms and large fines.

Some of the private corporate partners of the NSA spy programs are very willing to give in to the demands of the NSA because their cooperation is financially very rewarding. Subsequent documents have demonstrated these lucrative financial arrangements between the NSA's Special Source Operations division (SSO) and PRISM's private partners are in the millions of dollars.

The surveillance industry in general is thriving. The mass surveillance industry is now a multi-billion dollar business that has experienced significant growth since 2001. According to data made public by *The Wall Street Journal* in November 2011, the retail market for surveillance tools had risen up from very little in 2001 to about $5 billion in 2011. It was later reported that the size of the surveillance market rose to $13.5 billion in 2012, and was expected to reach $39 billion by 2020.

PRISM and massive electronic surveillance has continued under Obama. The Obama administration's argument is that NSA surveillance programs such as PRISM have been necessary to prevent acts of terrorism. Whistleblower Edward Snowden responded, "Bathtub falls and police officers kill more Americans than terrorism, yet we've been asked to sacrifice our most sacred rights for fear of falling victim to it." Snowden also stated, "The NSA routinely lies in response to congressional inquiries about the scope of surveillance in America." The three quotes at the beginning of this chapter support his claims.

Edward Snowden, Hero or Traitor?

> "He's obviously violated the laws of America, for which he's responsible, but I think the invasion of human rights and American privacy has gone too far. I think that the secrecy that has been surrounding this invasion of privacy has been excessive, so I think that the bringing of it to the public notice has probably been, in the long term, beneficial."—President Jimmy Carter speaking about Edward Snowden

> "The results of your conduct have put some very brave people at risk . . . You did a lot of damage to your country, and you've put a lot of people who serve the country in difficult circumstances, under the cover of darkness, at risk. And you've got their blood on your hands."—Senator Lindsey Graham speaking about Edward Snowden

> "The government does not need to know more about what we are doing. We need to know more about what the government is doing. We should be thankful for individuals like Edward Snowden and Glenn Greenwald who see injustice being carried out by their own government and speak out, despite the risk. They have done a great service to the American people by exposing the truth about what our government is doing in secret."—Congressman Ron Paul

On June 14, 2013, United States federal prosecutors charged Edward Snowden with theft of government property, unauthorized communication of national defense information and "willful communication of classified communications intelligence information to an unauthorized person," the last two charges having been brought under the 1917 Espionage Act. They are considered treason.

Snowden fled the United States to avoid prison. On August 1, 2013, he landed at Sheremetyevo, one of Moscow's international airports. Snowden remained at the airport more than a month in the transit section while he applied for asylum in numerous countries to no avail. Finland, Germany, India, Poland, Norway, Austria, Italy, and the Netherlands cited technical grounds for not considering his application. Ecuador had initially offered Snowden a temporary travel document but later withdrew it. All of these countries had been put under extreme pressure by the United States to deny his asylum. Russia then granted him temporary asylum for one year. Snowden's attorney Anatoly Kucherena said the asylum could be extended indefinitely on an annual basis and that Snowden had gone to an undisclosed location which would be kept secret for security reasons. In response to the Russia granting asylum the White House said the US administration was "extremely disappointed" by the Russian government's decision and cancelled a planned summit between Obama and Russian President Putin. Senator Lindsey Graham said, "I hope we'll chase him to the ends of the earth, bring him to justice and let the Russians know there will be consequences if they harbor this guy."

The Director of the NSA General Keith Alexander said, "He (Snowden) betrayed the trust and confidence we had in him. This was an individual with top secret clearance whose duty it was to administer these networks. He betrayed that confidence and stole some of our secrets."

Former Vice President Dick Cheney the chief advocate for the electronic surveillance programs in the Bush administration called Snowden a "traitor," And said, "I think it's one of the worst occasions in my memory of somebody with access to classified information doing enormous damage to the national security interests of the United States."

Snowden is not without his supporters. Former US Senator Gordon Humphrey, a New Hampshire Republican, sent an email message of support to Snowden calling the NSA surveillance program a "massive violation of the United States Constitution."

In August 2013, Snowden was awarded the biennial German "Whistle-blower Prize." In October 2013 in Moscow he was presented with the "Sam Adams Award" by a group of former American intelligence officers and whistleblowers who believe he acted like a patriot in the best interest of the United States.

Snowden has defended his actions saying he is not a traitor, "Let's be clear: I did not reveal any US operations against legitimate military targets. I pointed out where the NSA has hacked civilian infrastructure such as universities, hospitals, and private businesses because it is dangerous. These nakedly, aggressively criminal acts are wrong no matter the target."

The rightwing zealots continue to attack Snowden saying whatever the motive, he revealed classified information to others and should be prosecuted. This is hypocrisy. The American government and these same rightwing zealots were not outraged when it was revealed that General David Petraeus, the former CIA Director, gave highly classified documents which included covert operatives and military strategies to his mistress Paula Broadwell so that she could write his biography. General Petraeus also admitted that when first confronted about the incident that he had lied to the FBI and had committed perjury which the government also chose to ignore. On March 4, Petraeus was only charged with a misdemeanor. He was given two years' probation and a fine for what should have been a very lengthy prison sentence. His crimes were for personal gain and to appease his mistress. Snowden committed a similar crime, but it was to protect the privacy and freedoms of the American people, yet no one is offering him probation and a fine.

And Nothing Changes

> "More generally, we believe that the longstanding laws and traditions concerning intelligence committee oversight (on electronic surveillance) have been effective and workable..."—Vito T. Potenza, Acting General Counsel National Security Agency testimony to Congress September 12, 2006

On October 28, 2013, a coalition of more than a hundred public advocacy organizations came together in a coalition named "Stop Watching Us," to demand that Congress investigate the full scope of the NSA's spying programs. Thousands of people protested the National Security Agency's surveillance programs with a march on the National Mall. The coalition collected 575,000 printed signatures on a protest petition and delivered it to Congressman Justin Amash. The letter asked members of Congress to repeal Section 215 of the Patriot Act and create a special committee to investigate and report the extent of the domestic spying and to hold accountable public officials who are responsible for the "unconstitutional surveillance."

The Congress has asked National Security Agency Director General Keith Alexander and the Director of National Intelligence James Clapper to testify before Congress. Since both have previously lied about the program in the past to Congress, it is likely they will lie again and it is unlikely that significant changes will be made. If they act as they have in the past they will tell Congress they will end the program, re-name it and continue as before as this has been the NSA's constant and unending pattern since World War II.

FINAL CONCLUSIONS

> "America does not have a functioning democracy at this point in time."—President Jimmy Carter in a 2013 closed door meeting of Atlantic Bridge

> "Not to know is bad. Not to wish to know is worse."—African Proverb

Americans naively believe they live in a free and democratic society where freedom of speech and political freedoms are taken for granted. This has never been true for the American left. Throughout the nineteenth and twentieth centuries and into today in the twenty-first century the left has been unjustly vilified and demonized even by American moderates and liberals. The leaders of the American left have also been harassed, spied on, unfairly charged with crimes and even assassinated by rightwing zealots in the American government.

Albert Parsons and three other socialists were unfairly executed for a riot where they were not even present in what is now known as a police riot. Eugene Debs and Mother Jones were imprisoned for their union activities and their political beliefs and Big Bill Haywood was falsely accused of crimes and forced into exile for the same reasons.

In the 1920s, under the Attorney General A. Mitchell Palmer thousands of Jews, Russians, socialists and labor leaders were beaten, imprisoned and deported as suspected communists. In the 1950s, thousands were harassed and imprisoned and had their careers and livelihoods destroyed at the hands of Joe McCarthy and other politicians. Liberals like Hubert Humphrey and other members of the Americans for Democratic Action advocated against and wrote laws to send communists and socialists to prison camps.

Generals Joe Stilwell and George C. Marshall and statesmen like Dean Acheson, Owen Lattimore and John S. Service had their reputations destroyed by the right for contradicting their insane and wishful thinking rightwing foreign policies.

The civil rights leader W.E.B. Du Bois was tried and although he was found innocent, he still had had his passport taken and was not allowed to travel abroad. Dr. Martin Luther King Jr. was harassed, illegally wiretapped, accused of being a communist, blackmailed and eventually assassinated.

Gus Hall, Angela Davis and other American communists were illegally imprisoned although they never committed any crime. Hall spent eight years in prison that the Supreme Court later found unconstitutional. He illegally had his driver's license revoked because of his political beliefs. Davis was harassed by the FBI as a student and was illegally fired from her professorship at UCLA by Governor Ronald Reagan and she was later imprisoned for a crime she didn't commit.

In the 1960s and 1970s, anti-war activists, feminists, gay activists, and civil rights advocates were all spied upon, harassed and had their reputations destroyed by the FBI, and many were charged and went to prison for crimes they didn't commit.

The OSS/CIA became the army of the rightwing in America. By recruiting the Mafia and the Nazi Gestapo and Nazi scientists into their organization they corrupted themselves. They have committed horrendous crimes and acts of violence in the name of their rightwing political agenda and justified these horrible acts in the name of national security. They dealt in inhumane medical experimentation, mind control, drug smuggling, assassination, bribery, and torture to achieve their rightwing ends. They made war on the left in America. They dominate the American and foreign media to spread their lies and protect themselves. They have lied many times to presidents and Congress and have consistently destroyed public and government records to cover-up their high crimes and misdemeanors in the false name of national security. Whistleblowers and the press who opposed them were discredited, imprisoned or died mysterious deaths.

The FBI was used as a national police against the left and the civil rights and anti-war movements. They too engaged in illegal spying, intimidation, character assassination, blackmail, and actual assassinations. They planted false evidence, lied and perjured themselves in silencing "their enemies" and thereby corrupted the American legal and court systems.

Believe what you must about the assassinations of JFK, RFK, and MLK, but it makes little difference who you believe killed them, their assassinations changed the course of American history and helped drive America much further to the right.

The American right destroyed any politicians that disagreed or prevented their ever rightward drift. The rightwing rigged American elections with Nixon destroying the Paris Peace talks to win in 1968 and again when Reagan prevented the release of the American hostages in Iran to win in 1980. The 1988 election was rigged again by Bush Sr. using the shameful Willie Horton race-baiting campaign to win, and by the Supreme Court in 2000 making a political decision to steal and election for George W. Bush, and with Bush Jr. in 2004, using the false Swift Boat ads to discredit Kerry. The right attempted to rig the 2008 and 2012 elections with the "birther" and Tea party movements to discredit Obama. And they now can simply buy elections due another political decision of the Supreme Court. The Koch brothers, other billionaire's and multi-national corporations can now form political action committees and spend unlimited dollars to buy public opinion, spread lies and deception and buy the American elections.

The history of the deliberate destruction and assassination of the American left is undeniable. The American people are but pawns in a giant chess game pushed around and sacrificed with little regard by the rich and greedy kings of capitalism. American politics are firmly cemented to the right and have been steadily moving more to the right since the end of World War II.

But there is a glimmer of hope. The rise of previously alienated groups of women, minorities, non-Christians and others who have been abused, neglected and blamed by the right for every problem in America are coming into their own. As America becomes a minority majority their voices may change America, and that is exactly what the rightwing controllers fear. It is why they are engaging in massive voter suppression and in the shameless gerrymandering of congressional districts. Billionaires like the Koch brothers are pouring billions of dollars into the political and judicial process in the hopes of influencing and buying a rightwing outcome.

The freedoms of America will not be won on the battlegrounds of some foreign land with the spilling of the blood of others. It will not be won with guns, bullets and bombs or with planes, tanks and ships. The American freedom must be won in the minds of the American people, and this is the sole purpose of this book.

In conclusion it would be very easy for me to label America in her current condition as a fascist state based upon the case I have made in this book. Perhaps in the same regard it will be difficult for some readers to accept all this as our common shameful truth. But I do not need make claims of fascism and you do not have to read every word of this book nor do you need to have leftist view for us to agree that America has drifted too far to the right and because of this it has no balance. There is no longer an American left of any significance to counter-balance that continuous rightwing onslaught.

The American left was driven to extinction by unlawful, unconstitutional and frequently violent acts by those in government whose duty it was to protect these basic freedoms. However the way forward is not to wallow in the crimes of the past, but to recognize that many crimes were committed and that most of us are to blame for our indifference and ignorance and in the light of this recognition to build a new and better future.

There is a story about a German Lutheran Pastor who was discovered near death at the end of World War II in a Nazi concentration camp. When his liberators asked him what could a religious man have possibly done to be imprisoned? He replied, "Because I deserved to be." And after their puzzled silence he explained, "I didn't complain when the Nazis came for the Jews because I wasn't Jewish. I didn't complain when they took the Gypsies because I wasn't a Gypsy. I didn't complain when they came for the communists, the socialists, the disabled, the homosexuals or all the others. And when they finally came for me, there was no one left to complain."

The point of the this story is that we are all too often caught up in the drama of our daily lives and struggles to notice things larger than we are. We would rather live with the comfortable lie than to see the painful and horrible truth in our lives. To see injustice is to understand and to understand is the first step in change. There is an African proverb that says, "Not to know is bad. Not to wish to know is worse."

Good luck and may you have many better and more true and just tomorrows.

BIBLIOGRAPHY

Books:

A Question of Torture: CIA Interrogation, from the Cold War to the War on Terror, Alfred McCoy, 2007; Henry Holt & Co

A Religious History of the American People, Sidney E. Ahlstrom, 2004; Yale University Press

The Age of McCarthyism: A Brief History with Documents, Ellen Schrecker, 2002; Palgrave McMillan

All Fall Down: America's Tragic Encounter With Iran, Gary Sick, 2001; iUniverse

America's Nazi Secret, John Loftus, 2010; Trine Day

American Dynasty, Aristocracy, Fortune, and the Politics of Deceit in the House of Bush, Kevin Phillips, 2004; Penguin

American Dynasty, Kevin Phillips, 2004; The Penguin Group

The American Pope: The Life and Times of Cardinal Francis Spellman, John Cooney, 1984; New York Times Books

The Arrogance of Power: The Secret World of Richard Nixon, Anthony Summers, 2000; Viking

Bananas and Business: The United Fruit Company in Colombia, 1899–2000, Marcelo Bucheli, 2005; New York University Press

Bitter Fruit: The Story of the American Coup in Guatemala, Revised and Expanded, Stephen Schiesinger, Stephen Kinzer, John H. Coatsworth, 2005; David Rockefeller Center Studies on Latin America

Blowback: The First Full Account of America's Recruitment of Nazis and Its Disastrous Effect on the Cold War, Our Domestic and Foreign Policy, Christopher Simpson, 1989; Collier Books

The Brothers, John Foster Dulles, Allen Dulles, and Their Secret World War, Stephen Kinzer, 2013;Times Books, Henry Holt and Company, LLC

The COINTELPRO Papers: Documents from the FBI's Secret Wars Against Dissent in the United States, Ward Churchill, 1990; South End Press

Crisis on the Left: Cold War Politics and American Liberals, 1947–1954, Mary S. McAuliffe, 1978; University of Massachusetts Press

The Death of American Virtue, Ken Gormley 2011; Broadway Books

Defrauding America, Rodney Stich, 1994; Diablo Western Press

The Ends of Power, H.R. Haldeman with Joseph Di Mona, 1978; Times Books

Enemies, the History of the FBI, Tim Weiner, 2012; Random House

Eugene V. Debs: Citizen and Socialist, Nick Salvatore, 1982; University of Illinois Press

Fidel Castro, Robert E. Quirk, 1995; W. W. Norton & Company

From Columbus to Castro: The History of the Caribbean 1492–1969, Eric Williams, 1984; Vintage Books

From Hegel to Existentialism, Robert C. Solomon, 1983; Oxford University Press

Gold Warriors: America's Secret Recovery of Yamamoto's Gold, Sterling and Peggy Seagrave, 2003; Verso

Great Fortune, The Epic of Rockefeller Center, Daniel Okrent, 2004; Penguin Books

Gus Hall, Mark Isaakovitch Lapitskii, 1985; Progress Publishers

Hegel: A Biography, Terry Pinkard, 2000; Cambridge University Press

Hollywood's Celebrity Gangster, The Incredible Life and Times of Mickey Cohen, Brad Lewis, 2007; Consortium Book Sales

Hubert Humphrey: A Biography; Carl Solberg, 1984; Borealis Books

The Immaculate Deception: Bush Crime Family Exposed, General Russell S. Bowen, 2000; American West Publishers

In the Sleep Room: The Story of CIA Brainwashing Experiments in Canada, Anne Collins, 1988; Key Porter Books

Inevitable Revolutions: The United States in Central America, Walter LaFeber, 1993; W.W. Norton and Company

Intervention and Revolution, The United States in the Third World, Richard J. Barnet, 1968; World Publishing

JFK, the CIA, Vietnam, and the Plot to Assassinate John F. Kennedy, L. Fletcher Prouty, 2011; Skyhorse Publishing

Karl Marx: His Life and Environment, Sir Isaiah Berlin, 1996; Oxford University Press

Legacy of Ashes: The History of the CIA, Tim Weiner, 2007; Doubleday

Legacy of Secrecy, Lamar Waldron, 2010; ReadHowYouWant.com

The Life and Times of Joe McCarthy: A Biography, Thomas C. Reeves, 1997; Madison Books

Luce and His Empire, W. A. Swanberg, 1972; Scribner

The Making of the Slave Class, Jerry Carrier, 2010; Algora Publishing

The Man Who Killed Kennedy: The Case Against LBJ, Roger Stone, 2014; Skyhorse Publishing

Marx's General: The Revolutionary Life of Friedrich Engels, Tristram Hunt, 2010; Picador

Maverick Marine: General Smedley D. Butler and the Contradictions of American Military History, Hans Schmidt, 1998; University Press of Kentucky

Mother Jones: The Most Dangerous Woman in America, Elliott J. Gorn, 2002; Hill and Wang

National Insecurity: US Intelligence After the Cold War, Alfred W. McCoy, 2000; Temple University Press

Nixon's Darkest Secrets: The Inside Story of America's Most Troubled President, Don Fulsom, 2012; Thomas Dunne Books

Not in Your Lifetime, Anthony Summers, 1980; Marlowe

October Surprise, Barbara Honegger, 1980; Tudor

Official and Confidential: The Secret Life of J. Edgar Hoover, Anthony Summers, 1993; Putnam

Operation Paperclip, Annie Jacobsen, 2014; Little, Brown and Company

The Oswald Code, Alan Jules Weberman, 2014 CreateSpace Independent Publishing

Over Here: the First World War and American Society, David Kennedy, 2004; Oxford University Press

The Oxford History of the American People, Samuel Eliot Morison, 1965; Oxford University Press

Pius XII, The Holocaust, and the Cold War, Michael Phayer, 2008; Indiana University Press

Plausible Denial, Was the CIA Involved in the Assassination of JFK? Mark Lane, 1991; Thunder's Mouth Press

Politics of Hope, the Bitter Heritage: American Liberalism in the 1960s, Arthur Schlesinger Jr., 1962 Houghton Mifflin.

Price of Power, Seymour Hersh, 1984; Touchstone.

Quotations from Chairman Mao Tsetung, 1972; Foreign Languages Press, Peking

The Racial Matters: The FBI's Secret File on Black America, 1960–1972, Kenneth O'Reilly, 1989; The Free Press

The Real Odessa: How Peron Brought the Nazi War Criminals to Argentina, Uki Goñi, 2003; Granta UK

The Red Scare: The FBI and the Origins of Anti-Communism in the United States 1919–1943, Regin Schmidt, 2000; University of Copenhagen Press

The Residence: Inside the Private World of the White House, Kate Anderson Bower, 2015; Harper

The Rise and Fall of the Third Reich, William Shirer, 1960; Simon and Schuster

Rousseau's Political Writings: Discourse on Inequality, Discourse on Political Economy, On Social Contract, Norton Critical Editions, 1987; W.W. Norton & Company

Safe for Democracy: The Secret Wars of the CIA, John Prados, 2006, Rowman & Littlefield

Secret Agenda: The United States Government, Nazi Scientists and Project Paperclip 1945 to 1990, Linda Hunt, 1991, St Martin's Press

Secret History: The CIA's Classified Account of its Operations in Guatemala, 1952-1954, Nicholas Cullather, 1999; Stanford University Press

The Shock Doctrine: The Rise of Disaster Capitalism, Naomi Klein, 2010; Macmillan

Stilwell and the American Experience in China, 1911–45, Barbara Tuchman, 1972; McMillan

Tapestry, The History and Consequences of America's Culture, Jerry Carrier, 2014; Algora Publishing

Texas in the Morning: The Love Story of Madeleine Brown and President Lyndon Baines Johnson, Madeleine D. Brown, 1997; Conservatory Press

Understanding Power, Noam Chomsky, Peter Mitchell, 2002; The New Press

Unholy Trinity: The Vatican, The Nazis, and the Swiss Bankers, Mark Aarons and John Loftus, 1991; St. Martin's Press

Vietnam: Anatomy of a Peace. Gabriel Kolko, 1997; Routledge

Was Jonestown a CIA Medical Experiment? A Review of the Evidence, Michael Meiers, 1989; Edwin Mellon Press

Whiteout: The CIA, Drugs and the Press, Alexander Cockburn and Jeffery St. Clair 1999 Verso

Within Arm's Length: The Extraordinary Life and Career of a Special Agent in the United States Secret Service, Dan Emmett, 2012; iUniverse

Articles and Media Sources

"An Apology for a Guatemalan Coup, 57 Years Later," Elisabeth Malkin, October 20, 2011; *New York Times*

"Anti-communism in the 1950s", Wendy Wall; *Guilder Lehrman Institute of American History @ gilderlehrman.org*

"Boom Times for Surveillance Tech", Steven Musil, November 11, 2011, *CNT*

"Bush's Grandfather Directed Bank Tied to Man Who Funded Hitler,"October 17, 2003; *Associated Press*

"CIA and the Media", Carl Bernstein October 20, 1977; *Rolling Stone Magazine.*

"CIA Destroyed Videos Showing Interrogations: Harsh Techniques Seen in 2002 Tapes", Dan Eggen and Joby Warrick, December 7, 2007, *Washington Post*

"Clintons Joined S&L Operator in an Ozark Real Estate Venture", Jeff Gerth, March 8, 1992, *New York Times*

"Covert Operations: The billionaire brothers who are waging a war against Obama", Jane Mayer, August 10, 2010, *The New Yorker*

"Dark Money: Bombshell Report Exposes the Koch Brothers' 'Secret Bank'", September 12, 2013, *BillMoyers.com*

"Document Trove Exposes Surveillance Methods", Jennifer Valentino-Devries, Julia Angwin, and Steve Stecklow, November 19, 2011, *The Wall Street Journal*

"Earlier Denials Put Intelligence Chief in Awkward Position" Scott Shane and Jonathan Weisman, June 11, 2013, *New York Times*

"Editoriales Operacion Condor", Victor Flores Olea, April 10, 2006; *El Universal*

"Exclusive: Koch Brothers, Rick Scott and Jeb Bush Exposed in Florida Pipeline Scandal", Leslie Salzillo, February 2, 2015, *Daily Kos*

"Exclusive: Lee Atwater's Infamous 1981 Interview on the Southern Strategy", Rick Perlstein, November 13, 2012, *The Nation*

"Ex-Worker at C.I.A. Says He Leaked Data on Surveillance", Mark Mazetti and Michael S. Schmidt, June 9, 2013, *New York Times*

"Ford and the Führer", Ken Silverstein, January 24, 2000; *The Nation*

"Freedom Summer", Stanley Nelson, June 24, 2014; *American Experience, PBS*

"Gen. Butler Bares 'Fascist Plot' To Seize Government by Force; Says Bond Salesman, as Representative of Wall St. Group, Asked Him to Lead Army of 500,000 in March on Capital – Those Named Make Angry Denials", November 21, 1934; *The New York Times*

"Governor Bush and His Mythical Buddy", September 18, Editorial; *The Gainesville Sun, Gainesville.com*

"Guns, Drugs, and the CIA", Andrew and Leslie Cockburn, May 17, 1988; *Frontline, PBS*

"Harvard and the Making of a Unabomber", by Alston Chase, June 2000; *Atlantic Monthly*

"Iraq War Card", June 26, 2014; Moyers & Company, *BillMoyers.com*

"Khrushchev on Rosenbergs: Stoking Old Embers", McFadden, Robert, September 25, 2008; *New York Times*

"LBJ Tapes: Nixon Sabotaged Vietnam Peace Talks", James Joyner, March17, 2013; *BBC*

"Mind Control: My Mother, the CIA and LSD", Elizabeth Nickson, October 16, 1994; *The Observer*

"The Mob Mambo in pre-Castro Cuba", Valerie Ryan, March 16, 2007; *Seattle Times*

"Nixon Cited Missed Clues in Defense of a Rosenberg", Sam Roberts, September 13, 2008; *New York Times*

"NSA Is Building the Country's Biggest Spy Center (Watch What You Say)", James Bamford, March 15, 2012, *Wired*

"NSA Killed System That Sifted Phone Data Legally", Siobhan Gorman, May 18, 2006, *Baltimore Sun*

"Plot without Plotters", December 3, 1934 ; *Time Magazine.*

"Rectal Feeding, Threats to Children and More: 16 Awful Abuses from the CIA Torture Report", December 9, 2014, *Mother Jones*

"The Responsibilities Program of the FBI 1951–1955", Cathleen Thom and Patrick Chung, Volume 59, Issue 2, December 1997, *The Historian*

"Sarah Palin's $150,000 Wardrobe Malfunction", Booth More, October 22, 2008, *Los Angeles Times*

"Shaping the Tea Party Movement In to a Campaign Force", Kate Zernike, August 25, 2010, *The New York Times*

"South Korea Owns Up to Brutal Past", November 15, 2008, *The Sydney Morning Herald*

"Top Arkansas Lawyer Helped Hillary Clinton Turn Big Profit", Jeff Gerth, March 18, 1994, *New York Times*

"Tracking the Origins of a State Terror Network: Operation Condor", J. Patrice McSherry, 2002; *Latin American Perspectives* 29 (1): 36–60

"U.N. Chief's '61 Death: A Cold War Mystery", Ralph Slater, September 9, 2013; *Associated Press*

"US Military Wanted to Provoke War with Cuba", David Ruppe, May 1, 2001; *ABC News*

"US Practiced Torture after 9/11, Nonpartisan Review Concludes", Scott Shane, April 16, 2013, *New York Times*

"Vatican Gives Formal Apology for Inaction During Holocaust", William Drozdiak, March 17, 1998; *The Washington Post*

"Washington Letter", Richard Rovere, April 8, 1954; *The New Yorker*

"Witness Claims Second Shooter", April 30, 2012; *CNN*

Government Sources

"Art of War Papers, Lansdale, Magsaysay, America, and the Philippines, A Case Study of Limited Intervention Counterinsurgency", Andrew E. Lembke, Major, US Army, 2001 *Combat Institute Press*

"The Biography of Lee Harvey Oswald", Appendix 8, *The Warren Report*

"A Brief Synopsis of the Story of the Origin of the Pledge taken from the Detailed Narrative by Frances Bellamy, Author of the Pledge", *Congressional Record 91* (1945) House.

"Concerning Legislative Proposals to Update the Foreign Intelligence Surveillance Act (FISA)", September 12, 2006, *United States House of Representatives*

"*Final Report Of The Independent Counsel For Iran/Contra Matters, Volume I: Investigations and Prosecutions*", Lawrence E. Walsh Independent Counsel, August 4, 1993 Washington, D.C.

"History of the Italian Rat Line (10 April 1950)", IB Operating Officer Paul E. Lyon, 430th Counter Intelligence Corps (CIC), Headquarters of the US Forces in Austria. *Vide Jasenovac Archive.*

"The Iran-Contra Affair 20 Years On", November 20, 2006, George Washington University *National Security Archive Electronic Briefing Book 210*

"Justification for US Military Intervention in Cuba (TS)." Northwoods Memorandum for the US Secretary of Defense (March 13, 1962)

National Security Action Memorandum No. 263 11/21/63

"Recollections from the Church Committee's Investigation of NSA" L. Britt Snider, *CIA Library Historical Document*, Posted: April 14, 2007

"The US Invasion of Panama: The Truth Behind Operational 'Just Cause'", *The Independent Commission of Inquiry on the US Invasion of Panama 1991*

Printed in the United States
By Bookmasters